Active Filter
Design Handbook

Active Filter Design Handbook

For Use with Programmable Pocket Calculators and Minicomputers

G. S. Moschytz

and

P. Horn

Institut für Fernmeldetechnik
ETH, Zürich

JOHN WILEY & SONS

Chichester · New York · Brisbane · Toronto

Copyright © 1981 by John Wiley & Sons Ltd.

British Library Cataloguing in Publication Data:

Moschytz, George Samson
  Active filter design handbook.
  1. Electric filters, Active—Design and construction—Data processing
  2. Minicomputers
  3. Programmable calculators
  I. Title
  II. Horn, P.
  621.3815′32   TK 7872.F5   80-40845

  ISBN 0 471 27850 5

Filmset by Composition House Limited, Salisbury, Wiltshire, England,
and printed in Great Britain by Page Bros. (Norwich) Ltd.

Contents

vi

Preface

Before the age of integrated circuits and the availability of active filters most electrical engineering establishments employed their own filter specialists who alone understood the intricacies of classical LC filter design. Although they still exist—and are necessary for sophisticated filter design—the ranks of this breed of filter specialist are becoming thinner. This may be because ever more employers expect any one of their engineers to 'hook up' a filter—albeit an active one—as needed. This expectation stems from the widespread belief that an active filter is nothing more than a string of frequency-selective amplifiers which are readily assembled with the help of some design charts and tables taken from a handy trade journal. This attitude towards active filter design may be justified for the most simple and undemanding applications. In anything more sophisticated, a little more effort and know-how must be invested if the many stumbling-blocks that may otherwise be encountered are to be avoided. It is the purpose of this handbook to provide both the non-specialist and the professional active filter designer with that extra know-how with which he can effortlessly design *optimized low-cost active filters that will serve him well in most general applications.*

The material covered in the book and the filter circuits presented are the result of many years of activity by the authors as consultants and designers of active filters. During this time it became very apparent that a large number of relatively small electrical engineering companies exist who require a wide diversity of low-runner active filters and that with just a little additional information those active filters could be much improved. Too many manufacturers add last-minute active filters—designed with trade-journal data—to their systems and are surprised by stability problems and parasitic oscillations either during manufacture or—worse—later in the field. This handbook is intended primarily for these manufacturers.

In this handbook over twenty well-proven active filters for most possible applications are presented in detail. The selection of these filters is based on their low RC component count, minimum power (i.e. minimum number of amplifiers), low sensitivities to passive and active components, easy tunability, and good stability in practice. All the necessary design and tuning information is provided by design equations and flow charts which can be implemented by programmable hand calculators or minicomputers. Listings are included for the Texas Instruments SR-59 programmable hand calculator, in FORTRAN for the PDP-11/45 computer, and in BASIC for implementation on minicomputers. Because the design of active filters becomes more critical with increasing pole Q, the filters are broken down into the three categories 'low Q', 'medium Q', and 'high Q'. The flow charts for the medium- and high-Q filters include basic optimization routines that provide a degree of immunity from the effects of non-ideal operational amplifiers. The chapters for the design and tuning of these active filters (Chapters 5 and 6 respectively) represent the core of this book—and can be used independently of the other chapters. Nevertheless, certain fundamentals of active filter design have been included in introductory chapters in order to enable the designer to better understand the design chapters if he so desires.

In Chapter 1 the most basic fundamentals of classical filter concepts and theory are briefly outlined. In Chapter 2 the transfer function of a filter is introduced and its relationship to the frequency response and filter specifications is explained. In Chapter 3 the basic concepts necessary to understand the optimization of active filters, as applied in Chapter 5, are explained. This entails mainly the concepts of sensitivity and their use in the formulation of a figure-of-merit. In Chapter 4 the three filter categories are presented in general terms and in Chapter 5 they are presented in detail. Every possible second-order filter type is given in each of the three pole-Q categories; its design equations and flow charts for optimization are given and tuning information is added where applicable. In Chapter 6 the tuning of second-order active filters is presented in detail. These first six chapters deal almost exclusively with second-order filters. In Chapter 7 the design information necessary for the design of higher-order active filters, by cascading second-order building blocks, is presented, and finally, in Chapter 8, practical hints for the design of active filters are given. In this final chapter some of the most frequent—but rarely mentioned—pitfalls of active filter design are covered so that active filter design can be undertaken by almost anyone with a minimum of formal electrical engineering education to look back on—and that, after all, is the main purpose of this book.

CHAPTER 1

Introduction

1-1 FILTERS: A BRIEF INTRODUCTION

Filters, often called wave filters, are frequency-selective networks designed to 'pass' or transmit sinusoidal waves in one or more continuous frequency bands and to 'stop' or reject sinusoidal waves in the complementary bands. Filters with single passbands are typically classified as *lowpass, highpass*, and *bandpass*, depending on the bands of frequencies which are passed. For example, the passband of the bandpass filter illustrated in Fig. 1-1 extends from the frequency ω_1 to ω_2. There are other filter types such as *allpass, frequency-emphasizing*, and *frequency-rejection* filters. All of these types will be discussed in more detail in later sections. Another classification of filters is based on the network-theoretical concepts by which they were designed. It comprises *image-parameter filters* and *insertion-loss filters*.

An image-parameter filter consists of a cascade of two-port *sections* whose image impedances are *matched* at their junctions. If the filter were also matched at the end terminals, the 'image attenuation' would be zero in the passband. However, since the image impedance is frequency dependent and the terminations are usually resistive, the filter is not matched at its terminals at all frequencies. A non-zero attenuation in the passband is the result.

An alternative method of filter design is based on the insertion loss. Figure 1-2 shows a typical requirement for a bandpass filter. The insertion loss is required to remain below a certain passband maximum A_{max}, measured in decibels or nepers, in the range of frequencies from ω_{B_1} to ω_{B_2}, and to remain above a certain stopband minimum A_{min}, for frequencies lower than ω_{s_1} and above ω_{s_2}. The width of the intervals $\omega_{B_1} - \omega_{s_1}$ and $\omega_{s_2} - \omega_{B_2}$ is a measure of the required frequency selectivity. The incidental dissipation of the filter components causes the actual loss curve to depart considerably from the theoretical, especially near the edge of the band and in the vicinity of the infinite loss points. One feature of insertion-loss theory is that this non-ideal component behaviour is compensated for by a *predistortion* technique which, however, introduces a flat loss in the passband. Whereas the structure of the resulting insertion-loss filter is often the same as that of the equivalent image-parameter filter, for the same number of sections the insertion-loss filter gives a better filter performance. This improvement is obtained at the cost of much greater computational effort which was a significant deterrent before the present-day proliferation of computers. With today's vastly expanded computational capabilities, insertion-loss filter design has been made readily accessible in the form of filter tables such as those of Zverev.†

---

† A. I. Zverev, *Handbook of Filter Synthesis*, John Wiley and Sons, Inc., New York, 1967.

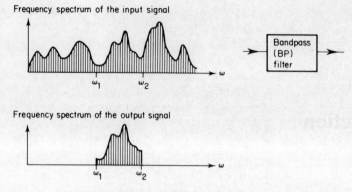

Fig. 1-1   Typical input and output frequency spectrum of bandpass
filter

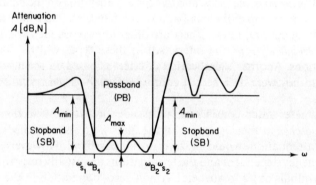

Fig. 1-2   Typical attenuation specifications for bandpass
filter

The filter design discussed in this book is therefore based on insertion-loss filter theory and, for certain applications as explained in Chapter 7, uses Zverev's *Handbook* as a take-off point.

1-2   ACTIVE FILTERS

In spite of the extensive resources that have gone into the perfection of LC filter theory, technology, and manufacture there is a widespread tendency to eliminate LC filters from modern electronic equipment, because integrated circuits have completely changed conventional systems and the performance criteria previously accepted in electronic designs. Thus LC filters, like all other circuit types that do not fit into the microminiaturization trend, are rapidly being replaced by filter types that do. Foremost among these are active filters which combine resistors, capacitors, and gain devices into active networks achieving filtering performance that is comparable or superior to that of their LC counterparts. Due to its excellent performance, reasonable price, and ready availability the operational amplifier is invariably used as the active gain device. The term 'active filters' comprises a host of different circuit concepts and design methods, the most important of which can be grouped into the following three categories.

Cascade Filter Design

This denotes isolated second-order filter sections (often referred to as biquadratic circuits or 'biquads') connected in cascade to realize the required higher-order transfer functions. The individual building blocks may be of second or third order and may comprise one or more operational amplifiers (opamps).

LC Filter Simulation

An LC filter structure is the starting point. This is then realized either by simulating each inductor by a gyrator–capacitor combination, or by transforming the initial filter structure such that it can be realized with general impedance converters (GICs), e.g. frequency-dependent negative resistances (FDNRs). Both gyrators and GICs are realizable with operational amplifiers.

Coupled Filters

Here the starting point is generally a cascade of first- or second-order active filters (preferably all-purpose building blocks) which are then coupled by additional negative feedback loops. The additional coupling is introduced in order to obtain the same stability with the resulting active filter cascade as is obtainable with simulated LC filter structures.

1-3 CASCADING SECOND-ORDER FILTERS

The connection of second-order filters in cascade or, briefly, 'cascade filter design' is the approach most widely used to design active filters meeting moderate demands. It is the method on which the designs described in this handbook are based.

The reasons for this choice are simple. In modern communication and data-processing systems much of the signal processing is achieved with digital LSI circuitry. As a consequence the demands on the peripheral analog active filters are often moderate and, in particular, the pole Q's are relatively low. On the other hand, the requirements on minimum power consumption are becoming ever more stringent. In applications of this kind the cascade design of single-amplifier second-order sections presents a near-to ideal solution to the filtering problem. For high-quality filters, i.e. those with higher pole Q's and requirements for very low sensitivity, multiple-amplifier sections, i.e. cascaded second-order sections using more than one amplifier each and, if need be, additional coupling between the sections, can be used.

Cascade design has the additional advantages of extreme design simplicity, simple component trimming and filter tuning, and minimum power. The latter comes about because the number of opamps per second-order filter section can be modified according to the performance quality desired. Thus a low-selectivity (i.e. low pole Q) filter can be built with one opamp, whereas the stability demands of a higher pole-Q section can be met with a two-amplifier section. Of the countless (single- and multiple-amplifier) second-order filter sections that are suitable for cascade design, those considered most suitable from the standpoint of ease of design and good performance have been selected for this handbook. Specifically, they were selected on the basis of

(a) minimum power,
(b) simple tuning and production techniques, and
(c) moderate tolerance specifications.

In most run-of-the-mill industrial applications such filters will be characterized by low production volumes and relatively unsophisticated technology. By the latter we mean thick-film rather than thin-film hybrid IC technology and, wherever possible (and still very widespread), manufacture of active filters using discrete components.

CHAPTER 2

Frequency Response and Transfer Functions

2-1 FROM SPECIFICATIONS TO TRANSFER FUNCTION

Most filter networks—and in particular those described in this book—belong to the family of linear lumped-parameter finite (LLF) networks. Those not falling into this category are, typically, nonlinear, distributed, non-finite—or any combination of these.

The output signal of an nth-order LLF network can be found in terms of the input signal by solving a linear nth-order differential equation of the form:

$$a_n \frac{d^n y}{dt^n} + a_{n-1} \frac{d^{n-1} y}{dt^{n-1}} + \cdots + a_1 \frac{dy}{dt} + a_0 y = b_m \frac{d^m x}{dt^m} + b_{m-1} \frac{d^{m-1} x}{dt^{m-1}} + \cdots + b_1 \frac{dx}{dt} + b_0 x$$

(2-1)

where $x(t)$ is the input signal, $y(t)$ the output signal, and $n \geq m$.

Applying the Laplace transform to this equation, we obtain the *transfer function* $T(s) = Y(s)/X(s)$ as the ratio of two polynomials $N(s)$ and $D(s)$, namely:

$$T(s) = \frac{N(s)}{D(s)} = \frac{b_m s^m + b_{m-1} s^{m-1} + \cdots + b_1 s + b_0}{a_n s^n + a_{n-1} s^{n-1} + \cdots + a_1 s + a_0}$$

[2-2]†

where $s = \sigma + j\omega$ is the complex frequency and $N(s)$ and $D(s)$ are polynomials in s with real coefficients a_i and b_j. Expressing $N(s)$ and $D(s)$ in their factored form, we obtain the poles and zeros of the transfer function:

$$T(s) = K \frac{(s - z_1)(s - z_2) \cdots (s - z_m)}{(s - p_1)(s - p_2) \cdots (s - p_n)}$$

$$= K \frac{\prod_{i=1}^{m} (s - z_i)}{\prod_{j=1}^{n} (s - p_j)}$$

(2-3)

The poles p_j and zeros z_i may be either real or complex conjugate. Combining a complex conjugate zero pair with a complex conjugate pole pair, we obtain the special case of a second-order transfer function:

$$T(s) = K \frac{(s - z)(s - z^*)}{(s - p)(s - p^*)} = K \frac{s^2 + (\omega_z/q_z)s + \omega_z^2}{s^2 + (\omega_p/q_p)s + \omega_p^2}$$

(2-4)

† Square brackets are used to emphasize important definitions or results.

5

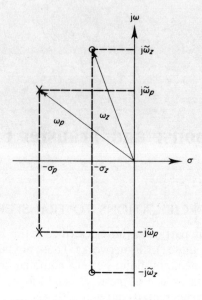

Fig. 2-1 Pole-zero diagram of
second-order transfer function

where

$$z, z^* = -\sigma_z \pm j\tilde{\omega}_z \qquad (2\text{-}5a)$$

$$p, p^* = -\sigma_p \pm j\tilde{\omega}_p \qquad (2\text{-}5b)$$

The poles and zeros can be displayed in the complex frequency or s plane as shown in Fig. 2-1. Note that

$$\omega_z^2 = \sigma_z^2 + \tilde{\omega}_z^2; \qquad \omega_p^2 = \sigma_p^2 + \tilde{\omega}_p^2 \qquad (2\text{-}6a)$$

and

$$q_z = \frac{\omega_z}{2\sigma_z}; \qquad q_p = \frac{\omega_p}{2\sigma_p} \qquad (2\text{-}6b)$$

To obtain the *frequency response* of the network described by eq. (2-1) we assume a sinusoidal input signal and, because the network is linear, obtain a sinusoidal response. The response is obtained by letting $s = j\omega$ in eq. (2-3); thus,

$$T(j\omega) = K \frac{\displaystyle\prod_{i=1}^{m}(j\omega - z_i)}{\displaystyle\prod_{j=1}^{n}(j\omega - p_j)} = |T(j\omega)| e^{j\phi(\omega)} \qquad (2\text{-}7)$$

Taking the logarithm of (2-7), we obtain

$$\ln T(j\omega) = \ln|T(j\omega)| + j \arg T(j\omega) \qquad (2\text{-}8)$$
$$= \alpha(\omega) + j\phi(\omega)$$

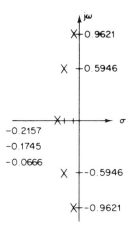

Fig. 2-2 Pole location
for transfer function
given by eq. (2-11)

where $\alpha(\omega)$ and $\phi(\omega)$ are the *gain* and *phase response* given in nepers and degrees, respectively. To obtain the gain response in decibels, we have

$$\alpha_{dB}(\omega) = 20 \log |T(j\omega)| = \frac{20}{\ln 10} \alpha(\omega) = 8.686\alpha(\omega) \qquad [2\text{-}9]$$

and to obtain the *group delay*:

$$\tau_g(\omega) = -\frac{d\phi(\omega)}{d\omega} \qquad [2\text{-}10]$$

As an example, consider the following fifth-order transfer function:

$$T(s) = \frac{K}{[s^2 + (\omega_{p_1}/q_{p_1})s + \omega_{p_1}^2][s^2 + (\omega_{p_2}/q_{p_2})s + \omega_{p_2}^2](s + \alpha)} \qquad (2\text{-}11)$$

Note that $T(s)$ has only finite poles since the numerator is a constant (the five zeros are said to be at infinity). The location of the poles are shown in Fig. 2-2 and the gain, phase, and group delay response in Fig. 2-3.

The transfer function $T(s)$ provides the gain response, i.e. the output/input ratio of our network, whereas filter specifications are very often expressed in terms of the *attenuation response*, i.e. the input/output ratio. For the active networks dealt with in this book the relationship between the gain and attenuation response is a very simple one. We assume throughout that the active filter is driven from a voltage source and that the output signal is taken from the output of an operational amplifier. Expressed differently, this means that the source impedance is zero and the load impedance infinite. We therefore have the operating conditions shown in Fig. 2-4, meaning that the transfer function will equal the output-to-input *voltage ratio*, i.e.

$$T(s) = \frac{V_{\text{out}}}{V_{\text{in}}}(s) \qquad (2\text{-}12)$$

8

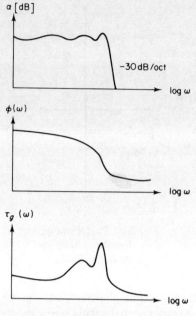

α [dB]

−30 dB/oct

log ω

φ(ω)

log ω

τ_g (ω)

log ω

Fig. 2-3   Gain, phase, and group-delay
response for transfer function given by
eq. (2-11)

The attenuation function $H(s)$ is then defined as

$$H(s) = \frac{V_{\text{in}}}{V_{\text{out}}}(s) = \frac{1}{T(s)} \tag{2-13}$$

For the sinusoidal input case we define the attenuation and phase response as

$$\begin{aligned} \ln H(j\omega) &= \ln|H(j\omega)| + j \arg H(j\omega) \\ &= A(\omega) + jB(\omega) \end{aligned} \tag{2-14}$$

and the attenuation response in decibels

$$A_{\text{dB}}(\omega) = 20 \log|H(j\omega)| \tag{2-15}$$

The attenuation response of the network function (2-11) is as shown in Fig. 2-5.

Because of the driving conditions used for active filters (see Fig. 2-4) we see that the attenuation response A_{dB} can be obtained very easily from the gain response α_{dB}. This in turn can be directly derived from the transfer function (see eq. 2-9). Comparing (2-9), (2-13), and (2-15), we find that

$$A_{\text{dB}}(\omega) = -\alpha_{\text{dB}}(\omega) \tag{2-16}$$

v_{in} Active filter v_{out}

Fig. 2-4   Typical operating conditions for active
filter

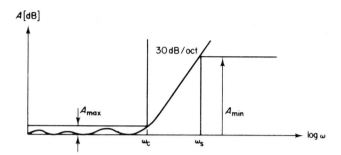

Fig. 2-5 Attenuation response corresponding to the transfer function given by eq. (2-11)

Furthermore, A_{dB} corresponds to the insertion loss discussed in Chapter 1 and therefore provides the link to conventional LC filter tables and other classical analytical tools. Note that the attenuation response (or insertion loss) shown in Fig. 2-5 is analogous to the bandpass tolerance specifications shown in Chapter 1 (Fig. 1-2). In the case of Fig. 2-5, however, we have a fifth-order lowpass filter where A_{max} and the cutoff frequency ω_c characterize the passband, the frequency span $\omega_s - \omega_c$ determines the selectivity, and A_{min} is the minimum loss in the stopband. Thus, in the case of active filters, the gain and attenuation response is directly related to the transfer function $T(s)$ by (2-8) and (2-13). This leads to the design procedure outlined in Fig. 2-6. From the given gain, phase, or attenuation specifications, a transfer function $T(s)$ must be found such that $|T(j\omega)|e^{j\phi(\omega)}$ satisfies these specifications. Once a suitable $T(s)$ has been found, the active filter design begins. It consists in finding an active filter circuit whose transfer function is $T(s)$. Whether additional constraints are placed on the circuit (e.g. minimum power, minimum sensitivity, maximum dynamic range) depends on the application.

The procedure outlined in Fig. 2-6 does not mean that it is always possible to derive a unique transfer function $T(s)$ from the specified gain, phase, or attenuation response. However, in most practical cases such a unique relationship does exist, as we shall see in

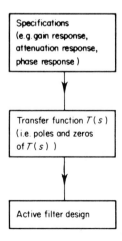

Fig. 2-6   Procedure for the design of active filters

Chapter 7. This direct relationship is particularly apparent for transfer functions of low order n, such as for second-order networks ($n = 2$). Such networks play the most important role in cascade filter design and will be discussed in what follows.

2-2   SECOND-ORDER NETWORK FUNCTIONS

The amplitude and phase response associated with a transfer function $T(s)$ can be obtained graphically from the pole-zero plot of $T(s)$. If $T(s)$ is given in terms of its poles and zeros:

$$T(s) = K \frac{(s - z_1)(s - z_2) \cdots (s - z_m)}{(s - p_1)(s - p_2) \cdots (s - p_n)} \tag{2-17}$$

then, for any frequency ω_0, the corresponding amplitude and phase can be obtained from the expression:

$$
\begin{aligned}
T(j\omega_0) &= |T(j\omega_0)| e^{j\phi(\omega_0)} \\
&= \frac{(j\omega_0 - z_1)(j\omega_0 - z_2) \cdots (j\omega_0 - z_m)}{(j\omega_0 - p_1)(j\omega_0 - p_2) \cdots (j\omega_0 - p_n)}
\end{aligned}
\tag{2-18}
$$

Each factor in (2-18) represents a complex phasor which can be displayed graphically in the s plane. With

$$(j\omega_0 - z_i) = A_{z_i}(\omega_0)\exp j\theta_{z_i}(\omega_0) \tag{2-19a}$$

$$(j\omega_0 - p_j) = A_{p_j}(\omega_0)\exp j\theta_{p_j}(\omega_0) \tag{2-19b}$$

we obtain, from (2-18),

$$|T(j\omega_0)| = \frac{A_{z_1} A_{z_2} \cdots A_{z_m}}{A_{p_1} A_{p_2} \cdots A_{p_n}} \tag{2-20a}$$

and

$$\phi(\omega_0) = (\theta_{z_1} + \theta_{z_2} + \cdots + \theta_{z_m} - \theta_{p_1} - \theta_{p_2} - \theta_{p_n}) \tag{2-20b}$$

Consider, for example, the transfer function

$$T(s) = K \frac{s^2 + \omega_z^2}{(s^2 + 2\sigma_p s + \omega_p^2)(s + \alpha)} \tag{2-21}$$

The corresponding poles and zeros in the s plane are shown in Fig. 2-7. With (2-9), the gain at ω_0 is

$$\alpha_{dB}(\omega_0) = 20 \log \frac{A_{z_1}(\omega_0)A_{z_2}(\omega_0)}{A_{p_1}(\omega_0)A_{p_2}(\omega_0)A_{p_3}(\omega_0)} \tag{2-22a}$$

and the phase is

$$\phi(\omega_0) = \theta_{z_1}(\omega_0) + \theta_{z_2}(\omega_0) - \theta_{p_1}(\omega_0) - \theta_{p_2}(\omega_0) - \theta_{p_3}(\omega_0) \tag{2-22b}$$

Note that $A_{z_1}(\omega_z) = 0$ and therefore $|T(j\omega_z)| = 0$, meaning that the *transmission zeros*, which are located on the imaginary axis at $\pm j\omega_z$, cause the amplitude to be zero at the frequency ω_z.

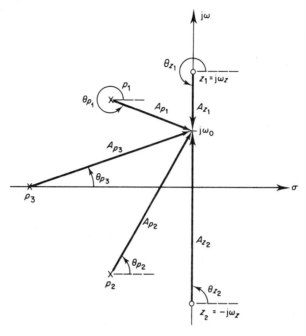

Fig. 2-7   Pole-zero diagram for transfer function of eq. (2-21)

After these preliminaries it is a simple matter to find the amplitude and phase characteristics associated with second-order transfer functions. These can be broken down into six basic functions as follows:

(a)   The *lowpass (LP) network* has a transfer function

$$T(s) = K \frac{\omega_p^2}{s^2 + 2\sigma_p s + \omega_p^2} \tag{2.23}$$

Note that†

$$2\sigma_p = \frac{\omega_p}{q_p} \quad \text{and} \quad 2\sigma_z = \frac{\omega_z}{q_z} \tag{2-24}$$

where σ_p and σ_z are the negative real parts of the pole and zero pairs p, p^* and z, z^*, respectively (see eq. 2-5). The pole plot is shown in Fig. 2-8(a) and the amplitude and phase response, for $q_p = 2$, in Fig. 2-8(b). It is useful to note that the graphical pole-zero representation for low-order network functions permits various critical frequencies and other characteristics of the frequency response to be obtained geometrically. Referring to Fig. 2-8a, the amplitude at any frequency ω is given by

$$|T(j\omega)| = \frac{K\omega_p^2}{\mu_1(\omega)\mu_2(\omega)} \tag{2-25}$$

† The negative real values σ_p and σ_z are useful when displaying the poles and zeros graphically in the s plane. The values ω_p and q_p are physically measurable quantities and are more appropriate when considering filter design; they are used in the design equations of Chapter 5.

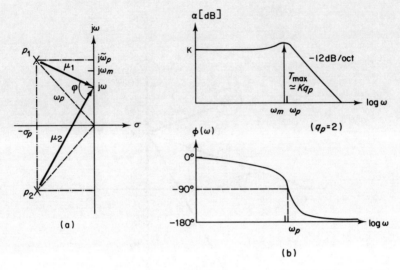

Fig. 2-8   Second-order lowpass function: (a) pole-zero diagram, (b) amplitude
and phase response

The area A of the triangle formed by the three points p_1, p_2 and $s = j\omega$ can be expressed by

$$A = \tfrac{1}{2}\mu_1\mu_2 \sin \varphi \qquad (2.26a)$$

and also by

$$A = \tfrac{1}{2}(2\tilde{\omega}_p \sigma_p) \qquad (2\text{-}26b)$$

Consequently, (2-25) can be written as

$$|T(j\omega)| = \frac{K\omega_p^2}{2\tilde{\omega}_p \sigma_p} \sin \varphi(\omega) \qquad (2\text{-}27)$$

In this equation the only frequency-dependent quantity is $\varphi(\omega)$. Thus, the maximum amplitude $T_{\max}$ occurs at frequency ω_m and is obtained when $\varphi = 90°$, namely,

$$T_{\max} = |T(\omega = \omega_m)| = \frac{K\omega_p^2}{2\tilde{\omega}_p \sigma_p} = \frac{Kq_p}{\sqrt{1 + 1/4q_p^2}}\bigg|_{q_p \gg 1} \approx Kq_p \qquad (2\text{-}28)$$

The frequency ω_m occurs at the intersection of the circle (the 'resonant-peaking circle') with diameter $p - p^*$ and the $j\omega$ axis; thus,

$$\omega_m = \sqrt{\tilde{\omega}_p^2 - \sigma_p^2} < \omega_p \qquad (2\text{-}29)$$

The frequency ω_m is always smaller than ω_p, since the poles p, p^* must be on the left of the $j\omega$ axis. It can also readily be seen from the diagram that the phase $\phi(\omega_p) = -90°$.

(b)   The *highpass (HP) network* has a transfer function:

$$T(s) = K \frac{s^2}{s^2 + 2\sigma_p s + \omega_p^2} \qquad (2\text{-}30)$$

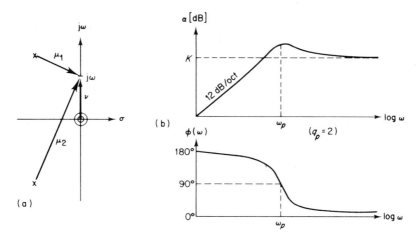

Fig. 2-9   Second-order highpass function: (a) pole-zero diagram, (b) amplitude and phase response

The pole-zero plot and the gain and phase response are shown in Fig. 2-9(a) and (b), respectively. The amplitude at any frequency ω is given by

$$|T(j\omega)| = K \frac{[v(\omega)]^2}{\mu_1(\omega)\mu_2(\omega)} \tag{2-31}$$

With this expression, the most important characteristics of the frequency response (which is symmetrical to that of the lowpass) may be derived.

(c)   The *bandpass (BP) network* has a transfer function:

$$T(s) = K \frac{2\sigma_p s}{s^2 + 2\sigma_p s + \omega_p^2} \tag{2.32}$$

The pole-zero plot is shown in Fig. 2-10(a) and the corresponding gain and phase response in Fig. 2-10(b). The amplitude response in terms of the s-plane phasors is given by

$$|T(j\omega)| = 2\sigma_p K \frac{v(\omega)}{\mu_1(\omega)\mu_2(\omega)} \tag{2-33}$$

For the second-order bandpass filter, the peak frequency ω_m is equal to the pole frequency ω_p. The peak amplitude is therefore given by

$$T_{max} = |T(\omega = \omega_m)| = K \tag{2-34}$$

Note that the 3-dB bandwidth of the second-order bandpass filter equals $2\sigma_p$ so that

$$Q = \frac{\text{peak frequency}}{\text{3-dB bandwidth}} = \frac{\omega_p}{2\sigma_p} = q_p \tag{2-35}$$

The equivalence of Q and q_p holds only for the second-order bandpass filter. The response in Fig. 2-10(b) is geometrically symmetrical, i.e. $\omega_p^2 = \omega_1 \omega_2$, where ω_1 and ω_2 are the 3-dB band edge frequencies.

14

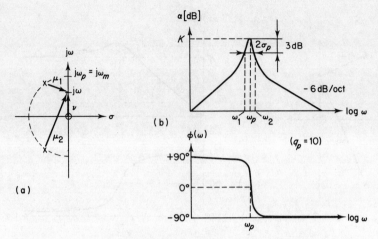

Fig. 2-10 Second-order bandpass function: (a) pole-zero diagram, (b) amplitude and phase response

(d) The *frequency-rejection network* (*FRN*), also called the *band-rejection* (*BR*) network, band-elimination network, or simply bandstop, is characterized by the transfer function

$$T(s) = K \frac{s^2 + 2\sigma_z s + \omega_z^2}{s^2 + 2\sigma_p s + \omega_p^2} \qquad (2\text{-}36a)$$

where

$$\sigma_z < \sigma_p \text{ (i.e. } q_z > q_p) \qquad (2\text{-}36b)$$

The pole-zero plot is shown in Fig. 2-11(a) and the amplitude and phase response in Fig. 2-11(b). The inequality (2-36b) implies that the zero pair dominates with respect to the pole pair (i.e. is always closer to the $j\omega$ axis). This is characteristic for a fre-

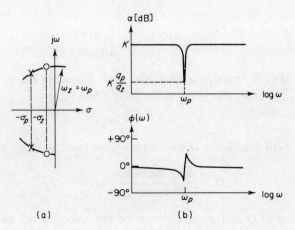

Fig. 2-11 Second-order frequency-rejection function: (a) pole-zero diagram, (b) amplitude and phase response

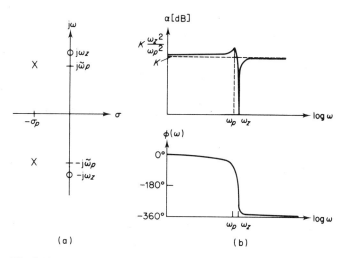

Fig. 2-12 Frequency-rejection function with 'frequency notch':
(a) pole-zero diagram, (b) amplitude and phase response

quency-rejection network. For the case where $\omega_p = \omega_z$, the minimum of the amplitude response occurs at

$$T_{min} = |T(j\omega_p)| = K\frac{\sigma_z}{\sigma_p} = K\frac{q_p}{q_z} \tag{2-37}$$

If $\sigma_z = 0$ (i.e. $q_z = \infty$), the zeros lie on the $j\omega$ axis (see Fig. 2-12a); we have a case similar to that of (2-21) in which the transmission zeros completely reject a sinusoidal signal, i.e. there is a 'notch' at the frequency ω_z (i.e. $|T(j\omega_z)| = 0$). This is shown in Fig. 2-12(b). If $\omega_z \neq \omega_p$, the symmetrical amplitude response of Fig. 2-11(b) becomes unsymmetrical. In general we have

$$|T(0)| = K\left(\frac{\omega_z}{\omega_p}\right)^2 \tag{2-38a}$$

and

$$|T(j\omega)|_{\omega \to \infty} = K \tag{2-38b}$$

Thus for $\omega_z > \omega_p$ we have a *lowpass notch (LPN)*, since $|T(0)| > |T(\infty)|$, and for $\omega_z < \omega_p$ a *highpass notch (HPN)*. The case shown in Fig. 2-12(b) corresponds to the LPN.

(e) The *frequency-emphasizing network (FEN)* has a transfer function:

$$T(s) = K\frac{s^2 + 2\sigma_z s + \omega_z^2}{s^2 + 2\sigma_p s + \omega_p^2} \tag{2-39a}$$

where

$$\sigma_z > \sigma_p \text{ (i.e. } q_z < q_p) \tag{2-39b}$$

Because the poles dominate with respect to the zeros (i.e. $\sigma_z > \sigma_p$) the frequencies in the vicinity of ω_p are emphasized and have bandpass character. The pole-zero plot (Fig. 2-13a) and the gain and phase response (Fig. 2-13b) demonstrate how the FEN and FRN can be considered to be the inverse of each other.

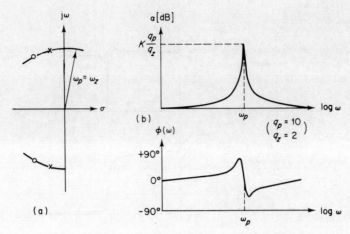

Fig. 2-13   Second-order frequency-emphasizing function: (a) pole-zero diagram, (b) amplitude and phase response

(f)   The second-order *allpass* (*AP*) *network* has the transfer function

$$T(s) = K \frac{s^2 - 2\sigma_0 s + \omega_0^2}{s^2 + 2\sigma_0 s + \omega_0^2} \tag{2-40}$$

The poles and zeros are symmetrical with respect to the jω axis (Fig. 2-14a), the amplitude is frequency independent (i.e. constant), and the phase has the frequency response

$$\phi(\omega) = -2 \cot^{-1}\left[q\left(\frac{\omega_0}{\omega} - \frac{\omega}{\omega_0}\right)\right] \tag{2-41a}$$

where

$$q = \frac{\omega_0}{2\sigma_0} \tag{2-41b}$$

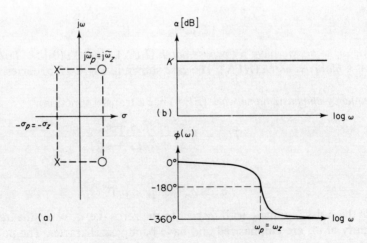

Fig. 2-14   Second-order allpass function: (a) pole-zero diagram, (b) amplitude and phase response

The delay, or slope of the phase curve, is then

$$\tau(\omega) = \frac{d\phi(\omega)}{d\omega} = -\frac{2q}{\omega_0}\frac{1 + (\omega_0/\omega)^2}{1 + q^2(\omega/\omega_0 - \omega_0/\omega)^2} \qquad (2\text{-}42)$$

At ω_0 we have

$$\tau(\omega_0) = -\frac{4q}{\omega_0} \qquad (2\text{-}43a)$$

whereas the maximum delay occurs at a slightly lower frequency, namely at

$$\omega_{\tau_{max}} = \omega_0\left[\sqrt{4 - \left(\frac{1}{q}\right)^2} - 1\right] \qquad (2\text{-}43b)$$

The amplitude and phase response of the second-order allpass network is shown in Fig. 2-14(b).

CHAPTER 3

Sensitivity and Figure-of-Merit

3-1 SOME USEFUL MEASURES OF SENSITIVITY

The components with which active filters are built are subject to change due to ambient variations (e.g. temperature and humidity) and aging. In order to measure the change in filter performance due to drift or change in component values the concept of network sensitivity has been introduced. With the *single-parameter relative sensitivity*

$$S_{x_i}^F = \frac{\partial [\ln F]}{\partial [\ln x_i]} \simeq \frac{\Delta F/F}{\Delta x_i/x_i} \qquad [3\text{-}1]$$

the relative variation of a network function or parameter F, due to a small change in a component x_i, is given by

$$\frac{\Delta F}{F} = S_{x_i}^F \frac{\Delta x_i}{x_i} \qquad (3.2)$$

Thus, the relative change in F due to the variation of N components is given by

$$\frac{\Delta F}{F} = \sum_{i=1}^{N} S_{x_i}^F \frac{\Delta x_i}{x_i} \qquad [3\text{-}3]$$

F can be any quantity characterizing a given network, such as the transfer function $T(s)$, the input impedance $Z(s)$, a coefficient of the transfer function c_j, the center frequency ω_p, and so on. Note that F can be a function of s, or simply a real or complex quantity, which is dependent on some or all of the N components x_i.

If we define the *variation* of a function F due to a relative change in a component x_i by

$$\frac{\Delta F}{F} = V_{x_i}^F = S_{x_i}^F \frac{\Delta x_i}{x_i} \qquad (3\text{-}4)$$

then the *worst-case* variation follows as

$$I = \left(\frac{\Delta F}{F}\right)_{\text{worst case}} = \sum_{i=1}^{N} |V_{x_i}^F| \qquad [3\text{-}5]$$

The so-called *Schoeffler criterion*, or the sum-of-squares, provides another useful figure-of-merit, namely

$$\Phi = \sum_{i=1}^{N} |V_{x_i}^F|^2 \qquad [3\text{-}6]$$

Table 3-1   Sensitivity relations

1.	$S_x^x = 1$	14.	$S_x^{1/y} = -S_x^y$
2.†	$S_x^{cx} = 1$	15.	$S_{1/x}^y = -S_x^y$
3.	$S_n^{xc^n} = n$	16.	$S_x^{y+c} = \dfrac{y}{y+c} S_x^y$
4.‡	$S_x^{y^n} = n S_x^y$	17.	$S_x^{u+v+\cdots} = \dfrac{1}{u+v+\cdots}(u S_x^u + v S_x^v + \cdots)$
5.	$S_x^{y^n} = \dfrac{1}{n} S_x^y$	18.	$S_{cx}^y = S_x^y$
6.	$S_x^{cy} = S_x^y$	19.	$S_{u/v}^y = \frac{1}{2}(S_u^y - S_v^y) = S_u^{y^{1/2}} - S_v^{y^{1/2}}$
7.	$S_x^y = S_{u_1}^y S_x^{u_1} + S_{u_2}^y S_x^{u_2} + \cdots$	20.	$S_x^{e^y} = y S_x^y$
	where $y = y(u_1, u_2, \ldots, u_n)$		
8.	$S_x^y = S_x^{|y|} + j\phi_y S_x^{\phi_y}$	21.	$S_x^{\ln y} = \dfrac{1}{\ln y} S_x^y$
9.	$S_x^{|y|} = \operatorname{Re} S_x^y$	22.	$S_x^{\sin y} = y \cot y S_x^y$
10.	$S_x^{y^*} = (S_x^y)^*$	23.	$S_x^{\cos y} = -y \tan y S_x^y$
11.	$S_x^{\phi_y} = \dfrac{1}{\phi_y} \operatorname{Im} S_x^y$	24.	$S_x^{\sinh y} = y \coth y S_x^y$
12.	$S_x^{uv\cdots} = S_x^u + S_x^v + \cdots$	25.	$S_x^{\cosh y} = y \tanh y S_x^y$
13.	$S_x^{u/v} = S_x^u - S_x^v$		

† c and n are constants.
‡ y, u, v are single-valued differentiable functions of x; also $y = |y| e^{j\phi_y}$.

The relative sensitivity of a function F can be computed by taking the derivative of F with respect to x, and multiplying by x/F, thus:

$$S_x^F = \left(\frac{dF}{dx}\right)\frac{x}{F} \qquad (3\text{-}7)$$

With (3-7) a list of useful sensitivity expressions can be derived as given in Table 3-1.

In some cases it is useful to define the *semi-relative sensitivity*

$$\mathscr{S}_x^F = F S_x^F = \frac{dF}{d[\ln x]} \qquad [3\text{-}8]$$

This is used, among other things, to characterize the pole or zero sensitivity to component change and is therefore sometimes called the *root sensitivity*. It is also useful when a change of the amplitude response to component change is of interest. Since the amplitude response $\alpha(\omega)$ and the phase response $\phi(\omega)$ are related to the transfer function $T(s = j\omega)$ (see Chapter 2, eq. 2-8) by

$$\alpha(\omega) = \operatorname{Re}[\ln T(j\omega)] \qquad (3\text{-}9a)$$

$$\phi(\omega) = \operatorname{Im}[\ln T(j\omega)] \qquad (3\text{-}9b)$$

it follows that, for a real component x,

$$\mathcal{S}_x^{\alpha(\omega)} = \frac{d\alpha(\omega)}{d[\ln x]} = \mathrm{Re}\left[\frac{d[\ln T(j\omega)]}{d[\ln x]}\right] = \mathrm{Re}[S_x^{T(j\omega)}] \qquad [3\text{-}10a]$$

Similarly,

$$\mathcal{S}_x^{\phi(\omega)} = \frac{d\phi(\omega)}{d[\ln x]} = \mathrm{Im}\left[\frac{d[\ln T(j\omega)]}{d[\ln x]}\right] = \mathrm{Im}[S_x^{T(j\omega)}] \qquad [3\text{-}10b]$$

Thus the change in amplitude response $\Delta\alpha(\omega)$ caused by a relative component change $\Delta x/x$ is given by

$$\Delta\alpha = \mathcal{S}_x^\alpha \frac{\Delta x}{x} = \mathrm{Re}\left[\frac{\Delta T}{T}\right]_{s=j\omega} \qquad (3\text{-}11)$$

From formula (9) in Table 3-1 we obtain

$$\Delta\alpha = \mathrm{Re}\left[\frac{\Delta T}{T}\right] = \mathrm{Re}[S_x^T]\frac{\Delta x}{x} = S_x^{|T|}\frac{\Delta x}{x} = \frac{\Delta|T|}{|T|} \qquad [3\text{-}12]$$

where $s = j\omega$ and we assume throughout that the component x is real. To obtain the worst-case amplitude error caused by the change of N components x, we therefore have, with (3-4) and (3-5),

$$I_\alpha = \Delta\alpha_{\text{worst case}} = \sum_{i=1}^{N} |\mathrm{Re}\, V_{x_i}^T|_{s=j\omega} \qquad (3\text{-}13)$$

The Schoeffler criterion then becomes:

$$\Phi_\alpha = \sum_{i=1}^{N} |\mathrm{Re}\, V_{x_i}^T|^2 \qquad (3\text{-}14)$$

The subscript α indicates that the function of interest is the amplitude response $\alpha(\omega)$. If it were the impedance Z, we would have

$$I_Z = \left(\frac{\Delta Z}{Z}\right)_{\text{worst case}} = \sum_{i=1}^{N} |V_{x_i}^T| \qquad (3\text{-}15a)$$

and

$$\Phi_Z = \sum_{i=1}^{N} |V_{x_i}^Z|^2 \qquad (3\text{-}15b)$$

3-2 GAIN-SENSITIVITY PRODUCT (GSP)

In the previous section we have assumed that the components x_i are passive and real. However, active filters are also subjected to variations of the active element which, most commonly, is the gain A of an operational amplifier. Ideally the gain A is infinite over an unlimited bandwidth; in practice it has a finite gain-bandwidth product. In general the dependence of a network function F on the opamp gain A can be expressed approximately in the form

$$F(A) \approx F_i + \frac{F_a}{A} \qquad (3\text{-}16)$$

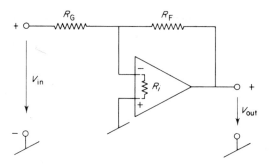

Fig. 3-1   Inverting operational amplifier

where F_i and F_a are independent of A. Calculating the sensitivity of F to A, we then obtain

$$S_A^F = -\left.\frac{F_a/F}{A}\right|_{A \to \infty} = 0 \qquad (3\text{-}17)$$

To be effective, the opamp must always be used in a frequency range in which its gain A is very large. Thus, according to (3-17), S_A^F tends to zero and is liable to elude any optimization process intended to minimize the sensitivity of F to component change. To prevent this from happening—and for various other reasons as well—it is useful to introduce the *gain-sensitivity product* (GSP) which is denoted by Γ, namely:

$$\Gamma_A^F = A S_A^F = -\left.\frac{F_a}{F}\right|_{A \to \infty} = -\frac{F_a}{F_i} \qquad [3\text{-}18]$$

This quantity remains finite for $A \to \infty$ and can therefore be included in the optimization process. The function F can represent any quantity that is relevant for the characterization of a network (e.g. transfer function, input impedance, pole, zero, ω_p, q_p, etc.).

Consider, for example, the inverting opamp shown in Fig. 3-1. The closed-loop gain β is given by

$$\beta = \frac{V_{out}}{V_{in}} = -\frac{R_F}{R_G}\left.\frac{1}{1 + \beta_0/A}\right|_{A \gg \beta_0} \approx -\frac{R_F}{R_G} \qquad (3\text{-}19a)$$

where

$$\beta_0 = \frac{R_F + R_G}{R_G} \qquad (3\text{-}19b)$$

The sensitivity of β to A is

$$S_A^\beta = \left.\frac{\beta_0}{A + \beta_0}\right|_{A \gg \beta_0} \to 0 \qquad (3\text{-}20a)$$

but the GSP is finite, namely,

$$\Gamma_A^\beta = \left.\frac{A\beta_0}{A + \beta_0}\right|_{A \gg \beta_0} \approx \beta_0 \qquad (3\text{-}20b)$$

Note that Γ_A^β decreases with β_0. Similarly, assuming an input resistance of the opamp equal to R_i ohms, the closed-loop input impedance is

$$Z_{in} = R_G + \frac{R_p}{1 + AB_0} \qquad (3.21a)$$

where

$$R_p = \frac{R_F R_i}{R_F + R_i} \quad \text{and} \quad B_0 = \frac{R_i}{R_F + R_i} \qquad (3\text{-}21b)$$

The sensitivity tends to zero with increasing gain A; thus

$$S_A^{Z_{in}} = \frac{R_F + R_i}{R_F + R_i + AR_i}\bigg|_{A \gg 1} \to 0 \qquad (3\text{-}22a)$$

but the GSP remains finite, namely,

$$\Gamma_A^{Z_{in}} = \frac{A(R_F + R_i)}{R_F + R_i + AR_i}\bigg|_{A \gg 1} = \frac{R_F + R_i}{R_i} \qquad (3\text{-}22b)$$

Note that $\Gamma_A^{Z_{in}}$ increases with R_F.

3-3 COEFFICIENT SENSITIVITY

If the network function $F(s)$ is given as a ratio of two polynomials with real coefficients, e.g.,

$$F(s) = \frac{\sum\limits_{i=1}^{m} b_i s^i}{\sum\limits_{j=1}^{n} a_j s^j} \qquad (3\text{-}23)$$

then the *coefficient sensitivity* gives the relative variation of a coefficient c_j caused by the relative change of a component x. As such, this definition is no different from any other relative sensitivity (see eq. 3-1), namely,

$$S_{x_i}^{c_j} = \frac{\partial[\ln c_j]}{\partial[\ln x_i]} \simeq \frac{\Delta c_j/c_j}{\Delta x_i/x_i} \qquad [3\text{-}24]$$

A complication arises, however, if the nominal value of the coefficient in question is zero, because then the quantity in eq. (3-24) goes to infinity. If, for example, the variation of F to a component x is to be obtained by way of the coefficient sensitivity, we obtain

$$V_{x_i}^F = (S_{c_j}^F S_{x_i}^{c_j}) \frac{\Delta x_i}{x_i} \qquad (3\text{-}25)$$

For a nominal $c_j = 0$ the first sensitivity term in eq. (3-25) equals zero, the second infinity. This can readily be prevented, however, by dividing the first and multiplying the second sensitivity term by c_j; thus,

$$V_{x_i}^F = \left(\frac{S_{c_j}^F}{c_j}\right)(c_j S_{x_i}^{c_j}) \frac{\Delta x_i}{x_i} \qquad [3\text{-}26]$$

In this way the benefit of using the relative sensitivity terms (e.g. the use of Table 3-1) is retained, while maintaining independence of the value of c_j. Similarly, the variation of F with respect to the gain A by way of the coefficient sensitivity is obtained as

$$V_A^F = \left(\frac{S_{c_j}^F}{c_j}\right)(c_j\Gamma_A^{c_j})\frac{\Delta A}{A^2} \qquad [3\text{-}27]$$

The calculation of a variation $\Delta F/F$ using the equations (3-26) and (3-27) is very useful. The first sensitivity term depends only on the initial network function $F(c_j, s)$ and takes on the form of a given frequency-dependent weighting function. The second term, which comprises the coefficient sensitivity, is generally the term to be minimized. This term will depend on the circuit selected for the realization of $F(c_j, s)$. Finally the relative component changes $\Delta x_i/x_i$ or $\Delta A/A^2$ depend entirely on the technology used for the filter realization and must generally be accepted as a given constraint. To decrease these changes requires the use of a higher-quality technology, which, in turn, results in a higher cost of the final network.

3-4   A FIGURE-OF-MERIT

When designing a single-amplifier second-order active filter there are generally more degrees of freedom than there are requirements or design equations. It is therefore possible to optimize the circuit in a variety of ways depending on the specifications. The degree of optimization that can be obtained is measured by a *figure-of-merit*. A useful figure-of-merit for an active filter is the degree of desensitization of the amplitude response to component changes that can be achieved. As we have seen, the achievable *minimum sensitivity* can be understood either in a worst-case or a sum-of-squares sense, as expressed by eqs. (3-13) and (3-14), respectively. Considering worst-case optimization, for example, the figure-of-merit for minimum amplitude-response sensitivity with respect to variations in the r resistors R_i, c capacitors C_j, and the gain A of a single-amplifier active filter is given by

$$I_\alpha = \sum_{i=1}^{r} |\text{Re}[V_{R_i}^{T(j\omega)}]| + \sum_{j=1}^{c} |\text{Re}[V_{C_j}^{T(j\omega)}]| + \left|\text{Re}[\Gamma_A^{T(j\omega)}]\frac{\Delta A}{A^2}\right| \qquad [3\text{-}28a]$$

The corresponding figure-of-merit in terms of the sum-of-squares follows from eq. (3-14) as

$$\Phi_\alpha = \sum_{i=1}^{r} |\text{Re}[V_{R_i}^{T(j\omega)}]|^2 + \sum_{j=1}^{c} |\text{Re}[V_{C_j}^{T(j\omega)}]|^2 + \left|\text{Re}[\Gamma_A^{T(j\omega)}]\frac{\Delta A}{A^2}\right|^2 \qquad [3\text{-}28b]$$

Minimizing either I_α or Φ_α as given by (3-28) involves the use of optimization computer routines that presently exceed the capacity of available pocket calculators. It can be shown, however, that a good indicator for the minimization of I_α or Φ_α is the minimization of the GSP, $\Gamma_A^{T(j\omega)}$ alone. One must simplify still further, however, since $\Gamma_A^{T(j\omega)}$ is a frequency-dependent function, which it is feasible to evaluate only at a limited number of frequencies. In the case of a second-order function this number of frequencies is quite small, since the characteristics of the corresponding network are most sensitive to component drift in the vicinity of the pole frequency. This will briefly be shown in what follows.

Consider a general second-order transfer function

$$T(s) = K\frac{\displaystyle\prod_{i=1}^{2}(s - z_i)}{\displaystyle\prod_{j=1}^{2}(s - p_j)} \qquad (3\text{-}29)$$

The variation of $T(s)$ to changes in the poles, zeros, and K is given by

$$\frac{dT(s)}{T(s)} = \frac{dK}{K} - \sum_{i=1}^{2} \frac{dz_i}{s - z_i} + \sum_{j=1}^{2} \frac{dp_j}{s - p_j} \tag{3-30}$$

If the pole Q, q_p is sufficiently high as to warrant optimization for minimum sensitivity, then (3-30) must be evaluated in the vicinity of the pole $p = p_1 = -\sigma_p + j\tilde{\omega}_p$ whose complex conjugate is $p^* = p_2 = -\sigma_p - j\tilde{\omega}_p$. In so doing, (3-30) can be approximated by†

$$\left.\frac{dT(s)}{T(s)}\right|_{s \approx j\tilde{\omega}_p} \approx \left.\frac{dp}{s - p}\right|_{s \approx j\tilde{\omega}_p} \tag{3-31}$$

Expression (3-31) must be evaluated at the frequencies at which $dT(j\omega)/T(j\omega)$ is most sensitive to component change. In the case of a general second-order network function this is at the frequencies $s = j(\omega_p \pm \sigma_p)$, which, in the case of a second-order bandpass network, corresponds to the -3-dB frequencies. Thus, (3-31) becomes

$$\left.\frac{dT(j\omega)}{T(j\omega)}\right|_{\omega_p \pm \sigma_p} = d\alpha(\omega_p \pm \sigma_p) + j\, d\phi(\omega_p \pm \sigma_p)$$

$$= \frac{1}{2}\left(\frac{dq_p}{q_p} - \frac{d\omega_p}{\omega_p}\right)(1 \mp j) + q_p \frac{d\omega_p}{\omega_p}(j \pm 1) \tag{3-32}$$

Limiting ourselves to a figure-of-merit with respect to the amplitude response as in (3-28), we obtain, from (3-32),

$$\Delta\alpha(\omega_p \pm \sigma_p) = \frac{1}{2}\frac{\Delta q_p}{q_p} \pm \frac{\Delta\omega_p}{\omega_p}(q_p \mp \tfrac{1}{2}) \tag{3-33}$$

Our figure-of-merit now corresponds either to the worst-case or to the sum-of-squares amplitude error at the frequencies $\omega_p \pm \sigma_p$. Considering the worst-case amplitude error, we obtain

$$I_\alpha = \Delta\alpha_{\text{worst case}} \approx \frac{1}{2}\left|\frac{\Delta q_p}{q_p}\right| + \left|q_p \frac{\Delta\omega_p}{\omega_p}\right| \tag{3-34}$$

where we assume that $q_p \gg 0.5$. In the following we shall consider only the amplitude variation due to a change in the amplifier gain A. With (3-28a), (3-34) then becomes

$$I_\alpha = \left|\text{Re}[\Gamma_A^{T(j\omega)}]\frac{\Delta A}{A^2}\right|_{\omega_p \pm \sigma_p} = V_A^{\alpha(\omega_p \pm \sigma_p)} = \tfrac{1}{2}|V_A^{q_p}| + |q_p V_A^{\omega_p}| \tag{3-35}$$

where

$$V_A^{\omega_p} = \Gamma_A^{\omega_p}\frac{\Delta A}{A^2} \tag{3-36a}$$

and

$$V_A^{q_p} = \Gamma_A^{q_p}\frac{\Delta A}{A^2} \tag{3-36b}$$

† G. S. Moschytz, *Linear Integrated Networks: Design*, Van Nostrand Reinhold Co., New York, 1975, p. 86.

To obtain the ω_p and q_p variation in (3-36), we utilize the fact that

$$\frac{d\omega_p}{\omega_p} = \text{Re}\left[\frac{dp}{p}\right] = \text{Re}[V_A^p] \tag{3-37a}$$

and

$$\frac{dq_p}{q_p} = -\sqrt{4q_p^2 - 1}\ \text{Im}\left[\frac{dp}{p}\right] = -\sqrt{4q_p^2 - 1}\ \text{Im}[V_A^p] \tag{3-37b}$$

Recognizing that the amplifier gain A is not constant, but will in practice itself be a function of frequency and therefore possess a real and imaginary part, i.e.

$$A(s = j\omega) = \text{Re}\ A(j\omega) + j\ \text{Im}\ A(j\omega) \tag{3-38}$$

we obtain, with (3-37),

$$\frac{\Delta\omega_p}{\omega_p} = V_A^{\omega_p} = \text{Re}\left[\Gamma_A^p\frac{\Delta A}{A^2}\right] = \text{Re}\left[\left(\Gamma_A^{\omega_p} - j\frac{\Gamma_A^{q_p}}{\sqrt{4q_p^2 - 1}}\right)\left(\text{Re}\left[\frac{\Delta A}{A^2}\right] + j\ \text{Im}\left[\frac{\Delta A}{A^2}\right]\right)\right] \tag{3-39a}$$

and

$$\frac{\Delta q_p}{q_p} = V_A^{q_p} = -\sqrt{4q_p^2 - 1}\ \text{Im}\left[\Gamma_A^p\frac{\Delta A}{A^2}\right]$$

$$= -\sqrt{4q_p^2 - 1}\ \text{Im}\left[\left(\Gamma_A^{\omega_p} - j\frac{\Gamma_A^{q_p}}{\sqrt{4q_p^2 - 1}}\right)\left(\text{Re}\left[\frac{\Delta A}{A^2}\right] + j\ \text{Im}\left[\frac{\Delta A}{A^2}\right]\right)\right] \tag{3-39b}$$

For all practical purposes, we can assume that $\Gamma_A^{\omega_p}$ and $\Gamma_A^{q_p}$ are real. Hence, the expressions in (3-39) simplify to

$$\frac{\Delta\omega_p}{\omega_p} = \Gamma_A^{\omega_p}\ \text{Re}\left[\frac{\Delta A}{A^2}\right] + \frac{\Gamma_A^{q_p}}{\sqrt{4q_p^2 - 1}}\ \text{Im}\left[\frac{\Delta A}{A^2}\right] \tag{3-40a}$$

and

$$\frac{\Delta q_p}{q_p} = -\sqrt{4q_p^2 - 1}\,\Gamma_A^{\omega_p}\ \text{Im}\left[\frac{\Delta A}{A^2}\right] + \Gamma_A^{q_p}\ \text{Re}\left[\frac{\Delta A}{A^2}\right] \tag{3-40b}$$

3-5 CONSIDERING THE FREQUENCY COMPENSATION

To evaluate eqs. (3-40) we must examine the frequency dependence of $A(s)$. For the filter sections tabulated in Chapter 5 *internal frequency compensation* is assumed, i.e. the opamps are compensated for a *single-pole roll-off.* Thus $A(s)$ has the form

$$A(s) = \frac{A_0\Omega}{s + \Omega} = \frac{\omega_g}{s + \Omega} \quad \text{lay element} \tag{3-41}$$

where Ω is the 3-dB frequency of the open-loop gain and $\omega_g = A_0\Omega$ is the *gain-bandwidth product.* Typically $A(s = j\omega)$ will have an amplitude and phase response as shown in Fig. 3-2. Note that over a relatively wide frequency band (approximately 300 Hz to 300 kHz) the amplitude has a -6dB/oct roll-off and a constant phase of $-90°$. Since this is most often the frequency range for which the active filters are intended, we can approximate $A(s)$ as follows:

$$A(s)|_{s=j\omega} \approx -j\frac{\omega_g}{\omega} \quad \text{integrator} \tag{3-42}$$

26

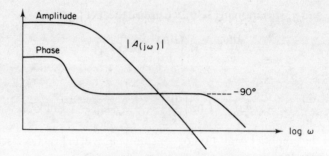

Fig. 3-2   Typical amplitude and phase response of opamp
with 'single-pole roll-off' frequency compensation

in which case

$$\text{Im}\left[\frac{\Delta A}{A}\right] = 0 \tag{3.43a}$$

With (3-42), it follows that

$$\text{Re}\left[\frac{\Delta A}{A^2}\right] = 0 \tag{3-43b}$$

and

$$\text{Im}\left[\frac{\Delta A}{A^2}\right] = \text{Im}\left[\frac{1}{A(s = j\omega)}\right]\frac{\Delta A}{A} \tag{3-43c}$$

Thus, with (3-40) and (3-43), we have for single-pole frequency compensation

$$\frac{\Delta\omega_p}{\omega_p} = V_A^{\omega_p} \approx \frac{\Gamma_A^{q_p}}{\sqrt{4q_p^2 - 1}}\,\text{Im}\left[\frac{\Delta A}{A^2}\right] \tag{3-44a}$$

and

$$\frac{\Delta q_p}{q_p} = V_A^{q_p} \approx -\sqrt{4q_p^2 - 1}\,\Gamma_A^{\omega_p}\,\text{Im}\left[\frac{\Delta A}{A^2}\right] \tag{3-44b}$$

If, in addition, ω_p is practically independent of A, then $\Gamma_A^{\omega_p} = 0$ and only (3-44a) remains to be inserted into eq. (3-35). If a more complicated external frequency compensation is used, or if the amplifier is used in a frequency range for which (3-42) is no longer valid, then all the terms in (3-40) must be used for the evaluation of (3-35).

For the case of internal frequency compensation, the expressions given by (3-44) are valid. Substituted in (3-35), the figure-of-merit for worst-case amplitude error becomes

$$I_\alpha = \left[\frac{1}{2}\left|\sqrt{4q_p^2 - 1}\,\Gamma_A^{\omega_p}\right| + \left|\frac{q_p\Gamma_A^{q_p}}{\sqrt{4q_p^2 - 1}}\right|\right]\left|\text{Im}\left[\frac{\Delta A}{A^2}\right]\right| \tag{3-45}$$

For $q_p \gg 1$ this simplifies to

$$I_\alpha = \left[q_p|\Gamma_A^{\omega_p}| + \tfrac{1}{2}|\Gamma_A^{q_p}|\right]\left|\text{Im}\left[\frac{\Delta A}{A^2}\right]\right| \tag{3-46}$$

For most of the circuits tabulated in Chapter 5, $\Gamma_A^{\omega_P} \approx 0$, so that

$$I_\alpha \sim \Gamma_A^{q_P} \qquad (3\text{-}47)$$

i.e it is sufficient to minimize the GSP with respect to q_p. For the remaining circuits both $\Gamma_A^{\omega_P}$ and $\Gamma_A^{q_P}$, weighted respectively as in (3-46), must be minimized. If the sum-of-squares quantity Φ_α as given by (3-28b) is used as the figure-of-merit, then for $q_p \gg 1$, the one-pole frequency compensation results in

$$\Phi_\alpha = [|q_p \Gamma_A^{\omega_P}|^2 + \tfrac{1}{4}|\Gamma_A^{q_P}|^2] \left| \mathrm{Im}\left[\frac{\Delta A}{A^2}\right] \right|^2 \qquad [3\text{-}48]$$

which in most cases also simplifies to a minimization of $\Gamma_A^{q_P}$.

If a more complicated scheme of frequency compensation than the single-pole roll-off implied in (3-44) is used, then the expressions given in (3-40) must be inserted in (3-35) or into the equivalent expression for Φ_α. Thus, for $q_p \gg 1$, we obtain, for example,

$$\begin{aligned}
I_\alpha &= \frac{1}{2}\left|\frac{\Delta q_p}{q_p}\right| + \left|q_p \frac{\Delta \omega_p}{\omega_p}\right| \\
&= \left| a\,\mathrm{Re}\left[\frac{\Delta A}{A^2}\right] - b\,\mathrm{Im}\left[\frac{\Delta A}{A^2}\right] \right| \\
&\quad + \left| a\,\mathrm{Im}\left[\frac{\Delta A}{A^2}\right] + b\,\mathrm{Re}\left[\frac{\Delta A}{A^2}\right] \right|
\end{aligned} \qquad (3\text{-}49)$$

where

$$a = \tfrac{1}{2}\Gamma_A^{q_P} \qquad (3\text{-}50a)$$

and

$$b = q_p \Gamma_A^{\omega_P} \qquad (3\text{-}50b)$$

From (3-49) it follows that

$$\left|\frac{\Delta \omega_p}{\omega_p}\right| = \left| \Gamma_A^{\omega_P}\,\mathrm{Re}\left[\frac{\Delta A}{A^2}\right] + \frac{1}{2q_p}\,\Gamma_A^{q_P}\,\mathrm{Im}\left[\frac{\Delta A}{A^2}\right] \right| \qquad (3\text{-}51a)$$

and

$$\left|\frac{\Delta q_p}{q_p}\right| = \left| \Gamma_A^{q_P}\,\mathrm{Re}\left[\frac{\Delta A}{A^2}\right] - 2q_p \Gamma_A^{\omega_P}\,\mathrm{Im}\left[\frac{\Delta A}{A^2}\right] \right| \qquad (3\text{-}51b)$$

Thus by using an appropriate frequency compensation, the real and imaginary parts of $(\Delta A/A^2)$ can be modified such that either $|\Delta \omega_p/\omega_p|$ or $|\Delta q_p/q_p|$, *but not both*, can be minimized.

The figures-of-merit given by (3-46) and (3-48) represent significantly simplified versions of the original quantities given by (3-28a) and (3-28b). This simplification is necessary if the design and optimization of second-order active filter sections is to be carried out on a minicomputer or even on a pocket calculator. Fortunately these simplified quantities are very good first-order measures for the degree of optimization attainable for any given second-order filter section. The minimum of I_α and Φ_α is relatively flat with respect to variations of passive components and largely dependent on the minimization of $\Gamma_A^{q_P}$ and, where applicable, of $q_p \Gamma_A^{\omega_p}$. If the complete expressions for I_α or Φ_α as given by (3-28) are to be used as figures-of-merit, because, say, the amplitude response $\alpha(\omega)$ is very sensitive to changes of the passive components, or because a considerable variation of the passive components is anticipated, then the minimization of I_α and Φ_α will require the use of a larger computer. A more extensive discussion of this type of optimization, in which all passive component sensitivities are included in the procedure, is quite straightforward, given the preliminaries presented above. Nevertheless, given our objectives, it is beyond the scope of this book.

CHAPTER 4

Building Blocks for Cascade Filter Design

4-1 LOW-Q BUILDING BLOCKS ($q_p \leq 2$)

Since the demands on active filters increase with the Q of their poles, it is reasonable to introduce a category of low-Q building blocks whose main characteristic is their utmost simplicity. This is particularly appropriate for communication systems in which the selectivity requirements for various pulse-shaping filters may be such as to permit the dominant pole Q to remain below, say, 2. To stipulate utmost simplicity for such second-order filter sections, or building blocks, implies

(a) minimum power (i.e. single opamp),
(b) minimum component count,
(c) minimum—or, if possible, no tuning requirements

The low-Q building blocks tabulated in Chapter 5 are based on the two active filter topologies shown in Fig. 4-1. The two are complementary to each other; the negative-feedback type in Fig. 4-1(a) uses the opamp in the open-loop mode and the positive-feedback type in Fig. 4-1(b) uses the opamp as a unity gain voltage follower. To describe these networks it is useful to introduce the following voltage transfer functions:

$$t_{12}(s) = \frac{n_{12}(s)}{\hat{d}(s)} = \frac{V_2}{V_1}\bigg|_{V_3 = 0}; \qquad t'_{12}(s) = \frac{n'_{12}(s)}{\hat{d}'(s)} = \frac{V'_2}{V'_1}\bigg|_{V'_3 = 0} \qquad (4\text{-}1a)$$

and

$$t_{32}(s) = \frac{n_{32}(s)}{\hat{d}(s)} = \frac{V_2}{V_3}\bigg|_{V_1 = 0}; \qquad t'_{32}(s) = \frac{n'_{32}(s)}{\hat{d}'(s)} = \frac{V'_2}{V'_3}\bigg|_{V'_1 = 0} \qquad (4\text{-}1b)$$

Note that the degree of the numerator polynomials is less than or equal to 2, that the denominator polynomials are second degree, and that they are the same for the two transfer functions of the same RC network.

With (4-1) we obtain for the negative-feedback (or class-3)† network

$$T(s) = \frac{V_{\text{out}}}{V_{\text{in}}} = -A\,\frac{t_{12}}{1 + At_{32}} \qquad (4\text{-}2)$$

---

† G. S. Moschytz, *Linear Integrated Networks: Design*, Van Nostrand Reinhold Co., New York, 1975, p. 133.

29

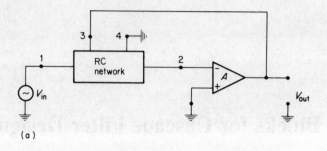

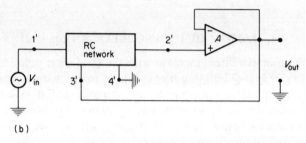

Fig. 4-1   Low-Q building blocks: (a) negative-feedback type
with opamp in open-loop mode, (b) positive-feedback type
with opamp in unity-gain mode

The opamp is in the open-loop mode; therefore $A \gg 1$ and

$$T(s)|_{A \gg 1} = -\frac{t_{12}(s)}{t_{32}(s)} = -\frac{n_{12}(s)}{n_{32}(s)} \tag{4-3}$$

Thus the zeros of $T(s)$ are the zeros of the passive forward transfer function $t_{12}(s)$ and the poles of $T(s)$ are the zeros of the passive feedback transfer function $t_{32}(s)$.

Introducing β as the closed-loop gain of the positive-feedback (or class-4†) network, we obtain

$$T(s) = \frac{V_{out}}{V_{in}} = \beta \frac{t'_{12}(s)}{1 - \beta t'_{32}(s)} \tag{4-4}$$

Since the closed-loop gain is unity, we have

$$T(s)|_{\beta = 1} = \frac{t'_{12}(s)}{1 - t'_{32}(s)} = \frac{n'_{12}(s)}{d'(s) - n'_{32}(s)} \tag{4-5}$$

Hence the zeros of $T(s)$ are the zeros of $t'_{12}(s)$ and the poles of $T(s)$ are the roots of the polynomial $d'(s) - n'_{32}(s)$. The poles and zeros of both building blocks in Fig. 4-1 are determined by the passive RC network. The gain is fixed either at unity or open-loop gain, and cannot be further adjusted. The pole Q is determined by the ratio of two resistors R_q and R, or two capacitors C_q and C, such that, in general

$$\frac{R_q}{R} \sim 4q_p^2 \qquad \text{or} \qquad \frac{C_q}{C} \sim 4q_p^2 \tag{4-6}$$

The GSP with respect to q_p has the general form:

$$\Gamma_A^{q_p} = kq_p^2 \tag{4-7}$$

† G. S. Moschytz, *Linear Integrated Networks: Design*, Van Nostrand Reinhold Co., New York, 1975, p. 133.

where the constant k is a function of the passive components. Note that the simplicity of the topologies in Fig. 4-1 are obtained at a price. Because of (4-6) the resistor or capacitor spread grows proportionately to $4q_p^2$. Furthermore, the GSP in eq. (4-7) is proportional to q_p^2. Thus the use of these simple filter building blocks is inherently limited to low-Q applications. By using them up to pole-Q values

$$q_p \leq 2 \tag{4-8}†$$

the disadvantages implied by (4-6) and (4-7) remain insignificant.

4-2 MEDIUM-Q BUILDING BLOCKS $(q_p \leq 20)$

Filter building blocks with q_p values up to, say, 20 are designated as 'medium-Q' building blocks for which the requirement of utmost simplicity can no longer be maintained. In order to avoid the q_p^2 proportionality of resistor spread and GSP that is present for low-q_p building blocks, some additional circuitry must be introduced, as shown in Fig. 4-2. The negative-feedback circuit shown in Fig. 4-2(a) differs from that of Fig. 4-1(a) in that a degree of positive feedback α has been included in the network, where

$$\alpha = \frac{R_q}{R_q + R} \tag{4-9}$$

This positive feedback modifies the transfer function of (4-2) as follows:

$$T(s) = \frac{V_{out}}{V_{in}} = -A\frac{t_{12}}{1 + A(t_{32} - \alpha)} \tag{4-10}$$

Hence, for open-loop gain, i.e. $A \gg 1$, we obtain

$$T(s)|_{A \gg 1} = -\frac{t_{12}(s)}{t_{32}(s) - \alpha} = -\frac{n_{12}(s)}{n_{32}(s) - \alpha \hat{d}(s)} \tag{4-11}$$

The resistor ratio α now provides an additional tuning parameter that can be used to tune q_p independently, to a first approximation, of the pole frequency ω_p.

The positive-feedback structure shown in Fig. 4-2(b) differs from that in Fig. 4-1(b) in that the closed-loop gain β is no longer unity but can be adjusted to a well-defined value, namely, assuming an ideal opamp,

$$\beta = 1 + \frac{R_q}{R} \tag{4-12}$$

The transfer function (4-4) now applies and we obtain

$$T(s) = \frac{V_{out}}{V_{in}} = \frac{n'_{12}(s)}{d'(s) - \beta n'_{32}(s)} \tag{4-13}$$

Here again β represents a tuning parameter with which q_p can be adjusted for, independently (to a first approximation) of the pole frequency ω_p.

---

† Naturally this upper limit is somewhat arbitrary and depends on the requirements for any given application.

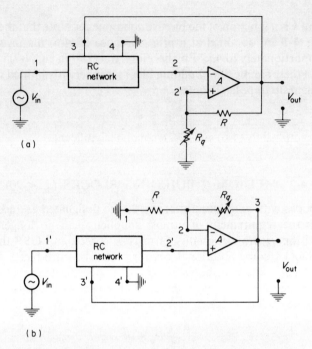

(a)

(b)

Fig. 4-2   Medium-Q building blocks: (a) negative-feedback
type, (b) positive-feedback type

For both circuits shown in Fig. 4-2 the relationship between R_q and q_p is of the form

$$R_q = k_1 - \frac{k_2}{q_p} \tag{4-14}$$

where k_1 and k_2 have the dimension ohms. This expression is shown graphically in Fig. 4-3. Note that the disadvantage of increased resistor spread with increasing q_p has been eliminated. On the other hand, another problem is apparent in Fig. 4-3, namely, that the exact value of R_q becomes increasingly critical as q_p becomes large. Hence the maximum value of q_p depends on the accuracy to which R_q can be adjusted to a required value. This in turn depends on the tuning equipment available and the technology with which the resistors are realized.

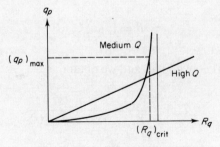

Fig. 4-3   Relationship between quality
factor q_p and tuning resistor R_q for
medium- and high-Q building blocks

Besides the problem of precision tuning for high-q_p values, which is implied by Fig. 4-3, a second, related, problem also exists. If we consider the sensitivity of q_p to a change in R_q, we obtain, from (4-14),

$$S^{q_p}_{R_q} = \frac{R_q}{k_2} q_p \tag{4-15}$$

i.e. the sensitivity is proportional to q_p. This proportionality to q_p of the sensitivity to a *passive* component is typical of the medium-Q circuits and cannot be avoided. Thus, with anything but the most high-quality (e.g. tantalum thin-film) resistors, $(q_p)_{max}$ should generally be limited by

$$q_p < 20 \tag{4-16}$$

In contrast to the low-Q circuits, where the gain-sensitivity product is proportional to q_p^2 (see eq. 4-7), it is proportional to q_p for the medium-Q circuits, i.e.

$$\Gamma^{q_p}_A \sim q_p \tag{4-17}$$

This is one more reason why the circuits used to realize the medium-Q building blocks can be used for q_p values up to an order of magnitude larger than the maximum q_p values recommended for the low-Q circuits.

4-3 HIGH-Q BUILDING BLOCKS ($q_p > 20$)

As explained in the previous section, the medium-Q building blocks tabulated in Chapter 5 are limited to q_p values in the order of 20 for two reasons; namely, (a) the critical tuning becomes increasingly difficult with increasing q_p (see Fig. 4-3) and (b) the q_p sensitivity to some of the passive components is proportional to q_p (e.g. see eq. 4-15). As a rule, single-amplifier active filters are therefore limited to medium-q_p values: higher-q_p values are attainable only by increasing the number of amplifiers.

A basic dual-amplifier configuration that is very suitable for high-Q applications is shown in Fig. 4-4(a). This network can be used to realize active impedances (i.e. active one-ports) as well as voltage transfer functions (i.e. active two-ports). In the case of voltage transfer functions the output voltage is taken from the output of one of the opamps, whereas the input voltage source is connected to a common input terminal as shown in Fig. 4-4(b).

Whether used as an active impedance or—as in the context of this book— to provide voltage transfer functions with complex conjugate poles, the design rules for the optimization of the network in Fig. 4-4 with respect to minimum sensitivity to component changes remain essentially the same. It can be shown that the circuits are optimum if the two capacitors (the circuits are canonic with respect to capacitors) used in the circuits are equal to a capacitor value C and if all resistors but one are equal to a resistor value R_0, where

$$R_0 = \frac{1}{\omega_p C} \tag{4-18}$$

and ω_p is the pole frequency. The remaining resistor, R_q, is used to determine the pole Q, and is given by

$$R_q = R_0 q_p = \frac{q_p}{\omega_p}\left(\frac{1}{C}\right) \tag{4-19}$$

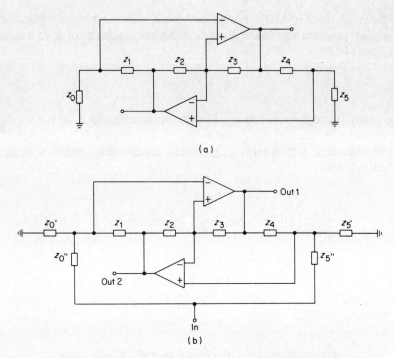

Fig. 4-4 High-Q building blocks: (a) basic dual-amplifier configuration
(b) configuration for voltage transfer functions

Note that this proportionality of R_q to q_p appreciably simplifies the tuning procedure (see Fig. 4-3). In practice the optimum resistor value R_o need not be realized exactly; it may be convenient to use a discrete resistor whose standard value, say R_d, is merely close to R_o. The difference between R_d and R_o can then be made up by a resistor, singled out for the purpose, whose value R_c is related to R_o and R_d by

$$R_c = \frac{R_o^2}{R_d} \tag{4-20}$$

Note that the circuit is particularly easy to tune. It is suitable for high-Q applications due to its low sensitivity to passive component variations (always less than unity), its easy tunability, and the simple design rules given above. These rules provide circuits that are optimum with respect to the gain-sensitivity product and that have minimum noise and maximum dynamic range.

CHAPTER 5

Design Equations and Flow Charts

5-1 THE DESIGN CRITERIA

In this chapter we provide the data necessary to design the second-order active filter types described in the preceding chapter. Seen as a whole, the circuits were selected to satisfy the general requirements of *minimum power, ease of tuning,* and *moderate tolerance specifications* as already outlined in Chapter 1. However, these requirements are by no means unique, and for any given filter function there are likely to be more than one circuit type that satisfies these requirements. Furthermore, the design equations for any given circuit provide more degrees of freedom than can be determined by the specifications and requirements outlined so far. This is no problem in practice, since additional specific requirements generally present themselves with the application for which a filter is intended. Nevertheless, for the purpose at hand, which is to provide well-proven active filters for a majority of the applications that the average engineer is likely to encounter, it is necessary—and, based on experience, it is possible—to compile a list of requirements and criteria that will cover most common applications. At the same time, such a list is sufficiently exhaustive as to make the choice of filter type, and the corresponding design equations, relatively easy. For the circuits presented in this chapter, the following list was used:

(a) Minimum number of passive components.
(b) Minimum number of opamps—and consequently minimum power.
(c) Minimum sensitivity of transfer characteristics to variations of the passive components.
(d) Minimum gain-sensitivity product in order to either reduce the need for highest quality opamps (e.g. wide bandwidth, low power, high open-loop gain) or, for a given opamp, to permit its use up to as high frequencies as possible.
(e) Simple tuning and production techniques.
(f) Minimum component spread, in particular when using hybrid-integrated (e.g. thick-film) passive components.

It should go without saying that all these requirements cannot be satisfied simultaneously for each individual circuit. However, within any given group (e.g. low-Q, medium-Q, and high-Q) there will be a subgroup of requirements that should primarily be fulfilled. The most conspicuous advantages and disadvantages resulting from this partial optimization will be briefly mentioned when the corresponding filter group is presented.

Having decided on a filter circuit, the actual design procedure begins. The purpose of the material presented in this chapter is to simplify this procedure for the designer to the greatest extent possible. To this end, the design equations for each of the twenty-three circuits presented here are expressed in terms of the most important design parameters (e.g. pole frequency, pole Q, etc.). A detailed flow chart is also presented for each circuit, which enables the designer to assemble a computer program (using any computer language) with which he can directly, or interactively, modify, improve, or simplify the circuit at hand. Each given flow chart has been translated into a pocket-calculator program (for the Texas Instruments SR-59 pocket calculator), into FORTRAN for use on a PDP-11-type computer, and into BASIC. The complete listings for these three program types are given, for each of the twenty-three circuits, in Appendices A, B, and C at the end of the book. Each program has been thoroughly laboratory tested by designing and building the corresponding filter section and checking the resulting response. Numerical examples based on these programs are given in Appendix D. Wherever applicable, i.e. in particular for most of the medium-Q and high-Q circuits, the pertinent tuning information is also given. This includes both the designation of the tuning resistors and the sequence in which they should be tuned.

In conclusion, we emphasize that every circuit presented in this chapter has been laboratory built and tested and found to be a recommendable circuit within the framework of the design criteria given above.

5-2 THE DESIGN EQUATIONS AND FLOW CHARTS

In the following three sections of this chapter, the circuit diagram and design equations for twenty-three second-order networks are given. They are grouped into three categories, namely, into low-Q networks (Section 5-3), medium-Q networks (Section 5-4), and high-Q networks (Section 5-5). For the most general second-order network, whose voltage transfer function is given by

$$T(s) = K \frac{s^2 + (\omega_z/q_z)s + \omega_z^2}{s^2 + (\omega_p/q_p)s + \omega_p^2} \tag{5-1}$$

a total of six design equations are given. These express the pole and zero parameters, as well as the gain constant K in terms of the circuit resistors R_i and capacitors C_j. In addition, the gain-sensitivity product (GSP) is also given in terms of the circuit components. Thus, for the general case, we have six design equations of the following form:

(a) For the pole parameters:

$$\omega_p = f_{\omega_p}(R_i, C_j) \tag{5-2}$$

$$q_p = f_{q_p}(R_i, C_j) \tag{5-3}$$

(b) For the zero parameters:

$$\omega_z = f_{\omega_z}(R_i, C_j) \tag{5-4}$$

$$q_z = f_{q_z}(R_i, C_j) \tag{5-5}$$

(c)   For the gain constant:

$$K = f_K(R_i, C_j) \tag{5-6}$$

(d)   For the gain-sensitivity product:

$$GSP = f_{GSP}(R_i, C_j) \tag{5-7}$$

Naturally, in the case of allpole networks (i.e. zeros at infinity) eqs. (5-4) and (5-5) do not apply. Furthermore, for all but the allpass network, the finite-zero networks (i.e. band-rejection networks) are assumed to have zeros nominally on the $j\omega$ axis (i.e. notch networks). For this case q_z is infinite and will not appear in a design equation. For allpass networks q_z is given by q_p, since $q_z = -q_p$.

Following the circuit diagram and the design equations for each circuit, a flow chart is given, which outlines the computation of all non-specified circuit components. In addition to specifying the network parameters (e.g. $\omega_p, q_p, \omega_z, K$), it is possible to specify the capacitor values and, in some cases, also the values of certain resistors. Each flow chart readily permits the computation of the remaining circuit components to be transferred to a pocket calculator (e.g. Texas Instruments SR-59 or Hewlett–Packard HP 67 or HP 97) or to a minicomputer (see Appendices A to D at the end of this book). The specified quantities then constitute the input data to the resulting analysis program. If the specification of some components is optional, this is indicated as such in the input box of the flow chart, e.g. R_i (optional) or C_j (optional). If an optional component is not specified, an appropriate value has been automatically assumed in the analysis programs given in the Appendices.

One network parameter than can generally not be arbitrarily specified is the gain constant K. The reason for this is twofold. First, the amplifier can provide only a limited gain, particularly when used in the closed-loop mode. Second, the topology of a given circuit may be such as to limit the gain constant to a maximum value K_0. In most of the design sequences given by the flow charts, the gain constant can, but need not, be specified, i.e. it is also optional. If the *specified value* K_{in} is larger than the *maximum available value* K_0, then the gain constant K obtained in the final circuit (and appearing in the 'print' box at the end of each flow chart) will, of necessity, be limited to K_0. If K_{in} is specified less than K_0, then the final gain constant K will equal K_{in}. Thus, three cases may occur with respect to the gain constant K:

(a) K_{in} (optional) is specified as less than K_0, i.e. $K_{in} < K_0$. Then

$$K = K_{in}$$

(b) K_{in} (optional) is specified as larger than K_0, i.e. $K_{in} > K_0$. Then, by default

$$K = K_0$$

(c) K_{in} (optional) is not specified. In the analysis program this corresponds to setting $K_{in} = 0$. Then, by default,

$$K = K_0$$

5-3   DESIGN DATA FOR LOW-Q NETWORKS ($q_p \leq 2$)

The sensitivity of the transfer characteristic (i.e. amplitude and phase response) to component variations is inherently low for low-Q networks. The sensitivity specifications for these networks will therefore be uncritical. For the same reason, no tuning requirements should be imposed on them. In terms of our list of design criteria, utmost circuit simplicity has top priority for this filter category. This means, in the first place, the use of a minimum number of passive components and of only one opamp, operated either in the unity-gain or the open-loop mode. In practice, highpass and lowpass networks with finite zeros (i.e. highpass and lowpass frequency-rejection networks or FRNs) generally require pole Q's higher than 2 so that they have not been included in this category.

The following abbreviations are used to designate the low-Q networks for which design data are given in this section:

1. LP–LQ   (Lowpass–Low Q)
2. BP–LQ-R   (Bandpass–Low Q-Resistive input)
3. BP–LQ-C   (Bandpass–Low Q-Capacitive input)
4. HP–LQ   (Highpass–Low Q)
5a. AP–Q.5-P   (Allpass–$Q < 0.5$-Positive)
5b. AP–Q.5-N   (Allpass–$Q < 0.5$-Negative)
6. AP–LQ   (Allpass–Low Q)
7. BR–LQ   (Band-rejection–Low Q)

1. LP–LQ

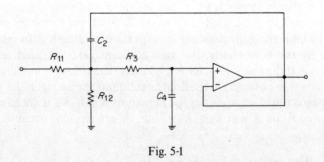

Fig. 5-1

$$T(s) = K \frac{\omega_p^2}{s^2 + (\omega_p/q_p)s + \omega_p^2} \qquad (1a)$$

$$R_1 = R_{11} \| R_{12} \qquad (1b) \qquad\qquad \omega_p^2 = \frac{1}{R_1 C_2 R_3 C_4} \qquad (1c)$$

$$q_p = \frac{\sqrt{R_3 C_2/R_1 C_4}}{1 + R_3/R_1} \qquad (1d) \qquad\qquad K = \frac{R_{12}}{R_{11} + R_{12}} \qquad (1e)$$

$$GSP = q_p \sqrt{\frac{C_2 R_1}{C_4 R_3}} \qquad (1f)$$

LP–LQ

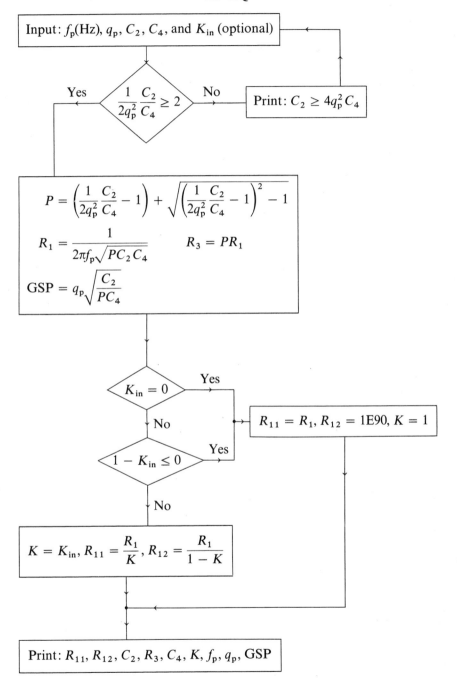

40

2. BP–LQ-R

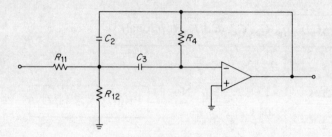

Fig. 5-2

$$T(s) = -K \frac{(\omega_p/q_p)s}{s^2 + (\omega_p/q_p)s + \omega_p^2} \qquad (2a)$$

$$R_1 = R_1 \| R_{12} \qquad (2b) \qquad\qquad \omega_p^2 = \frac{1}{R_1 C_2 C_3 R_4} \qquad (2c)$$

$$q_p = \frac{\sqrt{R_4 C_2/R_1 C_3}}{1 + C_2/C_3} \qquad (2d) \qquad\qquad K = \frac{R_{12}}{R_{11} + R_{12}} K_0 \qquad (2e)$$

$$K_0 = \text{GSP} = q_p^2 \left(1 + \frac{C_3}{C_2}\right) \qquad (2f)$$

BP–LQ-R

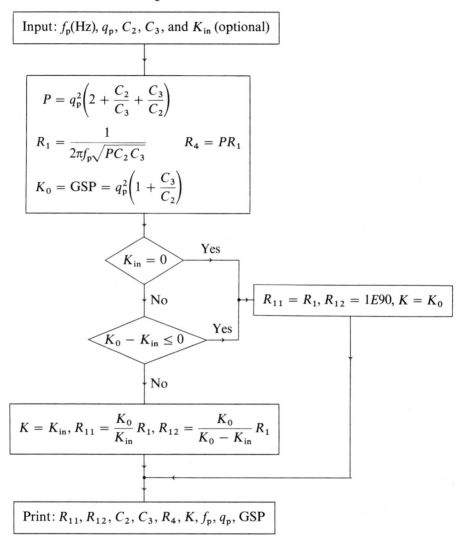

Input: f_p(Hz), q_p, C_2, C_3, and K_{in} (optional)

$$P = q_p^2\left(2 + \frac{C_2}{C_3} + \frac{C_3}{C_2}\right)$$

$$R_1 = \frac{1}{2\pi f_p\sqrt{PC_2C_3}} \qquad R_4 = PR_1$$

$$K_0 = GSP = q_p^2\left(1 + \frac{C_3}{C_2}\right)$$

$K_{in} = 0$ — Yes

No

$K_0 - K_{in} \leq 0$ — Yes

No

$R_{11} = R_1, R_{12} = 1E90, K = K_0$

$$K = K_{in}, R_{11} = \frac{K_0}{K_{in}}R_1, R_{12} = \frac{K_0}{K_0 - K_{in}}R_1$$

Print: $R_{11}, R_{12}, C_2, C_3, R_4, K, f_p, q_p$, GSP

42

3. BP–LQ-C

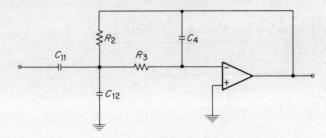

Fig. 5-3

$$T(s) = -K \frac{(\omega_p/q_p)s}{s^2 + (\omega_p/q_p)s + \omega_p^2} \qquad (3a)$$

$$C_1 = C_{11} + C_{12} \qquad (3b) \qquad\qquad \omega_p^2 = \frac{1}{C_1 R_2 R_3 C_4} \qquad (3c)$$

$$q_p = \frac{\sqrt{R_3 C_1/R_2 C_4}}{1 + R_3/R_2} \qquad (3d) \qquad\qquad K = \frac{C_{11}}{C_{11} + C_{12}} K_0 \qquad (3e)$$

$$K_0 = \text{GSP} = q_p \sqrt{\frac{C_1 R_2}{C_4 R_3}} \qquad (3f)$$

BP–LQ-C

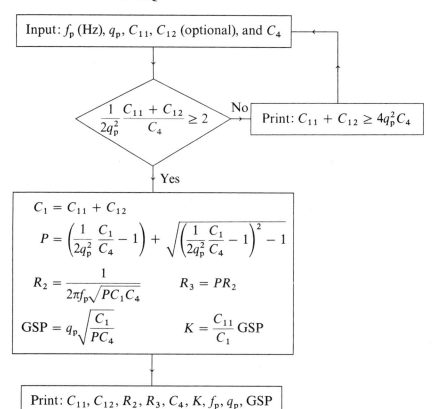

Input: f_p (Hz), q_p, C_{11}, C_{12} (optional), and C_4

$$\frac{1}{2q_p^2}\frac{C_{11} + C_{12}}{C_4} \geq 2$$

No → Print: $C_{11} + C_{12} \geq 4q_p^2 C_4$

Yes

$$C_1 = C_{11} + C_{12}$$

$$P = \left(\frac{1}{2q_p^2}\frac{C_1}{C_4} - 1\right) + \sqrt{\left(\frac{1}{2q_p^2}\frac{C_1}{C_4} - 1\right)^2 - 1}$$

$$R_2 = \frac{1}{2\pi f_p\sqrt{PC_1C_4}} \qquad R_3 = PR_2$$

$$GSP = q_p\sqrt{\frac{C_1}{PC_4}} \qquad K = \frac{C_{11}}{C_1} GSP$$

Print: $C_{11}, C_{12}, R_2, R_3, C_4, K, f_p, q_p$, GSP

4. HP–LQ

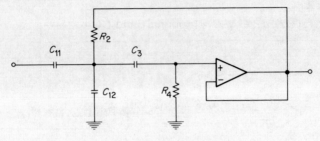

Fig. 5-4

$$T(s) = K \frac{s^2}{s^2 + (\omega_p/q_p)s + \omega_p^2} \qquad (4a)$$

$$C_1 = C_{11} + C_{12} \qquad (4b) \qquad\qquad \omega_p^2 = \frac{1}{C_1 R_2 C_3 R_4} \qquad (4c)$$

$$q_p = \frac{\sqrt{R_4 C_1 / R_2 C_3}}{1 + C_1/C_3} \qquad (4d) \qquad\qquad K = \frac{C_{11}}{C_{11} + C_{12}} \qquad (4e)$$

$$GSP = q_p^2 \left(1 + \frac{C_3}{C_1}\right) \qquad (4f)$$

HP–LQ

Input: f_p (Hz), q_p, C_{11}, C_{12} (optional), and C_3

$C_1 = C_{11} + C_{12}$

$P = q_p^2 \left(2 + \dfrac{C_3}{C_1} + \dfrac{C_1}{C_3} \right)$

$R_2 = \dfrac{1}{2\pi f_p \sqrt{PC_1 C_3}}$ $\qquad$ $R_4 = PR_2$

$GSP = q_p \sqrt{\dfrac{PC_3}{C_1}}$ $\qquad$ $K = \dfrac{C_{11}}{C_1}$

Print: $C_{11}, C_{12}, R_2, C_3, R_4, K, f_p, q_p, GSP$

5a. AP–Q.5-P

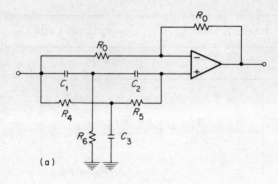

(a)

5b. AP–Q.5-N

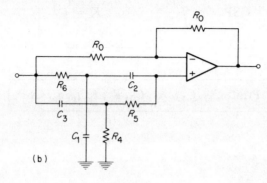

(b)

Fig. 5-5

$$T_P(s) = \frac{s^2 - (\omega_p/q_p)s + \omega_p^2}{s^2 + (\omega_p/q_p)s + \omega_p^2} \quad \text{(5a)}$$

$$T_N(s) = -\frac{s^2 - (\omega_p/q_p)s + \omega_p^2}{s^2 + (\omega_p/q_p)s + \omega_p^2} \quad \text{(5b)}$$

$$R_s = R_4 + R_5 \quad \text{(5c)}$$

$$C_s = \frac{C_1 C_2}{C_1 + C_2} \quad \text{(5d)}$$

$$\omega_p^2 = \frac{1}{R_4 R_5 C_s C_3} = \frac{1}{R_s R_6 C_1 C_2} \quad \text{(5e)}$$

$$q_p = \frac{1}{\omega_p(R_4 C_3 + R_s C_2)} \quad \text{(5f)}$$

AP–Q.5

$$\boxed{\text{Input:} f_p \text{ (Hz)}, q_p, C_1, C_2, C_3}$$

$$H = 1 - \frac{(C_1 + C_2)(C_2 + C_3) \cdot 4q_p^2}{C_1 C_2}$$

$H < 0$ — **Yes** → $\boxed{\text{Print:} C_1 = C_3 \geq C_2 \cdot 2q_p/(1 - 2q_p)}$

No

$$R_{4A}^\dagger = \frac{1 + \sqrt{H}}{2\omega_p q_p (C_2 + C_3)} \qquad R_{4B}^\dagger = \frac{1 - \sqrt{H}}{2\omega_p q_p (C_2 + C_3)}$$

$$R_{5A} = \frac{C_1 + C_2}{R_{4A} \omega_p^2 C_1 C_2 C_3} \qquad R_{5B} = \frac{C_1 + C_2}{R_{4B} \omega_p^2 C_1 C_2 C_3}$$

$$R_{6A} = \frac{1}{\omega_p^2 C_1 C_2 (R_{4A} + R_{5A})} \qquad R_{6B} = \frac{1}{\omega_p^2 C_1 C_2 (R_{4B} + R_{5B})}$$

$$\boxed{\text{Print:} C_1, C_2, C_3, R_{4A}, R_{5A}, R_{6A}, R_{4B}, R_{5B}, R_{6B}, f_p, q_p}$$

† Two solutions are obtained for resistors R_4 to R_6 (e.g. R_{4A} and R_{4B}); both solutions are valid for networks 5a and 5b. The values resulting in the smaller resistor spreads are recommended.

6. AP–LQ

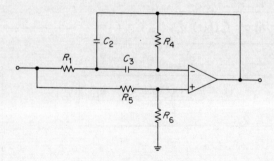

Fig. 5-6

$$T(s) = K \frac{s^2 - (\omega_p/q_p)s + \omega_p^2}{s^2 + (\omega_p/q_p)s + \omega_p^2} \qquad (6a)$$

$$\omega_p^2 = \frac{1}{R_1 C_2 C_3 R_4} \qquad (6b) \qquad\qquad 2\left(\frac{1}{R_4 C_2} + \frac{1}{R_4 C_3}\right) = \frac{1}{R_1 C_2} \frac{R_5}{R_6} \qquad (6c)$$

$$q_p = \frac{\sqrt{R_4/R_1}}{\sqrt{C_2/C_3} + \sqrt{C_3/C_2}} \qquad (6d) \qquad\qquad K = \frac{R_6}{R_5 + R_6} \qquad (6e)$$

$$\text{GSP} = q_p \sqrt{\frac{R_4 C_3}{R_1 C_2}} \qquad (6f)$$

AP–LQ

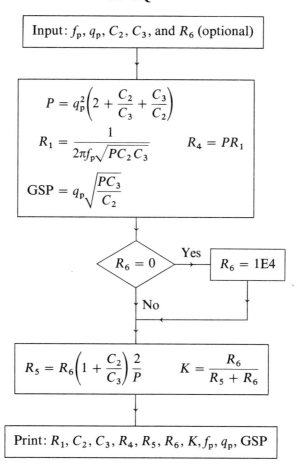

Input: f_p, q_p, C_2, C_3, and R_6 (optional)

$$P = q_p^2\left(2 + \frac{C_2}{C_3} + \frac{C_3}{C_2}\right)$$

$$R_1 = \frac{1}{2\pi f_p\sqrt{PC_2C_3}} \qquad R_4 = PR_1$$

$$GSP = q_p\sqrt{\frac{PC_3}{C_2}}$$

$R_6 = 0$ Yes $R_6 = 1E4$

No

$$R_5 = R_6\left(1 + \frac{C_2}{C_3}\right)\frac{2}{P} \qquad K = \frac{R_6}{R_5 + R_6}$$

Print: R_1, C_2, C_3, R_4, R_5, R_6, K, f_p, q_p, GSP

Note: Start with $C_2 = C_3$ or $C_2 > C_3$ for low GSP.

7. BR–LQ

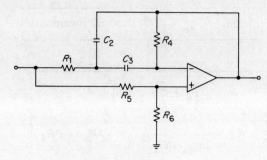

Fig. 5-7

$$T(s) = K \frac{s^2 + \omega_p^2}{s^2 + (\omega_p/q_p)s + \omega_p^2} \qquad (7a)$$

$$\omega_p^2 = \frac{1}{R_1 C_2 C_3 R_4} \qquad (7b)$$

$$\frac{1}{R_4 C_2} + \frac{1}{R_4 C_3} = \frac{1}{R_1 C_2} \frac{R_5}{R_6} \qquad (7c)$$

$$q_p = \frac{\sqrt{R_4/R_1}}{\sqrt{C_2/C_3} + \sqrt{C_3/C_2}} \qquad (7d)$$

$$K = \frac{R_6}{R_5 + R_6} \qquad (7e)$$

$$\mathrm{GSP} = q_p \sqrt{\frac{R_4 C_3}{R_1 C_2}} \qquad (7f)$$

BR–LQ

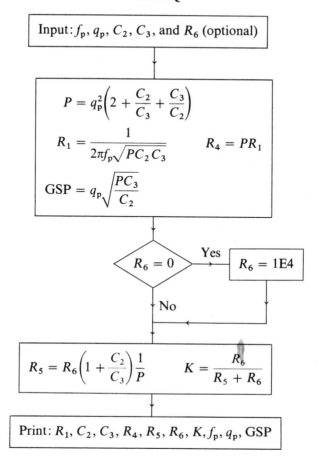

Input: f_p, q_p, C_2, C_3, and R_6 (optional)

$$P = q_p^2\left(2 + \frac{C_2}{C_3} + \frac{C_3}{C_2}\right)$$

$$R_1 = \frac{1}{2\pi f_p\sqrt{PC_2 C_3}} \qquad R_4 = PR_1$$

$$GSP = q_p\sqrt{\frac{PC_3}{C_2}}$$

$R_6 = 0$ — Yes → $R_6 = 1E4$

No

$$R_5 = R_6\left(1 + \frac{C_2}{C_3}\right)\frac{1}{P} \qquad K = \frac{R_6}{R_5 + R_6}$$

Print: R_1, C_2, C_3, R_4, R_5, R_6, K, f_p, q_p, GSP

Note: Start with $C_2 = C_3$ or $C_2 > C_3$ for low GSP.

5-4 DESIGN DATA FOR MEDIUM-Q NETWORKS ($q_p \le 20$)

The medium-Q circuits given in this section were selected on the basis of minimum gain-sensitivity product (GSP), minimum number of passive components, and use of only one opamp. Some kind of tuning, as discussed in detail in Chapter 6, is required for these circuits. Functional tuning (i.e. tuning of the operational circuits) has therefore been assumed and the necessary tuning data (i.e. tuning components and tuning sequence) is given. In most cases the tuning procedure is very simple. Only for one circuit (circuit 14, LPN/HPN–MQ) is the functional tuning relatively complicated and requires the computation of an optimum tuning sequence for each individual filter design. The optimum tuning sequence can be obtained by computing the sensitivity matrix with respect to all circuit components. This is described in detail in Chapter 6. An alternative circuit which may be tuned easily is filter No. 15, BR–LPN/HPN–MQ. This ease of tuning is acquired at the cost of more than the minimum number of capacitors, since an RC-loaded twin-T is used to obtain the frequency-notch characteristics.

The following abbreviations are used to designate the medium-Q networks for which design data are given in this section:

8. LP–MQ   (Lowpass–Medium Q)
9. BP–MQ-R   (Bandpass–Medium Q-Resistive input)
10. BP–MQ-C   (Bandpass–Medium Q-Capacitive input)
11. HP–MQ   (Highpass–Medium Q)
12. AP–MQ   (Allpass–Medium Q)
13. BR–MQ   (Band-rejection–Medium Q)
14. LPN/HPN–MQ   (Lowpass, Highpass notch–Medium Q)
15. BR–LPN/HPN–MQ   (Band-rejection–Lowpass, Highpass notch–Medium Q)

8. LP–MQ

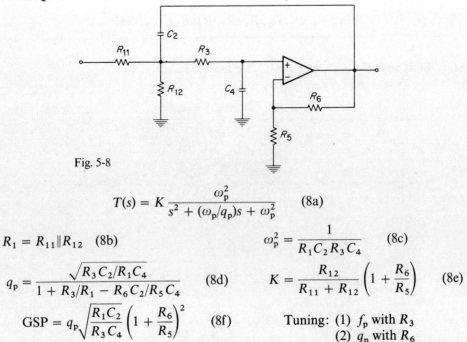

Fig. 5-8

$$T(s) = K \frac{\omega_p^2}{s^2 + (\omega_p/q_p)s + \omega_p^2} \qquad (8a)$$

$$R_1 = R_{11} \| R_{12} \quad (8b) \qquad\qquad \omega_p^2 = \frac{1}{R_1 C_2 R_3 C_4} \qquad (8c)$$

$$q_p = \frac{\sqrt{R_3 C_2 / R_1 C_4}}{1 + R_3/R_1 - R_6 C_2/R_5 C_4} \qquad (8d) \qquad K = \frac{R_{12}}{R_{11} + R_{12}}\left(1 + \frac{R_6}{R_5}\right) \qquad (8e)$$

$$GSP = q_p \sqrt{\frac{R_1 C_2}{R_3 C_4}}\left(1 + \frac{R_6}{R_5}\right)^2 \qquad (8f)$$

Tuning: (1) f_p with R_3
(2) q_p with R_6

LP–MQ

Input: f_p, q_p, C_2, C_4, K_{in} (optional), and R_5 (optional)

For minimal GSP: $P = \dfrac{C_2/C_4}{36q_p^2}\left[\sqrt{1 + 12q_p^2\left(1 + \dfrac{C_4}{C_2}\right)} + 1\right]^2$

Input: new P

$R_1 = \dfrac{1}{2\pi f_p\sqrt{PC_2 C_4}}$ $R_3 = PR_1$

IF $R_5 = 0$ THEN $R_5 = 1E4$

$R_6 = R_5\left[\dfrac{C_4}{C_2}(1 + P) - \sqrt{\dfrac{PC_4}{C_2}}\dfrac{1}{q_p}\right]$ $K_0 = 1 + \dfrac{R_6}{R_5}$

$GSP = q_p K_0^2 \sqrt{\dfrac{C_2}{PC_4}}$

$K_{in} = 0$ or $K_0 - K_{in} \leq 0$ — **Yes** → $R_{11} = R_1, R_{12} = 1E90, K = K_0$

No

$K = K_{in}, R_{11} = \dfrac{K_0}{K} R_1, R_{12} = \dfrac{K_0}{K_0 - K} R_1$

Print: $R_{11}, R_{12}, C_2, R_3, C_4, R_5, R_6, K, f_p, q_p, P, GSP$

9. BP–MQ-R

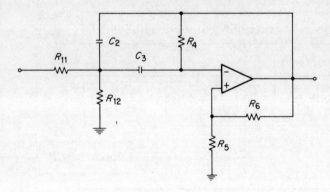

Fig. 5-9

$$T(s) = -K \frac{(\omega_p/q_p)s}{s^2 + (\omega_p/q_p)s + \omega_p^2} \qquad (9a)$$

$$R_1 = R_{11} \| R_{12} \qquad (9b)$$

$$\omega_p^2 = \frac{1}{R_1 C_2 C_3 R_4} \qquad (9c)$$

$$q_p = \frac{\sqrt{R_4 C_2/R_1 C_3}}{1 + C_2/C_3 - R_4 R_5/R_1 R_6} \qquad (9d)$$

$$K = \frac{R_{12}}{R_{11} + R_{12}} q_p \left(1 + \frac{R_5}{R_6}\right) \sqrt{\frac{R_4 C_3}{R_1 C_2}} \qquad (9e)$$

$$\text{GPS} = q_p \left(1 + \frac{R_5}{R_6}\right)^2 \sqrt{\frac{R_4 C_3}{R_1 C_2}} \qquad (9f)$$

Tuning: (1) f_p with R_4
(2) q_p with R_5

BP–MQ-R

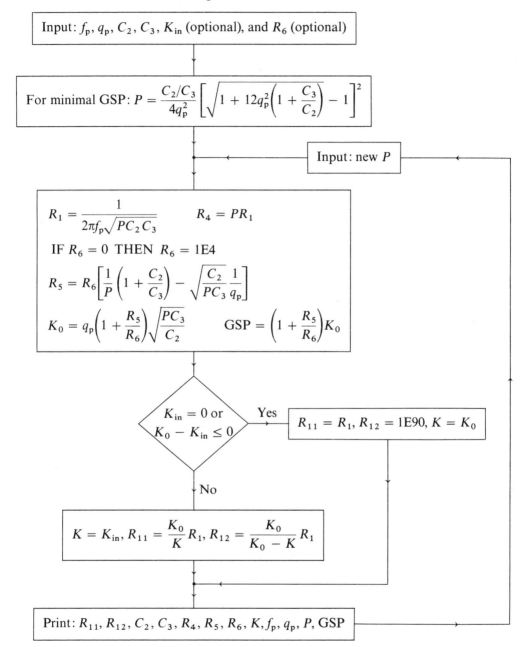

Input: f_p, q_p, C_2, C_3, K_{in} (optional), and R_6 (optional)

For minimal GSP: $P = \dfrac{C_2/C_3}{4q_p^2}\left[\sqrt{1 + 12q_p^2\left(1 + \dfrac{C_3}{C_2}\right)} - 1\right]^2$

Input: new P

$R_1 = \dfrac{1}{2\pi f_p\sqrt{PC_2 C_3}}$ $R_4 = PR_1$

IF $R_6 = 0$ THEN $R_6 = 1E4$

$R_5 = R_6\left[\dfrac{1}{P}\left(1 + \dfrac{C_2}{C_3}\right) - \sqrt{\dfrac{C_2}{PC_3}\dfrac{1}{q_p}}\right]$

$K_0 = q_p\left(1 + \dfrac{R_5}{R_6}\right)\sqrt{\dfrac{PC_3}{C_2}}$ $GSP = \left(1 + \dfrac{R_5}{R_6}\right)K_0$

$K_{in} = 0$ or $K_0 - K_{in} \leq 0$

Yes

$R_{11} = R_1,\ R_{12} = 1E90,\ K = K_0$

No

$K = K_{in},\ R_{11} = \dfrac{K_0}{K}R_1,\ R_{12} = \dfrac{K_0}{K_0 - K}R_1$

Print: R_{11}, R_{12}, C_2, C_3, R_4, R_5, R_6, K, f_p, q_p, P, GSP

56

10. BP–MQ-C

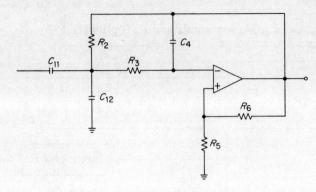

Fig. 5-10

$$T(s) = -K \frac{(\omega_p/q_p)s}{s^2 + (\omega_p/q_p)s + \omega_p^2} \qquad (10a)$$

$$C_1 = C_{11} + C_{12} \quad (10b) \qquad\qquad \omega_p^2 = \frac{1}{C_1 R_2 R_3 C_4} \quad (10c)$$

$$q_p = \frac{\sqrt{C_1 R_3/C_4 R_2}}{1 + R_3/R_2 - C_1 R_5/C_4 R_6} \quad (10d) \qquad K = \frac{C_{11}}{C_{11} + C_{12}} q_p \left(1 + \frac{R_5}{R_6}\right) \sqrt{\frac{C_1 R_2}{C_4 R_3}} \quad (10e)$$

$$\mathrm{GSP} = q_p \left(1 + \frac{R_5}{R_6}\right)^2 \sqrt{\frac{C_1 R_2}{C_4 R_3}} \quad (10f)$$

Tuning: (1) f_p with R_2 or R_3
(2) q_p with R_5

BP–MQ

Input: f_p, q_p, C_{11}, C_{12} (optional), C_4, and R_6 (optional)

For minimal GSP: $C_1 = C_{11} + C_{12}$, $P = \dfrac{C_1/C_4}{36q_p^2}\left[\sqrt{1 + 12q_p^2\left(1 + \dfrac{C_4}{C_1}\right)} + 1\right]^2$

Input: new P

$R_2 = \dfrac{1}{2\pi f_p\sqrt{PC_1C_4}}$ $R_3 = PR_2$

IF $R_6 = 0$ THEN $R_6 = 1E4$

$R_5 = R_6\left[\dfrac{C_4}{C_1}(1 + P) - \dfrac{1}{q_p}\sqrt{\dfrac{PC_4}{C_1}}\right]$

$K = \dfrac{C_{11}}{C_1}\left(1 + \dfrac{R_5}{R_6}\right)q_p\sqrt{\dfrac{C_1}{PC_4}}$

$\text{GSP} = q_p\left(1 + \dfrac{R_5}{R_6}\right)^2\sqrt{\dfrac{C_1}{PC_4}}$

Print: C_{11}, C_{12}, R_2, R_3, C_4, R_5, R_6, K, f_p, q_p, P, GSP

11. HP–MQ

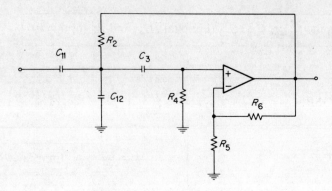

Fig. 5-11

$$T(s) = K \frac{s^2}{s^2 + (\omega_p/q_p)s + \omega_p^2} \qquad (11a)$$

$$C_1 = C_{11} + C_{12} \qquad (11b) \qquad\qquad \omega_p^2 = \frac{1}{C_1 R_2 C_3 R_4} \qquad (11c)$$

$$q_p = \frac{\sqrt{R_4 C_1/R_2 C_3}}{1 + C_1/C_3 - R_4 R_6/R_2 R_5} \qquad (11d) \qquad\qquad K = \frac{C_{11}}{C_1}\left(1 + \frac{R_6}{R_5}\right) \qquad (11e)$$

$$\mathrm{GSP} = q_p\left(1 + \frac{R_6}{R_5}\right)^2 \sqrt{\frac{R_4 C_3}{R_2 C_1}} \qquad (11f)$$

Tuning: (1) f_p with R_2 or R_4
(2) q_p with R_6

HP–MQ

Input: f_p, q_p, C_{11}, C_{12} (optional), C_3, and R_5 (optional)

For minimal GSP: $C_1 = C_{11} + C_{12}$, $P = \dfrac{C_1/C_3}{4q_p^2}\left[\sqrt{1 + 12q_p^2\left(1 + \dfrac{C_3}{C_1}\right)} - 1\right]^2$

Input: new P

$$R_2 = \frac{1}{2\pi f_p\sqrt{PC_1C_3}} \qquad R_4 = PR_2$$

IF $R_5 = 0$ THEN $R_5 = 1E4$

$$R_6 = R_5\left[\frac{1}{P}\left(1 + \frac{C_1}{C_3}\right) - \sqrt{\frac{C_1}{PC_3}\frac{1}{q_p}}\right]$$

$$K = \frac{C_{11}}{C_1}\left(1 + \frac{R_6}{R_5}\right)$$

$$GSP = q_p\left(1 + \frac{R_6}{R_5}\right)^2\sqrt{\frac{PC_3}{C_1}}$$

Print: C_{11}, C_{12}, R_2, C_3, R_4, R_5, R_6, K, f_p, q_p, P, GSP

12. AP–MQ

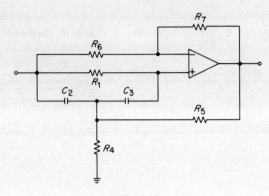

Fig. 5-12

$$T(s) = \frac{s^2 - (\omega_p/q_p)s + \omega_p^2}{s^2 + (\omega_p/q_p)s + \omega_p^2} \qquad (12a)$$

$$R_p = R_4 \| R_5 \qquad (12b) \qquad \qquad \omega_p^2 = \frac{1}{R_1 C_2 C_3 R_p} \qquad (12c)$$

$$q_p = \frac{\omega_p}{(1/R_p C_2)(R_7/R_6) - 1/R_1 C_2 - 1/R_1 C_3}$$

$$= \frac{\omega_p}{1/R_1 C_2 + 1/R_1 C_3 + 1/R_4 C_2 - (1/R_5 C_2)(R_7/R_6)} \qquad (12d)$$

$$\text{GSP} = q_p \frac{R_p}{R_5} \left(1 + \frac{R_7}{R_6}\right)^2 \sqrt{\frac{R_1 C_3}{R_p C_2}} \qquad (12e)$$

Tuning: (1) f_p with R_1
(2) $|T(f_p)| = 1$ with R_4
(3) q_p with R_7

AP–MQ

Input: f_p, q_p, C_2, C_3, and R_6 (optional)

For minimal GSP:

$$x = \frac{C_2}{C_3}, \quad P = \frac{2q_p^2(1 + x) - x}{6q_p^2(1 + x)^2}\left[\sqrt{1 + \left(\frac{6q_p^2(1 + x)^2}{2q_p^2(1 + x) - x}\right)^2 \cdot \frac{1}{3(1 + x)^2}} - 1\right]$$

Input: new P

$$R_1 = \frac{1}{2\pi f_p\sqrt{C_2 C_3 P}} \qquad R_p = PR_1$$

IF $R_6 = 0$ THEN $R_6 = 1E4$

$$R_7 = R_6\left[P\left(1 + \frac{C_2}{C_3}\right) + \frac{1}{q_p}\sqrt{\frac{PC_2}{C_3}}\right]$$

$$\alpha = 1 - \frac{2\sqrt{PC_2/C_3}}{q_p(1 + R_7/R_6)} \qquad R_5 = \frac{R_p}{\alpha} \qquad R_4 = \frac{R_p}{1 - \alpha}$$

$$\text{GSP} = \alpha q_p\left(1 + \frac{R_7}{R_6}\right)^2\sqrt{\frac{C_3}{PC_2}}$$

Print: R_1, C_2, C_3, R_4, R_5, R_6, R_7, f_p, q_p, P, GSP

13. BR–MQ

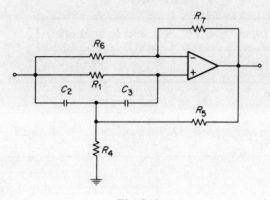

Fig. 5-13

$$T(s) = \frac{s^2 + \omega_p^2}{s^2 + (\omega_p/q_p)s + \omega_p^2} \qquad (13a)$$

$$R_p = R_4 \| R_5 \qquad (13b) \qquad \omega_p^2 = \frac{1}{R_1 C_2 C_3 R_p} \qquad (13c)$$

$$\frac{1}{R_1 C_2} + \frac{1}{R_1 C_3} = \frac{1}{R_p C_2} \frac{R_7}{R_6} \qquad (13d)$$

$$q_p = \frac{\omega_p}{1/R_1 C_2 + 1/R_1 C_3 + 1/R_4 C_2 - (1/R_5 C_2)(R_7/R_6)} \qquad (13e)$$

$$\text{GSP} = q_p \frac{R_p}{R_5} \left(1 + \frac{R_7}{R_6}\right)^2 \sqrt{\frac{R_1 C_3}{R_p C_2}} \qquad (13f)$$

Tuning: (1) f_p with R_1, (2) $|T(f_p)| = 0$ with R_4, (3) q_p with R_7

BR–MQ

Input: f_p, q_p, C_2, C_3, and R_6 (optional)

Starting value near the minimum of GSP: $P = \dfrac{1}{3(1 + C_2/C_3)}$

Input: new P

$R_1 = \dfrac{1}{2\pi f_p \sqrt{C_2 C_3 P}}$ $\qquad$ $R_p = PR_1$

IR $R_6 = 0$ THEN $R_6 = 1E4$

$R_7 = R_6\left(1 + \dfrac{C_2}{C_3}\right)P$

$\alpha = 1 - \dfrac{\sqrt{PC_2/C_3}}{q_p(1 + R_7/R_6)}$ $\qquad$ $R_5 = \dfrac{R_p}{\alpha}$ $\qquad$ $R_4 = \dfrac{R_p}{1 - \alpha}$

$\mathrm{GSP} = q_p\alpha\left(1 + \dfrac{R_7}{R_6}\right)^2 \sqrt{\dfrac{C_3}{PC_2}}$

Print: $R_1, C_2, C_3, R_4, R_5, R_6, R_7, f_p, q_p, P, \mathrm{GSP}$

14. LPN/HPN–MQ

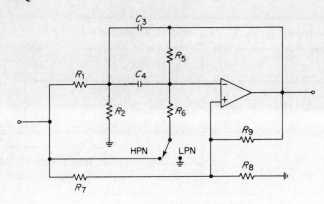

Fig. 5-14

$$T(s) = K \frac{s^2 + \omega_z^2}{s^2 + (\omega_p/q_p)s + \omega_p^2} \qquad (14a)$$

$$K = \frac{R_8}{R_7 + R_8} \qquad (14b)$$

$$\omega_p^2 = \frac{R_1 + R_2}{R_1 R_2 C_3 C_4} \left[\frac{1}{R_5} - \frac{R_7 R_8}{R_6 R_9 (R_7 + R_8)} \right] \qquad (14c)$$

LPN: *HPN:*

$$\omega_z^2 = \frac{(R_1 + R_2)(R_5 + R_6)}{R_1 R_2 C_3 C_4 R_5 R_6} \qquad (14d')$$

$$\omega_z^2 = \frac{R_1 + R_2}{R_1 R_2 C_3 C_4}$$

$$\times \left[\frac{1}{R_5} - \frac{R_7(R_8 + R_9)}{R_6 R_8 R_9} \right] \qquad (14d'')$$

$$\frac{C_4}{R_2} + \frac{(C_3 + C_4)(R_5 + R_6)}{R_5 R_6} = \frac{C_4 R_7(R_8 + R_9)}{R_1 R_8 R_9} \qquad (14e')$$

$$\frac{C_4}{R_2} + \frac{C_3 + C_4}{R_5} = \frac{R_7(R_8 + R_9)}{R_8 R_9} \left(\frac{C_4}{R_1} + \frac{C_3 + C_4}{R_6} \right) \qquad (14e'')$$

$$q_p = \frac{\omega_p}{\dfrac{C_3 + C_4}{C_3 C_4} \left[\dfrac{1}{R_5} - \dfrac{R_7 R_8}{R_6 R_9 (R_7 + R_8)} \right] - \dfrac{R_7 R_8 (R_1 + R_2)}{C_3 R_1 R_2 R_9 (R_7 + R_8)}} \qquad (14f)$$

LPN/HPN–MQ

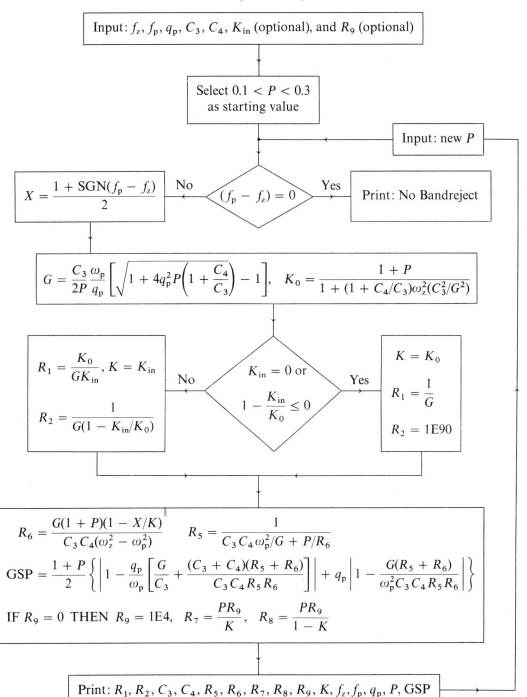

15. BR–LPN/HPN–MQ

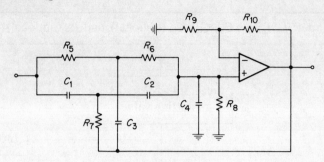

Fig. 5-15

$$T(s) = K \frac{s^2 + \omega_z^2}{s^2 + (\omega_p/q_p)s + \omega_p^2} \quad \text{(15a)}$$

$$C_s = \frac{C_1 C_2}{C_1 + C_2} \quad \text{(15b)}$$

$$K = \frac{1 + R_{10}/R_9}{1 + C_4/C_s} \quad \text{(15c)}$$

$$R_s = R_5 + R_6 \quad \text{(15d)}$$

$$\omega_z^2 = \frac{1}{R_5 R_6 C_s C_3} = \frac{1}{R_s R_7 C_1 C_2} \quad \text{(15e)}$$

$$\omega_p = \omega_z \sqrt{\frac{1 + R_s/R_8}{1 + C_4/C_s}} \quad \text{(15f)}$$

$$\hat{q} = \frac{1}{2\sqrt{(1 + C_2/C_1)(1 + C_2/C_3)}} \quad \text{(15g)}$$

$$q_p = \hat{q} \frac{(1 + C_4/C_s)(\omega_p/\omega_z)}{\hat{q}(1/R_8 C_s \omega_z + R_s C_4 \omega_z) - R_{10}/R_9} \quad \text{(15h)}$$

$$\text{GSP} = q_p \left(1 + \frac{R_{10}}{R_9}\right)^2 \frac{\sqrt{R_5 C_3/R_6 C_s} + \sqrt{R_s C_2/R_7 C_1}}{(1 + C_4/C_s)(\omega_p/\omega_z)} \quad \text{(15i)}$$

Tuning: (1) f_z with R_5, R_6 and R_7 iterative
(2) f_p with R_8
(3) q_p with R_{10}

BR–LPN/HPN–MQ

Input: f_z, f_p, q_p, C_1, C_2, C_3, C_4, and R_9 (optional)

$$\hat{q} = \frac{1}{2\sqrt{(1 + C_2/C_1)(1 + C_2/C_3)}} \qquad R_5 = \frac{1}{2\omega_z \hat{q}(C_2 + C_3)} \qquad C_s = \frac{C_1 C_2}{C_1 + C_2}$$

$$R_6 = \frac{(1 + C_2/C_1)}{R_5 \omega_z^2 C_2 C_3} \qquad R_s = R_5 + R_6$$

$$R_7 = \frac{1}{\omega_z^2 C_1 C_2 R_s} \qquad H = \left(1 + \frac{C_4}{C_s}\right)\frac{\omega_p^2}{\omega_z^2} - 1$$

No ← $H < 0$ → Yes

Print: $C_4 \geq \left(\dfrac{f_z^2}{f_p^2} - 1\right)\dfrac{C_1 C_2}{C_1 + C_2}$

$$R_8 = \frac{R_5 + R_6}{H}$$ ← No ← $H = 0$ → Yes → $R_8 = 1E90$

IF $R_9 = 0$ THEN $R_9 = 1E4$

$$R_{10} = R_9 \hat{q}\left[\frac{1}{R_8 C_s \omega_z} + R_s C_4 \omega_z - \frac{(1 + C_4/C_s)(\omega_p/\omega_z)}{q_p}\right]$$

$$\mathrm{GSP} = q_p\left(1 + \frac{R_{10}}{R_9}\right)^2 \frac{\sqrt{R_5 C_3/R_6 C_s} + \sqrt{R_s C_2/R_7 C_1}}{(1 + C_4/C_s)\cdot(\omega_p/\omega_z)} \qquad K = \frac{1 + R_{10}/R_9}{1 + C_4/C_s}$$

Print: C_1, C_2, C_3, C_4, R_5, R_6, R_7, R_8, R_9, R_{10}, f_z, f_p, q_p, K, GSP

5-5 DESIGN DATA FOR HIGH-Q NETWORKS ($q_p > 20$)

High-Q active networks require at least two opamps per second-order filter function. Whereas any second-order active network can be realized with two opamps, it is sometimes desirable to obtain more than one filter function (e.g. lowpass and bandpass) from the same building block. This is readily possible with three-opamp circuits, which we refer to as general-purpose filters. The filters in this high-Q category generally have lower sensitivities to active and passive components than do their single-amplifier counterparts. Furthermore, the functional tuning procedure is generally simpler, since the pole frequency and Q can often be tuned for, independently of one another.

The following abbreviations are used to designate the high-Q networks for which design data are given in this section:

16. LP–HQ   (Lowpass–High Q)
17. BP–HQ   (Bandpass–High Q)
18. HP–HQ   (Highpass–High Q)
19. AP–HQ   (Allpass–High Q)
20. BR–HQ   (Band-rejection–High Q)
21. LPN/HPN–HQ   (Lowpass, Highpass notch–High Q)
22. GP1   (General purpose 1)
23. GP2   (General purpose 2)

16. LP–HQ

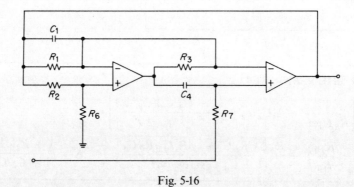

Fig. 5-16

$$T(s) = K \frac{\omega_p^2}{s^2 + (\omega_p/q_p)s + \omega_p^2} \quad (16a)$$

$$K = 1 + \frac{R_2}{R_6} \quad (16b)$$

$$\omega_p^2 = \frac{R_6}{R_2 R_3 R_7 C_1 C_4} \quad (16c)$$

$$q_p = \omega_p R_1 C_1 \quad (16d)$$

Tuning: (1) f_p with R_7, (2) q_p with R_1

LP–HQ

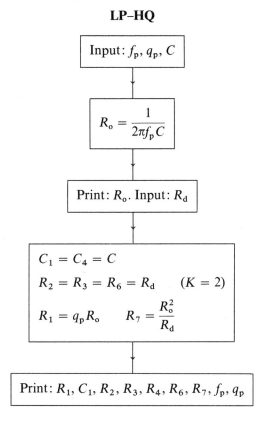

$$\boxed{\text{Input:}\ f_{\text{p}},\ q_{\text{p}},\ C}$$

$$\boxed{R_{\text{o}} = \frac{1}{2\pi f_{\text{p}} C}}$$

$$\boxed{\text{Print:}\ R_{\text{o}}.\ \text{Input:}\ R_{\text{d}}}$$

$$\boxed{\begin{aligned} &C_1 = C_4 = C \\ &R_2 = R_3 = R_6 = R_{\text{d}} \qquad (K = 2) \\ &R_1 = q_{\text{p}} R_{\text{o}} \qquad R_7 = \frac{R_{\text{o}}^2}{R_{\text{d}}} \end{aligned}}$$

$$\boxed{\text{Print:}\ R_1,\ C_1,\ R_2,\ R_3,\ R_4,\ R_6,\ R_7,\ f_{\text{p}},\ q_{\text{p}}}$$

Note: R_{o} is the *o*ptimal resistor for low GSP and R_{d} is the *d*iscrete resistor value, which should be close to R_{o}.

17. BP–HQ

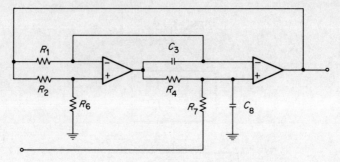

Fig. 5-17

$$T(s) = K \frac{(\omega_p/q_p)s}{s^2 + (\omega_p/q_p)s + \omega_p^2} \qquad (17a)$$

$$K = 1 + \frac{R_2}{R_6} \qquad (17b)$$

$$\omega_p^2 = \frac{R_2}{R_1 R_4 R_6 C_3 C_8} \qquad (17c)$$

$$q_p = \omega_p R_7 C_8 \qquad (17d)$$

Tuning: (1) f_p with R_4, (2) q_p with R_7

BP–HQ

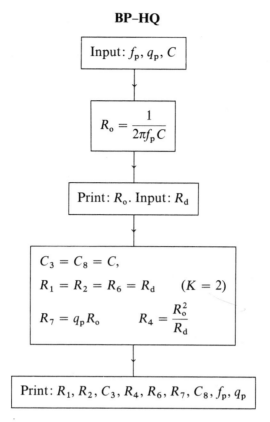

Note: R_o is the *o*ptimal resistor for low GSP and R_d is the *d*iscrete resistor value, which should be close to R_o.

72

18. HP–HQ

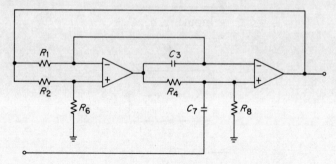

Fig. 5-18

$$T(s) = K \frac{s^2}{s^2 + (\omega_p/q_p)s + \omega_p^2} \qquad (18a)$$

$$K = 1 + \frac{R_2}{R_6} \qquad (18b)$$

$$\omega_p^2 = \frac{R_2}{R_1 R_4 R_6 C_3 C_7} \qquad (18c)$$

$$q_p = \omega_p R_8 C_7 \qquad (18d)$$

Tuning: (1) f_p with R_4, (2) q_p with R_8

HP–HQ

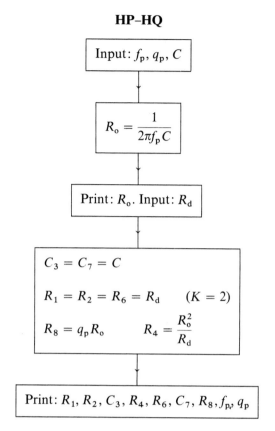

Note: R_o is the *o*ptimal resistor for low GSP and R_d is the *d*iscrete resistor value, which should be close to R_o.

74

19. AP–HQ

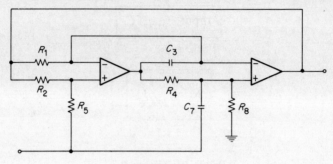

Fig. 5-19

$$T(s) = \frac{s^2 - (\omega_p/q_p)s + \omega_p^2}{s^2 + (\omega_p/q_p)s + \omega_p^2} \qquad (19a)$$

$$\omega_p^2 = \frac{R_2}{R_1 R_4 R_5 C_3 C_7} \qquad (19b)$$

$$q_p = \omega_p C_7 R_8 \qquad (19c)$$

$$R_2 = R_5 \qquad (19d)$$

Tuning: (1) f_p with R_4, (2) q_p with R_8

AP–HQ

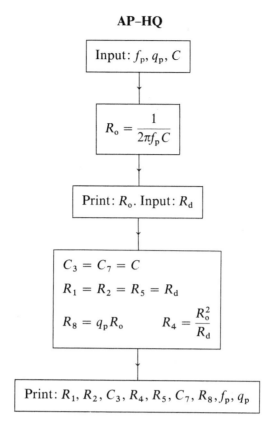

Note: R_o is the *optimal* resistor for low GSP and R_d is the *discrete* resistor value, which should be close to R_o

20. BR–HQ

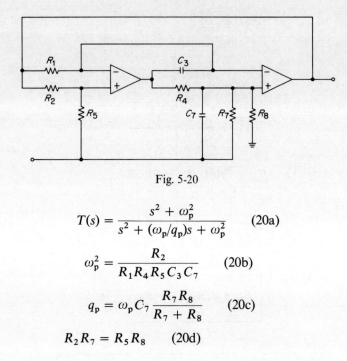

Fig. 5-20

$$T(s) = \frac{s^2 + \omega_p^2}{s^2 + (\omega_p/q_p)s + \omega_p^2} \qquad (20a)$$

$$\omega_p^2 = \frac{R_2}{R_1 R_4 R_5 C_3 C_7} \qquad (20b)$$

$$q_p = \omega_p C_7 \frac{R_7 R_8}{R_7 + R_8} \qquad (20c)$$

$$R_2 R_7 = R_5 R_8 \qquad (20d)$$

Tuning: (1) f_p with R_4, (2) $|T(f_p)| = 0$ and q_p with R_7 and R_8 (iterative)

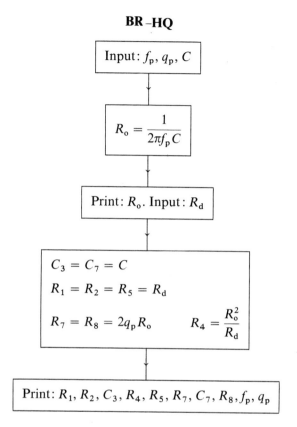

BR –HQ

Input: f_p, q_p, C

$$R_o = \frac{1}{2\pi f_p C}$$

Print: R_o. Input: R_d

$C_3 = C_7 = C$

$R_1 = R_2 = R_5 = R_d$

$R_7 = R_8 = 2q_p R_o \qquad R_4 = \dfrac{R_o^2}{R_d}$

Print: R_1, R_2, C_3, R_4, R_5, R_7, C_7, R_8, f_p, q_p

Note: R_o is the *o*ptimal resistor for low GSP and R_p is the *d*iscrete resistor value, which should be close to R_o.

21. LPN/HPN–HQ

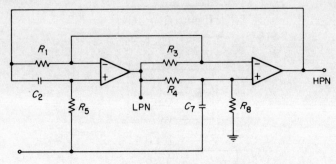

Fig. 5-21

$$T(s) = \frac{s^2 + \omega_z^2}{s^2 + (\omega_p/q_p)s + \omega_p^2} \qquad (21a)$$

$$\omega_p^2 = \frac{R_3}{R_1 R_4 R_5 C_2 C_7} \qquad (21b)$$

$$q_p = \omega_p C_7 R_8 \qquad (21c)$$

$$\omega_{zLPN} = \omega_p \sqrt{1 + \frac{R_4}{R_8}} \qquad (21d) \qquad \omega_{zHPN} = \omega_p \sqrt{1 - \frac{R_1 R_4}{R_3 R_8}} \qquad (21e)$$

Tuning: (1) f_z with R_4, (2) f_p with R_5, (3) q_p with R_8

LPN/HPN–HQ

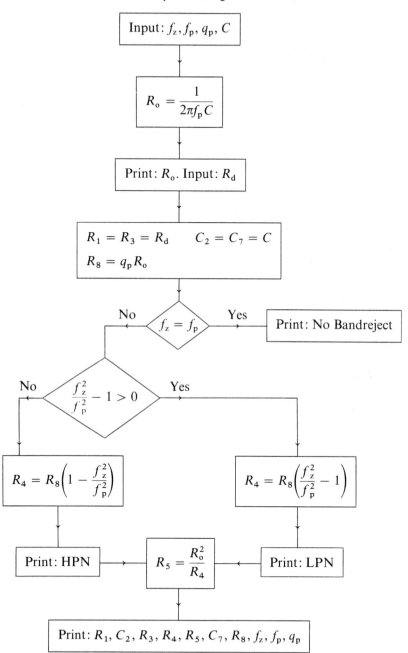

22. GP1

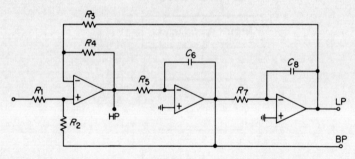

Fig. 5-23

$$T_{HP}(s) = K_{HP} \frac{s^2}{s^2 + (\omega_p/q_p)s + \omega_p^2} \quad \text{(22a)}$$

$$K_{HP} = \frac{1 + R_4/R_3}{R_1/R_2 + 1} \quad \text{(22b)}$$

$$T_{BP}(s) = -K_{BP} \frac{(\omega_p/q_p)s}{s^2 + (\omega_p/q_p)s + \omega_p^2} \quad \text{(22c)}$$

$$K_{BP} = \frac{R_2}{R_1} \quad \text{(22d)}$$

$$T_{LP}(s) = K_{LP} \frac{\omega_p^2}{s^2 + (\omega_p/q_p)s + \omega_p^2} \quad \text{(22e)}$$

$$K_{LP} = \frac{R_3/R_4 + 1}{R_1/R_2 + 1} \quad \text{(22f)}$$

$$\omega_p^2 = \frac{R_4}{R_3 R_5 R_7 C_6 C_8} \quad \text{(22g)}$$

$$q_p = \frac{1 + R_2/R_1}{1 + R_4/R_3} \sqrt{\frac{R_4}{R_3}} \quad \text{(22h)}$$

Tuning: (1) f_p with R_4, (2) q_p with R_2

GP1

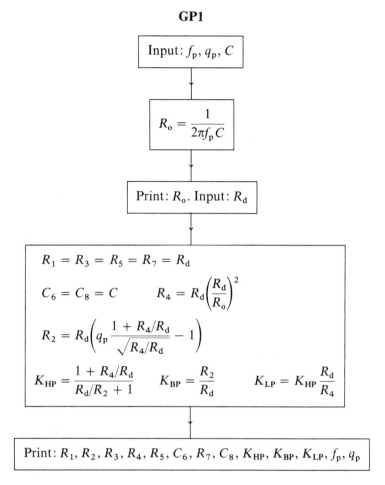

Input: f_p, q_p, C

$$R_o = \frac{1}{2\pi f_p C}$$

Print: R_o. Input: R_d

$R_1 = R_3 = R_5 = R_7 = R_d$

$C_6 = C_8 = C$ $\qquad R_4 = R_d\left(\frac{R_d}{R_o}\right)^2$

$R_2 = R_d\left(q_p \dfrac{1 + R_4/R_d}{\sqrt{R_4/R_d}} - 1\right)$

$K_{HP} = \dfrac{1 + R_4/R_d}{R_d/R_2 + 1}$ $\qquad K_{BP} = \dfrac{R_2}{R_d}$ $\qquad K_{LP} = K_{HP}\dfrac{R_d}{R_4}$

Print: R_1, R_2, R_3, R_4, R_5, C_6, R_7, C_8, K_{HP}, K_{BP}, K_{LP}, f_p, q_p

Note: R_o is the *o*ptimal resistor for low GSP and R_d is the *d*iscrete resistor value, which should be close to R_o.

82

23. GP2

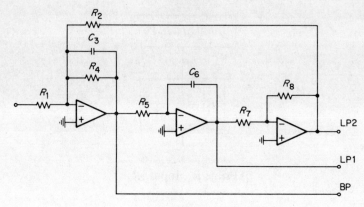

Fig. 5-23

$$T_{BP}(s) = -K_{BP} \frac{(\omega_p/q_p)s}{s^2 + (\omega_p/q_p)s + \omega_p^2} \qquad (23a)$$

$$K_{BP} = \frac{R_4}{R_1} \qquad (23b)$$

$$T_{LP1}(s) = K_{LP1} \frac{\omega_p^2}{s^2 + (\omega_p/q_p)s + \omega_p^2} \qquad (23c)$$

$$K_{LP1} = \frac{R_2 R_7}{R_1 R_8} \qquad (23d)$$

$$T_{LP2}(s) = -K_{LP2} \frac{\omega_p^2}{s^2 + (\omega_p/q_p)s + \omega_p^2} \qquad (23e)$$

$$K_{LP2} = \frac{R_2}{R_1} \qquad (23f)$$

$$\omega_p^2 = \frac{R_8}{R_2 R_5 R_7 C_3 C_8} \qquad (23g)$$

$$q_p = R_4 C_3 \omega_p \qquad (23h)$$

Tuning: (1) f_p with R_5, (2) q_p with R_4, (3) K with R_1

GP2

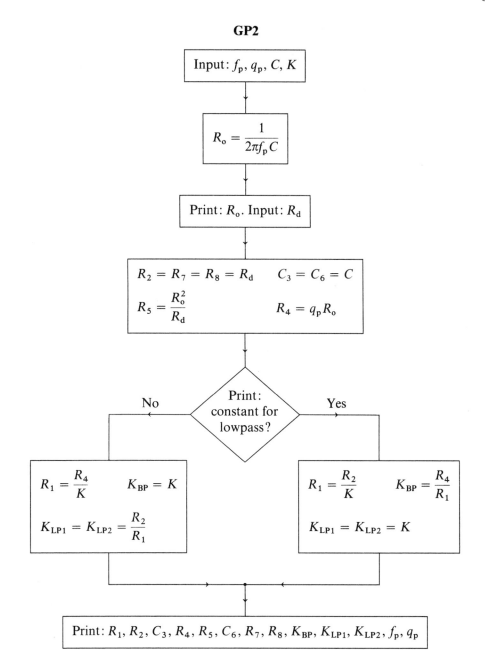

REFERENCES TO THE CIRCUITS

Circuit	Reference number
1. LP–LQ	2
2. BP–LQ-R	3
3. BP–LQ-C	3 (dual circuit)
4. HP–LQ	2
5. AP–Q.5	4
6. AP–LQ	7
7. BR–LQ	7
8. LP–MQ	2
9. BP–MQ-R	6
10. BP–MQ-C	6 (dual circuit)
11. HP–MQ	2
12. AP–MQ	1
13. BR–MQ	1
14. LPN/HPN–MQ	9
15. BR–LPN/HPN–MQ	5, 8
16. LP–HQ	11
17. BP–HQ	10, 11
18. HP–HQ	10, 11
19. AP–HQ	10, 11
20. BR–HQ	10
21. LPN/HPN–HQ	10
22. GP1	12
23. GP2	13

References

1. G. S. Moschytz, *Linear Integrated Networks: Design*, Van Nostrand Reinhold Co., New York, 1975.
2. R. P. Sallen and E. L. Key, 'A practical method of designing RC active filters,' *IRE Trans. Circuit Theory*, **CT-2**, 74–85 (March, 1955).
3. C. E. Cohn, 'Note on the simulation of higher-order linear systems with single operational amplifier,' *Proc. IEEE*, **1964**, 874 (July, 1964).
4. S. C. Dutta Roy, 'RC active all-pass networks using a differential-input operational amplifier,' *Proc. IEEE*, **1969**, 2055–2056 (November, 1969).
5. W. J. Kerwin and L. P. Huelsman, 'The design of high performance active RC band-pass filters', *IEEE Int. Conv. Rec.*, **14**, part 10, 74–88 (1966).
6. T. Deliyannis, 'High-Q factor circuit with reduced sensitivity', *Electronics Letters*, **4**, No. 26, 577–579 (December, 1968).
7. T. Deliyannis, 'RC active allpass sections', *Electronics Letters*, **5**, No. 3, 59–60 (February, 1969).
8. G. S. Moschytz, 'Sallen and Key filter networks with amplifier gain larger than or equal to unity', *IEEE Journal of Solid-State Circuits*, **1967**, 114–116 (September, 1967).
9. J. J. Friend, C. A., Harris, and D. Hilberman, 'STAR: an active biquadratic filter section', *IEEE Trans. Circuits and Systems*, **CAS-22**, No. 2, 115–121 (February, 1975).
10. N. Fliege: 'A new class of second-order RC-active filters with two operational amplifiers', *Nachrichtentechn. Zeitung*, **26**, Heft 6, 279–282, 1973.

11. W. B. Mikhael and B. B. Bhattacharyya, 'A practical design for insensitive RC-active filters', *IEEE Trans. Circuits and Systems*, **CAS-22**, 407–415 (May, 1975).

12. W. J. Kerwin, L. P., Huelsman, and R. W. Newcomb: 'State-variable synthesis for insensitive integrated circuit transfer functions', *IEEE J. Solid-State Circuits*, **SC-2**, 87–92 (September, 1967).

13. J. Tow, 'A step-by-step active-filter design', *IEEE Spectrum*, **6**, 64–68 (December, 1969).

CHAPTER 6

Tuning Active Filters

6-1 FUNCTIONAL AND DETERMINISTIC TUNING

As active filters are increasingly being developed for modern communication systems, so the question of how to tune them to specifications most efficiently, and at minimum cost, is becoming ever more important. Since the problem is most acute when the active filters are realized in hybrid-integrated (i.e. thin- or thick-film) form, the emphasis in this chapter will be on hybrid-integrated active filters. When using discrete components, the tuning procedure is similar and, if anything, simpler. This will be evident from the text.

In practice two basically different tuning methods can be distinguished, namely, *functional* and *deterministic* tuning.

Functional tuning implies tuning the critical parameters of a network while it is functional, i.e. in operation. Because the network is assembled as if for operation in the final system, any parasitics built into the network are automatically taken into account and 'tuned out' during the tuning process. Functional tuning is generally iterative, particularly if the tuning steps are interactive (see Fig. 6-1). The number of iterations increases with the degree of tuning accuracy required. The larger the number of iterative tuning steps, the more time consuming, and therefore the more costly, the tuning process will be. Functional tuning is generally preferable for laboratory purposes and when production quantities are moderate or low.

Deterministic tuning implies tuning—or trimming to value—individual components of a network as predicted by a combination of comprehensive network equations (in which parasitic effects are taken into account) and by component measurements (see Fig. 6-2). The solutions of the equations (generally obtained by an on-line computation facility) provide the values of the components to be tuned. Tuning is carried out 'to value'; hence it makes no difference whether the network is operational or not. Since the components to be tuned are generally resistors, this method consists of 'resistor trimming', in contrast to the tuning of network characteristics (e.g amplitude, phase, frequency) that occurs in functional tuning. The method is simple (e.g. 'to-value' trimming of resistors is essential in any hybrid-integrated circuits manufacturing plant) and rapid in execution (generally very few, if any, iterations are required). However, powerful computer programs are required to solve the non-linear network equations which must take first- and often second-order parasitic effects into account. Deterministic tuning is the more efficient of the two methods, but the necessary expenditure of an on-line computation facility, and the initial computational effort required, can generally be justified only by very high production volumes.

In practice it will very often be found useful to combine functional with deterministic tuning. The *initial* adjustments will be carried out by deterministic tuning, where the values

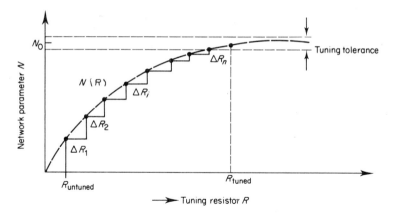

Fig. 6-1   Functionally tuning to a parameter value N_0 with the tuning resistor R

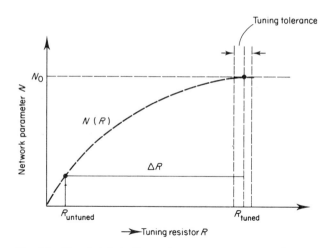

Fig. 6-2   Deterministically tuning to a parameter value N_0 with the tuning resistor R

are obtained from either the idealized network equations or from those containing at most first-order parasitic effects. To overcome more subtle second-order parasitics, a *fine-tuning* step is then undertaken in which the circuit is operational (i.e., assembled and powered) and a functional adjustment of one or more of the critical parameters is carried out. In this way the computational complexity inherent in deterministic-only tuning can be considerably reduced.

6-2   FUNCTIONAL TUNING

Functional tuning is based on a set of network equations in which the changes of the specified network characteristics $F_j, j = 1, 2, \ldots, m$, are related to incremental changes in the components x_i, $i = 1, 2, \ldots, n$, by the sensitivity matrix. Hence:

$$
\begin{bmatrix} \Delta F_1/F_1 \\ \\ \vdots \\ \\ \Delta F_m/F_m \end{bmatrix} = \begin{bmatrix} S_{x_1}^{F_1} & \cdots & S_{x_i}^{F_1} & \cdots & S_{x_n}^{F_1} \\ \\ \vdots & & & & \\ \\ S_{x_n}^{F_m} & \cdots & S_{x_i}^{F_m} & \cdots & S_{x_n}^{F_m} \end{bmatrix} \begin{bmatrix} \Delta x_1/x_1 \\ \vdots \\ \Delta x_i/x_i \\ \vdots \\ \Delta x_n/x_n \end{bmatrix} \tag{6-1}
$$

where the sensitivities $S_{x_i}^{F_j}$ are defined, as in Chapter 3, by

$$
S_{x_i}^{F_j} = \frac{dF_j}{dx_i}\frac{x_i}{F_j} \tag{6-2}
$$

Hence, if a_i ($i = 1, \ldots, n$) are the characteristic tuning parameters of a network function $F(a_i)$, and R_{a_j} are the corresponding tuning resistors (Fig. 6-3), then tuning the parameters from $a_i + \Delta a_i$ to a_i will adjust the network function from its initial form $F(a_i + \Delta a_i)$ to the desired form $F(a_i)$. Letting

$$
S_{R_{a_j}}^{a_i} = \frac{da_i/a_i}{dR_{a_j}/R_{a_j}} \tag{6-3}
$$

we then obtain the sensitivity relations:

$$
\begin{bmatrix} da_1/a_1 \\ \vdots \\ da_i/a_i \\ \vdots \\ da_n/a_n \end{bmatrix} = \begin{bmatrix} S_{R_{a1}}^{a_1} & S_{R_{a2}}^{a_1} & \cdots & S_{R_{an}}^{a_1} \\ & & & \\ S_{R_{a1}}^{a_i} & S_{R_{a2}}^{a_i} & \cdots & S_{R_{an}}^{a_i} \\ & & & \\ S_{R_{a1}}^{a_n} & S_{R_{a2}}^{a_n} & \cdots & S_{R_{an}}^{a_n} \end{bmatrix} \begin{bmatrix} dR_{a_1}/R_{a_1} \\ \vdots \\ dR_{a_j}/R_{a_j} \\ \vdots \\ dR_{a_n}/R_{a_n} \end{bmatrix} \tag{6-4a}
$$

or

$$
\left[\frac{da}{a}\right] = [S]\left[\frac{dR}{R}\right] \tag{6-4b}
$$

where $[S]$ is the sensitivity matrix.

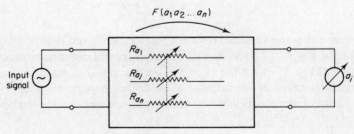

a_j = characteristic tuning parameters
R_{a_j} = trim components

Fig. 6-3 Functionally tuning the characteristic tuning parameters a_i with the corresponding resistors R_{a_j} to obtain the specified function $F(a_i)$

In order to allow for a non-interactive, and hence non-iterative, tuning procedure, *the sensitivity matrix must be a diagonal matrix*, meaning that all off-diagonal matrix elements must be zero (Fig. 6-4a). In practice this will rarely be the case. However, it may be possible to arrange the sensitivity matrix such that it is *triangular* with the upper triangular elements being zero (Fig. 6-4b). For each network characteristic a_k there is then a tuning element R_{a_k} that leaves all previously tuned parameters a_j $(j < k)$ unaffected. The tuning sequence is now critical; it results directly from the sensitivity matrix after the latter has been arranged in triangular form. The obtained sequence provides a single-pass (or 'one-shot'), non-interactive tuning procedure requiring no iterations. If a triangular matrix in the form of Fig. 6-4b cannot be obtained accurately, it must be approximated by arranging the matrix elements such that they decrease in value to the right of the diagonal (Fig. 6-4c). In this way, the number of tuning iterations can be minimized.

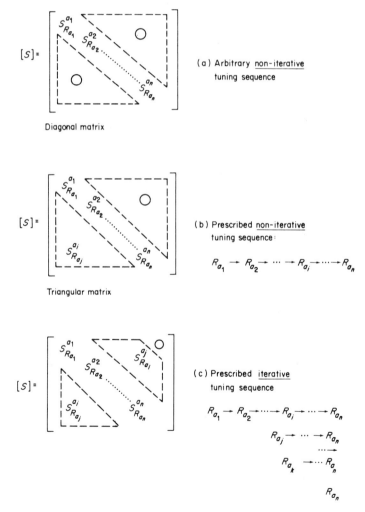

Fig. 6-4 Functional tuning strategies: (a) non-interactive, (b) interactive, onepass, (c) general interactive

Consider, for example, a second-order network possessing two conjugate complex poles $p_{1,2} = -\sigma_p \pm j\tilde{\omega}_p$. The corresponding transfer function has the form

$$T(s) = \frac{N(s)}{(s - p_1)(s - p_2)} \tag{6-5}$$

Assuming that the two poles p_1 and p_2 are specified and must be tuned for, we now derive the matrix equation corresponding to (6-4) with respect to the n resistors of the network. (Capacitors cannot be adjusted in hybrid-integrated circuits and are therefore not considered as tuning components.) We obtain

$$\begin{bmatrix} \dfrac{dp_1}{p_1} \\[2ex] \dfrac{dp_2}{p_2} \end{bmatrix} = \begin{bmatrix} \underbrace{u_{11} + jv_{11}}_{S_{R_1}^{p_1}} & u_{12} + jv_{12} & \cdots & u_{1n} + jv_{1n} \\[2ex] \underbrace{u_{21} + jv_{21}}_{S_{R_1}^{p_2}} & u_{22} + jv_{22} & \cdots & u_{2n} + jv_{2n} \end{bmatrix} \begin{bmatrix} dR_1/R_1 \\ \vdots \\ dR_n/R_n \end{bmatrix} \tag{6-6a}$$

or, in matrix form,

$$\left[\frac{dp}{p}\right] = [u + jv]\left[\frac{dR}{R}\right] \tag{6-6b}$$

The pole variation dp/p can now be related to the pole frequency and Q variations $d\omega_p/\omega_p$ and dq_p/q_p, respectively, as in Chapter 3 (see eq. 3-37); namely,

$$\frac{dp}{p} = \frac{d\omega_p}{\omega_p} - j\frac{1}{\sqrt{4q_p^2 - 1}}\frac{dq_p}{q_p} \tag{6-7}$$

where $\omega_p = \sqrt{\sigma_p^2 + \tilde{\omega}_p^2}$ and $q_p = \omega_p/2\sigma_p$. Thus it follows that in (6-6), for the pole p_1,

$$u_{1i} = S_{R_i}^{\omega_{p1}} \tag{6-8a}$$

and

$$v_{1i} = -(4q_{p1}^2 - 1)^{-1/2}S_{R_i}^{q_{p1}} \tag{6-8b}$$

In terms of the pole frequency ω_p and the pole Q, q_p, we therefore obtain, from (6-6a),

$$\begin{bmatrix} \dfrac{d\omega_{p1}}{\omega_{p1}} \\[2ex] \dfrac{d\omega_{p2}}{\omega_{p2}} \end{bmatrix} = \begin{bmatrix} u_{11} & u_{12} & \cdots & u_{1n} \\[2ex] u_{21} & u_{22} & \cdots & u_{2n} \end{bmatrix} \begin{bmatrix} \dfrac{dR_1}{R_1} \\ \vdots \\ \dfrac{dR_n}{R_n} \end{bmatrix} \tag{6-9a}$$

and

$$\begin{bmatrix} \dfrac{dq_{p1}}{q_{p1}} \\[2ex] \dfrac{dq_{p2}}{q_{p2}} \end{bmatrix} = -\sqrt{4q_p^2 - 1}\begin{bmatrix} v_{11} & v_{12} & \cdots & v_{1n} \\[2ex] v_{21} & v_{22} & \cdots & v_{2n} \end{bmatrix} \begin{bmatrix} \dfrac{dR_1}{R_1} \\ \vdots \\ \dfrac{dR_n}{R_n} \end{bmatrix} \tag{6-9b}$$

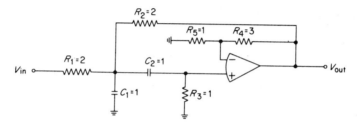

Fig. 6-5 Second-order bandpass network

Since p_1 and p_2 are complex conjugate, the variations of ω_{p_1}, ω_{p_2} and q_{p_1}, q_{p_2} will not be independent of each other and we need consider only the variation $d\omega_p/\omega_p$ and dq_p/q_p for a second-order network.

To illustrate the use of the sensitivity matrix to obtain the most efficient tuning sequence (i.e. with a minimum number of iterations) consider the second-order active bandpass network shown in Fig. 6-5. The voltage transfer function has the form

$$T(s) = K \frac{s}{(s - p_1)(s - p_2)} = K \frac{s}{s^2 + (\omega_p/q_p)s + \omega_p^2} \tag{6-10}$$

In practice, ω_p and q_p rather than the pole pair p_1 and p_2 will be specified, since the former are accurately measurable quantities. In addition, the constant K may be specified, although in general with a much wider tolerance than ω_p and q_p. Deriving the sensitivity matrix with respect to the five resistors of the network, we obtain

$$\begin{bmatrix} dK/K \\ d\omega_p/\omega_p \\ dq_p/q_p \end{bmatrix} = \begin{bmatrix} -1 & 0 & 0 & 1 & -1 \\ -0.25 & -0.25 & -0.5 & 0 & 0 \\ 0.25 & -1.75 & 1.5 & 1.5 & -1.5 \end{bmatrix} \begin{bmatrix} dR_1/R_1 \\ dR_2/R_2 \\ dR_3/R_3 \\ dR_4/R_4 \\ dR_5/R_5 \end{bmatrix} \tag{6-11}$$

The object is now to rearrange the sensitivity matrix in (6-11) such as to provide a tuning sequence comprising three resistors and requiring a minimum number of iterations. Clearly, neither a purely diagonal nor a triangular matrix can be obtained. The best we can do is with the resistors R_1, R_3, and R_4; namely,

$$\begin{bmatrix} dK/K \\ d\omega_p/\omega_p \\ dq_p/q_p \end{bmatrix} = \begin{bmatrix} -1 & 0 & 1 \\ -0.25 & -0.5 & 0 \\ 0.25 & 1.5 & 1.5 \end{bmatrix} \begin{bmatrix} dR_K/R_K \\ dR\omega_p/R\omega_p \\ dRq_p/Rq_p \end{bmatrix} \tag{6-12}$$

where $R_K = R_1$, $R_{\omega_p} = R_3$, and $R_{q_p} = R_4$. The optimum tuning sequence is then $R_1(K) \to R_3(\omega_p) \to R_4(q_p)$, whereby a slight error will be accrued in K since $S_{Rq_p}^K \neq 0$. This is not serious, however, since an error in K results in an error in the passband level of the filter response, whereas an error in ω_p or q_p results in an error of its centre frequency or selectivity, respectively. The former, rather than the latter, can generally be tolerated.

6-3 ACCURACY CONSIDERATIONS FOR FUNCTIONAL TUNING

When tuning for the frequency response of a network, we have the choice (in the case of minimum-phase† networks) of tuning to a specified amplitude or to a specified phase. The question is which of these two physical quantities provides a more convenient indicator for the tuning process? If we tune for an amplitude response as indicated in Fig. 6-6(a), we are concerned with the variation of the amplitude (e.g. in decibels) at a particular frequency ω_i with respect to the variation of a corresponding tuning resistor R_{α_i}. Thus, with the semi-relative sensitivity, introduced in Chapter 3, we have

$$[d\alpha(\omega_i)] = [\mathscr{S}_{R_{\alpha_i}}^{\alpha(\omega_i)}]\left[\frac{dR_{\alpha_i}}{R_{\alpha_i}}\right] \tag{6-13a}$$

where

$$\mathscr{S}_R^\alpha = \frac{d\alpha}{dR/R} \tag{6-13b}$$

Similarly, tuning for a phase response (Fig. 6-6b), the corresponding relationship between the phase $\phi(\omega_i)$ and the tuning resistor R_{ϕ_i} will be

$$[d\phi(\omega_i)] = [\mathscr{S}_{R_{\phi_i}}^{\phi(\omega_i)}]\left[\frac{dR_{\phi_i}}{R_{\phi_i}}\right] \tag{6-14a}$$

where

$$\mathscr{S}_R^\phi = \frac{d\phi}{dR/R} \tag{6-14b}$$

At first sight it would seem that the sensitivities (6-13b) and (6-14b) determine whether the amplitude α or the phase ϕ is a preferable tuning indicator for a given minimum-phase network. However, it can be shown‡ that no matter what the network, the phase is always a more accurate indicator with which to tune the response of a network. In fact, the tuning accuracy of the amplitude response of a second-order allpole network is within $\pm 2 \cdot \Delta\phi$ per cent. or $\pm 0.2 \cdot \Delta\phi$ decibels, when trimmed by means of a phase meter with an accuracy of $\pm \Delta\phi$ degrees. This is independent of the pole Q. Thus, with the attainable phase accuracy given by $\Delta\phi$ degrees, the resulting amplitude accuracy will be

$$\Delta\alpha \le 2\Delta\phi[\%] \approx 0.2\Delta\phi[\text{dB}] \tag{6-15}$$

It follows that a $1°$ phase error corresponds to a 0.2-dB error in amplitude. Phase meters with up to $0.1°$ phase accuracy are available at prices considerably lower than voltage meters with comparable accuracy (i.e. 0.02 dB). It follows that *wherever possible, functional tuning by phase is to be preferred over tuning by amplitude.* The pole-frequency error resulting from a phase error $\Delta\phi$ degrees is then

$$\frac{\Delta f_\text{p}}{f_\text{p}}[\%] = \frac{-\pi \cdot 100}{360 q_\text{p}}\Delta\phi \approx -\frac{\Delta\phi}{q_\text{p}} \tag{6-16}$$

---

† In contrast to non-minimum-phase networks, minimum-phase networks have no zeros in the right-half s plane. Except for allpass networks, all networks dealt with in this book are minimum phase.

‡ See G. S. Moschytz, *Linear Integrated Networks: Design*, Van Nostrand Reinhold Co., New York, 1975, p. 405.

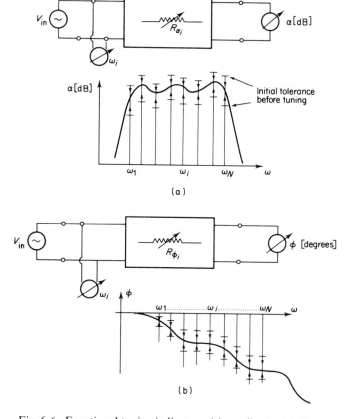

Fig. 6-6 Functional tuning indicators: (a) amplitude, (b) phase

where $\Delta\phi$ is measured in degrees and q_p is the pole Q. Note that the higher the q_p, the smaller the frequency error resulting from a given phase error. Thus, with a 0.1° phase error, the frequency error will be -0.1 per cent. if $q_p = 1$ and -0.01 per cent. if $q_p = 10$. The q_p accuracy associated with a phase error of $\Delta\phi$ degrees can be shown to be independent of q_p. It is approximately given by

$$\frac{\Delta q_p}{q_p} [\%] \approx -3.5 \cdot \Delta\phi \qquad [6\text{-}17]$$

provided that the phase is measured at the pole-frequency phase plus or minus 45°.

Consider, for example, the lowpass amplitude and phase characteristic shown in Fig. 6-7. From the corresponding transfer function

$$T(s) = K \frac{\omega_p^2}{s^2 + (\omega_p/q_p)s + \omega_p^2} \qquad (6\text{-}18)$$

we obtain the amplitude response (see Chapter 2)

$$\alpha(\omega) = \ln|T(j\omega)| \qquad (6\text{-}19a)$$

and the phase response

$$\phi(\omega) = \arg T(j\omega) \qquad (6\text{-}19b)$$

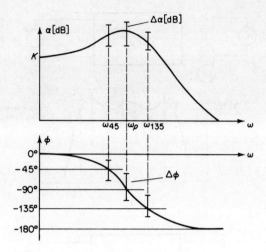

Fig. 6-7   Amplitude and phase characteristic of a
second-order lowpass network

To tune for the specified ω_p and q_p values, we tune for $-90°$ at the frequency $\omega_p/2\pi$ using an appropriate resistor R_{ω_p}, and for $-45°$ (or $-135°$) at the frequency $\omega_{45}/2\pi$ (or $\omega_{135}/2\pi$) using an appropriate resistor R_{q_p}. With a phase meter accurate to within $\Delta\phi$ degrees, the errors in amplitude, frequency, and q_p will be as given by (6-15), (6-16), and (6-17), respectively. K can also be tuned for; an error in K implies an error in the d.c. gain of the network.

6-4   DETERMINISTIC TUNING

For a given network, the deterministic tuning procedure follows the flow chart presented in Fig. 6-8. Thus, for the second-order lowpass network shown in Fig. 6-9, whose transfer function corresponds to that given by (6-18), we proceed as follows:†

(a)   Derive the three characteristic network parameters K, ω_p, and q_p as a function of the circuit components, i.e.

$$K = f_K(\beta, R_1, R_2, C_3, C_4)$$

$$\omega_p = f_{\omega_p}(R_1, R_2, R_4, C_3, C_4)$$

$$q_p = f_{q_p}(\beta, R_1, R_2, R_4, C_3, C_4)$$

(b)   Measure the capacitors C_3, C_4, and the closed-loop amplifier gain β.
(c)   Compute the following resistor values as a function of quantities that are either specified or measured, i.e.

$$R_1 = f_{R_1}(K, \omega_p, q_p, C_3, C_4, \beta)$$

$$R_2 = f_{R_2}(K, \omega_p, q_p, C_3, C_4, \beta)$$

$$R_4 = f_{R_4}(K, \omega_p, q_p, C_3, C_4, \beta)$$

(d)   Trim resistors R_1, R_2, and R_4 to the values computed under step (c).

† G. S. Moschytz, *Linear Integrated Networks: Design*, p. 408.

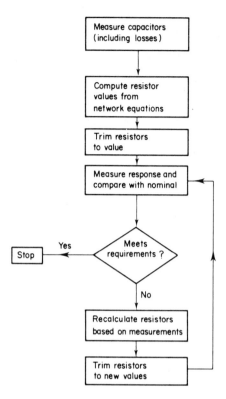

Fig. 6-8 Deterministic tuning sequence

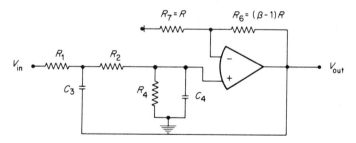

Fig. 6-9 Second-order lowpass network

In applying these four tuning steps which are typical for the deterministic tuning procedure, the following points should be kept in mind:

(a)   The equations derived in step (a) are the same *design equations* as those given for each individual circuit in Chapter 5. The derivation of the design equations precedes the tuning process and determines the *nominal* value of each component including the gain β. Thus the *design* or *nominal* value of each component is known before the tuning process is begun.

(b)   The equations derived in step (c) are *tuning equations* and not design equations. Besides containing specified quantities (e.g. K, ω_p, q_p) they also contain *measured* quantities (e.g. C_3, C_4, and β). Thus, in the example of Fig. 6-9, although the nominal value of β is known, the actual value of β obtained in manufacture is measured in step (b) by measuring the resistors R_6 and R_7. Note that at this point the amplifier is assumed to be ideal.

(c)   The circuits shown in Figs. 6-5 and 6-9 are assumed to be medium Q, rather than low Q, implying that tight tolerances are specified for q_p. Thus the closed-loop gain β is not equal to unity, but is somewhat larger (e.g. between one and two), in order to permit a final functional correction without affecting the pole frequency ω_p. The inclusion of the additional resistor (i.e. R_7 in Fig. 6-9) is a small price to pay for the increase in yield afforded by the possibility of a final touch-up tuning step. The resistor between the opamp output and inverting input terminal (e.g. R_6 in Fig. 6-9) is required in any case, in order to balance d.c. offset. The deterioration of gain stability incurred by the slightly larger-than-unity gain is negligible, particularly in the case of hybrid-integrated filters, thanks to the very close resistor tracking obtainable with either thick- or thin-film resistors. The combination of deterministic and functional tuning implied here will be further discussed in Section 6-6.

(d)   The measurement of capacitors (i.e. C_3 and C_4 in step (b) above) should preferably be carried out after the (chip) capacitors have been assembled on the substrate. (In the case of thin-film capacitors there is, of course, no other choice.) This permits parasitic capacitances and component drift due to circuit assembly to be taken into account during the measurement. Although methods exist for the accurate measurement of individual capacitors when they are connected to additional circuitry,† the preferred way of overcoming this problem is to provide provisional capacitor contacts to the substrate edges. These permit the accurate measurement of either single capacitors, or combinations of parallel or series pairs, as required for the subsequent computations.

To attain a one-pass tuning procedure, parasitic effects due to non-ideal circuit components must generally be taken into account in the tuning equations derived under step (c) above. This complicates the required computations considerably. The main parasitic effects that must be contended with are

(a)   Non-ideal characteristics of the active devices (e.g. frequency-dependent gain of the operational amplifiers). Referring to Fig. 6-10, this means that instead of using the constant gain β_0 in our equations, we must use $\beta(s)$; thus:

$$\beta_0 \rightarrow \beta(s) \approx \frac{\omega_g}{s + \omega_\alpha} \tag{6-20}$$

(b)   Losses and frequency dependence of capacitors. Thin-film capacitors, for example, are both lossy and frequency dependent. If the loss of a capacitor C_i is $\tan \delta_i$, then, instead of C_i, we must approximate C_i as follows:

$$C_i \rightarrow \frac{C_i}{1 + j \tan \delta_i} \approx \frac{C_i}{1 + j\delta_i} \approx C_i(1 - j\delta_i - \delta_i^2) \tag{6-21}$$

† G. S. Moschytz, *Linear Integrated Networks: Design*, p. 413.

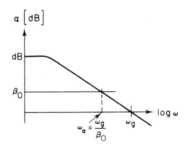

Fig. 6-10   Frequency-dependent
gain of an operational amplifier

Instead of frequency-independent capacitors, thin-film capacitors are frequency dependent according to the relationship:

$$C \rightarrow C(\omega) = C_o e^{-\omega \tau_c} \qquad (6\text{-}22)$$

whereby the time constant τ_c characterizes the technology used. Assuming that the value of $C(\omega)$ is measured at two frequencies (see Fig. 6-11), the value of $C(\omega_p)$ can be obtained by extrapolation as follows:

$$\log C(\omega_p) = \log C(\omega_1) + \tau_c(\omega_p - \omega_1) \qquad (6\text{-}23a)$$

where

$$\tau_c = \frac{\log[C(\omega_p)/C(\omega_1)]}{\omega_p - \omega_1} \qquad (6\text{-}23b)$$

(c)   Parasitic capacitances on the circuit substrate and resistive losses along conductance paths.

These parasitics must be taken into account, to the extent that the response of the final assembled circuit is to be as accurate as it would be if it had been tuned functionally. In doing so, the computations required under step (c) above become rapidly more complex, the equations highly non-linear, and of third, or even higher, order. With increasing complexity, only numerical solutions by computer can be expected, whereas, when assuming ideal components, analytical solutions are generally obtainable.

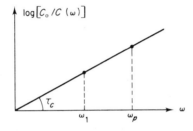

Fig. 6-11   Frequency dependence
of a thin-film capacitor

6-5 ACCURACY CONSIDERATIONS FOR DETERMINISTIC TUNING

Using the deterministic tuning procedure, the accuracy attained depends on the accuracy with which capacitors can be measured and with which resistors can be measured and trimmed. Assuming a worst-case measuring error of $\Delta C/C$ for all capacitors and a worst-case trimming error of $\Delta R/R$ for all resistors, the frequency error is

$$\left|\frac{\Delta\omega}{\omega}\right|_{\max} \leq \left|\frac{\Delta R}{R}\right|_{\max} + \left|\frac{\Delta C}{C}\right|_{\max} \qquad [6\text{-}24]$$

With a 0.1 per cent.-accurate capacitance bridge and the capability of trimming and measuring resistors to within 0.05 per cent., the worst-case frequency error will be 0.15 per cent.

The accuracy with which the capacitor losses are measured will also effect the frequency accuracy, adding a term to the two in (6-24). Assuming a loss-measurement error of $\Delta\delta$, we obtain the additional term:

$$\frac{\Delta\omega}{\omega} \approx \frac{1}{2q_p}\left(1 + \frac{1}{4q_p}\right)\Delta\delta \qquad (6\text{-}25)$$

This error is significantly smaller than the one represented by (6-24) and may often be ignored. Measuring the capacitor losses to within 10 per cent. accuracy (i.e. $\Delta\delta = 0.1$) and assuming a pole Q of only 2 (i.e. $q_p = 2$), the frequency error given by (6-25) is 0.02 per cent.

In general, any function F that is tuned to value using a resistor R_F will be accurate to within $F(1 \pm \Delta F/F)$, where

$$\frac{\Delta F}{F} = S_{R_F}^F \frac{\Delta R_F}{R_F} \qquad (6\text{-}26)$$

and $\Delta R_F/R_F$ is the trimming and measuring accuracy of the resistor R_F. Consider, for example, the case in which q_p is to be tuned deterministically by adjusting the closed-loop gain β. This, in turn, is determined by a resistor ratio, say R_β/R, where R_β is the trimming resistor (e.g. R_6 or R_7 in Fig. 6-9). The q_p accuracy follows as

$$\frac{\Delta q_p}{q_p} = S_\beta^{q_p} S_{R_\beta}^\beta \frac{\Delta R_\beta}{R_\beta} \qquad (6\text{-}27)$$

For the network of Fig. 6-9, eq. (6-27) becomes

$$\frac{\Delta q_p}{q_p} = \left(1 - \frac{1}{\beta}\right)\left(\frac{q_p}{\hat{q}} - 1\right)\frac{\Delta R_\beta}{R_\beta} \qquad (6\text{-}28)$$

where $R_\beta = R_6$. If R_7 were used for R_β the expression on the right-hand side of (6-28) would be negative. The pole Q of the passive RC network associated with the active filter is $\hat{q}$. It is obtained by setting β equal to zero in the expression for q_p, i.e.

$$\hat{q} = q_p(\beta = 0) \qquad (6\text{-}29)$$

With a capability for measuring and trimming R_β to within 0.05 per cent. accuracy, and with the typical values of $\beta = 2$, $\hat{q} = 0.4$, and $q_p = 20$, we obtain q_p accurately to within 1 per cent. Note that with currently available measuring equipment, deterministic tuning can readily compete with functional tuning in terms of accuracy, provided that a sufficiently thorough computational effort and adequate computer facilities are invested in the process.

6-6 COMBINING DETERMINISTIC WITH FUNCTIONAL TUNING

The main characteristics of functional and deterministic filter tuning are summarized in Table 6-1.

Functional tuning is conceptually simple and very effective in that all stray and parasitic effects of a practical circuit can be tuned out 'in situ' with the circuit in operation. The main disadvantages of the method are the required time-consuming iterations and the high-accuracy measurements of such parameters as phase, amplitude, and frequency. Such measurements are often alien to the typical hybrid-circuit manufacturing facility which is equipped for high-accuracy resistance and capacitance measurements only. Functional tuning thus becomes particularly useful for prototype and lab purposes, and for low-quantity production.

Deterministic tuning is based on the more sophisticated concept of predicting all relevant parasitic effects analytically and, by a combination of component measurements and computations of resistor values, trimming resistors to value such that the required network response is obtained. It is essentially a 'one-shot' process in that, ideally, each resistor need be trimmed only once. The disadvantages of the method are the complexity of initial computation and the luxury of on-line computing facilities. Given sufficiently high production quantities, however, such initial outlays in brain and computer power may readily be justified and subsequently amortized.

Because deterministic tuning entails only component measurement, computation, and (resistor) trimming, it is the preferred tuning method, provided the production quantities are large enough to justify the initial computational effort (i.e. deriving the network equations including parasitic effects) and the cost of on-line computation facilities. Very often, the initial computational effort can be significantly reduced by deriving the equations of the *idealized* network and, after initial deterministic tuning, correcting the resulting error by a *small* number of functional tuning steps. This procedure, outlined in Fig. 6-12, eliminates the numerous and time-consuming iterative tuning steps generally required by the purely functional tuning procedure. It accomplishes this by reserving a small number (typically one or two) appropriate resistors for a final touch-up, or vernier, functional adjustment after the circuit has previously been 'coarse adjusted' deterministically using simple, i.e. idealized, design equations. Thus, for the most common 'intermediate' situation,

Table 6-1   The main characteristics of functional and deterministic tuning

Functional	Deterministic
Network in operation	Network not in operation
Conceptually simple, directly applicable	Computationally complex, requires considerable preliminary analysis
Trim resistors to specified function values (e.g. amplitude, phase, frequency)	Measure components and compute resistor values, trim resistors to computed values
Requires accurate phase and frequency measurements	Requires accurate resistor and capacitor measurements
Tuning steps generally interactive	Resistor trimming non-interactive
Parasitic effects tuned out	Parasitics included in network equations
Iterative (time consuming)	One to two trimming steps
Tuning sequence derivable from sensitivity matrix	Requires on-line computation facilities and "... and routines for the solution of non-linear equations."
Suitable for lab purposes and low-production quantities	Suitable for high-production quantities

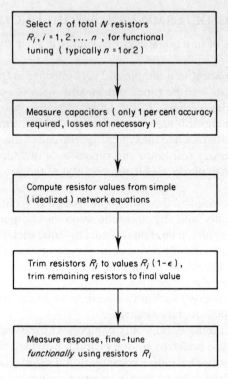

Fig. 6-12   Combining deterministic with
functional tuning

where production quantities are neither so high nor so low as to obviate the question of the
most suitable tuning method, a combination of functional and deterministic tuning
offers the best results.

6-7   TUNING SECOND-ORDER FILTER SECTIONS

In the context of this handbook, we are concerned with the tuning of the second-order
networks presented in Chapter 5. Normally, we would assume the kind of combined deterministic and functional tuning outlined in the previous section and presented in the flow
chart of Fig. 6-12. The initial deterministic tuning step would comprise the solution of the
idealized design equations while, at the same time, taking certain other constraints (e.g.
minimum sensitivity, minimum gain-sensitivity product, maximum dynamic range,
convenient component values) into account. The parasitic effects would not be included
since they are taken into account by the subsequent functional tuning step. Note that the
idealized design equations have already been solved in Chapter 5 and values for *all* circuit
components obtained. The component values result from a solution of the idealized design
equations and the simultaneous minimization of the gain-sensitivity product. This additional constraint can be satisfied in most cases since there exist more circuit components
than design equations. For the same reason, the values of certain components (generally
capacitors) can be selected from the viewpoint of practical feasibility and minimum cost
(i.e. larger values cost more). For the twenty-three circuits in Chapter 5 the initial computations necessary for the first deterministic tuning step are presumed to have been carried out

directly in that all nominal component values are obtained from the given computer programs. In the case of hybrid-integrated circuits, those components that are designated as tuning components (e.g. a resistor R_{ω_p} to tune the pole frequency ω_p, a resistor R_{q_p} to tune the pole Q, q_p) must be initially tuned to a value lower than nominal (typically 10 to 20 per cent.) because film resistors can only be tuned in an increasing direction. These 'tuning resistors' then permit the functional tuning step that completes the tuning procedure. It is this functional tuning step, related to the second-order filter circuits of Chapter 5, that will be outlined in the remainder of this chapter.

As we have seen in Section 6-3, functional tuning is most accurate when the phase, rather than the amplitude, is used as the quantity to be measured and tuned for. The necessary tuning data is most conveniently presented separately for the three basic categories of second-order networks, namely, allpole networks, networks with finite zeros, and non-minimum phase networks.

a. Allpole Networks

By allpole networks we mean those networks comprising a complex-conjugate pole pair and zeros only at the origin or infinity (i.e. lowpass, highpass, and bandpass networks). Consider the lowpass function

$$T(s) = K \frac{\omega_p^2}{s^2 + (\omega_p/q_p)s + \omega_p^2} \tag{6-30}$$

For $s = j\omega$ the amplitude and phase response is as shown in Fig. 6-13. For high q_p values (e.g. > 5), the peak frequency corresponds approximately to ω_p; q_p corresponds approximately to the ratio of ω_p and the 3-dB bandwidth. However, the amplitude response in the vicinity of ω_p is flat; therefore an accurate ω_p adjustment is difficult. This is a serious

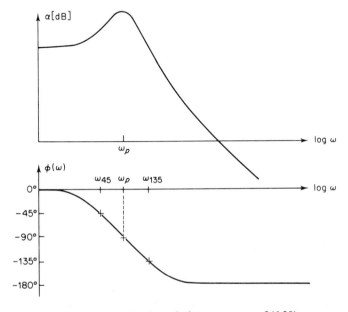

Fig. 6-13   Amplitude and phase response of (6.30)

disadvantage, since the pole frequencies should be adjusted for as accurately as possible (typically to within better than 0.2 per cent.).

A glance at Fig. 6-13 shows that, in contrast to the amplitude response, the phase has its *maximum slope* at ω_p and vicinity (i.e. covering the 3-dB frequency range). Thus, the phase curve provides a far less ambiguous measure for the parameters ω_p and q_p than the amplitude curve. For $s = j\omega$ the frequency response of $T(s)$ is

$$T(j\omega) = K \frac{\omega_p^2}{\omega_p^2 - \omega^2 + j\omega(\omega_p/q_p)} \tag{6-31}$$

and the phase

$$\phi(\omega) = -\tan^{-1}\left(\frac{\omega\omega_p}{q_p(\omega_p^2 - \omega^2)}\right) \tag{6-32}$$

A phase angle of $-90°$ is obtained for

$$\omega_{90} = \omega_p \tag{6-33}$$

For the phase angles $-45°$ and $-135°$ the argument of (6-32) is ± 1. Solving for ω we obtain

$$\omega_{45} = \frac{\omega_p}{2q_p}(\sqrt{4q_p^2 + 1} - 1) \tag{6-34a}$$

$$\omega_{135} = \frac{\omega_p}{2q_p}(\sqrt{4q_p^2 + 1} + 1) \tag{6-34b}$$

Solving for q_p, we have, for the lowpass network (LP),

$$(q_p)_{LP} = \frac{\omega_p}{\omega_{135} - \omega_{45}} \tag{6-35}$$

Note that (6-33) and (6-35) hold for all q_p values, including those less than 0.5. Furthermore, for the bandpass and highpass networks we must simply shift the phase curves by the constant amount introduced by their zeros (Fig. 6-14). This means adding 90° to the

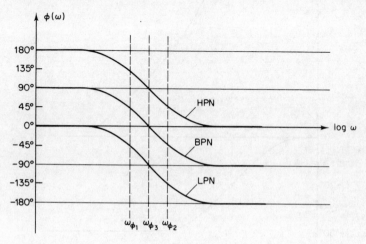

Fig. 6-14 Phase curves of general second-order networks: HPN, highpass network; BPN, bandpass network; LPN, lowpass network

phase curve of the bandpass network, and 180° to that of the highpass network. Thus, (6-33) and (6-35) become

$$\omega_p = \omega_{\phi_3} \tag{6-36a}$$

and

$$q_p = \frac{\omega_{\phi_3}}{\omega_{\phi_2} - \omega_{\phi_1}} \tag{6-36b}$$

where

For lowpass network: $\phi_1 = -45°$; $\phi_2 = -135°$; $\phi_3 = -90°$

For bandpass network: $\phi_1 = 45°$; $\phi_2 = -45°$; $\phi_3 = 0°$

For highpass network: $\phi_1 = 135°$; $\phi_2 = 45°$; $\phi_3 = +90°$

and

$$\omega_{\phi_1, \phi_2} = \frac{\omega_p}{2q_p}(\sqrt{4q_p^2 + 1} \mp 1) \tag{6-37}$$

The functional tuning procedure can now be summarized by the following two steps:

(a) ω_p adjustment. At ω_p adjust the network for the phase shift ϕ_3.
(b) q_p adjustment. Calculate ω_{ϕ_1} and ω_{ϕ_2} from (6-37) and adjust for ϕ_1 or ϕ_2 at the corresponding frequency.

The slope of $\phi(\omega)$, i.e. the delay $\tau(\omega)$, is obtained by taking the derivative of (6-32) (see Chapter 2, eq. 2-10). Thus

$$\tau(\omega) = -\frac{d\phi}{d\omega} = \frac{(\omega_p^2 + \omega^2)\omega_p q_p}{q_p^2(\omega_p^2 - \omega^2)^2 + \omega^2\omega_p^2} \tag{6-38}$$

Hence, at ω_p,

$$\tau(\omega_p) = -\frac{d\phi}{d\omega}\bigg|_{\omega = \omega_p} = \frac{2q_p}{\omega_p} \tag{6-39}$$

Thus, the larger the q_p, the steeper the phase slope, and the larger the delay τ. This is very useful, because the accuracy of the frequency adjustment becomes all the more important the higher q_p is specified, since it can be shown that the amplitude error at the 3-dB frequencies is $q_p \Delta\omega_p/\omega_p$. Fortunately, then, with increasing q_p a higher frequency accuracy becomes easier to attain.

According to the discussion on sensitivity matrices in Section 6-2, the tuning procedure outlined above will only be truly 'two-step' if we have a non-interactive, i.e. a diagonal or triangular, sensitivity matrix. If this is not the case, then the two steps outlined above must be repeated iteratively until the desired accuracy is obtained.

In the q_p adjustment described above, we have the choice of adjusting for either ϕ_1 or ϕ_2 at the respective frequency. By definition ω_{ϕ_2} is the higher of the two frequencies; thus if the operational amplifier introduces any parasitic phase lag, say $\Delta\phi$ degrees, this will be more apparent at ω_{ϕ_2} than at ω_{ϕ_1}. However, compensation of this parasitic phase at ω_{ϕ_2}, by tuning only to $(\phi_2 - \Delta\phi)$ degrees, may overcompensate the phase at ω_{ϕ_1}. Thus, which of the two frequencies to select for the q_p adjustment depends on which of the two, ω_{ϕ_1} or ω_{ϕ_2}, are in the more critical range of the filter band. Alternatively, an average value of parasitic phase can be compensated for at ω_p by tuning to $[\phi(\omega_p) - \Delta\phi/2]$ degrees; q_p is then tuned by adjusting for ϕ_1 or ϕ_2 at either of the frequencies ω_{ϕ_1} or ω_{ϕ_2}, respectively.

The functional tuning method described above entails the setting of an input sinusoidal signal generator to the required frequencies ω_p and, say, ω_{ϕ_2}, and then adjusting for ϕ_{ω_p} and ϕ_2, respectively. Naturally, for high tuning accuracy, the frequencies ω_p and ω_{ϕ_2} must be set accurately—a process that is time consuming with an oscillator of average accuracy or costly using, say, a frequency synthesizer. To eliminate the need for high-accuracy frequency setting, an oscillator of average accuracy (but high stability) combined with a high-accuracy frequency counter can be set to the *approximate* frequencies ω_p and ω_{ϕ_2}, say to ω'_p and ω'_{ϕ_2}, and the corresponding phase ϕ'_{ω_p} and ϕ'_2, calculated from (6-32). However, since $\tan^{-1} \phi(\omega'_p)$ will be very inaccurate if $\omega'_p \approx \omega_p$, the two frequencies to use, in this case, will be ω'_{ϕ_1} and ω'_{ϕ_2}, as calculated from (6-37). For the three network types we then have:

For lowpass network: $\qquad \phi'_1 = \phi(\omega'_{\phi_1}); \qquad\qquad \phi'_2 = \phi(\omega'_{\phi_2})$

For bandpass network: $\qquad \phi'_1 = 90° + \phi(\omega'_{\phi_1}); \quad \phi'_2 = 90° + \phi(\omega'_{\phi_2})$

For highpass network: $\qquad \phi'_1 = 180° + \phi(\omega'_{\phi_1}); \quad \phi'_2 = 180° + \phi(\omega'_{\phi_2})$

The tuning adjustments at ω'_{ϕ_1} and ω'_{ϕ_2} here take the place of the adjustments at ω_p and, say, ω_{ϕ_2}. Between them they tune the circuit for ω_p and q_p. Notice, however, that in contrast to the ω_p and ω_{ϕ_2} adjustment, the two tuning steps are now interactive since both ϕ'_1 and ϕ'_2 are functions of ω_p and q_p.

The tuning of the constant coefficient K is generally not very critical. If ω_p and q_p can be tuned for with relatively few iterative steps, it is rarely worth increasing this number for the sake of an accurate K. However, if high K accuracy is indeed required, it can generally be attained by a gain or attenuator adjustment somewhere preceding or following the network. In any event, the K adjustment is a gain adjustment setting the overall level of the output signal; in most cases the initial, or untuned K value, accurate to within a few per cent., will be quite sufficient.

b. Networks with Finite Zeros

Here we consider minimum-phase networks of the general form

$$T(s) = K \frac{s^2 + (\omega_z/q_z)s + \omega_z^2}{s^2 + (\omega_p/q_p)s + \omega_p^2} \qquad (6\text{-}40)$$

Beside the pole parameters ω_p and q_p we must now also adjust ω_z and q_z. The phase function is now

$$\phi(\omega) = \phi_z(\omega) - \phi_p(\omega) = \tan^{-1}\left[\frac{\omega\omega_z}{q_z(\omega_z^2 - \omega^2)}\right] - \tan^{-1}\left[\frac{\omega\omega_p}{q_p(\omega_p^2 - \omega^2)}\right] \qquad (6\text{-}41)$$

The contribution of the zeros has the same form as that of the poles but with the opposite sign.

In those cases in which the zeros are realized by a summing operation (see, for example, circuit 14 in Chapter 5), the zeros can be initially removed from the circuit by opening up

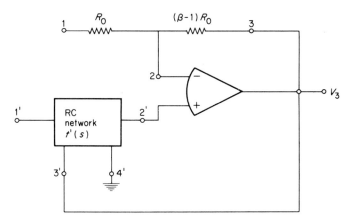

Fig. 6-15   Generalized version of circuit 15, Chapter 5

the summing path. The poles are then tuned separately as described above and the phase measured at the two frequencies ω'_{ϕ_1} and ω'_{ϕ_2}. Reconnecting the summing circuitry, the zeros are then tuned at ω'_{ϕ_2} such that

$$\phi(\omega'_{\phi_1}) = \tan^{-1}\left\{\frac{\omega'_{\phi_1}\omega_z}{q_z[\omega_z^2 - (\omega'_{\phi_1})^2]}\right\} - \tan^{-1}\left\{\frac{\omega'_{\phi_1}\omega_p}{q_p[\omega_p^2 - (\omega'_{\phi_1})^2]}\right\} \qquad (6\text{-}42)$$

and at ω'_{ϕ_2} such that the equivalent phase value $\phi(\omega'_{\phi_2})$ is obtained.

In other circuits (e.g. circuit 15, Chapter 5) the feedback loop responsible for the pole generation can be measured and tuned separately from the circuitry realizing the zeros, simply by measuring the network between appropriate terminals. Consider, for example, the generalized version of circuit 15 in Chapter 5 shown in Fig. 6-15. In regular operation, terminal 1 is gounded and the specified voltage transfer function is given by (see Chapter 4)

$$T'(s) = \frac{N(s)}{D(s)} = \frac{V_3}{V'_1} \approx \frac{t'_{12}}{t_{32} - t'_{32}} = \frac{\beta t'_{12}}{1 - \beta t'_{32}} \qquad (6\text{-}43)$$

where t'_{12} determines the zeros of $T'(s)$ and has the form

$$t'_{12} = \frac{V'_2}{V'_1}\bigg|_{V_3 = 0} = \frac{N(s)}{s^2 + (\omega_p/\hat{q})s + \omega_p^2} \qquad (6\text{-}44)$$

and t'_{32} is realized by a passive RC bandpass network with the form

$$t'_{32} = \frac{V'_2}{V'_3}\bigg|_{V_i = 0} = \frac{\omega_{32}s}{s^2 + (\omega_p/\hat{q})s + \omega_p^2} \qquad (6\text{-}45)$$

and

$$t_{32} = \frac{V_2}{V_3}\bigg|_{V_1 = 0} = \frac{1}{\beta} \qquad (6\text{-}46)$$

Both t'_{12} and t'_{32} are realized by the same passive RC network (but are fed from different input terminals) and therefore both have the same negative real poles (i.e. $\hat{q} < 0.5$).

Computing the transfer function between terminal 1 and the output, with terminal 1′ grounded, we obtain

$$T(s) = \frac{V_3}{V_1} \approx -\frac{t_{12}}{t_{32} - t'_{32}} \tag{6-47}$$

where t_{32} and t'_{32} are given by (6-45) and (6-46), and

$$t_{12} = \frac{V_2}{V_1}\bigg|_{V_3 = 0} = \frac{\beta - 1}{\beta} \tag{6-48}$$

$T(s)$ is independent of t'_{12} and therefore *independent of the zeros of the desired transfer function* $T'(s)$. On the other hand, the poles of $T(s)$ are precisely the poles of $T'(s)$. With (6-45)–(6-48) we obtain

$$T(s) = -(\beta - 1)\frac{s^2 + (\omega_p/\hat{q})s + \omega_p^2}{s^2 + (\omega_p/q_p)s + \omega_p^2} \tag{6-49}$$

where

$$q_p = \frac{\hat{q}}{1 - \beta(\omega_{32}/\omega_p)\hat{q}} \tag{6-50}$$

q_p is the pole Q of the specified denominator $D(s)$ in (6-43) and $T(s)$ is the frequency response of a frequency emphasizing network (FEN) (see Chapter 2, Section 2-2) *irrespective of the zeros of* $T'(s)$. Thus the poles of the FEN, seen between the terminals 1 and 3 of the general network, can be tuned first, followed by the separate tuning of the zeros.

The poles of (6-49) are tuned for as follows. From (6-41) we have

$$\phi(\omega) = \tan^{-1}\frac{\omega\omega_z/q_z(\omega_z^2 - \omega^2) - \omega\omega_p/q_p(\omega_p^2 - \omega^2)}{1 + (1/q_zq_p)[\omega^2\omega_z\omega_p/(\omega_z^2 - \omega^2)(\omega_p^2 - \omega^2)]} \tag{6-51}$$

and for $\omega_p = \omega_z$ this becomes

$$\phi(\omega) = \tan^{-1}\frac{\Omega[(q_p - q_z)/q_pq_z]}{\Omega^2 + 1/q_zq_p} \tag{6-52a}$$

where

$$\Omega = \frac{\omega_p}{\omega} - \frac{\omega}{\omega_p} \tag{6-52b}$$

For $\Omega = 0$, i.e. $\omega = \omega_p$, we have

$$\phi(\omega_p) = 180° \tag{6-53}$$

When the denominator of (6-52a) is zero, ϕ is 90° or 270°. Solving for the corresponding frequencies, we obtain

$$\omega_{90, 270} = \frac{\omega_p}{2\sqrt{q_pq_z}}(\sqrt{4q_pq_z + 1} \mp 1) \tag{6-54}$$

To tune for ω_p and q_p we select two frequencies, e.g. ω_p and ω_{90}, and tune for the corresponding phase. To compute ω_{90}, or ω_{270}, q_z is replaced by $\hat{q}$, which is computed either from the nominal network elements (i.e. q_p ($\beta = 0$) = $\hat{q}$) or measured according to (6-45).

The zeros are tuned after the circuit has been returned to its normal operating condition (terminal 1 grounded). It is preferable to tune the zeros using (6-43) rather than (6-44), since terminal 2' is a high-impedance point and therefore sensitive to external measuring equipment, whereas the output impedance at terminal 3 is low.

The expression for $\phi(\omega)$ in (6-52) is perfectly general for a second-order function for which $\omega_p = \omega_z$. Thus, depending on whether q_p is larger or smaller than q_z, it describes the phase response of a symmetrical frequency-emphasizing network (FEN) or frequency-rejection network (FRN) respectively.

In a frequency-rejection network (FRN) in which the zeros are close to, or on, the $j\omega$ axis (i.e. $q_z \to \infty$), the phase contribution of the zeros, $\phi_z(\omega)$, is restricted to a narrow frequency range around ω_z. This is shown in Fig. 6-16, where $\phi_z(\omega)$ is plotted for large q_z values. As a frame of reference for typical q_z values, one should bear in mind that the null depth of a symmetrical FRN (i.e. $\omega_z = \omega_p$) is proportional to q_p/q_z, so that for a -60-dB null and $q_p = 5$, q_z must be 5,000. Even in the case of a passive twin-T with $\hat{q} = 0.25$, q_z must be 250. For deeper null-depths, q_z must be increased accordingly. Thus, referring to Fig. 6-16, it follows that ω_z need not be separated much from ω_p before the phase contribution of the zeros to the phase of the poles can be neglected. In such cases, the poles and zeros can be tuned separately and between the same input–output terminals, instead of between two different terminal pairs as was described above.* Thus, for the range ω_z/ω_p less than 0.5 or greater than 2, the phase contribution of $\phi_z(\omega)$ on $\phi_p(\omega)$ in (6-41) can be neglected, and the poles can be tuned as in an allpole network. For the range of ω_z/ω_p between 0.9 to 1.1 the contribution of the zero phase to the pole phase is significant and the two must be tuned separately, as outlined above.

The fact that certain networks can be more easily tuned when their (finite) zeros are sufficiently far apart from the poles should be kept in mind during the pole-zero pairing

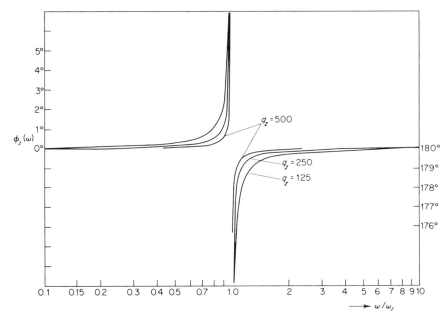

Fig. 6-16 Phase contribution of the zeros of a frequency-rejection network as a function of ω/ω_z

* Note that the zeros must be tuned *before* the poles.

process that will be discussed in Chapter 7. Thus, all things being equal, for tuning purposes it is usually preferable to pair poles with zeros that are as far apart as possible or at least have ω_z/ω_p ratios below 0.9 or above 1.1. Thus, for example, in applications having un-critical dynamic-range and signal-to-noise requirements, the pole-zero pairing may well proceed directly with a view to simplifying the tuning process. This means pairing the dominant or most critical poles with the zeros furthest away.

The band-rejection network represented by circuit 15 in Chapter 5 is noteworthy in that a certain well-defined part of the network, namely, the twin-T, realizes the zeros, while additional and separate components (the twin-T loading network) are available to tune the poles. This circuit therefore lends itself to a particularly simple form of tuning. The twin-T is first tuned for the zeros and subsequently, without any further adjustment of the twin-T, the twin-T loading network and the amplifier gain are used to tune the poles. These latter adjustments do not affect the previously tuned zeros in any way, provided that ω_z and ω_p are sufficiently far apart.

c. Non-minimum-Phase Networks

In the case of non-minimum-phase second-order networks, we restrict ourselves to allpass functions since any other function can always be expanded into the cascade of an allpass network and a network with finite zeros in the left-half plane. This expansion is achieved by adding a phantom pole and zero pair in the left-half s plane; thus,

$$T(s) = \frac{s^2 - (\omega_z/q_z)s + \omega_z^2}{s^2 + (\omega_p/q_p)s + \omega_p^2}$$

$$= \underbrace{\frac{s^2 - (\omega_z/q_z)s + \omega_z^2}{s^2 + (\omega_z/q_z)s + \omega_z^2}}_{T_1(s)} \underbrace{\frac{s^2 + (\omega_z/q_z)s + \omega_z^2}{s^2 + (\omega_p/q_p)s + \omega_p^2}}_{T_2(s)} \tag{6-55}$$

$T_1(s)$ represents an allpass network and $T_2(s)$ a minimum-phase network, as illustrated in Fig. 6-17.

A general second-order allpass function is given by the transfer function

$$T(s) = \frac{s^2 - (\omega_0/q)s + \omega_0^2}{s^2 + (\omega_0/q)s + \omega_0^2} \tag{6-56}$$

Very often this function is characterized by a 'stiffness' factor b instead of the root Q, where

$$b = 2q \tag{6-57}$$

From (6-52) it follows that

$$\phi(\omega) = -2\cot^{-1}\left[q\left(\frac{\omega_0}{\omega} - \frac{\omega}{\omega_0}\right)\right] \tag{6-58}$$

The delay or slope of the phase curve is then

$$\tau(\omega) = -\frac{d\phi(\omega)}{d\omega} = \frac{2q}{\omega_0} \frac{1 + (\omega_0/\omega)^2}{1 + q^2(\omega/\omega_0 - \omega_0/\omega)^2} \tag{6-59}$$

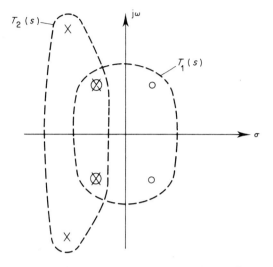

Fig. 6-17 Expansion of a non-minimum-phase second-order network function by adding a phantom pole-zero pair to obtain an allpass function $T_1(s)$ and a minimum-phase network function $T_2(s)$

and, at the frequency ω_0,

$$\tau(\omega_0) = \frac{4q}{\omega_0} \tag{6-60}$$

Note that the maximum delay occurs at a slightly lower frequency, namely, at

$$\omega_{\tau_{max}} = \omega_0 \left(\sqrt{4 - \frac{1}{q^2}} - 1 \right) \tag{6-61}$$

The allpass network is characterized by the two parameters ω_0 and q. From (6-58) we obtain

$$\phi(0) = 0°$$
$$\phi(\omega_0) = 180° \tag{6-62}$$
$$\phi(\omega \to \infty) = 360°$$

From (6-54) the frequencies at which the phase is 90° and 270°, respectively, are

$$\omega_{90,270} = \frac{\omega_0}{2q} \left(\sqrt{4q^2 + 1} \mp 1 \right) \tag{6-63}$$

Thus the procedure for tuning a second-order allpass network is as follows:

(a) To set $\omega_z = \omega_p = \omega_0$, $\phi(\omega_0)$ is adjusted for 180°.
(b) To set $-q_z = q_p = q$, the phase at ω_{90} or ω_{270} is adjusted for $-90°$ or $-270°$, respectively.

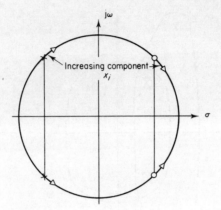

Fig. 6-18 Effect of step (b) of the tuning procedure for a second-order allpass network

As in the tuning of the other functions discussed above, we have indicated here which parameters (e.g. ω_z, ω_p, etc.) to tune and which measure (e.g. phase) to use in doing so. In practice, any given network must be examined individually to ascertain which components to use for the adjustment of each parameter and the best sequence to follow. In Chapter 5 this information, together with the other design data, is specifically presented for each individual circuit.

It should be pointed out that some networks may require a different measure for tuning a particular parameter than others. Consider, for example, the case of the allpass network in which the tuning component x_i used for step (b) above moves the zeros away from the $j\omega$ axis while moving the poles closer to it (see Fig. 6-18). This will happen if q_z is inversely, and q_p directly, proportional to changes in the component x_i. In this case, the decrease in the phase contribution of the zeros is approximately cancelled by the increase in the phase contribution of the poles; thus, in spite of high $S_{x_i}^{q_p}$ and $S_{x_i}^{q_z}$ values, the overall phase will remain practically constant while adjusting x_i. In such a case the amplitude is a better measure for the q adjustment than the phase. For $q_p = -q_z = q$, the amplitude at ω_0 must be equal to the amplitude at d.c. or at any other frequency. Note, then, that whereas the phase measurements suggested above are in general the most suitable indicators for the adjustment of network parameters, a given network realization may still require a tuning indicator other than phase. One must therefore ascertain individually the optimum tuning indicator every time a basically different network type is used.

6-8 A SIMPLE PHASE NETWORK FOR THE TUNING OF ACTIVE FILTERS

In the previous section we have seen that, for best accuracy, second-order filter sections should be tuned 'by phase' rather than 'by amplitude'. Above all, this means that the desired pole frequency and Q are tuned by adjusting appropriate 'tuning components' such that a specified phase value is measured at a prescribed frequency. Phase measurements are not as common as amplitude measurements and the necessity of acquiring a phase meter— typically with an accuracy of well below one degree—may sometimes be considered a drawback. In this section we suggest a method of circumventing the need for a phase meter

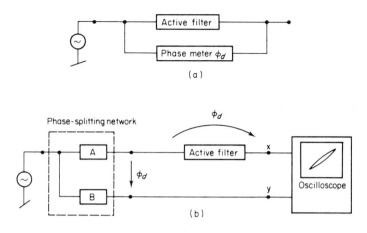

Fig. 6-19   Measuring the phase ϕ_d of an active filter: (a) direct set-up,
(b) with additional phase-splitting network

by providing simple, readily built auxiliary circuits with which active filters can be phase-tuned accurately enough for most applications.

Phase measurements are required primarily for the adjustment of the pole frequencies. (The notch frequencies of a band-rejection network and the right-half plane zeros of an all-pass network can generally be adjusted for by using an amplitude measurement as explained in the previous section.) Fortunately, the phase values required for pole frequency and Q adjustments are well defined and occur in multiples of $45°$ (see Fig. 6-14), namely, $0°$, $\pm 45°$, $\pm 90°$, $\pm 135°$. Thus, by designing phase-splitting networks that provide multiples of $45°$ accurately, and over a sufficiently wide frequency band, the pole frequencies can be adjusted for without the need for a phase meter. The pole tuning is carried out with the help of the Lissajous figures on an oscilloscope.

Consider an active filter network whose phase difference between input and output is ϕ_d degrees, as shown in Fig. 6-19(a). We now add a phase-splitting network with the same phase shift ϕ_d to the measuring set-up, as shown in Fig. 6-19(b). Connecting the output of the filter and the phase-splitting network to the x and y inputs, respectively, of an oscilloscope, the resulting Lissajous figure will be a straight line with a slope of $45°$ or $135°$, depending on whether the phase shift between x and y is zero or $180°$. Thus to tune the active filter pole frequency and Q, the corresponding phase ϕ_d (which is a multiple of $45°$) is obtained by tuning the corresponding tuning components until the initial ellipse degenerates to a straight line.

A dual phase-splitting network that provides both a constant $45°$ phase shift and a constant $90°$ phase shift over a frequency band between 10 Hz and 100 kHz is shown in Fig. 6-20. The networks A and B that provide the $45°$ phase shift consist of cascaded second-order allpass networks as shown in Fig. 6-21(a) and (b), respectively. Similarly, the cascaded second-order allpass circuits making up the $90°$ phase-shifting networks C and D are shown in Fig. 6-22(a) and (b), respectively. The corresponding pole (zero) frequencies and pole (zero) Q's are listed in Table 6-2. Note that all the pole and zero Q's are less than 0.5, i.e. each pole-zero pair lies on the real axis, symmetrically to the origin.

The allpass networks used for the $45°$ phase-splitting networks A and B (Fig. 6-21) correspond to circuit 12 (AP–MQ) given in Chapter 5. It was found sufficient to tune the

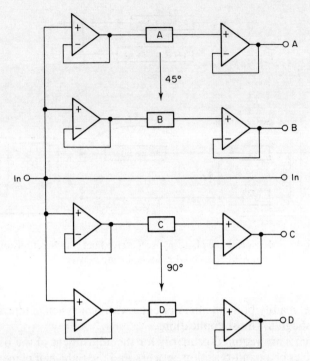

Fig. 6-20 Phase-splitting network; networks A and B
provide 45° phase shift, networks C and D provide 90°
phase shift

circuits deterministically, i.e. using the design equations in Chapter 5 to compute the
resistor values corresponding to the measured capacitor values. No additional functional
tuning step was required since the maximum phase error occurring at 100 kHz, which was
0.7°, was considered sufficiently small.

The allpass circuits used for the 90° phase-splitting networks C and D (Fig. 6-22) correspond to circuit 5a (AP–Q.5-P) in Chapter 5. A degree of functional tuning was found to
be necessary for these circuits in that the null-depth of the twin-T circuits was tuned for a
minimum at the respective pole frequencies (see Table 6-2). In order to reduce the remaining
phase error, a 10 pF capacitor was applied to the last allpass section of network D. As a
result, a 3° phase error at 100 kHz was reduced to 0.6° At frequencies below 100 kHz the
phase error was appreciably less.

The worst-case phase accuracy attainable both with the 45° and the 90° phase-splitting
network is in the order of 0.6°. According to eq. (6-15), this corresponds to an attainable
amplitude accuracy in the order of 0.12 dB, which is sufficient for most practical purposes.
The phase accuracy can be further improved by ensuring that the coaxial cables connecting
the active filter output signal (x) and the phase-splitting network output signal (y) to the
oscilloscope are as short, and of equal length, as possible. In order to equalize remaining
phase differences in the cables, and in the input amplifiers of the oscilloscope, initial calibrat-
ing measurements without the active filter can be made. Furthermore, interchanging the
x and y cables, a mean frequency can be established corresponding to the phase shift ϕ_d
actually required.

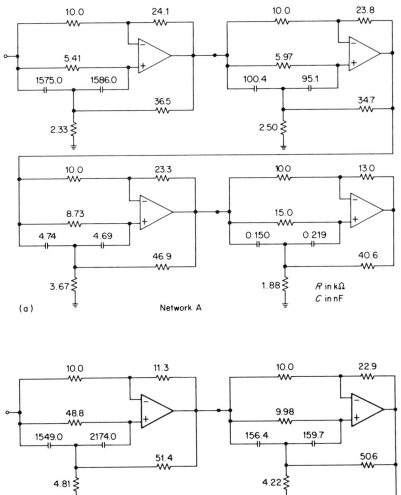

Fig. 6-21   A 45° phase-splitting network: (a) network A, (b) network B

114

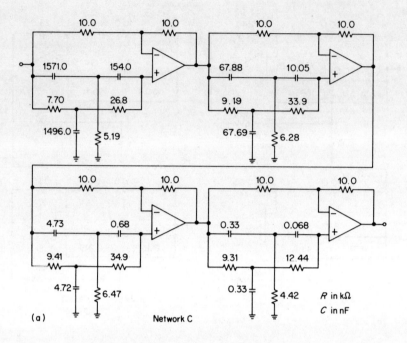

(a) Network C

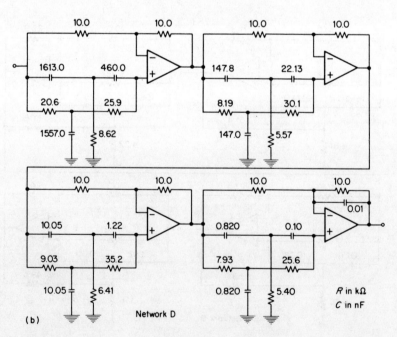

(b) Network D

Fig. 6-22   A 90° phase-splitting network: (a) network C, (b) network D

Table 6-2

Network	Pole (zero) frequencies (Hz)	Pole (zero) pairs; f_p (Hz)
A	$f_1 = 14.36$ $f_2 = 59.5$ $f_3 = 225.23$ $f_4 = 847.4$ $f_5 = 3,187.6$ $f_6 = 12,027$ $f_7 = 47,479$ $f_8 = 601,216$	$f_{p1} = 29.23$ $q_{p1} = 0.3958$ $f_{p2} = 436.9$ $q_{p2} = 0.473$ $f_{p3} = 6,191.7$ $q_{p3} = 0.4070$ $f_{p4} = 168,950$ $q_{p4} = 0.2605$
B	$f_1 = 1.66$ $f_2 = 21.06$ $f_3 = 83.14$ $f_4 = 313.7$ $f_5 = 1,180$ $f_6 = 4,440$ $f_7 = 16,806$ $f_8 = 69,615$	$f_{p1} = 5.92$ $q_{p1} = 0.2605$ $f_{p2} = 161.5$ $q_{p2} = 0.4070$ $f_{p3} = 2,288.9$ $q_{p3} = 0.4073$ $f_{p4} = 34,200$ $q_{p4} = 0.3958$
C	$f_1 = 11.65$ $f_2 = 50.29$ $f_3 = 190.8$ $f_4 = 718.1$ $f_5 = 2,701$ $f_6 = 10,182$ $f_7 = 39,636$ $f_8 = 296,534$	$f_{p1} = 24.2$ $q_{p1} = 0.3908$ $f_{p2} = 370.2$ $q_{p2} = 0.4073$ $f_{p3} = 5,244.1$ $q_{p3} = 0.4071$ $f_{p4} = 108,413$ $q_{p4} = 0.3225$
D	$f_1 = 3.372$ $f_2 = 25.23$ $f_3 = 98.22$ $f_4 = 370.2$ $f_5 = 1,393$ $f_6 = 5,240$ $f_7 = 19,887$ $f_8 = 85,830$	$f_{p1} = 9.224$ $q_{p1} = 0.3225$ $f_{p2} = 190.7$ $q_{p2} = 0.4071$ $f_{p3} = 2,701.5$ $q_{p3} = 0.4073$ $f_{p4} = 41,314$ $q_{p4} = 0.3908$

CHAPTER 7

Designing nth-Order Active Filters

7-1 THE nth-ORDER TRANSFER FUNCTION

One of the most basic problems in filter design is the so-called *approximation problem*. In terms of active filter design and the concepts discussed in Chapter 2 it entails finding a rational nth-order transfer function of the form

$$T(s) = \frac{N(s)}{D(s)} = \frac{b_m s^m + b_{m-1} s^{m-1} + \cdots + b_1 s + b_0}{a_n s^n + a_{n-1} s^{n-1} + \cdots + a_1 s + a_0} \tag{7-1}$$

such that, for $s = j\omega$,

$$\alpha(\omega) = \operatorname{Re} \ln T(j\omega) = \ln |T(j\omega)| \tag{7-2a}$$

and

$$\phi(\omega) = \operatorname{Im} \ln T(j\omega) = \arg T(j\omega) \tag{7-2b}$$

correspond to a specified amplitude and phase response, respectively. In general the poles of $T(s)$, i.e. the roots of $D(s)$, are complex conjugate. Using the designations introduced in Chapter 2, the general transfer function can therefore be expressed as a product of second-order transfer functions:

$$T(s) = \prod_{j=1}^{n/2} T_j(s) = \prod_{j=1}^{n/2} \frac{n_j(s)}{d_j(s)} \tag{7-3}$$

where $d_j(s)$ is assumed to be an even function with complex-conjugate roots, and the roots of $n_j(s)$, if finite, will either be on the $j\omega$ axis or symmetrical to the poles in the right-half s plane. In the general case, $T_j(s)$ has the form

$$T_j(s) = K_j \frac{s^2 + (\omega_{z_j}/q_{z_j})s + \omega_{z_j}^2}{s^2 + (\omega_{p_j}/q_{p_j})s + \omega_{p_j}^2} \tag{7-4}$$

If n is odd, then the product in (7-3) is multiplied by a first-order term of the general form

$$T_\alpha(s) = K_\alpha \frac{s + \alpha_z}{s + \alpha_p} \tag{7-5a}$$

or of the lowpass form

$$T_\alpha(s) = \frac{K_\alpha}{s + \alpha} \tag{7-5b}$$

116

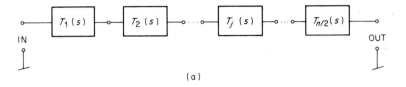

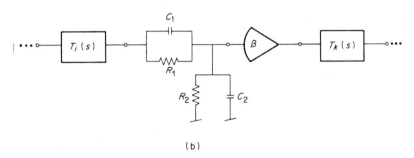

Fig. 7-1   Cascading second-order filter building blocks: (a) n even, (b) adding a
first-order section when n is odd

Assuming that n is even, the transfer function $T(s)$ as given by (7-3) can be realized by cascading $n/2$ second-order filter building blocks of the kind presented in Chapter 5. This is shown in Fig. 7-1(a). The output of each building block is taken from an opamp and therefore has a very low output impedance. As a consequence, the individual building blocks are isolated from each other and can be cascaded in any sequence. However, as outlined in Section 7-8, an optimum sequence may exist, such as to maximize the dynamic range of the resulting nth-order filter. If n is odd, then a first-order section of the kind shown in Fig. 7-1(b) can be used to provide the general function $T_\alpha(s)$ given by (7-5a). In terms of (7-5a) we then have

$$K_\alpha = \beta \frac{C_1}{C_p} \tag{7-6a}$$

$$\alpha_z = \frac{1}{R_1 C_1} \tag{7-6b}$$

$$\alpha_p = \frac{1}{R_p C_p} \tag{7-6c}$$

where $R_p = R_1 R_2 (R_1 + R_2)^{-1}$ and $C_p = C_1 + C_2$.

For the case of a first-order lowpass section, as given by (7-5b), we require only R_1 and C_2 in Fig. 7-1(b), where

$$K_\alpha = \frac{\beta}{R_1 C_2} \tag{7-6d}$$

and

$$\alpha = \frac{1}{R_1 C_2} \tag{7-6e}$$

A first-order highpass section is readily obtained by retaining only C_1 and R_2 in Fig. 7-1(b).

From the foregoing discussion it follows that, once $T(s)$ has been obtained, the procedure for filter design by cascading second- (or third-) order building blocks can readily be implemented. $T(s)$, in general given directly in terms of its poles and zeros, is decomposed into pole-zero pairs (see Section 7-7), each of which represents a second-order function $T_j(s)$ as in (7-4). Each function $T_j(s)$ is realizable by a circuit listed in Chapter 5. The resulting building blocks are then cascaded as in Fig. 7-1 to provide the desired nth-order function $T(s)$.

If $T(s)$ is initially given as a ratio of polynomials as in (7-1), the roots of $N(s)$ and $D(s)$ must first be calculated in order to obtain $T(s)$ in the form of (7-3). The question of which pole pair to combine with which zero pair for each $T_j(s)$ will be discussed briefly in Section 7-7. Although theoretically each of the possible $(n/2)!$ pole-zero pair combinations results in the same overall function $T(s)$, it can be shown that an optimum choice for maximum dynamic range and minimum noise does exist. First, however, we must direct our attention to the central question still remaining at this point, namely, that of finding the most suitable transfer function $T(s)$ capable of providing the specified amplitude and phase response. This will be the topic for most of the remainder of this chapter.

7-2 THE BASIC FILTER TYPES

The most important filter types are best discussed based on the characteristics of a lowpass filter. In Section 7-5 we shall see how all other filter types (e.g. bandpass, highpass, etc.) can readily be related to the characteristics of a normalized lowpass filter. Thus, having solved the approximation problem (i.e. the derivation of a rational function $T(s)$ to satisfy a specified amplitude and phase response) in the 'lowpass domain', it is relatively simple to obtain the corresponding other filter characteristics.

The linear amplitude response of the ideal lowpass filter is shown in Fig. 7-2(a), the corresponding insertion loss in decibels being shown in Fig. 7-2(b). The ideal lowpass filter is characterized by (a) zero loss and ripple in the passband, (b) an infinite attenuation slope at the cutoff frequency f_c (i.e. a zero transition region), and (c) infinite attenuation in the stopband. For obvious reasons, the ideal lowpass filter with this kind of response is often called a 'brick wall' filter. In general, a linear phase response is also assumed. The ideal

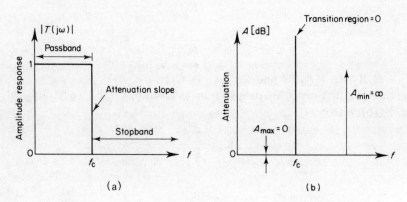

Fig. 7-2 Characteristics of an ideal lowpass filter: (a) amplitude response, (b) insertion loss

lowpass filter is distinguished by the fact that *no rational transfer function T(s) exists to describe it accurately.* Thus, any analytical description of the ideal lowpass filter can, at best, be an approximation. Many such approximations have been derived in the field of classical network theory. The best, and most commonly used ones can be grouped into the basic types whose characteristics are shown qualitatively in Fig. 7-3. Briefly, they can be described as follows.

a. Maximally Flat or Butterworth Filters

The maximally flat or Butterworth approximation of an ideal lowpass filter is shown in Fig. 7-3(a). The Butterworth filter is a compromise in many respects. It has a maximally flat response in the passband, but this is achieved at the expense of phase linearity (see Fig. 7-4) and steepness of attenuation slope. However, the attenuation slope of the Butterworth filter is quite good, it has a reasonably good impulse response, and, because it provides an excellent general-purpose approximation to the ideal filter response, it is one of the most commonly used filter types.

b. Equiripple or Chebyshev Filters

If steepness of attenuation slope, especially in the region of cutoff, is more important than passband flatness or phase linearity, the Chebyshev response, shown in Fig. 7-3(b) is often applicable. The Chebyshev filter exhibits increased overshoot when driven by a step function, and is designed with a prescribed ripple (i.e. equiripple) in the passband, e.g. 0.01 dB up to a possible 3-dB ripple. In return for the lack of smooth response in the passband, there are advantages in a very much higher rate of cutoff around the edge of the passband. The response curve at frequencies beyond the cutoff region runs parallel to, but nearer to, the passband than that of the equivalent-order Butterworth filter.

Both the Butterworth and the Chebyshev lowpass filters achieve infinite attenuation only at infinite frequency, i.e. all the zeros of transmission occur at infinite frequency. At any other frequency some signals will pass through the filter, i.e. also in the stopband. If infinite attenuation at particular frequencies in the stopband is required, the inverse Chebyshev response, shown in Fig. 7-3(c), may be used. There is no ripple in the passband, but ripple does exist in the stopband and attenuation is infinite at certain frequencies (so-called attenuation poles).

c. Elliptic or Chebyshev–Cauer Filters

Elliptic or Chebyshev–Cauer filters (also sometimes called complete Chebyshev, double Chebyshev, Darlington, or Zolotarev filters) have ripple in the passband *and* stopband, descend rapidly to a prescribed attenuation outside the passband, and maintain a specified minimum attenuation to undesirable frequencies outside the passband. Like the inverse Chebyshev filters, at certain finite frequencies in the stopband they have infinite attenuation, i.e. attenuation poles. The response is shown in Fig. 7-3(d). Elliptic filters are probably the most efficient filters in terms of component count, for approximating the amplitude response of an ideal filter. For a given filter order it is possible to produce filters more economically with either a very sharp cutoff or a very high attenuation in the stopband. On the other hand, the attenuation does not drop off smoothly to infinity outside the passband, but is maintained at a predetermined level. Note that the Chebyshev and the inverse Chebyshev filters are special cases of the more general Chebyshev–Cauer filters.

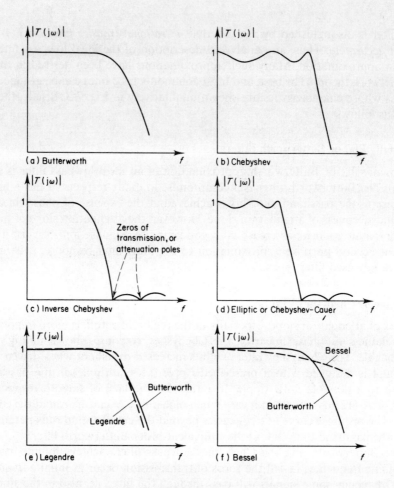

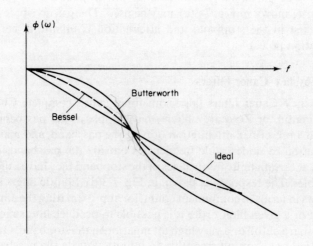

(g) Ideal, Butterworth, and Bessel phase response

Fig. 7-3 Response of basic filter types: (a–f) amplitude, (g) phase

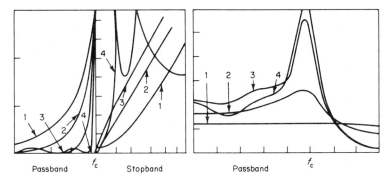

Fig. 7-4 Comparison of fifth-order filters for attenuation and group delay: (1) Bessel, (2) Butterworth, (3) Chebyshev (0.1 dB), (4) Chebyshev–Cauer (0.1 dB). (Reproduced from *Filter Specification and Selection* by kind permission of ELECTRON, IPC Business Press, and the agreement of the author Mr. W. Meek of Kemo)

d. Optimum-Monotonic or Legendre Filters

As has been emphasized, a Butterworth filter has a maximally flat passband response and the Chebyshev family of filters provides a good attenuation slope. In some applications, the attenuation slope of a Butterworth filter is inadequate and the ripple of a Chebyshev filter is not tolerable. Designing a Chebyshev filter that will have a very small or zero ripple does not help because Chebyshev and Butterworth filters are of the same family; a Chebyshev filter with zero ripple is a Butterworth filter. A solution in this instance may be to use a Legendre or optimum-monotonic filter. The amplitude response for such a filter is shown in Fig. 7-3(e). For purposes of comparison the response of a Butterworth filter is also shown. Notice that the Legendre response is not as flat as that of the maximally flat Butterworth response in the passband, but that the attentuation slope of the Legendre response is steeper. A typical property of Butterworth and Legendre filters is their monotonic character, i.e. for any value of gain there is a unique frequency. This is in contrast to the Chebyshev filters in which a particular value of gain will occur at several frequencies because of ripple. The Legendre characteristic attempts to combine the best characteristics of the Butterworth and Chebyshev characteristics. Here the attenuation slope is made as steep as possible with the restriction that the characteristic remains monotonic.

e. Linear-Phase or Bessel Filters

So far filters have been discussed mainly in terms of their amplitude responses, which are plots of gain (or attenuation) versus frequency. However, these plots do not describe the complete transmission properties of a filter; for example, the phase characteristic of a network is one of the most important parameters of a filter designed for the transmission of square-wave or pulse signals. When a rectangular pulse is passed through a Butterworth, Chebyshev, or Legendre filter, overshoot or ringing will appear on the pulse at the output. If this is undesirable, one of the members of the so-called Gaussian family of filters can be used, the most common of which is called a Bessel filter, because Bessel polynomials occur in the denominator of the transfer functions. Bessel filters are also sometimes called Thomson filters after the originator of the design method (W. E. Thomson, 1949).

If ringing or overshoot must be avoided when pulses are filtered, the phase shift between the input and output of a filter must be a linear function of frequency; stated differently, the rate of change of the phase with respect to frequency, or the group delay (see eq. 2-10 in Chapter 2), must be constant. The net effect of a constant group delay in a filter is that all frequency components of a signal transmitted through it are delayed by the same amount, i.e. there is no *dispersion* of signals passing through the filter. Accordingly, since a pulse contains signals of different frequencies, no dispersion takes place, i.e. its shape will be retained, when it is filtered by a network that has a linear-phase response or constant group delay. Just as the Butterworth filter is the best approximation to the ideal of 'perfect flatness of the amplitude response' in the filter passband, so the Bessel filter provides the best approximation to the ideal of 'perfect flatness of the group delay' in the passband, because it has a maximally flat group-delay response. However, this applies only to lowpass filters because highpass and bandpass Bessel filters do not have the linear-phase property.

Figure 7-3(f) compares the amplitude response of a Bessel filter with that of a Butterworth filter of the same order. Note that the Bessel filter is a poorer approximation to the ideal, both in flatness in the passband and in steepness of attenuation. There is no point in the passband at which the loss becomes zero; it falls off very gradually towards the cutoff (or 3 dB) frequency and then continues to fall just as gradually towards the eventual cutoff slope determined by the order of the filter. This attenuation slope will run parallel with the Butterworth and Chebyshev curves, but will be further from the passband.

Figure 7-3(g) compares the phase response of an ideal lowpass filter with that of a Butterworth and a Bessel filter. For an ideal filter the phase shift is linear with frequency; its group delay is constant at all frequencies. The Butterworth filter group delay is not constant because the plot of the phase angle versus frequency is non-linear. By contrast the Bessel filter has a reasonably linear phase angle versus frequency response in the passband; it therefore provides a good approximation to constant group delay. This is shown in more detail in Fig. 7-4, in which the attenuation and group delay for a fifth-order Bessel, Butterworth, Chebyshev, and Chebyshev–Cauer (the latter both with a 0.1-dB ripple) are shown.

Typical responses of various filters to a square-wave input are illustrated qualitatively in Fig. 7-5. The ringing in the Butterworth and Chebyshev filters that is the result of their non-linear-phase characteristics is evident; the absence of ringing in the Bessel filter shows

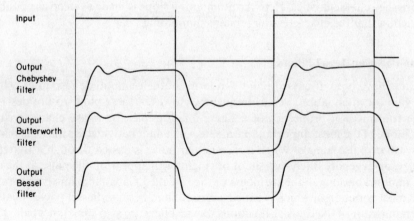

Fig. 7-5   Square-wave response of various filters

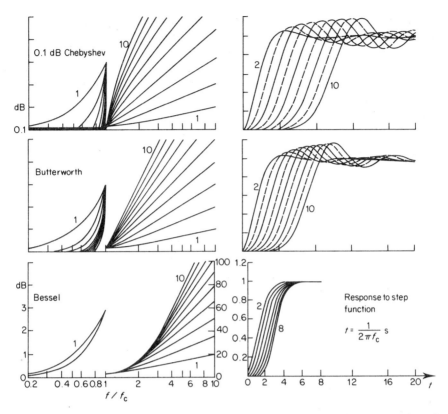

Fig. 7-6 Attenuation curves and step-function responses for Bessel, Butterworth, and Chebyshev (0.1 dB) filters. (Reproduced from *Filter Specification and Selection* by kind permission of ELECTRON, IPC Business Press, and the agreement of the author Mr. W. Meek of Kemo)

how well this type of filter approximates the desired linear-phase response. As expected, the response of the Chebyshev filter is inferior to the other two since its phase response is even less linear than that of the Butterworth filter (see Fig. 7-4). This is shown in detail in Fig. 7-6, where the attenuation curves and step-function responses for the Bessel, Butterworth, and Chebyshev (0.1-dB ripple) are shown for filters up to tenth order.

Transitional filters exist that have compromise characteristics trading off the best properties of two types of filters. One of the most common is the *Butterworth–Thomson* filter that attempts to combine the maximally flat amplitude of the Butterworth with the maximally flat group delay of the Bessel, or Thomson, filter.

7-3 THE TRANSFER FUNCTIONS OF ALLPOLE OR POLYNOMIAL FILTERS

Allpole filter networks are those whose transfer functions have no finite zeros. The typical nth-order transfer function has the form

$$T(s) = \frac{K}{D(s)} = \frac{K}{\prod_{j=1}^{n} (s - p_j)} \tag{7-7}$$

Thus, the numerator is a constant and the transfer function consists only of an nth-order polynomial in the denominator. Allpole filters are therefore referred to also as polynomial filters. The n zeros of $T(s)$ are said to be at infinity (note that $\lim_{\omega \to \infty} |T(j\omega)| = 0$). Of the basic filter types discussed in the previous section, Butterworth, Chebyshev, Legendre, Bessel, and transitional Butterworth–Thomson filters are allpole filters. By contrast, inverse Chebyshev and Chebyshev–Cauer filters are said to have *finite zeros*. In this case the numerator of $T(s)$ is also a polynomial whose roots (the zeros of $T(s)$) are finite, i.e. they lie in conjugate pairs on the $j\omega$ axis. In either case the *order n* of $T(s)$ refers to the order of the denominator polynomial $D(s)$, i.e. to the number of poles of $T(s)$. To realize an nth-order allpole network, it will be necessary to cascade $n/2$ allpole second-order networks as outlined in Section 7-1. If $T(s)$ had finite zeros, a corresponding number of second-order networks would have to have finite zeros. In any event, the allpole network will always be easier to realize than a network with finite zeros. In particular, the problem of tuning the finite zeros (see Chapter 6, Section 6-7) falls away, which is one of the main advantages of the allpole filter. Other advantages, such as the more linear phase characteristic and hence the better pulse response, were mentioned in the preceding section.

To determine which of the basic allpole networks is most suitable for a given application, it is useful to have a side-by-side comparison of their amplitude, phase, and delay characteristics. These characteristics are determined by the location, in the s plane, of the n poles of $T(s)$. Thus the poles of a Butterworth filter lie on a semi-circle in the left-half s plane, those of a Chebyshev filter on an ellipse which becomes narrower with increasing ripple and those of a Bessel filter on a curve outside the Butterworth semi-circle. This is shown qualitatively in Fig. 7-7. With the designations given in Fig. 7-8 (see also Chapter 2, Section 2-2), the amplitude response of an nth-order allpole filter is given by

$$|T(j\omega)| = \frac{K}{|D(j\omega)|} = \frac{K}{\prod_{j=1}^{n} A_{p_j}(\omega)} \tag{7-8}$$

With

$$A_{p_j}(\omega) = |s - p_j|_{s=j\omega}$$
$$= \sqrt{\sigma_{p_j}^2 + (\omega - \tilde{\omega}_{p_j})^2} \tag{7-9}$$

the amplitude response is given by

$$|T(j\omega)| = \frac{K}{\prod_{j=1}^{n} \sqrt{\sigma_{p_j}^2 + (\omega - \omega_{p_j})^2}} \tag{7-10}$$

By a suitable choice of K, the amplitude response can be normalized such that the maximum response is unity for all values of ω. Except for the Chebyshev filter with n odd, the maximum always occurs at $\omega = 0$, i.e. $|T(0)| = 1$. Applying this normalization in order to permit a valid comparison, the amplitude characteristics of the most important allpole lowpass networks are shown in Fig. 7-9. Note that the characteristics are plotted in decibels according to the expression for α_{dB} in eq. (2-9), Chapter 2. Furthermore, the characteristics are also normalized in frequency with respect to the 3-dB loss frequency ω_{3dB}, i.e. $\omega = \omega_{3dB} = 1$ rad/s. This normalization is common for Butterworth and Legendre filters, but not for the remaining filters whose characteristics are shown in Fig. 7-9. However, for the purpose of comparison as intended in Fig. 7-9, only one frequency normalization can be used.

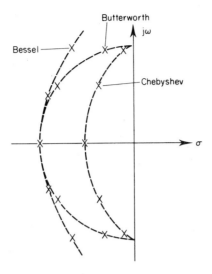

Fig. 7-7 Comparison of pole locations of Bessel, Butterworth, and Chebyshev filters

The phase response of $T(j\omega)$ is given by

$$\phi(\omega) = \arg T(j\omega) = -\sum_{j=1}^{n} \theta_{pj} \tag{7-11}$$

From Fig. 7-8 it follows that

$$\theta_{pj} = \tan^{-1}\left(\frac{\omega - \tilde{\omega}_{pj}}{-\sigma_{pj}}\right) \tag{7-12}$$

so that

$$\phi(\omega) = -\sum_{j=1}^{n} \tan^{-1}\left(\frac{\omega - \tilde{\omega}_{pj}}{-\sigma_{pj}}\right) \tag{7-13}$$

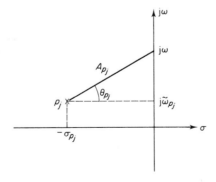

Fig. 7-8 Pole designations pertaining to eqs. (7-8) to (7-10)

126

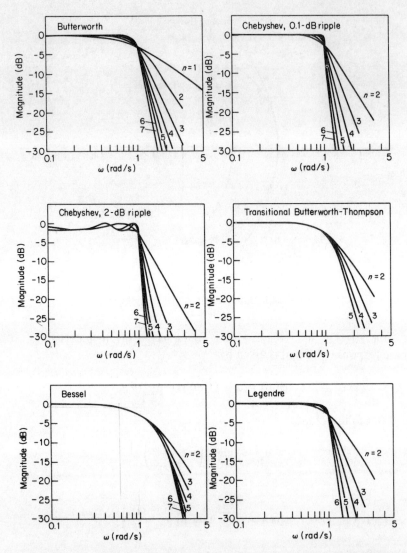

Fig. 7-9 Normalized amplitude responses of various lowpass allpole filters. (Reproduced by kind permission of A. S. McAllister from *Modern Low-Pass Filter Characteristics* by C. P. Eggen and A. S. McAllister, Electro-Technology, August 1966)

The phase characteristics corresponding to (7-13) of the basic allpole filter types are plotted, over the normalized frequency axis (i.e. $\omega = \omega_{3\text{dB}} = 1$), in Fig. 7-10. Although phase linearity is the parameter of importance here, it is not readily discernible from the graphs shown. In fact, the *rate of change* of the phase with frequency is a clearer criterion by which to judge phase linearity, and this is nothing but the group delay, as pointed out in the previous section. From Chapter 2 (eq. 2-10) we have

$$\tau_g(\omega) = -\frac{d\phi(\omega)}{d\omega} \tag{7-14}$$

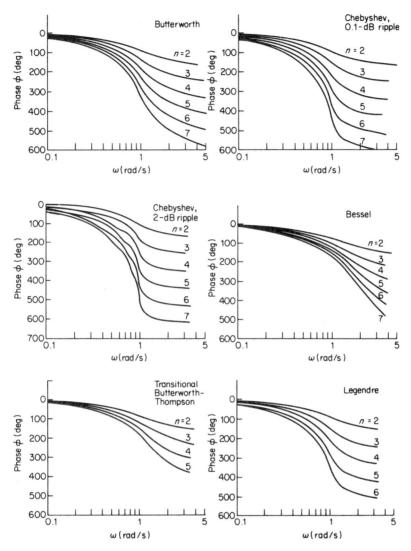

Fig. 7-10 Normalized phase responses of various lowpass allpole filters. (Reproduced by kind permission of A. S. McAllister from *Modern Low-Pass Filter Characteristics* by C. P. Eggen and A. S. McAllister, Electro-Technology, August, 1966)

and with (7-13) we obtain, for the allpole filter,

$$\tau_g(\omega) = \sum_{j=1}^{n} \frac{\sigma_{pj}}{\sigma_{pj}^2 + (\omega - \omega_{pj})^2} \qquad [7\text{-}15]$$

Plotting the group delay for the filters characterized in Figs. 7-9 and 7-10, we obtain the delay curves shown in Fig. 7-11. Because of the frequency normalization with respect to ω_{3dB} the delay τ_g given in seconds in Fig. 7-11 is similarly normalized. The actual time delay is obtained by dividing the normalized group delay by the value of the 3-dB cutoff

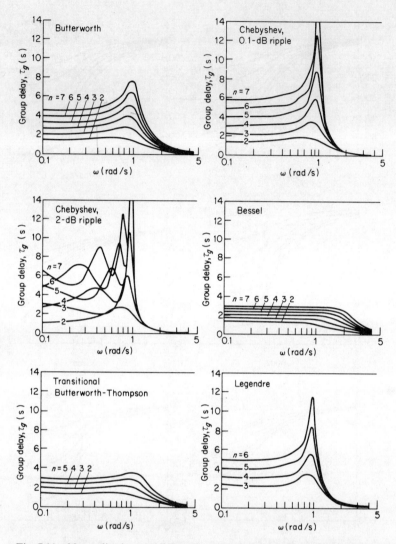

Fig. 7-11 Normalized group delay of various lowpass allpole filters. (Reproduced by kind permission of A. S. McAllister from *Modern Low-Pass Filter Characteristics* by C. P. Eggen and A. S. McAllister, Electro-Technology, August, 1966)

frequency. Thus, if the delay of a normalized filter is τ_g seconds at a particular frequency, the delay of the filter with a 3-dB frequency of f_{3dB} Hz is

$$T_g[s] = \frac{\tau_g}{\omega_{3dB}} = \frac{\tau_g}{2\pi f_{3dB}} \qquad (7\text{-}16)$$

where both τ_g and T_g are given in seconds and only the *value* of ω_{3dB} is used in (7-16). For example, the normalized fifth-order 0.1-dB ripple Chebyshev filter has a group delay of $\tau_g = 4$ s at $\omega = 0.1$ rad/s. If this filter is built with a 3-dB bandwidth of $f_{3dB} = 10$ kHz, the delay at 10 kHz is

$$T_g(10\text{ kHz}) = \frac{4}{2\pi \times 10^5} = 6.37\ \mu s$$

Based on the filter characteristics of the allpole filters plotted in Figs. 7-9 to 7-11, it may be possible to decide on a filter characteristic satisfying the specifications of a given application. If so, the desired transfer function $T(s)$ can be obtained by referring to the corresponding normalized pole locations given in Table 7-1. Consider, for example, the fifth-order 2-dB ripple Chebyshev filter. From Table 7-1 we obtain

$$p_1 = -0.2157$$

$$p_{2,3} = -0.1745 \pm j0.5946 \qquad (7\text{-}17)$$

$$p_{4,5} = -0.0666 \pm j0.9621$$

With

$$p_\mu = -\sigma + j\tilde{\omega} \qquad (7\text{-}18)$$

and

$$p_\nu = -\sigma - j\tilde{\omega}$$

we have

$$(\omega_p)_{\mu,\nu} = \sqrt{p_\mu p_\nu} = \sqrt{\sigma^2 + \tilde{\omega}^2} \qquad (7\text{-}19a)$$

$$\left(\frac{\omega_p}{q_p}\right)_{\mu,\nu} = -(p_\mu + p_\nu) = 2\sigma \qquad (7\text{-}19b)$$

and

$$(q_p)_{\mu,\nu} = \frac{\sqrt{\sigma^2 + \tilde{\omega}^2}}{2\sigma} \qquad (7\text{-}19c)$$

Thus, for the poles in (7-17), we obtain

$$(\omega_p)_{2,3} = 0.6197 \qquad (q_p)_{2,3} = 1.7756 \qquad (7\text{-}20a)$$

and

$$(\omega_p)_{4,5} = 0.9644 \qquad (q_p)_{4,5} = 7.240 \qquad (7\text{-}20b)$$

The desired transfer function therefore has the form

$$[T(S)]_{\text{Chebyshev 2dB}} = \frac{K}{(S + 0.2157)(S^2 + 0.349S + 0.384)(S^2 + 0.133S + 0.930)} \qquad (7\text{-}21)$$

This is the transfer function normalized with respect to the transmission level and 3-dB cutoff frequency. For a given 3-dB cutoff frequency ω_{3dB}, each normalized frequency term must be multiplied by ω_{3dB}, such that the resulting transfer function $T(s)$ remains dimensionless; thus

$$T(s) = \frac{K\omega_{3dB}^5}{(s + 0.2157\omega_{3dB})(s^2 + 0.349\omega_{3dB}s + 0.384\omega_{3dB}^2)(s^2 + 0.133\omega_{3dB}s + 0.930\omega_{3dB}^2)} \qquad (7\text{-}22)$$

where $s = S\omega_{3dB}$. To obtain a given level, say at $\omega = 0$, K must be selected accordingly. For $|T(0)| = 1$, K must be selected equal to unity. More will be said on the question of scaling in Section 7-5.

Table 7-1 Pole locations for the filters in Figs. 7-9 to 7-11 (normalized with respect to ω_{3dB}). (Reproduced by kind permission of A. S. McAllister from *Modern Low-Pass Filter Characteristics* by C. P. Eggen and A. S. McAllister, Electro-Technology, August, 1966)

	$n = 2$	$n = 3$	$n = 4$	$n = 5$	$n = 6$	$n = 7$
Butterworth	$s_{1,2} = -0.7071 \pm j0.7071$	$s_1 = -1.0000 \pm j0$ $s_{2,3} = -0.5000 \pm j0.8660$	$s_{1,2} = -0.9239 \pm j0.3827$ $s_{3,4} = -0.3827 \pm j0.9239$	$s_1 = -1.0000 \pm j0$ $s_{2,3} = -0.8090 \pm j0.5878$ $s_{4,5} = -0.3090 \pm j0.9511$	$s_{1,2} = -0.9659 + j0.2588$ $s_{3,4} = -0.7071 \pm j0.7071$ $s_{5,6} = -0.2588 \pm j0.9659$	$s_1 = -1.0000 + j0$ $s_{2,3} = -0.9010 \pm j0.4339$ $s_{4,5} = -0.6235 \pm j0.7818$ $s_{6,7} = -0.2225 \pm j0.9749$
Chebyshev, 0.1-dB ripple	$s_{1,2} = -0.6104 \pm j0.7106$	$s_1 = -0.6979 \pm j0$ $s_{2,3} = -0.3489 \pm j0.8683$	$s_{1,2} = -0.5257 \pm j0.3833$ $s_{3,4} = -0.2177 \pm j0.9254$	$s_1 = -0.4749 \pm j0$ $s_{2,3} = -0.3842 \pm j0.5884$ $s_{4,5} = -0.1467 \pm j0.9521$	$s_{1,2} = -0.3916 \pm j0.2590$ $s_{3,4} = -0.2867 \pm j0.7076$ $s_{5,6} = -0.1049 \pm j0.9666$	$s_1 = -0.3527 \pm j0$ $s_{2,3} = -0.3178 \pm j0.4341$ $s_{4,5} = -0.2199 \pm j0.7822$ $s_{6,7} = -0.0785 \pm j0.9754$
Chebyshev 2-dB ripple	$s_{1,2} = -0.3741 \pm j0.7572$	$s_1 = -0.3572 \pm j0$ $s_{2,3} = -0.1786 \pm j0.8938$	$s_{1,2} = -0.2486 \pm j0.3896$ $s_{3,4} = -0.1029 \pm j0.9406$	$s_1 = -0.2157 \pm j0$ $s_{2,3} = -0.1745 \pm j0.5946$ $s_{4,5} = -0.0666 \pm j0.9621$	$s_{1,2} = -0.1738 \pm j0.2609$ $s_{3,4} = -0.1272 \pm j0.7128$ $s_{5,6} = -0.0465 \pm j0.9737$	$s_1 = -0.1544 \pm j0$ $s_{2,3} = -0.1391 \pm j0.4364$ $s_{4,5} = -0.0962 \pm j0.7865$ $s_{6,7} = -0.0343 \pm j0.9807$
Transitional Butterworth–Thompson	$s_{1,2} = -0.8615 \pm j0.6977$	$s_1 = -1.1249 \pm j0$ $s_{2,3} = -0.6942 \pm j0.9368$	$s_{1,2} = -1.0858 \pm j0.3987$ $s_{3,4} = -0.5843 \pm 1.0605$	$s_1 = -1.1771 \pm j0$ $s_{2,3} = -1.0059 \pm j0.6428$ $s_{4,5} = -0.5103 \pm j1.1442$		
Bessel	$s_{1,2} = -1.1016 \pm j0.6364$	$s_1 = -1.3226 \pm j0$ $s_{2,3} = -1.0474 \pm j0.9992$	$s_{1,2} = -1.3700 \pm j0.4102$ $s_{3,4} = -0.9952 \pm j1.2571$	$s_1 = -1.5023 \pm j0$ $s_{2,3} = -1.3808 \pm j0.7179$ $s_{4,5} = -0.9576 \pm j1.4711$	$s_{1,2} = -1.5716 \pm j0.3209$ $s_{3,4} = -1.3819 \pm j0.9715$ $s_{5,6} = -0.9307 \pm j1.6620$	$s_1 = -1.6827 \pm j0$ $s_{2,3} = -1.6104 \pm j0.5886$ $s_{4,5} = -1.3775 \pm j1.1904$ $s_{6,7} = -0.9089 \pm j1.8346$
Legendre		$s_1 = -0.6200 \pm j0$ $s_{2,3} = -0.3450 \pm j0.9010$	$s_{1,2} = -0.5500 \pm j0.3590$ $s_{3,4} = -0.2320 \pm j0.9460$	$s_1 = -0.4680 \pm j0$ $s_{2,3} = -0.3880 \pm j0.5890$ $s_{4,5} = -0.1540 \pm j0.9680$	$s_{1,2} = -0.4390 \pm j0.2400$ $s_{3,4} = -0.3090 \pm 0.6980$ $s_{5,6} = -0.1152 \pm j0.9780$	

7-4 GRAPHICAL AND ANALYTICAL AIDS FOR THE DESIGN OF GENERAL nth-ORDER FILTERS

In the previous section some representative characteristics for each of the most important allpole or polynomial filters were given. They permit a preliminary selection of a filter transfer function to be made, based on the specifications of a given application. If nothing suitable can be found, then the following graphical and analytic aids will be useful, since they extend to allpole filters of higher order, and cover filters with finite zeros, i.e. inverse Chebyshev and Chebyshev–Cauer filters, as well. As is customary in most filter handbooks, this material will be presented in terms of attenuation, rather than gain, characteristics. Furthermore, it is limited to lowpass filters since the frequency transformations in Section 7-6 readily permit the extension to other filter types.

The first step in designing a filter of any kind is to establish its complexity, i.e. the necessary number n of its poles. This in turn will determine the number of second- (or third-) order sections required to realize the nth-order transfer function $T(s)$. To determine the order n of $T(s)$ for any filter, the following information, illustrated in Fig. 7-12, is usually required:

(a) The passband ripple A_{max}
(b) The minimum stopband attenuation A_{min}
(c) The transition region characterized by the ratio of the first frequency of minimum attenuation f_s and the ripple bandwidth f_c.

As we shall see in the following, this information can be used to determine n in nomograph form for Butterworth, Chebyshev, and Chebyshev–Cauer filters.

a. Maximally Flat or Butterworth Filters

Butterworth filters have no ripple in the passband. Nevertheless, a maximum attenuation A_{max} covering a frequency span up to the cutoff frequency f_c will be specified all the same. Thus, the order n can be related to the typical filter parameters shown in Fig. 7-13(a) by the following expression:

$$n = \frac{\log[(10^{0.1A_{min}} - 1)/(10^{0.1A_{max}} - 1)]}{2 \log(\omega_s/\omega_c)} \qquad [7\text{-}23]$$

where A_{min} and A_{max} are given in decibels.

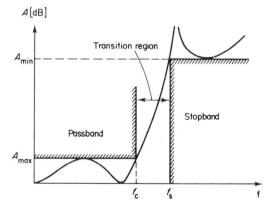

Fig. 7-12   Basic specifications of typical lowpass filter

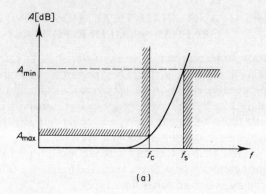

(a)

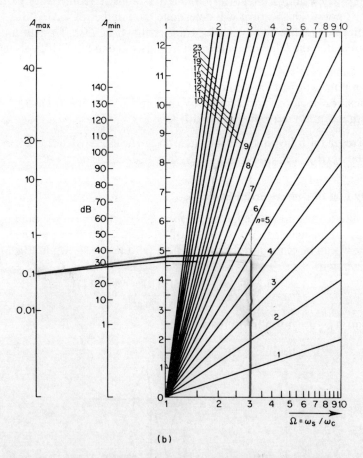

(b)

Fig. 7-13 Butterworth lowpass filter: (a) specifications, (b) nomograph for order *n*. (Reproduced by permission of John Wiley & Sons, Inc., from *Handbook of Filter Synthesis* by A. I. Zverev, John Wiley and Sons, Inc., New York, 1967)

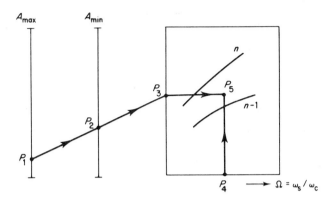

Fig. 7-14 Schematic procedure for use of the nomograph.
(Reproduced by permission of John Wiley & Sons, Inc., from
Handbook of Filter Synthesis by A. I. Zverev, John Wiley and
Sons, Inc., New York, 1967)

Example

For a filter specified to have $A_{max} = 0.1$ dB, $A_{min} = 30$ dB, and $\omega_s/\omega_c = 1.5$, eq. (7-23) gives $n = 13.15$. Since n must be an integer, a network of fourteenth order is required to meet the specifications.

   Instead of calculating n from (7-23) for every given filter specification, a very convenient nomograph can be set up for it. This is shown in Fig. 7-13(b). To estimate the filter order n, a straight line is drawn between the specified A_{max} and A_{min} and extended to the left side of the nomograph as indicated in Fig. 7-14. Extending from the left-hand point (P_3) parallel to the Ω axis to the required ratio ω_s/ω_c yields the order n of the required transfer function $T(s)$. Having obtained n, the coefficients of the corresponding denominator polynomial $D(s)$ can be obtained from Table 7-2. In this table $D(s)$ is given as the product of complex-conjugate and negative real roots (part a), and the q_p values for the complex-conjugate pairs are also listed (part b). The individual poles, for filters up to seventh order were given in Table 7-1. They are related to the quantities in Table 7-2 by the expressions given in eqs. (7-19). For active filter design the form of $D(s)$ given in part a of Table 7-2, i.e. in terms of complex-conjugate poles, is most useful. Thus, for example, the normalized transfer function for a fifth-order Butterworth filter is obtained as

$$T(s) = \frac{K}{(s^2 + 1.618s + 1)(s^2 + 0.618s + 1)(s + 1)} \tag{7-24}$$

The corresponding active filter can be realized as a cascade of two second-order active allpole networks with a pole Q of 1.62 and 0.62, respectively (see Table 7-2, part b), and of a first-order RC section as indicated in Fig. 7-1(b). An alternative is to cascade a third-order and a second-order lowpass filter. In this case the pole pair with the lower q_p value should preferably be combined with the third pole. Thus, instead of (7-24), $T(s)$ would take on the form

$$T(s) = \frac{K}{(s^3 + 2.618s^2 + 2.618s + 1)(s^2 + 0.618s + 1)} \tag{7-25}$$

Table 7-2   Denominator polynomials of Butterworth filters (normalized with respect to ω_c)

(a) Normalized denominator polynomials in factored form

n	
1	$(1 + s)$
2	$(1 + 1.414s + s^2)$
3	$(1 + s)(1 + s + s^2)$
4	$(1 + 0.765s + s^2)(1 + 1.848s + s^2)$
5	$(1 + s)(1 + 0.618s + s^2)(1 + 1.618s + s^2)$
6	$(1 + 0.518s + s^2)(1 + 1.414s + s^2)(1 + 1.932s + s^2)$
7	$(1 + s)(1 + 0.445s + s^2)(1 + 1.247s + s^2)(1 + 1.802s + s^2)$
8	$(1 + 0.390s + s^2)(1 + 1.111s + s^2)(1 + 1.663s + s^2)(1 + 1.9\,2s + s^2)$
9	$(1 + s)(1 + 0.347s + s^2)(1 + s + s^2)(1 + 1.532s + s^2)(1 + 1.879s + s^2)$
10	$(1 + 0.313s + s^2)(1 + 0.908s + s^2)(1 + 1.414s + s^2)(1 + 1.782s + s^2)(1 + 1.975s + s^2)$

(b) Pole quality factor q_p for complex-conjugate pole pairs

n	2	3	4	5	6	7	8	9	10
q_p	0.71	1.00	1.31	1.62	1.93	2.25	2.57	2.88	3.19
			0.54	0.62	0.71	0.80	0.90	1.0	1.10
					0.52	0.55	0.60	0.65	0.71
							0.51	0.53	0.56
									0.51

If realized with second-order sections, circuit 1 (LP–LQ) in Chapter 5 can be used since q_p is smaller than 2 for both circuits. If realized as a combination of a second-order and a third-order section, then the third-order lowpass section can be designed using the guidelines provided in the literature†.

b. Equiripple or Chebyshev Filters

Chebyshev filters have an equiripple response in the passband and a monotonic slope in the stopband. Referring to the characteristic filter parameters shown in Fig. 7-15(a), the order n is obtained as

$$n = \frac{\cosh^{-1}[(10^{0.1A_{min}} - 1)/(10^{0.1A_{max}} - 1)]^{1/2}}{\cosh^{-1}(\omega_s/\omega_c)} \qquad [7\text{-}26]$$

where A_{min} and A_{max} are given in decibels.

Example

For the same example as above, i.e. $A_{max} = 0.1$ dB, $A_{min} = 30$ dB and $\omega_s/\omega_c = 1.5$, we obtain from (7-26) that $n = 6.26$, meaning that n must be selected as the next highest integer 7. Notice how the order n is reduced from 14 for the Butterworth to 7 for the Chebyshev filter, merely by introducing a ripple of 0.1 dB. By increasing the ripple, the attenuation slope can be increased still further and the order reduced even more. In general, however, the permissible ripple in the passband is specified and is not subject to modification.

† G. S. Moschytz, *Linear Integrated Networks: Design*, Van Nostrand Reinhold Co., New York, 1975, pp. 247.

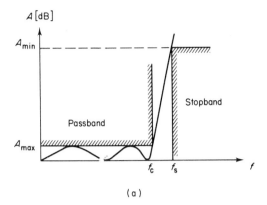

(a)

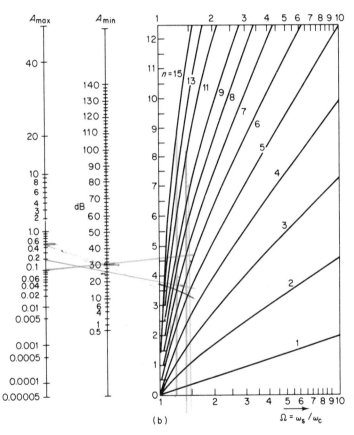

(b)

$\Omega = \omega_s / \omega_c$

Fig. 7-15   Chebyshev lowpass filters: (a) specifications, (b) nomograph for order n. (Reproduced by permission of John Wiley & Sons Inc., from *Handbook of Filter Synthesis* by A. I. Zverev, John Wiley and Sons, Inc., New York, 1967)

The expression in (7-26) can also be represented in the form of a nomograph as shown in Fig. 7-15(b). The nomograph is used following the procedure indicated in Fig. 7-14. Once n is established for a given inband ripple (i.e. the value of A_{max}) the corresponding polynomial $D(s)$ can be obtained from Table 7-3. Here $D(s)$, factored in terms of negative

Table 7-3 Denominator polynomials of Chebyshev filters (normalized with respect to ω_c)

(a) Normalized denominator polynomials in factored form

n	(i) 0.1-dB Ripple ($e = 0.153$)
1	$(6.552 + s)$
2	$(3.314 + 2.372s + s^2)$
3	$(0.969 + s)(1.690 + 0.969s + s^2)$
4	$(1.330 + 0.528s + s^2)(0.623 + 1.275s + s^2)$
5	$(0.539 + s)(1.195 + 0.333s + s^2)(0.636 + 0.872s + s^2)$
6	$(1.129 + 0.229s + s^2)(0.696 + 0.627s + s^2)(0.263 + 0.856s + s^2)$
7	$(0.377 + s)(1.092 + 0.168s + s^2)(0.753 + 0.470s + s^2)(0.330 + 0.679s + s^2)$
8	$(1.069 + 0.128s + s^2)(0.799 + 0.364s + s^2)(0.416 + 0.545s + s^2)(0.146 + 0.643s + s^2)$
9	$(0.290 + s)(1.054 + 0.101s + s^2)(0.834 + 0.290s + s^2)(0.498 + 0.445s + s^2)$
	$(0.201 + 0.546s + s^2)$
10	$(1.044 + 0.082s + s^2)(0.862 + 0.237s + s^2)(0.568 + 0.369s + s^2)(0.274 + 0.465s + s^2)$
	$(0.092 + 0.515s + s^2)$

n	(ii) 0.5-dB Ripple ($e = 0.349$)
1	$(2.863 + s)$
2	$(1.516 + 1.426s + s^2)$
3	$(0.626 + s)(1.142 + 0.626s + s^2)$
4	$(1.064 + 0.351s + s^2)(0.356 + 0.847s + s^2)$
5	$(0.362 + s)(1.036 + 0.224s + s^2)(0.477 + 0.586s + s^2)$
6	$(1.023 + 0.155s + s^2)(0.590 + 0.424s + s^2)(0.157 + 0.580s + s^2)$
7	$(0.256 + s)(1.016 + 0.114s + s^2)(0.677 + 0.319s + s^2)(0.254 + 0.462s + s^2)$
8	$(1.012 + 0.087s + s^2)(0.741 + 0.248s + s^2)(0.359 + 0.372s + s^2)(0.088 + 0.439s + s^2)$
9	$(0.198 + s)(1.009 + 0.069s + s^2)(0.789 + 0.198s + s^2)(0.453 + 0.304s + s^2)$
	$(0.156 + 0.373s + s^2)$
10	$(1.007 + 0.056s + s^2)(0.826 + 0.162s + s^2)(0.532 + 0.252s + s^2)(0.238 + 0.318s + s^2)$
	$(0.056 + 0.352s + s^2)$

n	(iii) 1-dB Ripple ($e = 0.509$)
1	$(1.965 + s)$
2	$(1.103 + 1.098s + s^2)$
3	$(0.494 + s)(0.994 + 0.494s + s^2)$
4	$(0.987 + 0.279s + s^2)(0.279 + 0.674s + s^2)$
5	$(0.289 + s)(0.988 + 0.179s + s^2)(0.429 + 0.468s + s^2)$
6	$(0.991 + 0.124s + s^2)(0.558 + 0.340s + s^2)(0.125 + 0.464s + s^2)$
7	$(0.205 + s)(0.993 + 0.091s + s^2)(0.653 + 0.256s + s^2)(0.230 + 0.370s + s^2)$
8	$(0.994 + 0.070s + s^2)(0.724 + 0.199s + s^2)(0.341 + 0.298s + s^2)(0.070 + 0.352s + s^2)$
9	$(0.159 + s)(1.00 + 0.06s + s^2)(0.78 + 0.16s + s^2)(0.44 + 0.24s + s^2)(0.14 + 0.30s + s^2)$
10	$(0.996 + 0.045s + s^2)(0.814 + 0.130s + s^2)(0.521 + 0.203s + s^2)(0.227 + 0.255s + s^2)$
	$(0.045 + 0.283s + s^2)$

n	(iv) 2-dB Ripple ($e = 0.765$)

n	
1	$(1.308 + s)$
2	$(0.823 + 0.804s + s^2)$
3	$(0.369 + s)(0.886 + 0.369\ s + s^2)$
4	$(0.929 + 0.210s + s^2)(0.222 + 0.506s + s^2)$
5	$(0.218 + s)(0.952 + 0.135s + s^2)(0.393 + 0.353s + s^2)$
6	$(0.966 + 0.094s + s^2)(0.533 + 0.257s + s^2)(0.100 + 0.351s + s^2)$
7	$(0.155 + s)(0.975 + 0.069s + s^2)(0.635 + 0.194s + s^2)(0.212 + 0.280s + s^2)$
8	$(0.980 + 0.053s + s^2)(0.710 + 0.151s + s^2)(0.327 + 0.226s + s^2)(0.057 + 0.266s + s^2)$
9	$(0.121 + s)(0.984 + 0.042s + s^2)(0.764 + 0.121s + s^2)(0.428 + 0.185s + s^2)$
	$(0.132 + 0.227s + s^2)$
10	$(0.987 + 0.034s + s^2)(0.806 + 0.099s + s^2)(0.512 + 0.153s + s^2)(0.218 + 0.193s + s^2)$
	$(0.036 + 0.214s + s^2)$

n	(v) 3-dB Ripple ($e = 1$)

n	
1	$(1.002 + s)$
2	$(0.708 + 0.645s + s^2)$
3	$(0.299 + s)(0.839 + 0.299s + s^2)$
4	$(0.903 + 0.170s + s^2)\ (0.196 + 0.411s + s^2)$
5	$(0.178 + s)(0.936 + 0.110s + s^2)(0.377 + 0.287s + s^2)$
6	$(0.955 + 0.076s + s^2)(0.522 + 0.209s + s^2)(0.089 + 0.285s + s^2)$
7	$(0.126 + s)(0.966 + 0.056s + s^2)(0.627 + 0.158s + s^2)(0.204 + 0.228s + s^2)$
8	$(0.974 + 0.043s + s^2)(0.704 + 0.123s + s^2)(0.321 + 0.184s + s^2)(0.050 + 0.217s + s^2)$
9	$(0.098 + s)(0.980 + 0.034s + s^2)(0.760 + 0.098s + s^2)(0.423 + 0.151s + s^2)$
	$(0.127 + 0.185s + s^2)$
10	$(0.983 + 0.028s + s^2)(0.802 + 0.080s + s^2)(0.508 + 0.125s + s^2)(0.214 + 0.158s + s^2)$
	$(0.032 + 0.175s + s^2)$

(b) Pole-quality factor q_p for complex-conjugate pole pairs

0.1 dB

n	2	3	4	5	6	7	8	9	10
q_p	0.77	1.34	2.18	3.28	4.63	6.23	8.08	10.18	12.52
			0.62	0.91	1.33	1.85	2.45	3.14	3.92
					0.60	0.85	1.18	1.59	2.04
							0.59	0.82	1.13
									0.59

0.5 dB

n	2	3	4	5	6	7	8	9	10
q_p	0.86	1.71 ·	2.94	4.54	6.51	8.84	11.53	14.58	17.92
			0.71	1.18	1.81	2.58	3.47	4.49	5.61
					0.68	1.09	1.61	2.21	2.89
							0.68	1.06	1.53
									0.67

Table 7-3 cont'd.

Table 7-3 cont'd.

1 dB

n	2	3	4	5	6	7	8	9	10
q_p	0.96	2.02	3.56	5.56	8.00	10.90	14.24	18.03	22.26
			0.78	1.40	2.20	3.16	4.27	5.53	6.94
					0.76	1.30	1.96	2.71	3.56
							0.75	1.55	1.86
									0.75

2 dB

n	2	3	4	5	6	7	8	9	10
q_p	1.13	2.55	4.59	7.23	10.46	14.28	18.69	23.68	29.27
			0.93	1.78	2.84	4.12	5.58	7.25	9.11
					0.90	1.65	2.53	3.54	4.66
							0.89	1.60	2.41
									0.89

3 dB

n	2	3	4	5	6	7	8	9	10
q_p	1.30	3.07	5.58	8.82	12.78	17.46	22.87	29.00	35.85
			1.08	2.14	3.46	5.02	6.83	8.87	11.15
					1.04	1.98	3.08	4.32	5.70
							1.03	1.93	2.94
									1.03

real poles and complex-conjugate pole pairs (part a), and the corresponding pole Q's (part b) are given for $A_{max} = 0.1$ dB, 0.5 dB, 1 dB, 2 dB, and 3 dB, respectively, for transfer functions up to tenth order. With the factored form of $D(s)$ given in part a of Table 7-3, active Chebyshev filters can be realized by cascading second- and third-order sections as described above for the Butterworth filters.

It can be shown that the poles of a Chebyshev transfer function $T(s)$ (i.e. the roots of $D(s)$) can be derived from those of the corresponding Butterworth function. As we know, the Butterworth poles lie on the unity semi-circle in the left-half plane, as shown for a fifth-order filter in Fig. 7-16. Each Butterworth pole pair has the form

$$p_B = -\sigma_B \pm j\tilde{\omega}_B \tag{7-27a}$$

The poles of a Chebyshev filter lie on an ellipse that falls inside the Butterworth unit circle (see Fig. 7-16). The ellipse eccentricity ε is determined by the amount of ripple in the pass-band. Each Chebyshev pole p_C can be obtained from p_B by multiplying σ_B by ε; thus, from (7-27a),

$$p_C = -\varepsilon\sigma_B \pm j\tilde{\omega}_B \tag{7-27b}$$

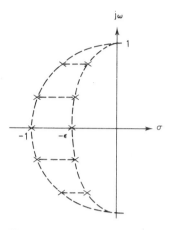

Fig. 7-16 Deriving the Chebyshev poles (on ellipse) from the
Butterworth poles (on semi-
circle)

Note that the imaginary part of p_C is assumed equal to $\tilde{\omega}_B$, which is true only to a first approximation. The eccentricity ε depends on the 'ripple factor' e, where

$$e = \sqrt{10^{0.1 A_{max}} - 1} \tag{7-28a}$$

or, solved for A_{max},

$$A_{max} = 10 \log(1 + e^2)[\text{dB}] \tag{7-28b}$$

The ripple factor e increases from zero to unity as the passband ripple A_{max} increases from 0 to 3 dB. It is related to the amplitude-response ripple as shown in Fig. 7-17, and is given in Table 7-3 for the corresponding ripple values. The eccentricity ε, which is also the factor by which the real part of Butterworth poles must be multiplied to obtain the corresponding Chebyshev poles, see eq. (7-27b), depends on the ripple factor e as follows:

$$\varepsilon = \tanh\left(\frac{1}{n} \sinh^{-1}\frac{1}{e}\right) \tag{7-29}$$

Notice from Fig. 7-17 that the passband cutoff frequency ω_c is not equal to the 3-dB frequency ω_{3dB}. In fact, the two coincide only for $e = 1$ or $A_{max} = 3$ dB. For $0 < e < 1$,

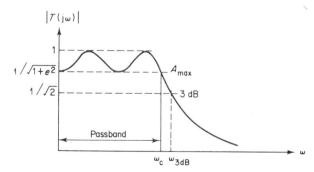

Fig. 7-17 Ripple factor e and 3-dB frequency for Chebyshev
filters

Table 7-4   The relative passband ω_c/ω_{3dB} for Chebyshev filters

e	A_{max} [dB]		1	2	3	4	5	6	7	8	9	10
							n					
0.153	0.1		0.153	0.515	0.720	0.824	0.881	0.915	0.936	0.951	0.961	0.968
0.349	0.5		0.349	0.719	0.857	0.915	0.944	0.960	0.971	0.978	0.982	0.985
0.509	1		0.509	0.821	0.913	0.950	0.967	0.978	0.983	0.987	0.990	0.992
0.765	2		0.765	0.931	0.968	0.982	0.988	0.992	0.994	0.995	0.996	0.997
1.00	3		0.998	0.999	1	1	1	1	1	1	1	1

ω_{3dB} is larger than ω_c, i.e. $\omega_{3dB}/\omega_c > 1$. The relationship between ω_{3dB}, the order n, and the ripple factor e is given by

$$\omega_{3dB} = \cosh\left(\frac{1}{n}\cosh^{-1}\frac{1}{e}\right)\omega_c \qquad (7\text{-}30)$$

The ratio ω_c/ω_{3dB}, which tells how close to the ω_{3dB} frequency the passband reaches, is given in Table 7-4 for the ripple and n values used in Table 7-3. Note that for a fixed n there is a trade-off between the ripple and cutoff frequency ω_c; for a small ripple, the pass-band, given by ω_c, is narrow. To obtain both a small ripple *and* a wide passband ω_c, the order n must be chosen sufficiently large.

c. Elliptic or Chebyshev–Cauer Filters

Elliptic filters have equal ripple in the passband and in the stopband. The transfer functions are characterized by poles and finite zeros and the attenuation response by attenuation zeros and poles. The latter are shown schematically in Fig. 7-18(a). The relationship between the filter order n and the quantities in Fig. 7-18(a) are more complicated than those for the Butterworth and Chebyshev filters and will therefore not be given here. Nevertheless, the nomograph, which represents this relationship, is just as convenient as the previous ones and is given in Fig. 7-18(b). Using this nomograph for the same filter example as was used above, i.e. $A_{max} = 0.1$ dB, $A_{min} = 30$ dB, and $\omega_s/\omega_c = 1.5$, we find that n is now reduced to 5. Thus, by the introduction of two zero pairs, a pole pair of the Chebyshev filter can be eliminated. This illustrates once again that in terms of amplitude response alone, the elliptic filters are the most efficient. Naturally, when the phase response is also of importance, i.e. for the transmission and filtering of pulses, then the relatively poor performance of the elliptic filter may dictate a different choice.

As we know, elliptic filters are not allpole filters, i.e. the denominator *and* the numerator are given in terms of polynomials whose poles and zeros must be known, in order to build the corresponding active filters. If we recall that the tabulation of Chebyshev denominator polynomials in the previous section already required a reasonable amount of space—and was by no means comprehensive at that—then it will be clear that the tabulation of Chebyshev–Cauer filters far exceeds the scope of this handbook. Since excellent tables for the design of these filters exist in handbook form, we shall select one and briefly explain its use for the derivation of Chebyshev–Cauer transfer functions.

The recommended handbook is that of Zverev† and the tabulation of Chebyshev–Cauer filters—or CC filters, as they are referred to in that book—essentially begins on

† A. I. Zverev, *Handbook of Filter Synthesis*, John Wiley and Sons, Inc., New York, 1967.

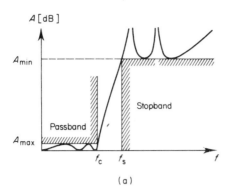

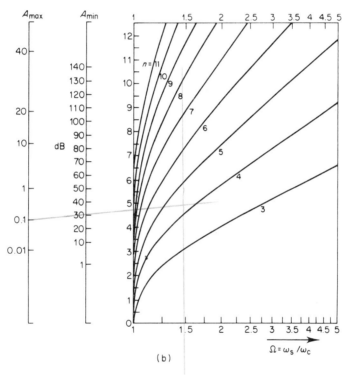

Fig. 7-18 Chebyshev–Cauer lowpass filters: (a) specifications, (b) nomograph for order n. (Reproduced by permission of John Wiley and Sons, Inc., from *Handbook of Filter Synthesis* by A. I. Zverev, John Wiley and Sons, Inc., New York, 1967)

page 169. A typical page of this section of Zverev's book is shown in Fig. 7-19.† The parameters required to select a particular filter according to given specifications will be explained below. Some of these parameters, such as A_{max} and Ω_s, which is a measure for the attenuation slope, are transformed in such a way as to permit clear and easily usable tables.

---

† Recently another excellent and comparable handbook has been published; namely, R. Saal and W. Entenmann, *Handbook of Filter Design*, AEG, Telefunken, Berlin, 1979. The nomenclature in both handbooks is essentially the same; however, the tabulated pole-zero data in Saal's handbook are accurate to within ten places as compared to five in Zverev's handbook.

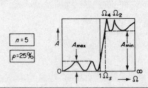

θ	Ω_k	A_{min}	σ_0	σ_1	σ_3	Ω_1	Ω_2	Ω_3	Ω_4
c	∞	∞	0.42450	−0.13118	−0.34343	1.0332	∞	0.6386	∞
1.0	57.2987	212.22	0.42454	−0.13115	−0.34342	1.0331	97.4775	0.6385	60.2470
2.0	28.6537	182.11	0.42465	−0.13109	−0.34341	1.0331	48.7389	0.6387	30.1274
3.0	19.1073	164.49	0.42484	−0.13098	−0.34340	1.0331	32.4927	0.6389	20.0893
4.0	14.3356	151.99	0.42511	−0.13082	−0.34338	1.0331	24.3697	0.6392	15.0176
5.0	11.4737	142.29	0.42545	−0.13063	−0.34335	1.0331	19.4959	0.6397	12.0620
6.0	9.5668	134.36	0.42587	−0.13039	−0.34332	1.0331	16.2468	0.6402	10.0565
7.0	8.2055	127.65	0.42637	−0.13010	−0.34329	1.0331	13.9260	0.6408	8.6247
8.0	7.1853	121.84	0.42695	−0.12978	−0.34324	1.0331	12.1854	0.6415	7.5516
9.0	6.3925	116.70	0.42761	−0.12941	−0.34319	1.0330	10.8316	0.6422	6.7175
10.0	5.7588	112.11	0.42834	−0.12899	−0.34313	1.0330	9.7486	0.6431	6.0507
11.0	5.2408	107.94	0.42916	−0.12854	−0.34307	1.0330	8.8625	0.6441	5.5057
12.0	4.8097	104.14	0.43006	−0.12804	−0.34299	1.0330	8.1241	0.6452	5.0520
13.0	4.4454	100.63	0.43104	−0.12749	−0.34291	1.0329	7.4993	0.6463	4.6684
14.0	4.1336	97.39	0.43210	−0.12690	−0.34282	1.0329	6.9638	0.6476	4.3401
15.0	3.8637	94.36	0.43325	−0.12627	−0.34272	1.0328	6.4997	0.6490	4.0559
16.0	3.6280	91.52	0.43448	−0.12560	−0.34261	1.0328	6.0936	0.6504	3.8076
17.0	3.4203	88.85	0.43580	−0.12489	−0.34248	1.0328	5.7353	0.6520	3.5888
18.0	3.2361	86.33	0.43720	−0.12413	−0.34235	1.0327	5.4168	0.6536	3.3946
19.0	3.0716	83.94	0.43870	−0.12333	−0.34220	1.0326	5.1318	0.6554	3.2212
20.0	2.9238	81.66	0.44029	−0.12248	−0.34204	1.0326	4.8753	0.6572	3.0654
21.0	2.7904	79.50	0.44197	−0.12160	−0.34187	1.0325	4.6433	0.6592	2.9246
22.0	2.6695	77.43	0.44375	−0.12067	−0.34168	1.0324	4.4323	0.6613	2.7970
23.0	2.5593	75.45	0.44562	−0.11970	−0.34147	1.0324	4.2397	0.6634	2.6807
24.0	2.4586	73.54	0.44759	−0.11869	−0.34125	1.0323	4.0631	0.6657	2.5743
25.0	2.3662	71.71	0.44967	−0.11763	−0.34101	1.0322	3.9007	0.6681	2.4767
26.0	2.2812	69.95	0.45185	−0.11654	−0.34074	1.0321	3.7507	0.6706	2.3868
27.0	2.2027	68.25	0.45413	−0.11540	−0.34046	1.0320	3.6119	0.6732	2.3038
28.0	2.1301	66.60	0.45653	−0.11422	−0.34015	1.0319	3.4829	0.6759	2.2270
29.0	2.0627	65.01	0.45904	−0.11301	−0.33981	1.0318	3.3629	0.6787	2.1556
30.0	2.0000	63.47	0.46166	−0.11175	−0.33945	1.0317	3.2508	0.6817	2.0892
31.0	1.9416	61.97	0.46440	−0.11045	−0.33906	1.0315	3.1460	0.6847	2.0274
32.0	1.8871	60.51	0.46727	−0.10911	−0.33864	1.0314	3.0476	0.6879	1.9695
33.0	1.8361	59.10	0.47027	−0.10773	−0.33819	1.0313	2.9553	0.6912	1.9154
34.0	1.7883	57.72	0.47339	−0.10631	−0.33770	1.0311	2.8683	0.6946	1.8646
35.0	1.7434	56.37	0.47666	−0.10485	−0.33718	1.0310	2.7864	0.6981	1.8170
36.0	1.7013	55.06	0.48006	−0.10336	−0.33662	1.0308	2.7089	0.7018	1.7722
37.0	1.6616	53.78	0.48361	−0.10182	−0.33601	1.0306	2.6356	0.7056	1.7299
38.0	1.6243	52.53	0.48731	−0.10025	−0.33535	1.0304	2.5662	0.7095	1.6901
39.0	1.5890	51.30	0.49117	−0.09864	−0.33465	1.0302	2.5003	0.7135	1.6525
40.0	1.5557	50.10	0.49519	−0.09699	−0.33390	1.0300	2.4377	0.7177	1.6170
41.0	1.5243	48.92	0.49939	−0.09531	−0.33309	1.0298	2.3781	0.7220	1.5833
42.0	1.4945	47.76	0.50376	−0.09359	−0.33222	1.0296	2.3213	0.7265	1.5515
43.0	1.4663	46.63	0.50832	−0.09183	−0.33129	1.0294	2.2672	0.7311	1.5213
44.0	1.4396	45.51	0.51307	−0.09004	−0.33029	1.0291	2.2154	0.7358	1.4926
45.0	1.4142	44.42	0.51803	−0.08822	−0.32922	1.0288	2.1660	0.7407	1.4654
46.0	1.3902	43.34	0.52320	−0.08636	−0.32807	1.0286	2.1187	0.7457	1.4396
47.0	1.3673	42.27	0.52859	−0.08446	−0.32684	1.0283	2.0733	0.5709	1.4150
48.0	1.3456	41.23	0.53422	−0.08254	−0.32551	1.0280	2.0299	0.7562	1.3916
49.0	1.3250	40.19	0.54010	−0.08058	−0.32410	1.0277	1.9881	0.7617	1.3693
50.0	1.3054	39.17	0.54624	−0.07860	−0.32258	1.0273	1.9480	0.7673	1.3481
51.0	1.2868	38.16	0.55266	−0.07658	−0.32096	1.0270	1.9095	0.7731	1.3279
52.0	1.2690	37.17	0.55937	−0.07453	−0.31922	1.0266	1.8724	0.7791	1.3087
53.0	1.2521	36.18	0.56639	−0.07246	−0.31736	1.0262	1.8366	0.7852	1.2903
54.0	1.2361	35.21	0.57374	−0.07036	−0.31537	1.0259	1.8021	0.7915	1.2728
55.0	1.2208	34.24	0.58144	−0.06823	−0.31323	1.0254	1.7689	0.7980	1.2561
56.0	1.2062	33.29	0.58952	−0.06608	−0.31095	1.0250	1.7368	0.8046	1.2402
57.0	1.1924	32.34	0.59799	−0.06390	−0.30850	1.0246	1.7057	0.8114	1.2250
58.0	1.1792	31.40	0.60690	−0.06170	−0.30588	1.0241	1.6757	0.8184	1.2104
59.0	1.1666	30.46	0.61626	−0.05948	−0.30308	1.0236	1.6467	0.8255	1.1966
60.0	1.1547	29.53	0.62612	−0.05725	−0.30008	1.0231	1.6185	0.8328	1.1834
θ	Ω_k	A_{min}	σ_0	σ_1	σ_3	Ω_1	Ω_2	Ω_3	Ω_4

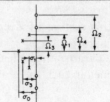

All σ_i values are negative.

Fig. 7-19 A page from A. I. Zverev's *Handbook of Filter Synthesis*, John Wiley and Sons, Inc., New York, 1967. (Reproduced by permission of John Wiley & Sons, Inc.)

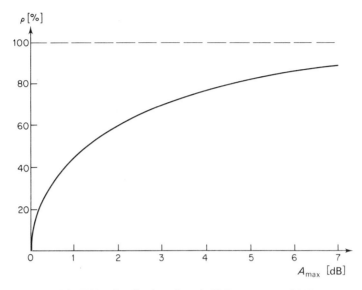

Fig. 7-20   Qualitative plot of $\rho[\%]$ versus $A_{max}[dB]$

The parameters are as follows:

(a)   The polynomial order n. This is obtained from the nomograph in Fig. 7-18(b) as explained above.

(b)   The reflection coefficient ρ. This quantity is proportional to the ripple A_{max} in the passband. However, A_{max} is unsuitable for tabulation purposes since it can theoretically vary from zero to relatively large values. A set of concise tables requires a measure that is limited between well-defined values and can, preferably, be given in linear, integer quantities. The reflection coefficient, which is related to A_{max} as follows:

$$\rho = \sqrt{|1 - 10^{-0.1 A_{max}}|} \qquad [7\text{-}31]$$

serves this purpose admirably. The qualitative plot of ρ versus A_{max} in Fig. 7-20 shows this clearly. As A_{max}, plotted in decibels, increases indefinitely, ρ, plotted in per cent., increases from 0 to 100.

   The Zverev tables are ordered according to integer numbers of ρ in per cent., namely, $\rho = 1, 2, 3, 4, 5, 8, 10, 15, 20, 25$, and 50 per cent. The corresponding values of A_{max} are listed in Table 7-5. Thus an inband ripple of 0.3 dB corresponds approximately to $\rho = 25$ per cent. Notice that the integer values of ρ permit only relatively few values of A_{max} to be obtained accurately. To be on the safe side of a design, the value of A_{max} must therefore be rounded down to the next lower value of ρ. Thus, for $A_{max} = 0.1$ dB, a value of $\rho = 15$ per cent. should be used.

(c)   The modular angle θ. The modular angle θ is related to Ω_s, which is a measure for the attenuation slope between passband and stopband, i.e., referring to Fig. 7-18,

$$\Omega_s = \frac{\omega_s}{\omega_c} \qquad (7\text{-}32)$$

As is the case with A_{max}, Ω_s is also an unsuitable value for the purpose of tabulation. Typically, Ω_s, which must be larger than unity (since 'brick wall' filters are not physically realizable), will have values between unity and, say, five. Theoretically, however,

Table 7-5 Relationship between the reflection coefficient ρ and the inband ripple A_{max}

$|\rho|\,[\%]$	$A_{max}\,[dB]$
0	0
1	0.00043
2	0.0017
3	0.0039
4	0.007
5	0.011
8	0.028
10	0.044
15	0.099
20	0.18
25	0.28
35	0.57
50	1.25

Ω_s can be arbitrarily large. The question is how to transform Ω_s into a measure that permits a classification in linear terms while giving emphasis to the low values of Ω_s ranging just beyond unity. The measure used, namely, the modular angle θ, accomplishes this objective perfectly. It is related to Ω_s as follows:

$$\theta = \sin^{-1}\left(\frac{1}{\Omega_s}\right) \tag{7-33}$$

The plot of θ versus Ω_s, shown schematically in Fig. 7-21, demonstrates that θ is limited between $0°$ amd $90°$ and that the most linear and spread-out portion of the curve covers the values of Ω_s just beyond unity. Thus, for example, $\Omega_s = 1.5$ cor-

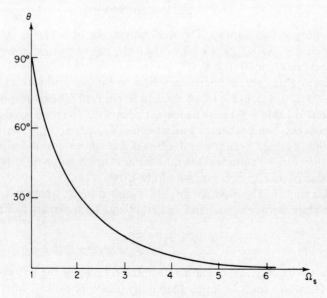

Fig. 7-21   Qualitative plot of θ [degrees] versus Ω_s

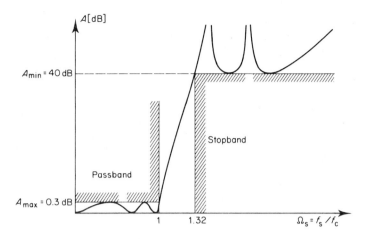

Fig. 7-22 Example of filter specifications for Chebyshev–Cauer filter

responds to a modular angle $\theta = 42°$. Again, to be on the safe side in any given design, the linear distribution of θ in tables requires a rounding off of Ω_s.

(d) The symmetry factor K. This value indicates the required equal or unequal loading resistances of a filter. It is relevant only for passive LC filters and can be ignored for the purposes of active RC filter design as dealt with in this handbook.

Example

As an illustrative example we shall now find the Chebyshev–Cauer, or CC, transfer function corresponding to the filter specifications given in Fig. 7-22. From the nomograph in Fig. 7-18(b) we first find the order $n = 5$, from Table 7-5 we find $\rho = 25$ per cent., and from eq. (7-33) we compute $\theta = 49°$. In terms of Zverev's handbook, the desired filter is classified as

$$\underset{\substack{\text{Chebyshev–Cauer}}}{\text{CC}} \quad \underset{\substack{\text{Polynomial} \\ \text{order } n}}{05} \quad \underset{\substack{\text{Reflection} \\ \text{coefficient} \\ \rho[\%]}}{25} \quad \underset{\substack{\text{Modular} \\ \text{angle} \\ \theta[°]}}{49} \tag{7-34}$$

In Zverev's handbook, the tables for Chebyshev–Cauer, or CC, filters can be found on page 169 onwards. Individual tables are characterized by the order n and the reflection coefficient ρ. Thus for $n = 5$ and $\rho = 25$ per cent. (i.e. on page 220) we find the table shown in Fig. 7-19. There, for $\theta = 49°$ we find the normalized real and imaginary values for the poles and zeros of $T(s)$, as indicated by the sketch below the table. Note that Zverev uses circles to designate poles and crosses to designate zeros.† The poles and zeros of transfer functions are commonly designated the other way around (e.g. see Fig. 7-7). However, Zverev's designation corresponds to the *attenuation* response shown above each table, and thus to attenuation zeros (in the passband) and attenuation poles (in the stopband). Using a designation for poles and zeros that corresponds to the designation used elsewhere

† This has been reversed in Fig. 7.19.

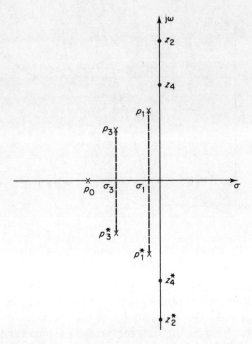

Fig. 7-23   Pole-zero plot for filter specified in
Fig. 7-22

in this and other books on active filters (see Fig. 7-23), we obtain the following normalized poles and zeros for $\theta = 49°$:

$$p_0 = -\sigma_0 = -0.54010$$

$$p_1, p_1^* = \sigma_1 \pm j\Omega_1 = -0.08058 \pm j1.0277$$

$$p_3, p_3^* = \sigma_3 \pm j\Omega_3 = -0.32410 \pm j0.7617$$

$$z_2, z_2^* = \pm j\Omega_2 = \pm j1.9881 \qquad (7\text{-}35)$$

$$z_4, z_4^* = \pm j\Omega_4 = \pm j1.3693$$

The corresponding normalized transfer function then results as

$$T(s) = K \frac{(s^2 + 3.9525)(s^2 + 1.8750)}{(s + 0.5401)(s^2 + 0.1612s + 1.0627)(s^2 + 0.6482s + 0.68523)} \qquad (7\text{-}36)$$

The ω_p and q_p values can be obtained from the expressions given by (7-19), where our $\tilde{\omega}$ values correspond to the Ω of Zverev. The transfer function in (7-36) is normalized with respect to the transmission level and the cutoff frequency ω_c. For a given cutoff frequency ω_c the transfer function must be scaled accordingly, i.e. each normalized frequency term must be multiplied by ω_c such that the resulting $T(s)$ remains dimensionless. This was shown in (7-21) and (7-22) and will be discussed in more detail in Section 7-5. Similarly, to obtain a given level, say at $\omega = 0$, K must be selected accordingly. For $|T(0)| = 1$, K must be selected such that

$$K \frac{3.9525 \times 1.8750}{0.5401 \times 1.0627 \times 0.68523} = 1 \qquad (7\text{-}37)$$

or $K = 0.053$.

Note that in Zverev's handbook a second page exists for each n and ρ value, which gives the normalized inductor and capacitor values for the corresponding LC filter (e.g. page 221 in our example). Naturally, for the cascade design of active RC filters, this second page has no significance.

d. Linear Phase, or Bessel Filters

Bessel filters are allpole filters, i.e. their numerator is a constant and the denominator $D(s)$ a polynomial of nth order (see eq. 7-7). As pointed out in Section 7-2 in the discussion of Bessel filters, the important parameter of these filters, beside their amplitude selectivity, is their linearity of phase or constancy of group delay. It was pointed out that these filters are often used in the transmission of pulse or square-wave signals and that the transient response of these filters is therefore of utmost importance. Thus, for example, Fig. 7-6 showed that the step response of the Bessel filter is superior to that of a Butterworth or Chebyshev filter in that the overshoot of the Bessel filter is appreciably less than that of the other two. This improvement in step response is obtained at the cost of filter selectivity, since the attenuation slope of the Bessel filter is much less steep, as is also shown in Fig. 7-6. Thus, a practical criterion for the selection of a Bessel filter would go along the line of asking for 'something like a Butterworth filter, but with a superior step response'. To this end it is useful to compare the overshoot of Butterworth and Bessel filters as in Table 7-6 for filters up to $n = 5$. The Bessel filters have only a tenth of the overshoot of the Butterworth filters and improve as the order n is increased, while the Butterworth filters get worse. As we know from Fig. 7-7, it is the fact that the poles of the Bessel filter are further removed from the $j\omega$ axis than those of the Butterworth filters that accounts for this superior step response and for the inferior frequency selectivity. Thus, for each Butterworth polynomial there is a corresponding Bessel polynomial whose roots are shifted away from the imaginary axis. These polynomials are listed in Table 7-7 for n up to ten. As in Tables 7-2 and 7-3, the Bessel polynomials are given as the product of complex-conjugate and negative real roots (part a) and the Q factors q_p of the corresponding complex-conjugate poles (part b).

The basis for comparison of Bessel with Butterworth filters is often not restricted to step-response overshoot and selectivity. For the same order filter, the rise time of the Butterworth step response is actually *less* than that of the Bessel filter, as the comparison in Table 7-8 shows. Thus, if we consider the Bessel and Butterworth filters as two extremes, where the former provides a *maximally flat delay* and the latter a *maximally flat magnitude* response, then it is natural to ask whether a set of functions can be found that have steady-state and transient characteristics that lie somewhere in between these two extremes. Consider Fig. 7-24, where the Butterworth poles are given by

$$p_B = r_B e^{j(\pi - \theta_B)} = e^{j(\pi - \theta_B)} \tag{7-38a}$$

and the Bessel poles by

$$p_T = r_T e^{j(\pi - \theta_T)} \tag{7-38b}$$

A pole p whose location varies smoothly between the Butterworth and Bessel locations can now be obtained by introducing a parameter m such that

$$p = p_B \left(\frac{p_T}{p_B}\right)^m \tag{7-39}$$

Table 7-6   Overshoot of Butterworth and Bessel
filters

Order	Butterworth (%)	Bessel (%)
1	0	0
2	4.3	0.43
3	8.15	0.75
4	10.9	0.83
5	12.8	0.76

Table 7-7   Denominator polynomials of Bessel filters (normalized for $\tau_g(1) = 1$ s)

(a) Normalized denominator polynomials in factored form

n	
1	$(1.000 + s)$
2	$(3.000 + 3.000s + s^2)$
3	$(2.322 + s)(6.459 + 3.678s + s^2)$
4	$(9.140 + 5.792s + s^2)(11.488 + 4.208s + s^2)$
5	$(3.647 + s)(14.272 + 6.704s + s^2)(18.156 + 4.649s + s^2)$
6	$(18.801 + 8.497s + s^2)(20.853 + 7.471s + s^2)(26.514 + 5.032s + s^2)$
7	$(4.972 + s)(25.666 + 9.517s + s^2)(28.937 + 8.140s + s^2)(36.597 + 5.371s + s^2)$
8	$(31.977 + 11.176s + s^2)(33.935 + 10.410s + s^2)(38.569 + 8.737s + s^2)(48.432 + 5.678s + s^2)$
9	$(6.297 + s)(62.041 + 5.959s + s^2)(49.789 + 9.277s + s^2)(43.647 + 11.209s + s^2)$ $(40.589 + 12.259s + s^2)$
10	$(77.443 + 6.218s + s^2)(62.626 + 9.772s + s^2)(54.839 + 11.935s + s^2)(50.582 + 13.231s + s^2)$ $(48.668 + 13.844s + s^2)$

(b) Quality factor q_p for complex-conjugate pole pairs

n	2	3	4	5	6	7	8	9	10
q_p	0.58	0.69	0.81	0.92	1.02	1.13	1.23	1.32	1.42
			0.52	0.56	0.61	0.66	0.71	0.76	0.81
					0.51	0.53	0.56	0.59	0.62
							0.51	0.52	0.54
									0.50

Table 7-8   Rise time of Butterworth and
Bessel filters

Order	Butterworth	Bessel
1	2.20	2.20
2	2.15	2.73
3	2.29	3.07
4	2.43	3.36
5	2.56	3.58

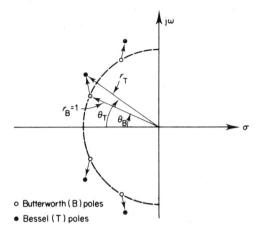

Fig. 7-24 On the derivation of Bessel poles from
Butterworth poles

Note that for $m = 0$, $p = p_B$, i.e. we have the maximally flat magnitude, or Butterworth, response, and for $m = 1$, $p = p_T$ and we have the maximally flat delay or Bessel response. For each value of $0 \leq m \leq 1$ a set of poles is defined in terms of the Butterworth and Bessel poles such that

$$p = r\,e^{j\theta} \qquad (7\text{-}40a)$$

where

$$r = r_T^m \qquad (7\text{-}40b)$$

$$\theta = m\theta_T + (1 - m)\theta_B \qquad (7\text{-}40c)$$

The filters with these poles are called *transitional Butterworth–Thomson* filters. As m is decreased from unity, the bandwidth of the magnitude response increases, whereas the phase is maximally linear for $m = 1$ and becomes less linear as m decreases. In addition, the rise time becomes longer and the overshoot smaller as m is increased from zero to unity. Naturally there is nothing to prevent m from being extended beyond the zero-to-unity range if the resulting response thereby becomes more desirable.

e. Inverse Chebyshev Filters

The inverse Chebyshev filter is similar to the Butterworth filter in that it is maximally flat in the passband, but, unlike the latter, it has attenuation poles in the stopband. Thus, with respect to the stopband, it is similar to the Chebyshev–Cauer filter and, like the latter, it is not an allpole filter but has a transfer function consisting of a ratio of polynomials; in other words, the transfer function has finite zeros (see the gain response shown in Fig. 7-3c). Because of these finite zeros the inverse Chebyshev filter has a much sharper transition region than the corresponding Butterworth filter. However, interestingly enough, its transition region is no sharper than that of the corresponding Chebyshev filter. Thus, if we consider the attenuation response of a typical inverse Chebyshev filter, as shown in Fig. 7-25(a), we find that the order n of the denominator polynomial $D(s)$, as specified by A_{max}, A_{min}, and f_s/f_c, is identical to the order n of the corresponding Chebyshev filter (see

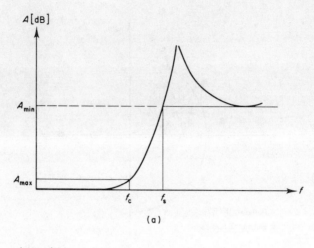

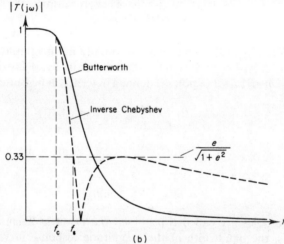

Fig. 7-25 Inverse Chebyshev filter: (a) attenuation response, (b) comparison with Butterworth filter

Fig. 7-15a) satisfying the same specifications. Thus, the ripple in the passband of the Chebyshev filter combined with its monotonic attenuation slope in the stopband is just as effective —in terms of filter selectivity—as the maximally flat inband characteristics combined with finite attenuation poles of the inverse Chebyshev filter. The obvious question, then, is why one would use inverse Chebyshev filters at all, if they achieve no more than the more easily realizable Chebyshev filters. (Remember that allpole filters, e.g. Chebyshev filters, are always more easily realizable, i.e. more easily tunable and require fewer components, than filters with finite zeros such as inverse Chebyshev filters.) The answer is twofold. For one thing the maximally flat inband characteristics give the inverse Chebyshev filter better delay characteristics and therefore make it more suitable for pulse filtering purposes than a regular Chebyshev filter. For another, the pole Q's, q_p, are lower for the inverse Chebyshev than for the corresponding Chebyshev filter. This is plausible if we think of the inverse Chebyshev filter as a Butterworth filter whose attenuation slope is pulled down sharply at discrete frequencies (i.e. the attenuation poles), as shown qualitatively in Fig. 7-25(b). We recall that the pole Q's of Butterworth filters are appreciably lower than those of the corresponding Chebyshev filters (see Tables 7-2 and 7-3) and can therefore think of the inverse Chebyshev filter as a 'Butterworth filter with an equiripple stopband'.

Since the inverse Chebyshev filter is closely related to the Chebyshev filter (the former is equiripple in the stopband, the latter in the passband) the corresponding transfer function can readily be derived from that of the Chebyshev filter. To obtain the order n we use the nomograph for Chebyshev filters in Fig. 7-15(b) or eq. (7-26) since the order is the same for both filter types for a given set of specifications. The denominator $D_{iC}(s)$ of the inverse Chebyshev filter is obtained from the 'regular' Chebyshev denominator polynomial $D_C(s)$ by setting

$$D_{iC}(s) = s^n D_C(s) \tag{7-41}$$

This is a result of the fact that the amplitude functions which yield $D_{iC}(s)$ and $D_C(s)$ are identical except that ω is replaced by $1/\omega$ in one of them. Note that $D_C(s)$, the Chebyshev polynomial, is normalized with respect to the cutoff frequency ω_c. A comparison of Figs. 7-17 and 7-25(b), and some regard for the derivation of the one response from the other, will make clear that $D_{iC}(s)$ is normalized with respect to the stopband frequency ω_s. Thus, in contrast to the Chebyshev filter (see eq. 7-30), the 3-dB cutoff frequency in the passband of the inverse Chebyshev filter is given by

$$\omega_{3dB} = \left[\cosh\left(\frac{1}{n} \cosh^{-1} \frac{1}{e}\right) \right]^{-1} \omega_s \tag{7-42}$$

where $\omega_{3dB} < \omega_s$.

From Fig. 7-25 it follows that a specified stopband attenuation A_{min} corresponds to a ripple factor e where the attenuation in the stopband is $e(1 + e^2)^{-1/2}$. The inband attenuation A_{max} of the corresponding Chebyshev polynomial $D_C(s)$ is $(1 + e^2)^{-1/2}$ where the same ripple factor e applies. Thus, for example, if $n = 3$ and $e = 0.5$ then from Table 7-3 we obtain

$$D_C(s) = (0.626 + s)(1.142 + 0.626s + s^2)$$

where we use the smaller value of $e = 0.349$ to guarantee a factor of safety in the stopband. From (7-41) it follows that

$$D_{iC}(s) = s^3 \left(0.626 + \frac{1}{s}\right)\left(1.142 + \frac{0.626}{s} + \frac{1}{s^2}\right)$$

$$= 0.715(s + 1.597)(s^2 + 0.548s + 0.876)$$

The numerator polynomial $N(s)$ of $T(s)$ is found from the expression

$$N(s)N(-s) = \omega^{2n} C_n^2\left(\frac{1}{\omega}\right)\bigg|_{\omega^2 = -s^2} \tag{7-43}$$

where $C_n(\omega)$ is a so-called *Chebyshev polynomial* of nth degree as listed in Table 7-9. These polynomials play an important role in the derivation of all equiripple functions, i.e. also those of Chebyshev filters. However, in the latter their presence is not necessarily apparent due to the many tables and other design aids in which they have tacitly been taken into account. In (7-43) the product of two polynomials is defined, namely, $N(s)$ and $N(-s)$. However, since the zeros of $N(s)$ must be on the $j\omega$ axis, those of $N(-s)$ will be identical,

Table 7-9 Normalized Chebyshev polynomials
$C_n(\omega)$

n	$C_n(\omega)$
0	1
1	ω
2	$2\omega^2 - 1$
3	$4\omega^3 - 3\omega$
4	$8\omega^4 - 8\omega^2 + 1$
5	$16\omega^5 - 20\omega^3 + 5\omega$
6	$32\omega^6 - 48\omega^4 + 18\omega^2 - 1$
7	$64\omega^7 - 112\omega^5 + 56\omega^3 - 7\omega$
8	$128\omega^8 - 256\omega^6 + 160\omega^4 - 32\omega^2 + 1$

i.e. both polynomials contain the *same* factors, all of which have the form $(s^2 + \alpha)$. Thus, from Table 7-9, for our example of $n = 3$, we find

$$C_3(\omega) = 4\omega^3 - 3\omega$$

and, from (7-43),

$$N(s)N(-s) = \omega^6 \left(\frac{4}{\omega^3} - \frac{3}{\omega}\right)^2 \Bigg|_{\omega^2 = -s^2}$$

$$= (4 - 3\omega^2)^2|_{\omega^2 = -s^2} = (3s^2 + 4)^2$$

Consequently, $N(s) = 3s^2 + 4$ and the transfer function is given by

$$T(s) = K \frac{3s^2 + 4}{(s + 1.597)(s^2 + 0.548s + 0.876)}$$

where we have disregarded the constant 0.715 in $D_{iC}(s)$ and lumped it in with the constant K. As in previous examples, K will be determined by the level at a specified frequency, e.g. for $|T(0)| = 1$, K must be approximately 1.6.

Finally, although unnecessary for the derivation of the transfer functions, it may be of interest to compare the gain response of the Chebyshev filter $|T_C(j\omega)|$ and that of the inverse Chebyshev filter $|T_{iC}(j\omega)|$ as expressed in terms of the Chebyshev polynomials $C_n(\omega)$ and the ripple factor e. For the Chebyshev filter we have

$$|T_C(j\omega)| = \frac{1}{\sqrt{1 + e^2 C_n^2(\omega)}} \qquad \text{[7-44]}$$

A glance at the Chebyshev polynomials in Table 7-9 shows that, for n odd,

$$|T_C(0)| = 1 \qquad \text{(7-45a)}$$

and, for n even,

$$|T_C(0)| = \frac{1}{\sqrt{1 + e^2}} \qquad \text{(7-45b)}$$

Equation (7-45b) corresponds to the ripple in the passband (see Fig. 7-17). Since the $C_n(\omega)$ polynomials are normalized with respect to the cutoff frequency ω_c, it follows that $C_n(\omega = \omega_c) = C_n(1) = 1$ for all n. Thus, for $\omega = \omega_c$,

$$|T_C(1)| = \frac{1}{\sqrt{1 + e^2}} \tag{7-45c}$$

which is also shown in Fig. 7-17.

For the inverse Chebyshev filters we have

$$|T_{iC}(j\omega)| = \frac{eC_n(1/\omega)}{\sqrt{1 + e^2 C_n^2(1/\omega)}} \tag{7-46}$$

Hence for all n we have

$$|T_{iC}(0)| = 1 \tag{7-47a}$$

and for $\omega = \omega_s$ (see Fig. 7-25b) and all n,

$$|T_{iC}(1)| = \frac{e}{\sqrt{1 + e^2}} \tag{7-47b}$$

Equation (7-47b) corresponds to the ripple in the stopband.

7-5 FREQUENCY AND LEVEL SCALING

a. Frequency Scaling

The lowpass transfer functions, given in terms of their poles and zeros in this chapter, have all been normalized with respect to some reference frequency ω_r. This is done for convenience of tabulation. Introducing the normalized frequencies,

$$\Omega = \frac{\omega}{\omega_r} \tag{7-48a}$$

and

$$S = \frac{s}{\omega_r} \tag{7-48b}$$

a typical second-order transfer function will have the form

$$T(S) = K\frac{S^2 + (\Omega_z/q_z)S + \Omega_z^2}{S^2 + (\Omega_p/q_p)S + \Omega_p^2} \tag{7-49}$$

The designations in (7-48) are useful when outlining the procedure for frequency normalizing and scaling. In discussing the various types of lowpass filters and their poles and zeros in the previous sections of this chapter, care was taken to indicate to which reference frequency the corresponding polynomials and related quantities were normalized. With the exception of the inverse Chebyshev filters where it is the stopband frequency ω_s, the

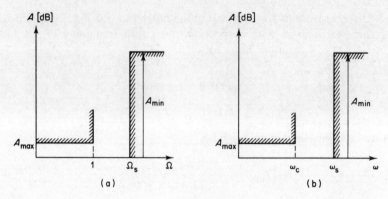

Fig. 7-26 Lowpass filter: (a) normalized specifications, (b) practical specifications

cutoff frequency ω_c, which is the passband-edge frequency of a lowpass filter, is generally used. (Note, however, that for the curves in Figs. 7-9 to 7-11 the 3-dB frequency ω_{3dB} is used for ω_r; this is also commonly used for Butterworth and Legendre filter functions.) Thus, the normalized lowpass filter specifications are generally given as shown in Fig. 7-26(a). For $\Omega \leq 1$ the passband loss should be lower than A_{max} and for $\Omega \geq \Omega_s$ the stopband attenuation should be greater than A_{min}. In practice the lowpass filter specifications will be given as in Fig. 7-26(b), i.e. the normalized transfer function must be *scaled* by the reference frequency $\omega_r = \omega_c$. For the example in (7-49) the corresponding scaled—or unnormalized—transfer function is therefore obtained using (7-48), namely,

$$T(s) = K \frac{s^2 + \omega_c(\Omega_z/q_z)s + \omega_c^2\Omega_z^2}{s^2 + \omega_c(\Omega_p/q_p)s + \omega_c^2\Omega_p^2} \tag{7-50}$$

Note that in either case the network function must maintain the same dimension. In the case of transfer functions as in (7-49) and (7-50) both must be dimensionless.

b. Level Scaling

As we have seen in various examples so far, the value of the constant K that is initially obtained when deriving a transfer function does not necessarily provide the signal level actually specified. Naturally this signal level can be specified only at a given frequency. In the case of lowpass filters it is generally specified for d.c., i.e. for zero frequency. If a constant K' is obtained that does not provide the signal level L actually specified, say at a frequency ω_L, then the new value of K must be obtained from

$$T(\omega_L) = \frac{N(\omega_L)}{D(\omega_L)} = L \tag{7-51a}$$

For the example given by (7-49) we obtain, for $\omega_L = 0$,

$$K = L\frac{\Omega_p^2}{\Omega_z^2} \tag{7-51b}$$

If $K > K'$, an additional amplifier may be necessary to achieve the desired d.c. level L; if $K < K'$, a resistive or capacitive attenuator can be introduced in the active filter cascade.

7-6 FREQUENCY TRANSFORMATIONS

The filter functions discussed so far apply to the design of lowpass filters. Fortunately, we do not have to deal separately with the equivalent functions for the other types of filters such as highpass and bandpass (see Chapter 2) since, with the help of simple frequency transformations, the corresponding filter functions for these other filter types can readily be obtained. In discussing these frequency transformations we shall, as in the preceding section, use S as the original variable and s, which in the preceding section was the scaled variable, as the transformed variable.

a. Lowpass to Highpass Transformation

Highpass filters are specified as shown qualitatively in Fig. 7-27. Both the actual and the normalized frequency axis are shown, and, as is customary, the reference frequency ω_r has been selected equal to the passband-edge frequency ω_c, i.e. $\omega_r = \omega_c$. The highpass transfer function $T_{HP}(s)$ can be obtained from the normalized lowpass function $T_{LP}(s)$ by letting

$$S = \frac{s}{\omega_r} \quad \xrightarrow{LP \to HP} \quad \left.\frac{\omega_r}{s}\right|_{\omega_r = \omega_c} = \frac{\omega_c}{s} \tag{7-52}$$

i.e.

$$T_{HP}(s) = T_{LP}\left(\frac{\omega_r}{s}\right) \tag{7-53}$$

In designing a highpass filter the reverse procedure is also required, i.e. the highpass specifications are given in terms of Fig. 7-27 and the corresponding normalized lowpass characteristics in terms of Fig. 7-26 must be found. Thus for a given set of highpass specifications A_{min}, A_{max}, ω_s, and ω_r we first obtain the corresponding normalized lowpass characteristics A_{min}, A_{max}, $\Omega_c = 1$, and, with (7-52),

$$\Omega_s = \frac{\omega_s}{\omega_r} \quad \xrightarrow{HP \to LP} \quad \Omega_s = \frac{\omega_r}{\omega_s} \tag{7-54}$$

With these normalized lowpass requirements we can find the corresponding transfer function $T_{LP}(S)$ and then, using the frequency transformation (7-52), obtain $T_{HP}(s)$ as in (7-53).

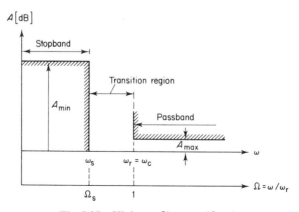

Fig. 7-27   Highpass filter specifications

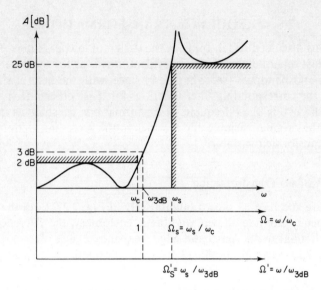

Fig. 7-28 Normalized lowpass filter for highpass filter design example

Example

Find the transfer function $T_{HP}(s)$ for a Chebyshev highpass filter specified as follows:

$$A_{min} = 25 \text{ dB}, A_{max} = 2 \text{ dB}, \omega_c = 1{,}000 \text{ rad/s, and } \omega_s = 500 \text{ rad/s.}$$

The equivalent characteristics of the normalized lowpass filter are shown in Fig. 7-28. They are

$$A_{min} = 25 \text{ dB}, A_{max} = 2 \text{ dB}, \Omega_c = 1, \text{ and } \Omega_s = 2$$

Notice that for the lowpass filter ω_c and ω_s are reversed, i.e. $\omega_c = 500$ rad/s and $\omega_s = 1000$ rad/s. Using the Chebyshev 2-dB ripple curves shown in Fig. 7-9 to find the required filter order, we find that for $n = 3$ the specifications are satisfied. However, the curves in Fig. 7-9 are not normalized with respect to ω_c but to ω_{3dB}. The difference is shown in the two normalized axes Ω and Ω' in Fig. 7-28. From Table 7-4 we find for $n = 3$ and $A_{max} = 2$ dB that $\omega_c/\omega_{3dB} = 0.968$ and therefore $\omega_{3dB}(n = 3) = 500/0.968 = 516$ rad/s. Consequently, $\Omega'_r = \omega_s/\omega_{3dB} = 1000/516 = 1.94$. A glance at the curves in Fig. 7-9 shows that for this normalized frequency of 1.94 (rather than 2 as originally assumed) the order $n = 3$ may be somewhat marginal; thus we select $n = 4$. From Table 7-1 we then find the corresponding normalized (with respect to ω_{3dB}) poles

$$p_{1,2} = -0.2486 \pm j0.3896$$

$$p_{3,4} = -0.1029 \pm j0.9406$$

With the relations given in (7-19) we therefore obtain the lowpass transfer function

$$T_{LP}(S) = \frac{1}{(S^2 + 0.497S + 0.214)(S^2 + 0.206S + 0.895)}$$

The corresponding highpass filter function $T_{HP}(s)$ is obtained by replacing S by $\omega_r/s = \omega_{3dB}/s$. Since we now have $n = 4$, we must find the corresponding new ω_{3dB}. From Table 7-4 we find $\omega_c/\omega_{3dB} = 0.982$ and hence ω_{3dB} $(n = 4) = 509$ rad/s. Substituting S by $509/s$ in $T_{LP}(S)$ we obtain:

$$T_{HP}(s) = \frac{5s^4}{(s^2 + 1182s + 1.211 \times 10^6)(s^2 + 117s + 0.289 \times 10^6)}$$

This transfer function will have a 2-dB ripple Chebyshev highpass filter response and will meet the prescribed requirements.

b. Lowpass to Bandpass Transformation

The specifications for a bandpass filter response are shown qualitatively in Fig. 7-29. It is assumed that the bandpass is geometrically symmetrical, i.e.

$$\omega_{B_1}\omega_{B_2} = \omega_{s_1}\omega_{s_2} = \omega_r^2 \tag{7-55}$$

To obtain the geometrically symmetrical bandpass function corresponding to a normalized lowpass function, we must let

$$S = \frac{S}{\omega_r} \xrightarrow{\text{LP} \to \text{BP}} \frac{s^2 + \omega_r^2}{Bs} \tag{7-56a}$$

where

$$B = \omega_{B_2} - \omega_{B_1} \tag{7-56b}$$

and

$$\omega_r = \sqrt{\omega_{B_1}\omega_{B_2}} = \sqrt{\omega_{s_1}\omega_{s_2}} \tag{7-56c}$$

B is the passband bandwidth of the filter. Thus the bandpass transfer function $T_{BP}(s)$ is obtained from $T_{LP}(s)$ by letting

$$T_{BP}(s) = T_{LP}\left(\frac{s^2 + \omega_r^2}{Bs}\right) \tag{7-57}$$

In practice the bandpass characteristics will be given in terms of Fig. 7-29 and these must be transformed into those of a corresponding normalized lowpass function. Having

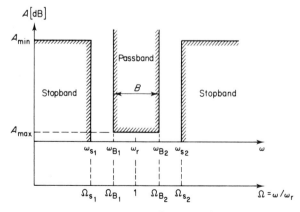

Fig. 7-29   Bandpass filter specifications

obtained this, the various design aids for normalized lowpass filters given in this chapter can be used to find the corresponding normalized lowpass transfer function. With (7-57) this is then converted back into a bandpass transfer function satisfying the original specifications.

To obtain the normalized lowpass function corresponding to Fig. 7-26 from the bandpass specifications given in terms of Fig. 7-29 we must let

$$\Omega_s = \frac{\omega_{s_2} - \omega_{s_1}}{\omega_{B_2} - \omega_{B_1}} \tag{7-58}$$

Thus for a given set of specifications for a geometrically symmetrical bandpass filter (Fig. 7-29), i.e. A_{max}, A_{min}, ω_{s_1}, ω_{B_1}, ω_{s_2}, ω_{B_2}, where (7-55) holds, we first obtain the corresponding normalized lowpass characteristics A_{max}, A_{min}, $\Omega_c = 1$, and, with (7-58), Ω_s. Having found the corresponding normalized lowpass function $T_{LP}(S)$ the corresponding bandpass function is found by using (7-57).

If the original bandpass characteristics do not correspond to those of a geometrically symmetrical filter, then the specifications can be modified as follows. The stopband attenuation can be increased and the non-symmetrical band-edge frequency decreased in the direction of more stringent filter requirements. The resulting more stringent geometrically symmetrical filter will then be guaranteed to satisfy the less stringent requirements of the original geometrically non-symmetrical specifications.

Example

Find the transfer function $T_{BP}(s)$ for a Chebyshev bandpass filter specified as follows:

$$A_{max} = 0.1 \text{ dB}, A_{min} = 20 \text{ dB}, f_{s_1} = 300 \text{ Hz}, f_{B_1} = 500 \text{ Hz}, f_{B_2} = 3000 \text{ Hz}, f_{s_2} = 6000 \text{ Hz}$$

Note that the filter is not geometrically symmetrical since $f_{B_1}f_{B_2} \neq f_{s_1}f_{s_2}$. To obtain geometrical symmetry the upper frequency f_{s_2} can be decreased to a frequency f'_{s_2} as shown in Fig. 7-30, such that (7-55) holds; namely,

$$f'_{s_2} = \frac{f_{B_1}f_{B_2}}{f_{s_1}} = 5,000 \text{ Hz}$$

If the stopband attenuation at low and high frequencies had been specified differently, i.e. $A_{min_1} \neq A_{min_2}$ as indicated in Fig. 7-30, then A_{min_2} would be increased such as to equal A_{min_1}, or vice versa.

The normalized lowpass characteristics are now given by

$$A_{max} = 0.1 \text{ dB}, A_{min} = 20 \text{ dB}, \Omega_c = 1, \Omega_s = \frac{5000-300}{3000-500} = 1.88$$

Using the nomograph in Fig. 7-15 we find that a Chebyshev filter with $n = 4$ will satisfy the prescribed requirements. From Table 7-3 we obtain

$$T_{LP}(S) = \frac{1}{(S^2 + 0.528S + 1.330)(S^2 + 1.275S + 0.623)}$$

With (7-55) and (7-56a) we replace S by

$$\frac{s^2 + 4\pi^2(1.5 \times 10^6)}{(2\pi \times 2500)s}$$

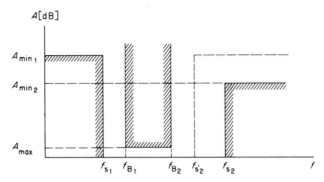

Fig. 7-30   Conversion of non-symmetrical into symmetrical
bandpass filter specifications

Substituting this term into $T_{LP}(S)$ according to (7-57) is rather cumbersome. However, the lowpass function will invariably have second-order terms of the general form

$$T_{LP}(S) = \frac{1}{S^2 + aS + b} \tag{7-59}$$

Thus, with the substitution

$$S = \frac{s^2 + \alpha}{\beta s} \tag{7-60}$$

each second-order term becomes a fourth-order term of the form

$$T_{BP}(s) = \frac{Ks^2}{s^4 + a_3 s^3 + a_2 s^2 + a_1 s + a_0} \tag{7-61a}$$

where

$$K = \beta^2 \tag{7-61b}$$

$$a_0 = \alpha^2 \tag{7-61c}$$

$$a_1 = a\alpha\beta \tag{7-61d}$$

$$a_2 = 2\alpha + b\beta \tag{7-61e}$$

$$a_3 = a\beta \tag{7-61f}$$

Notice that the lowpass to bandpass frequency transformation doubles the order of the corresponding nth-order lowpass denominator and introduces a term s^n in the numerator. This means that for every lowpass pole, two bandpass poles are obtained. It should be noted that the Q's (i.e. q_p) of the newly transformed bandpass poles are invariably higher than those of the original lowpass poles.

Rather than go through the substitution procedure outlined by (7-59) to (7-61) it is possible to obtain the bandpass pole pairs corresponding to the individual lowpass poles graphically.† Although the results may not be numerically accurate enough for filter design, they do give a first-order indication of the required pole frequencies and, more important, the pole Q's.

† A. Premoli, 'A frequency transformation chart for RC-active band-pass filters', *Alta Frequenza*, 41, No. 6, 468–469 (June, 1972).

The normalized version of the frequency transformation in eq. (7-56) is given by

$$S = \frac{p^2 + 1}{bp} \tag{7-62a}$$

where S is the lowpass complex frequency normalized with respect to ω_r. Given in polar coordinates, we let

$$S = M\,e^{j\Phi} \tag{7-62b}$$

The complex bandpass frequency, normalized with respect to ω_r, is p. In polar coordinates we let

$$p = \frac{S}{\omega_r} = m\,e^{j\phi} \tag{7-62c}$$

Finally, b is the inband bandwidth B normalized with respect to ω_r, i.e., with (7-56b),

$$b = \frac{B}{\omega_r} = \frac{\omega_{B_2} - \omega_{B_1}}{\omega_r} \tag{7-62d}$$

The Q factors of the lowpass and bandpass poles are given respectively by

$$Q_L = \frac{1}{2 \cos \Phi} \tag{7-63a}$$

and

$$Q_B = \frac{1}{2 \cos \phi} \tag{7-63b}$$

To find the bandpass pole pair corresponding to individual lowpass poles we can now use the frequency transformation chart shown in Fig. 7-31. A lowpass pole S_i is characterized by A_i and Q_{L_i}, where

$$A_i = M_i b \tag{7-64}$$

The bandpass poles $p_{\mu, v}$ are then obtained from the chart, by reading the quality factor Q_B and the modulus pair m_μ and m_v where

$$m_\mu = \frac{1}{m_v} \geq 1 \tag{7-65}$$

Example

We consider a normalized third-order lowpass filter with a real pole and a complex pole pair given by the parameters

$$M_1 = 0.97, Q_{L_1} = 0.5, M_2 = 1.3, Q_{L_2} = 1.34$$

Assuming a relative bandwidth of the bandpass filter as $b = 0.1$, we obtain

$$A_1 = bM_1 = 0.097, A_2 = bM_2 = 0.13$$

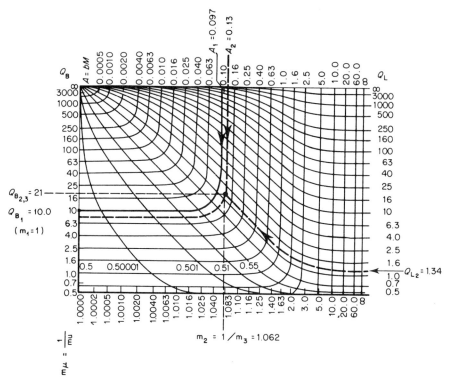

Fig. 7-31   Frequency transformation chart for bandpass filter design. (Reproduced from *A Frequency Transformation Chart for RC Active Band-Pass Filters* by A. Premoli, Alta Frequenza, June, 1972, by kind permission of A. Premoli, Associazione Electrotechnica et Electtronica Italiana)

Entering the chart as shown in Fig. 7-31, we obtain the corresponding three pole pairs in terms of m and Q_B, namely,

$$m_1 = 1, \, Q_{B_1} = 10.0, \, m_2 = \frac{1}{m_3} = 1.062, \text{ and } Q_{B_{2,3}} = 21$$

Note that the chart in Fig. 7-31 permits a speedy evaluation of the bandpass Q factors to be made once the normalized lowpass poles are known. The transformation carried out in this example is qualitatively shown in Fig. 7-32. It demonstrates how the low Q factors of the third-order lowpass filter are significantly increased in the corresponding sixth-order bandpass filter. Typically, in a stagger-tuned bandpass filter comprising three second-order bandpass filters, the Q factors of the lower and higher section are equal and larger than that of the centre section.

c. Lowpass to Bandstop Transformation

The specifications for a bandstop filter are shown qualitatively in Fig. 7-33. The bandstop filter is the inverse of a bandpass filter in that the passband and stopband have been interchanged. Remember that also the highpass filter is the inverse of the lowpass by similar reasoning (passband and stopband interchanged), and is obtained from the lowpass by

162

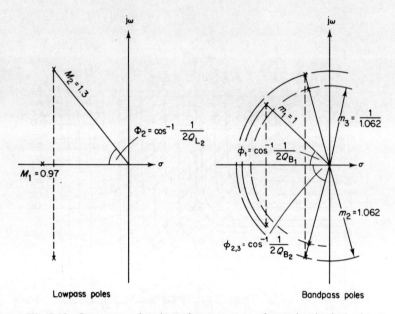

Lowpass poles   Bandpass poles

Fig. 7-32   Lowpass to bandpass frequency transformation in the s plane

substituting $1/S$ by S. Accordingly, the bandstop characteristic can be obtained by inverting the lowpass to bandpass frequency transformation. Referring to (7-56a) we obtain

$$S = \frac{S}{\omega_r} \xrightarrow{\text{LP} \to \text{BS}} \frac{Bs}{s^2 + \omega_r^2} \tag{7-66a}$$

where

$$B = \omega_{c_2} - \omega_{c_1} \tag{7-66b}$$

and

$$\omega_r = \sqrt{\omega_{c_1}\omega_{c_2}} = \sqrt{\omega_{s_1}\omega_{s_2}} \tag{7-66c}$$

B is the stopband bandwidth and (7-66c) implies geometric symmetry. Thus the bandstop transfer function $T_{BS}(s)$ is obtained from the normalized lowpass function $T_{LP}(S)$ by letting

$$T_{BS}(s) = T_{LP}\left(\frac{Bs}{s^2 + \omega_r^2}\right) \tag{7-67}$$

In practice the bandstop characteristics given in terms of Fig. 7-33 must first be transformed into those of a normalized lowpass function. Given the bandstop filter parameters $A_{\max}, A_{\min}, \omega_{c_1}, \omega_{s_1}, \omega_{s_2}$, and ω_{c_2}, where geometric symmetry is assumed (see eq. 7-66c), the corresponding normalized lowpass filter is given by the parameters: $A_{\max}, A_{\min}, \Omega_c = 1$, and

$$\Omega_s = \frac{\omega_{c_2} - \omega_{c_1}}{\omega_{s_2} - \omega_{s_1}} \tag{7-68}$$

With these parameters the desired normalized lowpass transfer function $T_{LP}(S)$ can be found using the tables and other design aids given in this chapter. Substituting S by $Bs/(s^2 + \omega_r^2)$ in $T_{LP}(S)$ the corresponding bandstop function $T_{BS}(s)$ is obtained as indicated by (7-67). Because of the direct analogy between the bandpass and bandstop transfer function

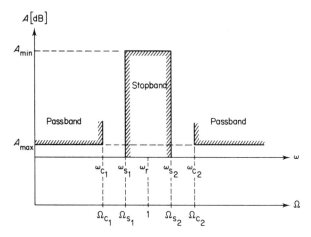

Fig. 7-33   Bandstop filter specifications

derivations, there is no need to pursue the bandstop case here any further. Note that in the event of geometrically non-symmetrical bandstop requirements, these are modified to more stringent geometrically symmetrical requirements just as was shown in the bandpass case. The resulting geometrically symmetrical bandstop filter is then sure to fulfill the requirements of the specified non-symmetrical filter.

7-7   POLE-ZERO PAIRING

The question of pole-zero pairing is an intricate one; a detailed discussion of the problem exceeds the scope of this book, and can be found in the literature.† However, some brief guidelines and rules of thumb will be given since they are often sufficient when designing general-purpose active filters.

By pole-zero pairing we mean the decomposition of an nth-order filter function into the product of second-order terms, each of which can be realized by one of the second-order building blocks given in Chapter 5. That such a decomposition is by no means unique will be clear from the following brief discussion.

Consider the pole-zero plot corresponding to a fourth-order bandpass filter shown in Fig. 7-34. The corresponding transfer function has the form

$$T(s) = K \frac{s^2}{(s^2 + (\omega_{p_1}/q_{p_1})s + \omega_{p_1}^2][s^2 + (\omega_{p_2}/q_{p_2})s + \omega_{p_2}^2]} \tag{7-69}$$

This function can be decomposed into a product of two second-order expressions:

$$T(s) = T_1(s)T_2(s) \tag{7-70}$$

where

$$T_1(s) = K_1 \frac{s^2}{s^2 + (\omega_{p_1}/q_{P_1})s + \omega_{p_1}^2} \tag{7-71a}$$

and

$$T_2(s) = \frac{K_2}{s^2 + (\omega_{p_2}/q_{p_2})s + \omega_{p_2}^2} \tag{7-71b}$$

† G. S. Moschytz, *Linear Integrated Networks: Design,* Van Nostrand Reinhold, New York, 1975, p. 15.

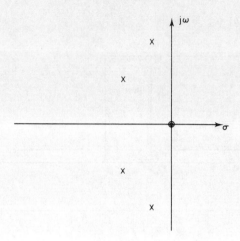

Fig. 7-34 Pole-zero plot corresponding to
eq. (7-69)

i.e. $T_1(s)$ is a highpass and $T_2(s)$ a lowpass function. However, $T(s)$ can also be decomposed into a product

$$T(s) = T'_1(s)T'_2(s) \tag{7-72}$$

where

$$T'_1(s) = K'_1 \frac{s}{s^2 + (\omega_{p_1}/q_{p_1})s + \omega_{p_1}^2} \tag{7-73a}$$

and

$$T'_2(s) = K'_2 \frac{s}{s^2 + (\omega_{p_2}/q_{p_2})s + \omega_{p_2}^2} \tag{7-73b}$$

In this case both $T'_1(s)$ and $T'_2(s)$ correspond to bandpass networks. The difference in frequency response between the corresponding highpass–lowpass decomposition and the bandpass–bandpass decomposition is qualitatively shown in Fig. 7-35. Which of these two decompositions, or pole-zero pairings, is the better one cannot be answered in a general way. It depends on the criterion, or criteria, used to define the optimum pole-zero pairing strategy. There are various criteria according to which pole-zero pairing can be carried out, and their importance will depend on the application at hand and on the available active devices and passive components. The most important criteria are as follows:

(a) *Maximizing the dynamic range.* This is important if the active filter is required to process signals of large amplitude while the signal distortion is to remain acceptably small. Clearly, the input signals can be well controlled against overload of the first stage, but overload of individual sections within the active filter may not be recognizable. The output signal level of any section $T_j(s)$ may overload the following stage without any noticeable effects at the output of the overall filter, while the overall frequency response, if measured carefully, might be found to be far from the specified and designed characteristic.

(b) *Minimizing inband losses.* This criterion is closely related to criterion (a). It may be that, in order to overcome inband losses or to actually provide gain, the gain per filter stage is increased to the point of overloading following stages, thereby again

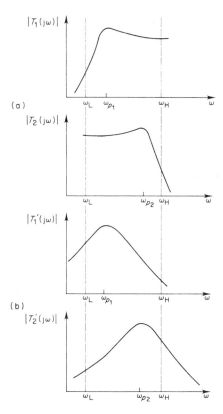

Fig. 7-35 Frequency responses corresponding to different pole-zero pairings of (7-69): (a) pairing for (7-71), (b) pairing for (7-73)

causing signal distortion. It has been found that there exists an *optimum decomposition* of $T(s)$ into pole-zero pairs, an *optimum distribution* of the constants K_j, and an *optimum sequence* of the cascaded sections $T_j(s)$, such as to minimize inband losses, or even to provide gain, without introducing signal distortion.

(c) *Maximizing the signal-to-noise ratio.* This will be of importance when the incoming signal levels are very low and degradation due to noise generated within the active element of the network may ensue. One of the disadvantages of active, as compared to passive, networks is that the active elements within the former generate noise. Thus the signal-to-noise ratio is an important parameter here, where the noise referred to is the noise generated *within* the active network.

(d) *Minimizing overall transmission sensitivity.* It can be shown that in a certain network type the pole-zero pairing has a direct effect on the transmission sensitivity to variations of the active devices used.

(e) *Minimizing d.c. offset.* Active filters, in contrast to passive ones, may introduce an unacceptable d.c. offset voltage at the output. For example, this may be the case with lowpass filters which are used to filter out unwanted harmonics of a signal whose zero crossings are critical.

(f) *Simplifying the tuning procedure.* Some second-order active filters are simpler to tune than others, depending on their transfer function and method of realization. A bandpass filter may be simpler to tune (or occur more often in a given system) than a lowpass or highpass filter. Thus, confronted with our example above, of decomposing (7-69), the decomposition (7-73) may be preferable, from this point of view, than the decomposition given by (7-71).

One of the most common and important criteria for pole-zero pairing is the first one listed above, namely, that of maximizing the dynamic range. This becomes increasingly significant with high-order networks possessing finite zeros on the $j\omega$ axis. The procedure for optimum pole-zero pairing, i.e. for obtaining the 'optimum pole-zero assignment', is relatively involved in this case and can be found in the literature.† The objective of the procedure can be briefly summarized as follows:

In order to maximize the dynamic range and the inband gain of an nth-order filter network, the poles and zeros of the individual second- or third-order sections should be chosen such that the response of each section is guaranteed to be as flat as possible within the frequency band of interest.

As a rule of thumb, this optimum pole-zero assignment for 'maximum flatness' in the passband is obtained by *combining the high-Q poles of T(s) with zeros that are as close to them as possible.*

Consider, for example, the fifth order transfer function

$$T(s) = K\frac{(s^2 + \omega_{z_1}^2)(s^2 + \omega_{z_2}^2)}{(s - p_0)(s - p_1)(s - p_1^*)(s - p_2)(s - p_2^*)} \tag{7-74}$$

where

$$\omega_{z_1} = 29.2 \text{ krad/s}$$

$$\omega_{z_2} = 43.2 \text{ krad/s}$$

$$p_0 = 16.8 \text{ krad/s}$$

$$p_1, p_1^* = -9.7 \pm j17.5 \text{ krad/s}$$

$$p_2, p_2^* = -2.36 \pm j22.4 \text{ krad/s}$$

The pole-zero plot is shown in Fig. 7-36 and the frequency response $|T(j\omega)|$ in Fig. 7-37. With the following pole-zero assignment (solid lines in Fig. 7-36):

$$T_0(s) = \frac{16.8}{s - p_0} \tag{7-75a}$$

$$T_1(s) = 0.47 \frac{s^2 + \omega_{z_1}^2}{(s - p_1)(s - p_1^*)} \tag{7-75b}$$

$$T_2(s) = 0.27 \frac{s^2 + \omega_{z_2}^2}{(s - p_2)(s - p_2^*)} \tag{7-75c}$$

† G. S. Moschytz, *Linear Integrated Networks: Design*, Van Nostrand Reinhold Co., New York, 1975.

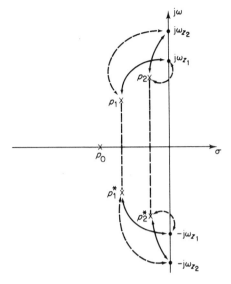

Fig. 7-36 The pole-zero plot for (7-74)

we obtain the frequency responses shown in Fig. 7-38. Notice that the coefficients K_0, K_1, and K_2 were selected such that $|T_j(0)| = 1$. This makes a comparison of the frequency responses clearer. Applying the criterion for the maximum dynamic range, we obtain the pole-zero assignment indicated by broken lines in Fig. 7-36. This results in the transfer functions

$$T_0(s) = \frac{16.8}{s - p_0} \tag{7-76a}$$

$$T'_1(s) = 0.21 \frac{(s^2 + \omega_{z_2}^2)}{(s - p_1)(s - p_1^*)} \tag{7-76b}$$

$$T'_2(s) = 0.6 \frac{s^2 + \omega_{z_1}^2}{(s - p_2)(s - p_2^*)} \tag{7-76c}$$

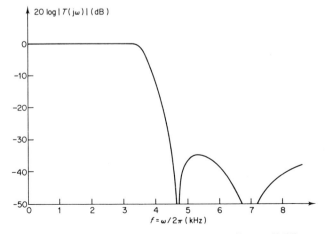

Fig. 7-37 Frequency response corresponding to (7-74)

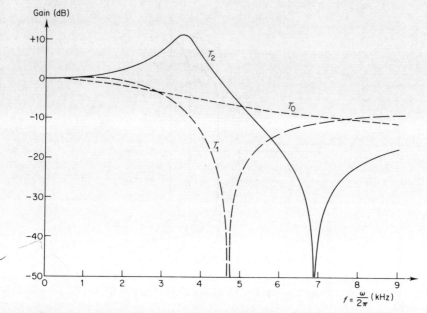

Fig. 7-38   Frequency response corresponding to pole-zero assignment (7-75)

and the frequency responses plotted in Fig. 7-39. A comparison of the responses in Figs. 7-38 and 7-39 shows that by combining the high-Q poles p_2, p_2^* with the zeros lying *closest* to them (i.e. ω_{z_1}, $\omega_{z_1}^*$), $|T_2'(j\omega)|$ becomes flatter in the passband (between 0 Hz and 3 kHz). $T_0(s)$ remains the same in each case and can, of course, be combined with either one of the complex pole pairs to form a third-order function. Its effects on the frequency response will not be very noticeable in any case.

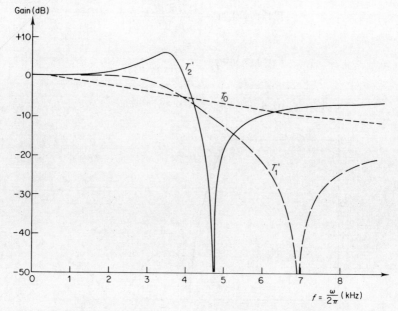

Fig. 7-39   Frequency responses corresponding to pole zero assignment (7-76)

It should be noted in the example given above that, besides the pole-zero assignment, another degree of freedom in decomposing a given network function $T(s)$ is the so-called *gain distribution*. This refers to the choice of the individual constants K_j associated with each second- or third-order function $T_j(s)$. The constants K_j are subject to the constraint that

$$\prod_{j=1}^{n/2} K_j = K \qquad (7\text{-}77)$$

where K is the gain constant of the nth order function $T(s)$ and n has been assumed to be even in (7-77). The constraint (7-77) is, of course, in no way conclusive; there are an infinite number of ways of distributing K_j factors such that (7-77) is satisfied. Thus the gain distribution provides a free parameter with which criteria similar to those associated with the pole-zero assignment problem can be taken into consideration. There exist, in fact, procedures for optimizing the gain distribution for maximum dynamic range or for minimum sensitivity which are outlined in the literature referenced above. Broadly speaking, the criterion for maximum dynamic range again aims at maximum flatness in the passband and endeavours to avoid large level differences between individual filter stages. Thus the optimization is based on attaining 'equal average levels' in the passband of the cascaded nth-order network.

7-8 THE OPTIMUM SEQUENCE

The previous section dealt with the optimum decomposition of the nth-order network function $T(s)$ into a product of second- or third-order functions $T_j(s)$ by appropriate pole-zero pairing strategies and gain distribution. The only degree of freedom remaining after these two optimization steps have been carried out is to establish the optimum sequence in which the resulting filter building blocks are to be cascaded. Thus, for example, an eighth-order function

$$T(s) = \prod_{j=1}^{4} T_j(s) \qquad (7\text{-}78)$$

can be obtained by arranging the four sections in any of twenty-four (i.e. 4!) possible sequences, some of which are shown in Fig. 7-40. Since we can assume that the individual sections are isolated from each other, the cascading sequence will not have any effect on the

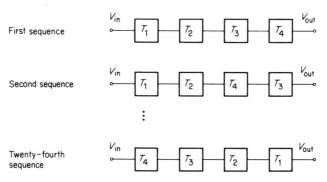

Fig. 7-40 Some of the twenty-four possible cascading sequences of a four-section network

overall sensitivity. This leaves the optimum dynamic range as the most important criterion according to which the cascading sequence should be determined.

The actual algorithms used to obtain the optimum cascading sequence are similar to those used for the optimum pole-zero pairing and are no less complex. Thus a detailed discussion is also beyond the scope of this handbook and can be found in the literature.† For a maximum dynamic range, the objectives are also similar to those of the pole-zero assignment problem. In the assignment problem we endeavour to maintain as flat a frequency response of the individual sections in the passband as possible; here we endeavour to cascade the sections such that, *at the interface between any two sections, the signal spectrum over the passband remains as flat as possible*. Frequently, the resulting optimum sequence for the maximum dynamic range turns out to be the one in which *the pole Q of the cascaded second-order networks increases from input to output*.

In some cases, considerations other than dynamic-range optimization may have to be taken into account for the filter sequence. It may, for example, be important to have a lowpass or a bandpass section for the first stage, in order to keep high frequencies from the amplifiers, and thereby avoid slew-rate problems. Similarly, it may be desirable to have a highpass or a bandpass characteristic associated with the last stage in order to remove power-supply ripple, or noise created by the amplifiers themselves, from the output signal. If such constraints are imposed on the first and last stages, for instance, the remaining sequence can still be determined according to the guidelines described above.

† G. S. Moschytz, *Linear Integrated Networks: Design*, Van Nostrand Reinhold Co., New York, 1975, p. 54.

CHAPTER 8

Practical Hints for Active Filter Design

The study of active filter theory, however intense, does not make an active filter work. This fact becomes clear in the first hours of a filter laboratory course. Many students who have never had any difficulties with theoretical problems are often surprised by their first practical experience with an operational amplifier. The opamp is more complicated in practice than an ideal gain element combining one output with two input nodes. The theoretical study of a second-order active filter with a single complex pole pair is easy to understand, but putting the theory into practice will very likely cause problems, particularly for beginners in the field.

This chapter has been written as an introduction for beginners and as a quick reference for those already skilled in using opamps but not in designing active filters.

8-1   THE QUICKEST WAY TO THE DESIGN OF AN ACTIVE FILTER

The *first step* in designing an active filter will be to write and test a computer program (see Appendix D) for the active filter stages chosen from Chapter 5.

The *second step* is to run the program until solutions are found which satisfy the requirements, while taking into account the considerations discussed in Section 8-2.

The *third step* is to build a filter using the component values calculated in the second step. In most cases these will represent a compromise between several requirements. In general this step will be followed by the deterministic tuning, described in Chapter 6, Section 6-4.

The *fourth step* (which should be the last) is to carry out the measurement of the active filter. This entails measuring the response first of the individual filter sections and then of the overall filter cascade. In some cases, particularly for higher frequencies and Q factors, this step has to be followed by the functional tuning of individual stages as described in Chapter 6, Section 6-2.

Programming problems which occur during the first step will most likely occur during the transfer of the given programs into the computer. The programs themselves have been thoroughly checked and double-checked so that mistakes in them are not anticipated. As a check for the correct transfer to the computer, numerical examples are given in Appendix D.

The second step may leave many questions open for the inexperienced designer when running a program for more sophisticated networks (e.g. circuits 14 and 15 in Chapter 5). For networks needing several input values, such as capacitors, a starting parameter, an optional resistor, and/or a constant, all of which can be independently selected and may influence the resulting gain-sensitivity product (GSP), it is recommended that several runs of the program are carried out. This permits the designer to investigate the behavior of the network for the given parameters, such as the pole and zero frequencies and the Q factors. Running several samples for a particular network will give a feeling for the direction in which input variables can be changed without obtaining a too-high value of GSP or without increasing the spread of passive elements excessively. Attention should be paid to the following Section 8-2, in which the close relationship between the selection of active and passive elements is discussed.

The best way to obtain practical design values for a network is first to select the capacitors and measure them accurately, second, to input the measured values into the particular program, and third, to change the remaining free parameters of the program until practical resistor values are obtained. By rule of thumb the resulting GSP should be less than or approximately equal to, $4Q$, if the GSP is calculated by the program.

In most cases for low- and medium-Q networks the programs calculate first an optimum value of a parameter P, whereby for given capacitors the GSP value is minimal. The program then allows a change of the parameter P. This change is very useful if discrete values of certain resistors (e.g. those which are not later required for functional tuning) are to be used. The second advantage of being able to change the parameter P is that it may be possible to reduce the component spread without causing an undesirable increase of the GSP. This is because the GSP characteristic is very flat near its minimum.

After the final computation the network can be built, whereby the remaining non-discrete resistors are deterministically tuned for.

In the fourth step the nominal parameters are measured (e.g. pole frequencies, Q factors, attenuation) as required in the program input. The accuracy of the resulting filter will depend on the accuracy with which the capacitors and resistors are measured and on how ideal the opamp is. The opamp can be assumed to be reasonably ideal for low-Q factors and low frequencies; at higher frequencies a frequency and Q shift will be measured which may or may not be acceptable. If unacceptable, the resulting shift can be eliminated either by functional tuning (see Section 6-2 of Chapter 6), by selecting a better circuit for higher Q factors, or by predistorting the circuit parameters.

In the case of predistortion, the originally required parameters are multiplied by the inverse of the multiplicative factor obtained from the measured distortion. This step is repeated until a match is achieved. For example, if the frequency required is 10,000 Hz, but the measurement is 9.850 Hz (due to non-idealities), the multiplicative factor is 0.985. The predistorted frequency is 10,152.3 Hz and will be used as a new input value of the program for the computation of the predistorted resistor values. It should be noted, however, that for a single circuit functional tuning is much more rapid than the predistortion procedure, which is commonly used for large production quantities of a given circuit.

8-2   THE SELECTION OF ACTIVE AND PASSIVE COMPONENTS

There are many characteristics of greater and lesser importance which should be taken into account in the selection of an operational amplifier for active filter design. The most important characteristics are open-loop gain and phase, their temperature stability, output and input impedances, noise, slew rate, and distortion. The temperature stability of the open-loop gain and phase, or a plot of the frequency response at different temperatures, is often omitted from the manufacturer's specifications of an opamp. The phase–frequency plot near the unity-gain frequency, with a capacitive load as parameter, is also a very important indicator of the opamp's stability and is sometimes missing from the specifications as well. For relatively large production quantities of active filters it is therefore recommended to select the optimum opamp in terms of price and performance, based on measurements carried out especially for a given application. For low-Q and low-frequency applications the 741-type opamp has been found satisfactory. The 4741 quad opamp from Harris has been found very favourable; besides its low price and the advantages common to other similar opamps, it also has exceptional temperature stability of the open-loop gain and very low noise. It is to be assumed that by the time this book is in print other manufacturers will also provide temperature-stable and high-frequency opamps for a reasonable price, which will extend the usable frequency and Q range of active filters.

After the selection of an opamp based on a careful examination, combined with possible measurements, of its characteristics, the boundaries of the resistor values to be used in the RC network can be determined. These depend on the opamp's input and output resistors. It should be noted that the computer programs of the active networks presented here assume an ideal opamp with zero output and infinite input resistance. In practice the resistor values to be used in the RC network should be greater than the output resistance or less than the input resistance of the opamp, generally by at least a factor of ten. Using this rule of thumb with an older 741 type opamp with 100 Ω output and 1 MΩ input resistance, one finds a relatively narrow range of permitted resistor values, namely, between 1 kΩ and 100 kΩ. Indeed, after careful study of the opamp's specs, one finds that many characteristics are only valid for a load resistor greater than 2 kΩ (although the given characteristics are measured with a load resistor of 10 kΩ). Thus the remaining resistor range is actually even smaller, namely, less than two decades. This fact should be taken into consideration by running the programs and changing the input capacitor values such as to stay within the limited resistor range permitted by the opamp specs.

8-3   SOLVING STABILITY PROBLEMS

Active filters may have stability problems for a number of reasons, in which case, instead of a filter, one may end up with an oscillator. The main sources for instability are (a) opamps that have been too critically frequency compensated, (b) the existence of high-frequency parasitic poles, and (c) an excessive capacitive load on the opamp. In troubleshooting filter instabilities, the first step is to check for proper interconnection of all passive components and all opamp terminals. Furthermore, it must not be forgotten that an amplifier usually needs two symmetrical power-supply voltages and often also requires external frequency-compensating elements. Naturally, it also pays to study the specification sheets of the opamps before use and to compare the active filter network diagram in this book with that of the built-up circuit.

If the active filter network being checked continues to oscillate, it is recommended to short the input terminal of the circuit to ground. This is because there are many filters which are stable only with the input grounded. In practice, this means that they must be driven from a voltage source with a *low* output impedance. Thus, if the oscillation disappears after the input has been shorted to ground, then it was caused by too high an output impedance of the preceding, or driving, stage. Connecting a voltage follower or a buffer amplifier with low output impedance to the input of the active filter circuit should therefore solve this problem. However, even if the oscillation still continues, all further investigations should be made with the input of the filter grounded.

When connecting the output terminal of the opamp to an oscilloscope, a high-impedance probe with low input capacitance should be used. If such a probe is not available, a resistor (e.g. 10 kΩ) should be used in series with the probe, because alone the capacitance of the oscilloscope interconnecting cable may be sufficient to cause opamp oscillation.

In general, there are two basic types of oscillation that may occur in an active filter. The frequency of the first kind is close to the pole frequency of the filter network and usually has a higher amplitude than the oscillation of the second kind whose frequency is close to the unity-gain frequency of the opamp.

If the closed-loop gain of the opamp is too high or, in other words, if the resistors which determine the Q factor are not properly tuned, the first kind of oscillation near the pole frequency takes place. In this case the remedy is to lower or increase the appropriate resistors. The resistors in question will be those reserved for the functional tuning of the Q factor of the active filter poles.

The oscillation of the second kind, which occurs at much higher frequencies (i.e. near the unity-gain frequency of the opamp), is the more serious of the two and is caused by improper frequency compensation of the opamp. If externally compensated opamps are used, the compensation network (sometimes only a single capacitor) might not be properly dimensioned. Besides checking the opamp data sheet and application notes for additional information on the frequency compensation, the following practical hints should be observed. A small capacitor (the value of which can be between 10 pF and several 100 pF) should be placed in parallel with the other capacitors of the compensation network (if any), in parallel with the resistor going from the output to the negative input of the opamp, or in parallel with the resistor going from the positive opamp input terminal to ground. The desired effect is to decrease the voltage passing from the opamp output to its positive input, while increasing the voltage passing from the opamp output to its negative input, in order to decrease the opamp gain at high frequencies.

If these steps do not eliminate the parasitic oscillation, then the opamp should be measured alone, i.e. without the components associated with the active filter circuit, but with the same closed loop gain, and the steps outlined above repeated. If the opamp still oscillates and no further information is available from the manufacturer, then a less-critical opamp must be used.

8-4   EXTERNAL FREQUENCY COMPENSATION

Although the object of this chapter is to give practical hints for the design of active filters without going into theoretical detail, a few equations in this section will be useful in explaining the benefits that are attainable through the use of external frequency compensation of an opamp. In Chapter 3, eqs. (3-40a) and (3-40b), the relative shift in the pole frequency ω_p and the quality factor q_p of a network pole p_0, due to a change in the open-loop gain A of the opamp, is given in terms of the gain sensitivity product Γ. It can be shown that very similar expressions are obtained if the shift of ω_p and q_p, caused by the fact that the open-loop opamp gain is *finite* and not infinite, is calculated. The following expressions are obtained:

$$\left(\frac{\Delta\omega_p}{\omega_p}\right)_f = -\Gamma_A^{\omega_p}\,\mathrm{Re}\left[\frac{1}{A(p_0)}\right] - \frac{\Gamma_A^{q_p}}{\sqrt{4q_p^2 - 1}}\,\mathrm{Im}\left[\frac{1}{A(p_0)}\right] \tag{8-1a}$$

$$\left(\frac{\Delta q_p}{q_p}\right)_f = \Gamma_A^{\omega_p}\sqrt{4q_p^2 - 1}\,\mathrm{Im}\left[\frac{1}{A(p_0)}\right] - \Gamma_A^{q_p}\,\mathrm{Re}\left[\frac{1}{A(p_0)}\right] \tag{8-1b}$$

where the subscript 'f' indicates that the relative variations $\Delta\omega_p/\omega_p$ and $\Delta q_p/q_p$ are due to 'finite' gain.

As it happens, almost all single-opamp networks given in Chapter 5 (the only exception is circuit 14) have in common that the GSP of the pole frequency ω_p is equal to zero. Therefore, for these networks, the equations (8-1) simplify to:

$$\left(\frac{\Delta\omega_p}{\omega_p}\right)_f = -\frac{\Gamma_A^{q_P}}{\sqrt{4q_p^2 - 1}}\, \mathrm{Im}\left[\frac{1}{A(p_0)}\right] \tag{8-2a}$$

$$\left(\frac{\Delta q_p}{q_p}\right)_f = -\Gamma_A^{q_P}\, \mathrm{Re}\left[\frac{1}{A(p_0)}\right] \tag{8-2b}$$

For an internal frequency compensation—or external compensation using a single capacitor—both of which cause a so-called 'single-pole roll-off' (SPRO) type of compensation, eqns. (3-42) and (3-43) of Chapter 3 can be used. In particular, eq. (3-43b) is significant. Rewritten in the present context, it becomes

$$\mathrm{Re}\left[\frac{1}{A(p_0)}\right]_{\mathrm{SPRO}} \approx 0 \tag{8-3}$$

It follows from (8-2) and (8-3) that in the case of SPRO compensation a shift of the pole frequency ω_p, and not of the quality factor q_p, should be expected due to the finite gain of the opamp.

Without going into details, it can also be shown that in the case of a somewhat more sophisticated frequency compensation, namely, the 'double-pole single-zero' (DPSZ) compensation, we obtain instead of eq. (8-3) the complementary expression that

$$\mathrm{Im}\left[\frac{1}{A(p_0)}\right]_{\mathrm{DPSZ}} \approx 0 \tag{8-4}$$

Thus, in the case of DPSZ compensation, a q_p shift, and not an ω_p shift, will be caused by finite opamp gain. The implication of the preceding discussion is that the ω_p and q_p shifts caused by finite gain (and bandwidth) of the opamp can be controlled by the type of frequency compensation used. This is all the more important because it can be shown that, of the two, a frequency shift is much more detrimental to a specified high selectivity frequency response than a q_p shift. Thus, given the choice, a frequency shift should be avoided

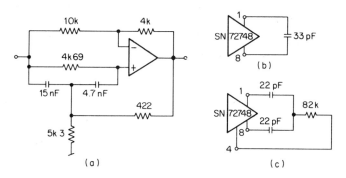

Fig. 8-1   Second-order allpass circuit (circuit 12, Chapter 5):
(a) circuit diagram, (b) single-pole roll-off (SPRO) compensation,
(c) double-pole single-zero (DPSZ) compensation.

176

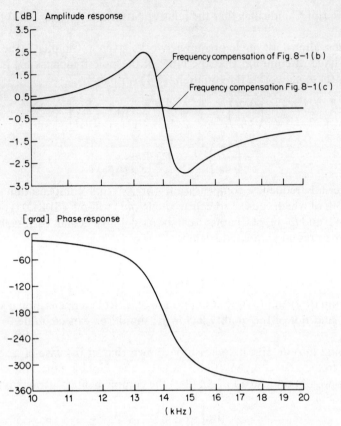

Fig. 8-2 Amplitude and phase response of second-order allpass circuit using SPRO and DPSZ frequency compensation.

if at all possible. It is therefore worthwhile to consider the DPSZ frequency compensation in any applications requiring high frequency selectivity (i.e. high-pole Q factors) or operating at high frequencies relative to the available bandwidth of the opamp.

To give an example of the effectiveness of DPSZ frequency compensation, consider the allpass network ((AP–MQ), circuit 12 in Chapter 5) which is shown in Fig. 8-1(a). Using an SN 72748 type opamp the SPRO frequency compensation shown in Fig. 8-1(b) and the DPSZ compensation shown in Fig. 8-1(c) were compared when used in the allpass network. The resulting measured amplitude and phase responses are shown in Fig. 8-2. Using the SPRO compensation the maximum amplitude error was close to 3 dB whereas with the DPSZ it was less than 0.1 dB. Naturally, in these measurements, nothing was changed in each case but the frequency compensation of the opamp. This is a demonstration of how effective the DPSZ compensation can be in a critical application.

References and Additional Reading

I FILTER THEORY AND DESIGN

H. J. Blinchikoff and A. I. Zverev, *Filtering in the Time and Frequency Domains*, John Wiley and Sons, New York, 1976.

D. S. Humpherys, *The Analysis, Design, and Synthesis of Electrical Filters*, Prentice-Hall, Inc., Englewood Cliffs, New Jersey, 1970.

D. E. Johnson, *Introduction to Filter Theory*, Prentice-Hall, Inc., Englewood Cliffs, New Jersey, 1976.

J. D. Rhodes, *Theory of Electrical Filters*, John Wiley and Sons, New York, 1976.

G. C. Temes and J. W. LaPatra, *Introduction to Circuit Synthesis and Design*, McGraw-Hill Book Co., New York, 1977.

G. C. Temes and S. K. Mitra (Eds.), *Modern Filter Theory and Design*, John Wiley and Sons, New York, 1973.

II ACTIVE FILTER THEORY AND DESIGN

A. Budak, *Passive and Active Network Analysis and Synthesis*, Houghton Mifflin Co., Boston, 1974.

G. Daryanani, *Principles of Active Network Synthesis and Design*, John Wiley and Sons, New York, 1976.

W. E. Heinlein and W. H. Holmes, *Active Filters for Integrated Circuits*, Springer-Verlag, New York, 1974.

L. P. Huelsman (Ed.), *Active RC Filters: Theory and Application*, Benchmark Papers in Electrical Engineering and Computer Science, Vol. 15, Dowden, Hutchinson and Ross, Inc., Stroudsburg, Pennsylvania, 1976.

D. E. Johnson and J. L. Hilburn, *Rapid Practical Designs of Active Filters*, John Wiley and Sons, New York, 1975.

H. Y-F. Lam, *Analog and Digital Filters: Design and Realization*, Prentice-Hall, Inc., Englewood Cliffs, New Jersey, 1979.

C. S. Lindquist, *Active Network Design with Signal Filtering Applications*, Stewart and Sons, Long Beach, California, 1977.

S. K. Mitra: *Analysis and Synthesis of Linear Active Networks*, John Wiley and Sons, New York, 1969.

G. S. Moschytz, *Linear Integrated Networks: Fundamentals*, Van Nostrand Reinhold Co., New York, 1974.

G. S. Moschytz, *Linear Integrated Networks: Design*, Van Nostrand Reinhold Co., New York, 1975.

G. S. Moschytz, *Single-Amplifier Active Filters: A Review*, Monograph, Scientia Electrica, Birkhäuser-Verlag, Basel, Switzerland, 1980, also: Scientia Electrica, Vol. 26, No. 1, pp. 1–46, 1980.

A. S. Sedra and P. O. Brackett, *Filter Theory and Design: Active and Passive*, Matrix Publishers, Inc., Illinois, 1978.

A. B. Williams, *Active Filter Design*, Artech House, Inc., Dedham, Massachusetts, 1975.

III SENSITIVITY THEORY AND FILTER TUNING

K. Geher, *Theory of Network Tolerances*, Akadémiai Kiadó, Budapest, 1971.

S. K. Mitra, *Analysis and Synthesis of Linear Active Networks*, John Wiley and Sons, New York, 1969.

178

G. S. Moschytz, 'The sensitivity problem in active filters, *Scientia Electrica* (Birkhäuser Verlag, Basel, Switzerland), **21**, No. 4, 81–105 (1975).

G. S. Moschytz, *Linear Integrated Networks: Design*, Van Nostrand Reinhold Co., New York, 1975.

G. S. Moschytz, 'Functional and deterministic tuning of hybrid-integrated active filters', *Electrocomponent Science and Technology*, **5**, 79–89 (1978).

IV   APPROXIMATION THEORY

R. W. Daniels, *Approximation Methods for Electronic Filter Design*, McGraw-Hill Book Co., New York, 1974.

K. L. Su, *Time-Domain Synthesis of Linear Networks*, Prentice-Hall, Inc., Englewood Cliffs, New Jersey, 1971.

G. C. Temes and S. K. Mitra (Eds.), *Modern Filter Theory and Design*, John Wiley and Sons, New York, 1973, Chap. 2.

V   FILTER TABLES

M. Biey and A. Premoli, "Tables for Active Filter Design (based on Cauer and MCPER functions)," Georgi Publishing Co., St. Saphorin, Switzerland, 1980.

E. Christian and E. Eisenmann, *Filter Design Tables and Graphs*, John Wiley and Sons, Inc., New York, 1966.

G. E. Hansell, *Filter Design and Evaluation*, Van Nostrand Reinhold Co., New York, 1969.

R. Saal, *Handbook of Filter Design*, Allgemeine Elektrizitäts-Gesellschaft AEG-Telefunken, Berlin, 1979.

J. K. Skwirzynski, *Design Theory and Data for Electrical Filters*, Van Nostrand Reinhold Co., New York, 1965.

A. I. Zverev, *Handbook of Filter Synthesis*, John Wiley and Sons, New York, 1967.

VI   COMPUTER-AIDED NETWORK ANALYSIS, OPTIMIZATION, AND DESIGN

621.372   D. A. Calahan, *Computer-Aided Network Design*, McGraw-Hill Book Co., New York, 1972.

L. O. Chua and P. M. Lin, *Computer-Aided Analysis of Electronic Circuits*, Prentice-Hall, Inc., Englewood Cliffs, New Jersey, 1975.

R. W. Daniels, *An Introduction to Numerical Methods and Optimization Techniques*, North-Holland, New York, 1978.

S. W. Director (Ed.), *Computer-Aided Circuit Design: Simulation and Optimization*, Benchmark Papers in Electrical Engineering and Computer Science, Vol. 5, Dowden, Hutchinson and Ross, Inc., Stroudsburg, Pennsylvania, 1973.

S. W. Director, *Circuit Theory: A Computational Approach*, John Wiley and Sons, New York, 1975.

J. Staudhammer, *Circuit Analysis by Digital Computer*, Prentice-Hall, Inc., Englewood Cliffs, New Jersey, 1975.

G. Szentirmai (Ed.), *Computer-Aided Filter Design*, IEEE Press, Inc., New York, 1973.

J. Vlach, *Computerized Approximation and Synthesis of Linear Networks*, John Wiley and Sons, New York, 1969.

VII   POCKET CALCULATORS AND MINICOMPUTERS

J. A. Ball, *Algorithms for RPN Calculators*, John Wiley and Sons, New York, 1978.

T. H. Crowley, *Understanding Computers* (Paperback), McGraw-Hill, New York, 1967.

P. C. Sanderson, *Minicomputers*, Newnes-Butterworths, London, 1976.

J. M. Smith, *Scientific Analysis on the Pocket Calculator*, John Wiley and Sons, New York, 1975.

VIII   OPAMP CIRCUIT DESIGN

G. B. Clayton, *Operational Amplifiers*, Butterworth, London, 1971.

G. E. Tobey, J. G. Graeme, and L. P. Huelsman, *Operational Amplifiers*, McGraw-Hill Book Co., New York, 1971.

J. V. Wait, L. P., Huelsman, and G. A. Korn, *Introduction to Operational Amplifier Theory and Applications*, McGraw-Hill Book Co., New York, 1975.

Program Records for the SR-59 Pocket Calculator

The program records for the Texas Instruments SR-59 pocket calculator for each of the twenty-three networks presented in Chapter 5 are given on the following pages.

The description of the program, the running procedure, the keys, labels, flags, and data registers are to be found on the first page of each program record. The program listing starts on the second page. In those cases in which the space on the preprinted first page is too little, the list of the used data registers is continued on the last page of that particular circuit program.

Before running a new program, all program data registers should be cleared by depressing the appropriate keys or by switching the calculator off and on again. This should be done particularly in those cases in which optional values are not pre-set. In such a case the program takes the values from the register of the optional input variable and this value should be zero and not the value remaining from a preceding program.

TITLE / TITEL / TITRE	1. LP-LQ	PAGE / SEITE / PAGE	1 OF / VON / DE 3	TI PROGRAMMABLE

PROGRAM RECORD
PROGRAMM-BERICHT
FICHE PROGRAMME

| PROGRAMMER / PROGRAMMIERER / PROGRAMMEUR | Horn | DATE / DATUM / DATE | 15.8.78 |

| Partitioning (Op 17) / Speicher-Bereichsverteilung / Partition (Op 17) | 4 7 9 . 5 9 | Library Module / Software-Modul / Module enfichable | – | Printer / Drucker / Imprimante | YES | Cards / Karten / Cartes | 1 |

PROGRAM DESCRIPTION ● PROGRAMM BESCHREIBUNG ● DESCRIPTION DU PROGRAMME

Calculate resistors R_{11}, R_{12}, R_3.

K can be required between $0 \to 1$

without requirement is $K = 1$ ($R_{12} \to \infty$).

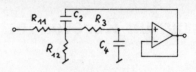

realizability condition: $\boxed{C_2 \geqslant 4q_p^2 C_4}$

otherwise message "C_4 TOO BIG"

$$T(s) = \frac{K\,\omega_p^2}{s^2 + \dfrac{\omega_p}{q_p}s + \omega_p^2}$$

USER INSTRUCTIONS ● BENUTZER INSTRUKTIONEN ● MODE D'EMPLOI

STEP / SCHRITT / SEQUENCE	PROCEDURE / PROZEDUR / PROCEDURE	ENTER / EINGABE / INTRODUIRE	PRESS / BEFEHL / APPUYER SUR		DISPLAY / ANZEIGE / AFFICHAGE
1	Text preparation if printer is available		2nd	A'	14 24 22.
2	Frequency [Hz]	f_p	A		f_p
3	Quality	q_p	B		q_p
4	C_2 [F]	C_2	C		C_2
5	C_4 [F]	C_4	D		C_4
6	if required $0 < K \leqslant 1$	K	E		K
7	RUN		2nd	E'	0.00

USER DEFINED KEYS / PROGRAMM-ADRESSTASTEN / TOUCHES UTILISATEUR

A	f_p
B	q_p
C	C_2
D	C_4
E	K
A'	TEXT
B'	
C'	
D'	
E'	RUN

DATA REGISTERS / DATENSPEICHER / REGISTRES-MEMOIRE (INV List)

0 0	indirect address	3 0	indirect address
0 1	GSP	1	
0 2	q_p	2	
0 3	f_p	3	
0 4	K	2 4	R_1
0 5	C_4	2 5	C_2/C_4
0 6	R_3	2 6	$[C_3/(2C_4\,q_p^2)] - 1$
0 7	C_2	2 7	P
0 8	R_{12}	2 8	$1-K$
0 9	R_{11}	1 9	K required

LABELS (Op 08)

INV	lnx	CE	CLR	x≥t	x² √
√x̄	1/x √	STO	RCL	SUM	yˣ
EE	(	)	÷	GTO	X
SBR	–	RST	+	R/S	.
+/–	=	CLR	INV	log	CP

FLAGS / FLAGS / DRAPEAUX	0	1	2	3	4	5	6	7	8	9

Text in 31-39, 42-43

000	76	LBL
001	17	B'
002	57	ENG
003	73	RC*
004	30	30
005	69	OP
006	04	04
007	73	RC*
008	00	00
009	69	OP
010	06	06
011	01	1
012	22	INV
013	44	SUM
014	30	30
015	97	DSZ
016	00	00
017	00	00
018	02	02
019	98	ADV
020	92	RTN
021	76	LBL
022	11	A
023	42	STO
024	03	03
025	92	RTN
026	76	LBL
027	12	B
028	42	STO
029	02	02
030	92	RTN
031	76	LBL
032	13	C
033	42	STO
034	07	07
035	92	RTN
036	76	LBL
037	14	D
038	42	STO
039	05	05
040	92	RTN
041	76	LBL
042	15	E
043	42	STO
044	19	19
045	92	RTN
046	76	LBL
047	16	A'
048	03	3
049	05	5
050	00	0
051	02	2
052	00	0
053	02	2
054	42	STO
055	39	39
056	85	+
057	01	1
058	95	=
059	42	STO
060	38	38
061	01	1
062	05	5
063	00	0
064	03	3
065	42	STO
066	37	37
067	03	3
068	05	5
069	00	0
070	04	4
071	42	STO
072	36	36
073	01	1
074	05	5
075	00	0
076	05	5
077	42	STO
078	35	35
079	02	2
080	06	6
081	42	STO
082	34	34
083	02	2
084	01	1
085	42	STO
086	33	33
087	03	3
088	04	4
089	42	STO
090	32	32
091	02	2
092	02	2
093	03	3
094	06	6
095	03	3
096	03	3
097	42	STO
098	31	31
099	03	3
100	07	7
101	03	3
102	02	2
103	03	3
104	02	2
105	42	STO
106	42	42
107	01	1
108	04	4
109	02	2
110	04	4
111	02	2
112	02	2
113	42	STO
114	43	43
115	92	RTN
116	76	LBL
117	10	E'
118	02	2
119	32	X:T
120	43	RCL
121	07	07
122	55	÷
123	43	RCL
124	05	05
125	55	÷
126	42	STO
127	25	25
128	02	2
129	55	÷
130	43	RCL
131	02	02
132	33	X²
133	95	=
134	77	GE
135	33	X²
136	69	OP
137	00	00
138	43	RCL
139	35	35
140	69	OP
141	01	01
142	43	RCL
143	42	42
144	69	OP
145	02	02
146	43	RCL
147	43	43
148	69	OP
149	03	03
150	69	OP
151	05	05
152	98	ADV
153	25	CLR
154	92	RTN
155	76	LBL
156	33	X²
157	75	-
158	01	1
159	95	=
160	42	STO
161	26	26
162	33	X²
163	75	-
164	01	1
165	95	=
166	34	ΓX
167	85	+
168	43	RCL
169	26	26
170	95	=
171	42	STO
172	27	27
173	65	×
174	43	RCL
175	05	05
176	65	×
177	43	RCL
178	07	07
179	95	=

180	34	√X
181	65	×
182	02	2
183	65	×
184	89	π
185	65	×
186	43	RCL
187	03	03
188	95	=
189	35	1/X
190	42	STO
191	24	24
192	65	×
193	43	RCL
194	27	27
195	95	=
196	42	STO
197	06	06
198	43	RCL
199	25	25
200	55	÷
201	43	RCL
202	27	27
203	95	=
204	34	√X
205	65	×
206	43	RCL
207	02	02
208	95	=
209	42	STO
210	01	01
211	09	9
212	42	STO
213	00	00
214	03	3
215	09	9
216	42	STO
217	30	30
218	25	CLR
219	32	X⌂T
220	43	RCL
221	19	19
222	67	EQ
223	35	1/X
224	94	+/-
225	85	+
226	01	1
227	95	=
228	22	INV
229	77	GE
230	35	1/X
231	67	EQ
232	35	1/X
233	42	STO
234	28	28
235	43	RCL
236	24	24
237	55	÷
238	43	RCL
239	19	19

240	42	STO
241	04	04
242	95	=
243	42	STO
244	09	09
245	43	RCL
246	24	24
247	55	÷
248	43	RCL
249	28	28
250	95	=
251	42	STO
252	08	08
253	71	SBR
254	17	B'
255	25	CLR
256	92	RTN
257	76	LBL
258	35	1/X
259	43	RCL
260	24	24
261	42	STO
262	09	09
263	01	1
264	52	EE
265	09	9
266	00	0
267	42	STO
268	08	08
269	01	1
270	42	STO
271	04	04
272	61	GTO
273	02	02
274	53	53
275	03	3
276	92	RTN

TITLE / TITEL / TITRE	2. BP-LQ-R	PAGE / SEITE / PAGE	1 OF / VON / DE 3	TI PROGRAMMABLE

PROGRAMMER / PROGRAMMIERER / PROGRAMMEUR: Horn

DATE / DATUM / DATE: 7.8.78

PROGRAM RECORD
PROGRAMM-BERICHT
FICHE PROGRAMME

Partitioning (Op 17) / Speicher-Bereichsverteilung / Partition (Op 17): 4 7 9 5 9

Library Module / Software-Modul / Module enfichable: --

Printer / Drucker / Imprimante: YES   Cards / Karten / Cartes: 1

PROGRAM DESCRIPTION ● PROGRAMM BESCHREIBUNG ● DESCRIPTION DU PROGRAMME

Calculate resistors R_{11}, R_{12}, R_4.

K will be maximum if not defined.

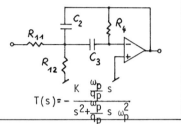

$$T(s) = -\frac{K \frac{\omega_p}{q_p} s}{s^2 + \frac{\omega_p}{q_p} s + \omega_p^2}$$

USER INSTRUCTIONS ● BENUTZER INSTRUKTIONEN ● MODE D'EMPLOI

STEP SCHRITT SEQUENCE	PROCEDURE / PROZEDUR / PROCEDURE	ENTER / EINGABE / INTRODUIRE	PRESS / BEFEHL / APPUYER SUR	DISPLAY / ANZEIGE / AFFICHAGE
1	Text preparation if printer is available		2nd A'	22 36 33.
2	Frequency [Hz]	f_p	A	f_p
3	Quality	q_p	B	q_p
4	C_2 [F]	C_2	C	C_2
5	C_3 [F]	C_3	D	C_3
6	if required $\quad K = |T(j\omega_p)|$	K	E	K
7	RUN		2nd E'	0.00

USER DEFINED KEYS / PROGRAMM-ADRESSTASTEN / TOUCHES UTILISATEUR		DATA REGISTERS / DATENSPEICHER / REGISTRES-MEMOIRE (INV [ ])		LABELS (Op 08)
A	f_p	0⁰ indirect address	3⁰ indirect address	
B	q_p	0₁ GSP	1	
C	C_2	0₂ q_p	2	
D	C_3	0₃ f_p	3	
E	K	0₄ K_p	2₄ $K_{max} - K$	
A'	TEXT	0₅ R_4	2₅ K_{max}	
B'		0₆ C_3	2₆ C_3/C_2	
C'		0₇ C_2	2₇ $R_1 = R_{11} \| R_{12}$	
D'		0₈ R_{12}	2₈ $p = R_4/R_1$	
E'	RUN	0₉ R_{11}	1₉ K_{in}	

FLAGS / FLAGS / DRAPEAUX: 0 1 2 3 4 5 6 7 8 9

© 1977 Texas Instruments

Text in 31 - 39

P/N 0000 000 0309

000	76	LBL
001	17	B'
002	57	ENG
003	73	RC*
004	30	30
005	69	OP
006	04	04
007	73	RC*
008	00	00
009	69	OP
010	06	06
011	01	1
012	22	INV
013	44	SUM
014	30	30
015	97	DSZ
016	00	00
017	00	00
018	02	02
019	98	ADV
020	92	RTN
021	76	LBL
022	11	A
023	42	STO
024	03	03
025	92	RTN
026	76	LBL
027	12	B
028	42	STO
029	02	02
030	92	RTN
031	76	LBL
032	13	C
033	42	STO
034	07	07
035	92	RTN
036	76	LBL
037	14	D
038	42	STO
039	06	06
040	92	RTN
041	76	LBL
042	15	E
043	42	STO
044	19	19
045	92	RTN
046	76	LBL
047	16	A'
048	03	3
049	05	5
050	00	0
051	02	2
052	00	0
053	02	2
054	42	STO
055	39	39
056	85	+
057	01	1
058	95	=
059	42	STO
060	38	38
061	01	1
062	05	5
063	00	0
064	03	3
065	42	STO
066	37	37
067	85	+
068	01	1
069	95	=
070	42	STO
071	36	36
072	03	3
073	05	5
074	00	0
075	05	5
076	42	STO
077	35	35
078	02	2
079	06	6
080	42	STO
081	34	34
082	02	2
083	01	1
084	42	STO
085	33	33
086	03	3
087	04	4
088	42	STO
089	32	32
090	02	2
091	02	2
092	03	3
093	06	6
094	03	3
095	03	3
096	42	STO
097	31	31
098	92	RTN
099	76	LBL
100	10	E'
101	43	RCL
102	06	06
103	55	÷
104	43	RCL
105	07	07
106	95	=
107	42	STO
108	26	26
109	85	+
110	35	1/X
111	85	+
112	02	2
113	95	=
114	65	×
115	43	RCL
116	02	02
117	33	X²
118	95	=
119	42	STO

120	28	28
121	65	×
122	43	RCL
123	06	06
124	65	×
125	43	RCL
126	07	07
127	95	=
128	34	√X
129	65	×
130	02	2
131	65	×
132	89	π
133	65	×
134	43	RCL
135	03	03
136	95	=
137	35	1/X
138	42	STO
139	27	27
140	65	×
141	43	RCL
142	28	28
143	95	=
144	42	STO
145	05	05
146	09	9
147	42	STO
148	00	00
149	03	3
150	09	9
151	42	STO
152	30	30
153	43	RCL
154	26	26
155	85	+
156	01	1
157	95	=
158	65	×
159	43	RCL
160	02	02
161	33	X²
162	95	=
163	42	STO
164	01	01
165	43	RCL
166	26	26
167	65	×
168	43	RCL
169	28	28
170	95	=
171	34	√X
172	65	×
173	43	RCL
174	02	02
175	95	=
176	42	STO
177	25	25
178	43	RCL
179	19	19

180	67	EQ
181	35	1/X
182	94	+/-
183	85	+
184	43	RCL
185	25	25
186	95	=
187	22	INV
188	77	GE
189	35	1/X
190	67	EQ
191	35	1/X
192	42	STO
193	24	24
194	43	RCL
195	25	25
196	65	×
197	43	RCL
198	27	27
199	55	÷
200	43	RCL
201	19	19
202	42	STO
203	04	04
204	95	=
205	42	STO
206	09	09
207	65	×
208	43	RCL
209	04	04
210	55	÷
211	43	RCL
212	24	24
213	95	=
214	42	STO
215	08	08
216	71	SBR
217	17	B'
218	25	CLR
219	92	RTN
220	76	LBL
221	35	1/X
222	43	RCL
223	27	27
224	42	STO
225	09	09
226	01	1
227	52	EE
228	09	9
229	00	0
230	42	STO
231	08	08
232	43	RCL
233	25	25
234	42	STO
235	04	04
236	61	GTO
237	02	02
238	16	16
239	92	RTN

TITLE / TITEL / TITRE	3. BP - LQ - C	PAGE / SEITE / PAGE 1 OF / VON / DE 3	TI PROGRAMMABLE

PROGRAM RECORD
PROGRAMM-BERICHT
FICHE PROGRAMME

PROGRAMMER / PROGRAMMIERER / PROGRAMMEUR: Horn
DATE / DATUM / DATE: 9.8.78

Partitioning (Op 17) / Speicher-Bereichsverteilung / Partition (Op 17): | 4 7 . 9 5 9 | Library Module / Software-Modul / Module enfichable

Printer / Drucker / Imprimante: YES   Cards / Karten / Cartes: 1

PROGRAM DESCRIPTION ● PROGRAMM BESCHREIBUNG ● DESCRIPTION DU PROGRAMME

Calculate resistors R_2, R_3.

K can be changed by changing

of C_{11} and C_{12}.

For maximal K set C_{12} equal to zero.

realizability condition: $\boxed{C_{11} + C_{12} \geq 4q_p^2 \, C_4}$

otherwise message "C_4 TOO BIG"

$$T(s) = -\frac{K \frac{\omega_p}{q_p} s}{s^2 + \frac{\omega_p}{q_p} s + \omega_p^2}$$

USER INSTRUCTIONS ● BENUTZER INSTRUKTIONEN ● MODE D

STEP / SCHRITT / SEQUENCE	PROCEDURE / PROZEDUR / PROCEDURE	ENTER / EINGABE / INTRODUIRE	PRESS / BEFEHL / APPUYER SUR		DISPLAY / ANZEIGE / AFFICHAGE
1	Text preparation if printer is available		2nd	A'	14 24 22.
2	Frequency [Hz]	f_p	A		f_p
3	Quality	q_p	B		q_p
4	C_{11}	C_{11}	C		C_{11}
5	C_{12}	C_{12}	D		C_{12}
6	C_4	C_4	E		C_4
7	RUN		2nd	E'	GSP

USER DEFINED KEYS / PROGRAMM-ADRESSTASTEN / TOUCHES UTILISATEUR

A	f_p
B	q_p
C	C_{11}
D	C_{12}
E	C_4
A'	TEXT
B'	
C'	
D'	
E'	RUN

DATA REGISTERS / DATENSPEICHER / REGISTRES-MEMOIRE ([INV] [list])

0₀	indirect address
0₁	GSP
0₂	q_p
0₃	f_p
0₄	K
0₅	C_4
0₆	R_3
0₇	R_2
0₈	C_{12}
0₉	C_{11}

3₀	indirect address
1	
2	
3	
4	
2₅	C_1/C_4
2₆	$C_1 = C_{11} + C_{12}$
2₇	P
2₈	$C_1/(C_4 \cdot 2q_p^2) - 1$
9	

LABELS (Op 08)

INV	lnx	CE	CLR	x:t	x²
√	1/x	✔	STO	RCL	SUM	y^x
EE	(	)	÷	GTO	X
SBR	−	RST	+	R/S	.
+/−	=	CLR	INV	log	CP

FLAGS / FLAGS / DRAPEAUX

0	1	2	3	4	5	6	7	8	9

1977 Texas Instruments

Text in 31-39, 41-43

P N 0000 000 0309

000	76	LBL	060	38	38	120	92	RTN
001	17	B'	061	03	3	121	76	LBL
002	57	ENG	062	05	5	122	10	E'
003	73	RC*	063	00	0	123	02	2
004	30	30	064	03	3	124	32	X:T
005	69	OP	065	42	STO	125	43	RCL
006	04	04	066	37	37	126	09	09
007	73	RC*	067	85	+	127	85	+
008	00	00	068	01	1	128	43	RCL
009	69	OP	069	95	=	129	08	08
010	06	06	070	42	STO	130	95	=
011	01	1	071	36	36	131	42	STO
012	22	INV	072	01	1	132	26	26
013	44	SUM	073	05	5	133	55	÷
014	30	30	074	00	0	134	43	RCL
015	97	DSZ	075	05	5	135	05	05
016	00	00	076	42	STO	136	55	÷
017	00	00	077	35	35	137	42	STO
018	02	02	078	02	2	138	25	25
019	98	ADV	079	06	6	139	02	2
020	92	RTN	080	42	STO	140	55	÷
021	76	LBL	081	34	34	141	43	RCL
022	11	A	082	02	2	142	02	02
023	42	STO	083	01	1	143	33	X²
024	03	03	084	42	STO	144	95	=
025	92	RTN	085	33	33	145	77	GE
026	76	LBL	086	03	3	146	35	1/X
027	12	B	087	04	4	147	69	OP
028	42	STO	088	42	STO	148	00	00
029	02	02	089	32	32	149	43	RCL
030	92	RTN	090	02	2	150	41	41
031	76	LBL	091	02	2	151	69	OP
032	13	C	092	03	3	152	01	01
033	42	STO	093	06	6	153	43	RCL
034	09	09	094	03	3	154	42	42
035	92	RTN	095	03	3	155	69	OP
036	76	LBL	096	42	STO	156	02	02
037	14	D	097	31	31	157	43	RCL
038	42	STO	098	01	1	158	43	43
039	08	08	099	05	5	159	69	OP
040	92	RTN	100	00	0	160	03	03
041	76	LBL	101	05	5	161	69	OP
042	15	E	102	42	STO	162	05	05
043	42	STO	103	41	41	163	98	ADV
044	05	05	104	03	3	164	25	CLR
045	92	RTN	105	07	7	165	92	RTN
046	76	LBL	106	03	3	166	76	LBL
047	16	A'	107	02	2	167	35	1/X
048	01	1	108	03	3	168	75	-
049	05	5	109	02	2	169	01	1
050	00	0	110	42	STO	170	95	=
051	02	2	111	42	42	171	42	STO
052	00	0	112	01	1	172	28	28
053	02	2	113	04	4	173	33	X²
054	42	STO	114	02	2	174	75	-
055	39	39	115	04	4	175	01	1
056	85	+	116	02	2	176	95	=
057	01	1	117	02	2	177	34	√X
058	95	=	118	42	STO	178	85	+
059	42	STO	119	43	43	179	43	RCL

```
180   28   28
181   95   =
182   42   STO
183   27   27
184   65   ×
185   43   RCL
186   26   26
187   65   ×
188   43   RCL
189   05   05
190   95   =
191   34   √X
192   65   ×
193   02   2
194   65   ×
195   89   π
196   65   ×
197   43   RCL
198   03   03
199   95   =
200   35   1/X
201   42   STO
202   07   07
203   65   ×
204   43   RCL
205   27   27
206   95   =
207   42   STO
208   06   06
209   43   RCL
210   25   25
211   55   ÷
212   43   RCL
213   27   27
214   95   =
215   34   √X
216   65   ×
217   43   RCL
218   02   02
219   55   ÷
220   42   STO
221   01   01
222   43   RCL
223   26   26
224   65   ×
225   43   RCL
226   09   09
227   95   =
228   42   STO
229   04   04
230   09   9
231   42   STO
232   00   00
233   03   3
234   09   9
235   42   STO
236   30   30
237   71   SBR
238   17   B'
239   92   RTN
```

TITLE / TITEL / TITRE **4. HP - LQ**	PAGE / SEITE / PAGE **1** OF / VON / DE **3**	**TI PROGRAMMABLE** **PROGRAM RECORD** **PROGRAMM-BERICHT** **FICHE PROGRAMME**
PROGRAMMER / PROGRAMMIERER / PROGRAMMEUR **Horn**	DATE / DATUM / DATE **15.8.78**	
Partitioning (Op 17) / Speicher-Bereichsverteilung / Partition (Op 17) **4 7 9 5 9**	Library Module / Software-Modul / Module enfichable **–**	Printer / Drucker / Imprimante **YES** Cards / Karten / Cartes **1**

PROGRAM DESCRIPTION ● PROGRAMM BESCHREIBUNG ● DESCRIPTION DU PROGRAMME

Calculate resistors R_2, R_4

K can be changed between $0 \rightarrow 1$

by changing of C_{11} and C_{12}.
For maximal K = 1 set $C_{12} = 0$.

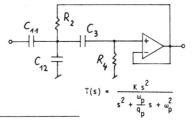

$$\tau(s) = \frac{K s^2}{s^2 + \frac{\omega_p}{q_p} s + \omega_p^2}$$

USER INSTRUCTIONS ● BENUTZER INSTRUKTIONEN ● MODE D'EMPLOI

STEP / SCHRITT / SEQUENCE	PROCEDURE / PROZEDUR / PROCEDURE	ENTER / EINGABE / INTRODUIRE	PRESS / BEFEHL / APPUYER SUR		DISPLAY / ANZEIGE / AFFICHAGE
1	Text preparation if printer is available		2nd	A'	22 36 33.
2	Frequency [Hz]	f_p	A		f_p
3	Quality	q_p	B		q_p
4	C_{11} [F]	C_{11}	C		C_{11}
5	if required C_{12} [F]	C_{12}	D		C_{12}
6	C_3 [F]	C_3	E		C_3
7	RUN		2nd	E'	0.00

USER DEFINED KEYS / PROGRAMM-ADRESSTASTEN / TOUCHES UTILISATEUR		DATA REGISTERS / DATENSPEICHER / REGISTRES-MEMOIRE (INV)		
A	f_p	0 0	indirect address	3 0	indirect address
B	q_p	0 1	GSP	1	
C	C_{11}	0 2	q_p	2	
D	C_{12}	0 3	f_p	3	
E	C_3	0 4	K	4	
A'	TEXT	0 5	R_4	5	
B'		0 6	C_3	2 6	P
C'		0 7	R_2	2 7	C_1/C_3
D'		0 8	C_{12}	2 8	$C_1 = C_{11} + C_{12}$
E'	RUN	0 9	C_{11}	9	

LABELS (Op 08)

[INV] [lnx] [CE] [CLR] [x:t] [x²]
[√x] [1/x] [STO] [RCL] [SUM] [yˣ]
[EE] [( ] [ )] [÷] [GTO] [X]
[SBR] [–] [RST] [+] [R/S] [.]
[+/–] [=] [CLR] [INV] [log] [CP]

FLAGS / FLAGS / DRAPEAUX 0 1 2 3 4 5 6 7 8 9

© 1977 Texas Instruments

TEXT in 31 - 39

P-N 0000 000 0309

000	76	LBL
001	17	B'
002	57	ENG
003	73	RC*
004	30	30
005	69	OP
006	04	04
007	73	RC*
008	00	00
009	69	OP
010	06	06
011	01	1
012	22	INV
013	44	SUM
014	30	30
015	97	DSZ
016	00	00
017	00	00
018	02	02
019	98	ADV
020	92	RTN
021	76	LBL
022	11	A
023	42	STO
024	03	03
025	92	RTN
026	76	LBL
027	12	B
028	42	STO
029	02	02
030	92	RTN
031	76	LBL
032	13	C
033	42	STO
034	09	09
035	92	RTN
036	76	LBL
037	14	D
038	42	STO
039	08	08
040	92	RTN
041	76	LBL
042	15	E
043	42	STO
044	06	06
045	92	RTN
046	76	LBL
047	16	A'
048	01	1
049	05	5
050	00	0
051	02	2
052	00	0
053	02	2
054	42	STO
055	39	39
056	85	+
057	01	1
058	95	=
059	42	STO

060	38	38
061	03	3
062	05	5
063	00	0
064	03	3
065	42	STO
066	37	37
067	01	1
068	05	5
069	00	0
070	04	4
071	42	STO
072	36	36
073	03	3
074	05	5
075	00	0
076	05	5
077	42	STO
078	35	35
079	02	2
080	06	6
081	42	STO
082	34	34
083	02	2
084	01	1
085	42	STO
086	33	33
087	03	3
088	04	4
089	42	STO
090	32	32
091	02	2
092	02	2
093	03	3
094	06	6
095	03	3
096	03	3
097	42	STO
098	31	31
099	92	RTN
100	76	LBL
101	10	E'
102	43	RCL
103	09	09
104	85	+
105	43	RCL
106	08	08
107	95	=
108	42	STO
109	28	28
110	55	÷
111	43	RCL
112	06	06
113	95	=
114	42	STO
115	27	27
116	85	+
117	35	1/X
118	85	+
119	02	2

```
120   95    =
121   65    ×
122   43   RCL
123   02    02
124   33   X²
125   95    =
126   42   STO
127   26    26
128   65    ×
129   43   RCL
130   28    28
131   65    ×
132   43   RCL
133   06    06
134   95    =
135   34   √X
136   65    ×
137   02    2
138   65    ×
139   89    π
140   65    ×
141   43   RCL
142   03    03
143   95    =
144   35   1/X
145   42   STO
146   07    07
147   65    ×
148   43   RCL
149   26    26
150   95    =
151   42   STO
152   05    05
153   43   RCL
154   26    26
155   55    ÷
156   43   RCL
157   27    27
158   95    =
159   34   √X
160   65    ×
161   43   RCL
162   02    02
163   95    =
164   42   STO
165   01    01
166   43   RCL
167   09    09
168   55    ÷
169   43   RCL
170   28    28
171   95    =
172   42   STO
173   04    04
174   09    9
175   42   STO
176   00    00
177   03    3
178   09    9
179   42   STO
```

```
180   30    30
181   71   SBR
182   17   B'
183   25   CLR
184   92   RTN
```

TITLE	5. AP - Q.5	PAGE 1 OF 3
TITEL		SEITE VON
TITRE		PAGE DE

TI PROGRAMMABLE
PROGRAM RECORD
PROGRAMM-BERICHT
FICHE PROGRAMME

PROGRAMMER / PROGRAMMIERER / PROGRAMMEUR: Horn
DATE / DATUM / DATE: 27.10.78

Partitioning (Op 17) / Speicher-Bereichsverteilung / Partition (Op 17): $4\,7\,9\,.\,5\,9$
Library Module / Software-Modul / Module enfichable: --
Printer / Drucker / Imprimante: YES
Cards / Karten / Cartes: 1

PROGRAM DESCRIPTION ● PROGRAMM BESCHREIBUNG ● DESCRIPTION DU PROGRAMME

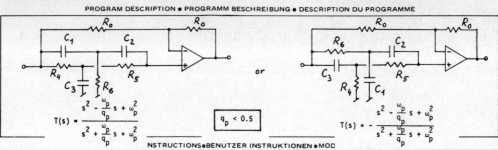

$$T(s) = \frac{s^2 - \frac{\omega_p}{q_p}s + \omega_p^2}{s^2 + \frac{\omega_p}{q_p}s + \omega_p^2}$$

$$q_p < 0.5$$

$$T(s) = - \frac{s^2 - \frac{\omega_p}{q_p}s + \omega_p^2}{s^2 + \frac{\omega_p}{q_p}s + \omega_p^2}$$

INSTRUCTIONS ● BENUTZER INSTRUKTIONEN ● MOD

STEP SCHRITT SEQUENCE	PROCEDURE PROZEDUR PROCEDURE	ENTER EINGABE INTRODUIRE	PRESS BEFEHL APPUYER SUR		DISPLAY ANZEIGE AFFICHAGE
1	Text preparation if printer is available		2nd	A'	14 24 22
2	enter pole-frequency [Hz]	F	A		F
3	enter quality < 0.5 !	Q	B		Q
4	C_1 [F]	C_1	C		C_1
5	C_2 [F]	C_2	D		C_2
6	C_3 [F]	C_3	E		C_3
7	RUN		2nd	E'	0.00
	repeat steps 4-7 for other C-values				

USER DEFINED KEYS PROGRAMM-ADRESSTASTEN TOUCHES UTILISATEUR		DATA REGISTERS DATENSPEICHER REGISTRES-MEMOIRE (INV Inst)		LABELS (Op 08) LABELS (Op 08) LABELS (Op 08)
A	f_p	00,30 indirect address	10 C_2	
B	q_p	01 q_p	11 C_1	
C	C_1	02 f_p	12 $C_1 + C_2$	
D	C_2	03 R_{6B}	13 $C_2 + C_3$	
E	C_3	04 R_{5B}	14 $2q_p$	
A'	TEXT	05 R_{4B}	15 $C_1 \cdot C_3$	
B'		06 R_{6A}	16 $\sqrt{H}$	
C'		07 R_{5A}	17 $2\pi\,f_p$	
D'		08 R_{4A}	18 ω_p^2	
E'	RUN	09 C_3	50,51,52 indirect address	

FLAGS FLAGS DRAPEAUX	0	1	2	3	4	5	6	7	8	9

Text in reg. 31 - 43

P/N 0000 000 0309

000	76	LBL
001	17	B'
002	22	INV
003	57	ENG
004	73	RC*
005	30	30
006	69	OP
007	04	04
008	57	ENG
009	73	RC*
010	00	00
011	69	OP
012	06	06
013	01	1
014	22	INV
015	44	SUM
016	30	30
017	97	DSZ
018	00	00
019	00	00
020	02	02
021	98	ADV
022	98	ADV
023	92	RTN
024	76	LBL
025	11	A
026	42	STO
027	02	02
028	92	RTN
029	76	LBL
030	12	B
031	42	STO
032	01	01
033	92	RTN
034	76	LBL
035	13	C
036	42	STO
037	11	11
038	92	RTN
039	76	LBL
040	14	D
041	42	STO
042	10	10
043	92	RTN
044	76	LBL
045	15	E
046	42	STO
047	09	09
048	92	RTN
049	76	LBL
050	16	A'
051	01	1
052	05	5
053	00	0
054	02	2
055	42	STO
056	41	41
057	85	+
058	01	1
059	95	=

060	42	STO
061	40	40
062	85	+
063	01	1
064	95	=
065	42	STO
066	39	39
067	03	3
068	05	5
069	00	0
070	05	5
071	01	1
072	03	3
073	42	STO
074	38	38
075	85	+
076	01	1
077	95	=
078	42	STO
079	35	35
080	85	+
081	09	9
082	09	9
083	95	=
084	42	STO
085	37	37
086	85	+
087	01	1
088	95	=
089	42	STO
090	24	24
091	85	+
092	09	9
093	09	9
094	95	=
095	42	STO
096	36	36
097	85	+
098	01	1
099	95	=
100	42	STO
101	33	33
102	02	2
103	01	1
104	42	STO
105	32	32
106	03	3
107	04	4
108	42	STO
109	31	31
110	03	3
111	07	7
112	03	3
113	02	2
114	03	3
115	02	2
116	42	STO
117	42	42
118	01	1
119	04	4

120	02	2
121	04	4
122	02	2
123	02	2
124	42	STO
125	43	43
126	92	RTN
127	76	LBL
128	10	E'
129	02	2
130	65	×
131	43	RCL
132	01	01
133	95	=
134	42	STO
135	14	14
136	33	X²
137	65	×
138	53	(
139	43	RCL
140	11	11
141	85	+
142	43	RCL
143	10	10
144	54	)
145	42	STO
146	12	12
147	65	×
148	53	(
149	43	RCL
150	10	10
151	85	+
152	43	RCL
153	09	09
154	54	)
155	42	STO
156	13	13
157	55	÷
158	53	(
159	43	RCL
160	11	11
161	65	×
162	43	RCL
163	09	09
164	54	)
165	42	STO
166	15	15
167	95	=
168	94	+/-
169	85	+
170	01	1
171	95	=
172	22	INV
173	77	GE
174	34	ΓX
175	34	ΓX
176	42	STO
177	16	16
178	06	6
179	42	STO

180	52	52
181	07	7
182	42	STO
183	51	51
184	08	8
185	42	STO
186	50	50
187	43	RCL
188	16	16
189	71	SBR
190	22	INV
191	03	3
192	42	STO
193	52	52
194	04	4
195	42	STO
196	51	51
197	05	5
198	42	STO
199	50	50
200	43	RCL
201	16	16
202	94	+/-
203	71	SBR
204	22	INV
205	01	1
206	01	1
207	42	STO
208	00	00
209	04	4
210	01	1
211	42	STO
212	30	30
213	71	SBR
214	17	B'
215	25	CLR
216	92	RTN
217	76	LBL
218	34	ГX
219	69	OP
220	00	00
221	43	RCL
222	40	40
223	69	OP
224	01	01
225	43	RCL
226	42	42
227	69	OP
228	02	02
229	43	RCL
230	43	43
231	69	OP
232	03	03
233	69	OP
234	05	05
235	98	ADV
236	91	R/S
237	92	RTN
238	76	LBL
239	22	INV
240	85	+
241	01	1
242	95	►=
243	55	÷
244	53	(
245	89	⫪
246	65	×
247	02	2
248	65	×
249	43	RCL
250	02	02
251	54	)
252	42	STO
253	17	17
254	55	÷
255	02	2
256	55	÷
257	43	RCL
258	01	01
259	55	÷
260	43	RCL
261	13	13
262	95	=
263	72	ST*
264	50	50
265	65	×
266	43	RCL
267	17	17
268	33	X²
269	42	STO
270	18	18
271	65	×
272	43	RCL
273	15	15
274	65	×
275	43	RCL
276	10	10
277	95	=
278	35	1/X
279	65	×
280	43	RCL
281	12	12
282	95	=
283	72	ST*
284	51	51
285	85	+
286	73	RC*
287	50	50
288	95	=
289	65	×
290	43	RCL
291	10	10
292	65	×
293	43	RCL
294	11	11
295	65	×
296	43	RCL
297	18	18
298	95	=
299	35	1/X
300	72	ST*
301	52	52
302	92	RTN

TITLE	6. AP - LQ	PAGE	1	OF	3	TI PROGRAMMABLE
TITEL		SEITE		VON		**PROGRAM RECORD**
TITRE		PAGE		DE		**PROGRAMM-BERICHT**

PROGRAM RECORD
PROGRAMM-BERICHT
FICHE PROGRAMME

PROGRAMMER Horn   DATE 23.8.78
PROGRAMMIERER   DATUM
PROGRAMMEUR   DATE

Partitioning (Op 17)   4 7 9 5 9   Library Module —   Printer YES   Cards 1
Speicher-Bereichsverteilung   Software-Modul   Drucker   Karten
Partition (Op 17)   Module enfichable   Imprimante   Cartes

PROGRAM DESCRIPTION ● PROGRAMM BESCHREIBUNG ● DESCRIPTION DU PROGRAMME

Calculate resistors R_1, R_4, R_5.
R_6 will be set equal to 10kΩ if not defined.

Start with $C_2 = C_3$ or $C_2 > C_3$

$$T(s) = K \frac{s^2 - \frac{\omega_p}{q_p} s + \omega_p^2}{s^2 + \frac{\omega_p}{q_p} s + \omega_p^2}$$

USER INSTRUCTIONS●BENUTZER INSTRUKTIONEN●

STEP SCHRITT SEQUENCE	PROCEDURE PROZEDUR PROCEDURE	ENTER EINGABE INTRODUIRE	PRESS BEFEHL APPUYER SUR		DISPLAY ANZEIGE AFFICHAGE
1	Text preparation if printer is available		2nd	A'	22 36 33.
2	Frequency [Hz]	f_p	A		f_p
3	Quality	q_p	B		q_p
4	C_2 [F]	C_2	C		C_2
5	C_3 [F]	C_3	D		C_3
6	if required R_6	R_6	E		R_6
7	RUN		2nd	E'	0.00

USER DEFINED KEYS PROGRAMM-ADRESSTASTEN TOUCHES UTILISATEUR		DATA REGISTERS DATENSPEICHER REGISTRES-MEMOIRE (INV LST)		LABELS (Op 08) LABELS (Op 08) LABELS (Op 08)
A	f_p	0₀ } indirect address	1₀ R_1	INV, lnx, CE, CLR, x:t, x²
B	q_p	0₁ GSP	1	√, 1/x, STO, RCL, SUM, y^x
C	C_2	0₂ q_p	2	EE, (,), +, GTO, X
D	C_3	0₃ f_p	3	SBR, −, RST, +, R/S, .
E	R_6	0₄ K	4	+/−, =, CLR, INV, log, CP
A'	TEXT	0₅ R_6	5	
B'	PRINT	0₆ R_5	6	
C'		0₇ R_4	2₇ C_2/C_3	
D'		0₈ C_3	2₈ $P = R_4/R_1$	
E'	RUN	0₉ C_2	9	

FLAGS FLAGS DRAPEAUX	0	1	2	3	4	5	6	7	8	9

Text in 31-40

P N 0000 000 0309

```
000   76  LBL        060   85   +
001   17  B'         061   01   1
002   57  ENG        062   95   =
003   73  RC*        063   42  STO
004   30   30        064   38   38
005   69  OP         065   03   3
006   04   04        066   05   5
007   73  RC*        067   00   0
008   00   00        068   05   5
009   69  OP         069   42  STO
010   06   06        070   37   37
011   01   1         071   85   +
012   22  INV        072   01   1
013   44  SUM        073   95   =
014   30   30        074   42  STO
015   97  DSZ        075   36   36
016   00   00        076   85   +
017   00   00        077   01   1
018   02   02        078   95   =
019   98  ADV        079   42  STO
020   92  RTN        080   35   35
021   76  LBL        081   02   2
022   11   A         082   06   6
023   42  STO        083   42  STO
024   03   03        084   34   34
025   92  RTN        085   02   2
026   76  LBL        086   01   1
027   12   B         087   42  STO
028   42  STO        088   33   33
029   02   02        089   03   3
030   92  RTN        090   04   4
031   76  LBL        091   42  STO
032   13   C         092   32   32
033   42  STO        093   02   2
034   09   09        094   02   2
035   92  RTN        095   03   3
036   76  LBL        096   06   6
037   14   D         097   03   3
038   42  STO        098   03   3
039   08   08        099   42  STO
040   92  RTN        100   31   31
041   76  LBL        101   92  RTN
042   15   E         102   76  LBL
043   42  STO        103   10  E'
044   05   05        104   04   4
045   92  RTN        105   00   0
046   76  LBL        106   42  STO
047   16  A'         107   30   30
048   03   3         108   01   1
049   05   5         109   00   0
050   00   0         110   42  STO
051   02   2         111   00   00
052   42  STO        112   43  RCL
053   40   40        113   09   09
054   01   1         114   55   ÷
055   05   5         115   43  RCL
056   00   0         116   08   08
057   03   3         117   95   =
058   42  STO        118   42  STO
059   39   39        119   27   27
```

```
120   85   +
121   35   1/X
122   85   +
123   02   2
124   95   =
125   65   ×
126   43   RCL
127   02   02
128   33   X²
129   95   =
130   42   STO
131   28   28
132   65   ×
133   43   RCL
134   08   08
135   65   ×
136   43   RCL
137   09   09
138   95   =
139   34   √X
140   65   ×
141   02   2
142   65   ×
143   89   π
144   65   ×
145   43   RCL
146   03   03
147   95   =
148   35   1/X
149   42   STO
150   10   10
151   65   ×
152   43   RCL
153   28   28
154   95   =
155   42   STO
156   07   07
157   43   RCL
158   28   28
159   55   ÷
160   43   RCL
161   27   27
162   95   =
163   34   √X
164   65   ×
165   43   RCL
166   02   02
167   95   =
168   42   STO
169   01   01
170   43   RCL
171   05   05
172   67   EQ
173   35   1/X
174   22   INV
175   77   GE
176   35   1/X
177   65   ×
178   53   (
179   01   1
```

```
180   85   +
181   43   RCL
182   27   27
183   54   )
184   55   ÷
185   43   RCL
186   28   28
187   65   ×
188   02   2
189   95   =
190   42   STO
191   06   06
192   55   ÷
193   43   RCL
194   05   05
195   85   +
196   01   1
197   95   =
198   35   1/X
199   42   STO
200   04   04
201   71   SBR
202   17   B'
203   25   CLR
204   92   RTN
205   76   LBL
206   35   1/X
207   01   1
208   52   EE
209   04   4
210   42   STO
211   05   05
212   61   GTO
213   01   01
214   77   77
215   92   RTN
```

TITLE / TITEL / TITRE	7. BR - LQ	PAGE / SEITE / PAGE: 1 OF / VON / DE 3	**TI PROGRAMMABLE** **PROGRAM RECORD** **PROGRAMM-BERICHT** **FICHE PROGRAMME**
PROGRAMMER / PROGRAMMIERER / PROGRAMMEUR	Horn	DATE / DATUM / DATE: 23.8.78	
Partitioning (Op 17) / Speicher-Bereichsverteilung / Partition (Op 17)	4 7 9 5 9	Library Module / Software-Modul / Module enfichable — —	Printer / Drucker / Imprimante YES Cards / Karten / Cartes 1

PROGRAM DESCRIPTION ● PROGRAMM BESCHREIBUNG ● DESCRIPTION DU PROGRAMME

Calculate resistors R_1, R_4, R_5.

R_6 will be set equal to $10k\Omega$ if not defined.

Start with $C_2 = C_3$ or $C_2 > C_3$

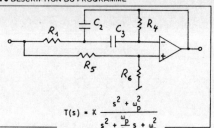

$$T(s) = K \frac{s^2 + \omega_p^2}{s^2 + \frac{\omega_p}{q_p} s + \omega_p^2}$$

USER INSTRUCTIONS ● BENUTZER INSTRUKTIONEN ● MODE [

STEP SCHRITT SEQUENCE	PROCEDURE PROZEDUR PROCEDURE	ENTER EINGABE INTRODUIRE	PRESS BEFEHL APPUYER SUR		DISPLAY ANZEIGE AFFICHAGE
1	Text preparation if printer is available		2nd	A'	22 36 33.
2	Frequency [Hz]	f_p	A		f_p
3	Quality	q_p	B		q_p
4	C_2 [F]	C_2	C		C_2
5	C_3 [F]	C_3	D		C_3
6	if required R_6	R_6	E		R_6
7	RUN		2nd	E'	0.00

USER DEFINED KEYS PROGRAMM-ADRESSTASTEN TOUCHES UTILISATEUR		DATA REGISTERS DATENSPEICHER REGISTRES-MEMOIRE (INV List)			LABELS (Op 08) LABELS (Op 08) LABELS (Op 08)
A	f_p	0_0 } indirect address 30	1_0	R_1	
B	q_p	0_1 GSP	1		
C	C_2	0_2 q_p	2		
D	C_3	0_3 f_p	3		
E	R_6	0_4 K	4		
A'	TEXT	0_5 R_6	5		
B'	PRINT	0_6 R_5	6		
C'		0_7 R_4	2_7 C_2/C_3		
D'		0_8 C_3	2_8 $P = R_4/R_1$		
E'	RUN	0_9 C_2	9		

FLAGS FLAGS DRAPEAUX	0	1	2	3	4	5	6	7	8	9

F N 0000 000 0309

Text in 31-40

000	76	LBL
001	17	B'
002	57	ENG
003	73	RC*
004	30	30
005	69	OP
006	04	04
007	73	RC*
008	00	00
009	69	OP
010	06	06
011	01	1
012	22	INV
013	44	SUM
014	30	30
015	97	DSZ
016	00	00
017	00	00
018	02	02
019	98	ADV
020	92	RTN
021	76	LBL
022	11	A
023	42	STO
024	03	03
025	92	RTN
026	76	LBL
027	12	B
028	42	STO
029	02	02
030	92	RTN
031	76	LBL
032	13	C
033	42	STO
034	09	09
035	92	RTN
036	76	LBL
037	14	D
038	42	STO
039	08	08
040	92	RTN
041	76	LBL
042	15	E
043	42	STO
044	05	05
045	92	RTN
046	76	LBL
047	16	A'
048	03	3
049	05	5
050	00	0
051	02	2
052	42	STO
053	40	40
054	01	1
055	05	5
056	00	0
057	03	3
058	42	STO
059	39	39
060	85	+
061	01	1
062	95	=
063	42	STO
064	38	38
065	03	3
066	05	5
067	00	0
068	05	5
069	42	STO
070	37	37
071	85	+
072	01	1
073	95	=
074	42	STO
075	36	36
076	85	+
077	01	1
078	95	=
079	42	STO
080	35	35
081	02	2
082	06	6
083	42	STO
084	34	34
085	02	2
086	01	1
087	42	STO
088	33	33
089	03	3
090	04	4
091	42	STO
092	32	32
093	02	2
094	02	2
095	03	3
096	06	6
097	03	3
098	03	3
099	42	STO
100	31	31
101	92	RTN
102	76	LBL
103	10	E'
104	04	4
105	00	0
106	42	STO
107	30	30
108	01	1
109	00	0
110	42	STO
111	00	00
112	43	RCL
113	09	09
114	55	÷
115	43	RCL
116	08	08
117	95	=
118	42	STO
119	27	27

120	85	+
121	35	1/X
122	85	+
123	02	2
124	95	=
125	65	×
126	43	RCL
127	02	02
128	33	X²
129	95	=
130	42	STO
131	28	28
132	65	×
133	43	RCL
134	08	08
135	65	×
136	43	RCL
137	09	09
138	95	=
139	34	√X
140	65	×
141	02	2
142	65	×
143	89	π
144	65	×
145	43	RCL
146	03	03
147	95	=
148	35	1/X
149	42	STO
150	10	10
151	65	×
152	43	RCL
153	28	28
154	95	=
155	42	STO
156	07	07
157	43	RCL
158	28	28
159	55	÷
160	43	RCL
161	27	27
162	95	=
163	34	√X
164	65	×
165	43	RCL
166	02	02
167	95	=
168	42	STO
169	01	01
170	43	RCL
171	05	05
172	67	EQ
173	35	1/X
174	22	INV
175	77	GE
176	35	1/X
177	65	×
178	53	(
179	01	1

180	85	+
181	43	RCL
182	27	27
183	54	)
184	55	÷
185	43	RCL
186	28	28
187	95	=
188	42	STO
189	06	06
190	55	÷
191	43	RCL
192	05	05
193	85	+
194	01	1
195	95	=
196	35	1/X
197	42	STO
198	04	04
199	71	SBR
200	17	B'
201	25	CLR
202	92	RTN
203	76	LBL
204	35	1/X
205	01	1
206	52	EE
207	04	4
208	42	STO
209	05	05
210	61	GTO
211	01	01
212	77	77
213	92	RTN

| TITLE / TITEL / TITRE | 8. LP - MQ | | | PAGE / SEITE / PAGE | 1 | OF / VON / DE | 3 | TI PROGRAMMABLE |

TI PROGRAMMABLE
PROGRAM·RECORD
PROGRAMM-BERICHT
FICHE PROGRAMME

| PROGRAMMER / PROGRAMMIERER / PROGRAMMEUR | Horn | DATE / DATUM / DATE | 4.8.78 |

Partition·ng (Op 17) / Speich·-Bereich· ·rteilung / Part (Op 17): 4 7 9 5 9 Library Module / Software-Modul / Module enfichable --

| Printer / Drucker / imprimante | YES | Cards / Karten / Cartes | 1 |

PROGRAM DESCRIPTION ● PROGRAMM BESCHREIBUNG ● DESCRIPTION DU PROGRAMME

Calculate values of the resistors R_{11}, R_{12}, R_3, R_6

R_5 will be set equal to $10k\Omega$ if not defined.

K will be maximum ($R_{12} \to \infty$) if not defined.

RUN-P calculates $P = R_3/R_{11} \parallel R_{12}$ for the minimal GSP.

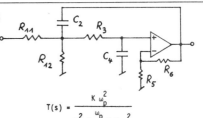

$$T(s) = \frac{K\,\omega_p^2}{s^2 + \frac{\omega_p}{q_p}s + \omega_p^2}$$

USER INSTRUCTIONS ● BENUTZER INSTRUKTIONEN ● MODI

STEP / SCHRITT / SEQUENCE	PROCEDURE / PROZEDUR / PROCEDURE	ENTER / EINGABE / INTRODUIRE	PRESS / BEFEHL / APPUYER SUR		DISPLAY / ANZEIGE / AFFICHAGE
1	Text preparation if printer is available		2nd	A'	22 36 33.
2	Frequency [Hz]	f_p	A		f_p
3	Quality	q_p	B		q_p
4	C_2 [F]	C_2	C		C_2
5	C_4 [F]	C_4	D		C_4
6	if required K	K	E		K
7	if required R_5 [Ω]	R_5	2nd	C'	R_5
8	Calculation of P for minimal GSP		2nd	D'	P
9	RUN with given P	P	2nd	E'	0.00
10	Repeat step 9 for new P				
	if required:				
11	delete print of R_{11}-Q		2nd	St flg	0
12	print R_{11}-Q (only once after step 9)				
13	cancel step 11		INV 2nd	St flg	0

USER DEFINED KEYS / PROGRAMM-ADRESSTASTEN / TOUCHES UTILISATEUR

A	f_p
B	q_p
C	C_2
D	C_4
E	K
A'	TEXT
B'	PRINT
C'	R_5
D'	RUN-P
E'	P-RUN

DATA REGISTERS / DATENSPEICHER / REGISTRES-MEMOIRE (INV list)

0⁰	indirect address	1⁰	R_{11}
0₁	q_p	1⁹	K_{IN}
0₂	f_p	2²	$K_{max}-K$
0₃	K	2³	$1 + \frac{R_6}{R_5}$
0₄	R_6	2⁴	$\sqrt{P \cdot C_4/C_2}$
0₅	R_5	2⁵	$R_1 = R_{11} \parallel R_{12}$
0₆	C_4	2⁶	P
0₇	R_3	2⁷	GSP
0₈	C_2	2⁰	C_4/C_2
0₉	R_{12}	3⁰	indirect address

LABELS (Op 08)

INV	lnx	CE	CLR	x:t	x² ✓
π	1/x	√ STO	RCL	SUM	y^x
EE	(	)	+	GTO	X
SBR	-	RST	+	R/S	.
+/-	=	CLR	INV	log	CP
		P→R			CMs
		|x|			int
	Pause	x:t	Nop	Op	Rad
	x=t	Σ+	x̄	Grad	St flg
	D.MS	π	list	Write	Dsz

FLAGS / FLAGS / DRAPEAUX: 0

© 1977 Texas Instruments

Text in reg. 28, 29, 31-40,   K in 19

P-N 0000 000 0309

204

000	76	LBL	060	42	STO	120	92	RTN
001	17	B'	061	40	40	121	76	LBL
002	57	ENG	062	85	+	122	19	D'
003	73	RC*	063	01	1	123	43	RCL
004	30	30	064	95	=	124	06	06
005	69	OP	065	42	STO	125	55	÷
006	04	04	066	39	39	126	43	RCL
007	73	RC*	067	01	1	127	08	08
008	00	00	068	05	5	128	95	=
009	69	OP	069	00	0	129	42	STO
010	06	06	070	03	3	130	20	20
011	01	1	071	42	STO	131	85	+
012	22	INV	072	38	38	132	01	1
013	44	SUM	073	03	3	133	95	=
014	30	30	074	05	5	134	65	×
015	97	DSZ	075	00	0	135	01	1
016	00	00	076	04	4	136	02	2
017	00	00	077	42	STO	137	65	×
018	02	02	078	37	37	138	43	RCL
019	98	ADV	079	01	1	139	01	01
020	98	ADV	080	05	5	140	33	X²
021	92	RTN	081	00	0	141	85	+
022	76	LBL	082	05	5	142	01	1
023	11	A	083	42	STO	143	95	=
024	42	STO	084	36	36	144	34	ΓX
025	02	02	085	03	3	145	85	+
026	92	RTN	086	05	5	146	01	1
027	76	LBL	087	00	0	147	95	=
028	12	B	088	06	6	148	33	X²
029	42	STO	089	42	STO	149	55	÷
030	01	01	090	35	35	150	43	RCL
031	92	RTN	091	85	+	151	20	20
032	76	LBL	092	01	1	152	55	÷
033	13	C	093	95	=	153	03	3
034	42	STO	094	42	STO	154	06	6
035	08	08	095	34	34	155	55	÷
036	92	RTN	096	02	2	156	43	RCL
037	76	LBL	097	06	6	157	01	01
038	14	D	098	42	STO	158	33	X²
039	42	STO	099	33	33	159	95	=
040	06	06	100	02	2	160	92	RTN
041	92	RTN	101	01	1	161	76	LBL
042	76	LBL	102	42	STO	162	10	E'
043	15	E	103	32	32	163	42	STO
044	42	STO	104	03	3	164	26	26
045	19	19	105	04	4	165	65	×
046	92	RTN	106	42	STO	166	43	RCL
047	76	LBL	107	31	31	167	08	08
048	18	C'	108	03	3	168	65	×
049	42	STO	109	03	3	169	43	RCL
050	05	05	110	42	STO	170	06	06
051	92	RTN	111	28	28	171	95	=
052	76	LBL	112	02	2	172	34	ΓX
053	16	A'	113	02	2	173	65	×
054	03	3	114	03	3	174	02	2
055	05	5	115	06	6	175	65	×
056	00	0	116	03	3	176	89	⊓
057	02	2	117	03	3	177	65	×
058	00	0	118	42	STO	178	43	RCL
059	02	2	119	29	29	179	02	02

180	95	=	240	55	÷	300	25	25
181	35	1/X	241	43	RCL	301	95	=
182	42	STO	242	05	05	302	42	STO
183	25	25	243	85	+	303	10	10
184	65	×	244	01	1	304	65	×
185	43	RCL	245	95	=	305	43	RCL
186	26	26	246	42	STO	306	03	03
187	95	=	247	23	23	307	55	÷
188	42	STO	248	33	X²	308	43	RCL
189	07	07	249	65	×	309	22	22
190	01	1	250	43	RCL	310	95	=
191	00	0	251	01	01	311	42	STO
192	42	STO	252	55	÷	312	09	09
193	00	00	253	43	RCL	313	87	IFF
194	04	4	254	24	24	314	00	00
195	00	0	255	95	=	315	03	03
196	42	STO	256	42	STO	316	19	19
197	30	30	257	27	27	317	71	SBR
198	43	RCL	258	43	RCL	318	17	B'
199	05	05	259	28	28	319	25	CLR
200	22	INV	260	69	OP	320	92	RTN
201	77	GE	261	04	04	321	76	LBL
202	35	1/X	262	43	RCL	322	35	1/X
203	67	EQ	263	26	26	323	01	1
204	35	1/X	264	69	OP	324	52	EE
205	65	×	265	06	06	325	04	4
206	53	(	266	43	RCL	326	42	STO
207	53	(	267	29	29	327	05	05
208	43	RCL	268	69	OP	328	61	GTO
209	06	06	269	04	04	329	02	02
210	55	÷	270	43	RCL	330	05	05
211	43	RCL	271	27	27	331	92	RTN
212	08	08	272	69	OP	332	76	LBL
213	65	×	273	06	06	333	33	X²
214	42	STO	274	98	ADV	334	43	RCL
215	20	20	275	43	RCL	335	25	25
216	43	RCL	276	19	19	336	42	STO
217	26	26	277	67	EQ	337	10	10
218	54	)	278	33	X²	338	01	1
219	34	√X	279	94	+/-	339	52	EE
220	42	STO	280	85	+	340	09	9
221	24	24	281	43	RCL	341	00	0
222	55	÷	282	23	23	342	42	STO
223	43	RCL	283	95	=	343	09	09
224	01	01	284	22	INV	344	43	RCL
225	94	+/-	285	77	GE	345	23	23
226	85	+	286	33	X²	346	42	STO
227	53	(	287	67	EQ	347	03	03
228	01	1	288	33	X²	348	61	GTO
229	85	+	289	42	STO	349	03	03
230	43	RCL	290	22	22	350	13	13
231	26	26	291	43	RCL	351	92	RTN
232	54	)	292	23	23			
233	65	×	293	55	÷			
234	43	RCL	294	43	RCL			
235	20	20	295	19	19			
236	54	)	296	42	STO			
237	95	=	297	03	03			
238	42	STO	298	65	×			
239	04	04	299	43	RCL			

TITLE / TITEL / TITRE	9. BP - MQ - R	PAGE / SEITE / PAGE	1 OF / VON / DE 3	**TI PROGRAMMABLE**

PROGRAM RECORD
PROGRAMM-BERICHT
FICHE PROGRAMME

PROGRAMMER / PROGRAMMIERER / PROGRAMMEUR	Horn	DATE / DATUM / DATE	3.8.78

Partitioning (Op 17) / Speicher-Bereichsverteilung / Partition (Op 17) | 4 , 7 . 9 5 9 | Library Module / Software-Modul / Module enfichable --

Printer / Drucker / Imprimante YES   Cards / Karten / Cartes 1

PROGRAM DESCRIPTION ● PROGRAMM BESCHREIBUNG ● DESCRIPTION DU PROGRAMME

Calculate values
of the resistors R_{11}, R_{12}, R_4, R_5
K will be maximum if not defined.
R_6 will be 10kΩ if not defined.

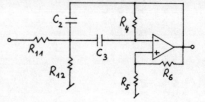

Parameter $P = \dfrac{R_4}{R_{11} /\!/ R_{12}}$

$$T(s) = - \frac{K \frac{\omega_p}{q_p} s}{s^2 + \frac{\omega_p}{q_p} s + \omega_p^2}$$

USER INSTRUCTIONS ● BENUTZER INSTRUKTIONEN ● MODE D'EMPLOI

STEP / SCHRITT / SEQUENCE	PROCEDURE / PROZEDUR / PROCEDURE	ENTER / EINGABE / INTRODUIRE	PRESS / BEFEHL / APPUYER SUR		DISPLAY / ANZEIGE / AFFICHAGE
1	Text preparation if printer is available		2nd	A'	22 36 33.
2	Frequency [Hz]	f_p	A		f_p
3	Quality	q_p	B		q_p
4	C_2 [F]	C_2	C		C_2
5	C_3 [F]	C_3	D		C_3
6	if required $K = |T(j\omega_p)|$	K	E		K
7	if required $R_6 = [\Omega]$	R_6	2nd	C'	R_6
8	Calculation of P for minimum GSP		2nd	D'	P
9	RUN with given P	P	2nd	E'	0.00
10	Repeat Step 9 for new P				
	if required:				
11	delete print of R_{11}-Q		2nd	St flg 0	
12	print R_{11}-Q (only once after step 9)		2nd	B'	
13	cancel step 11		Inv	2nd St flg	0

USER DEFINED KEYS / PROGRAMM-ADRESSTASTEN / TOUCHES UTILISATEUR		DATA REGISTERS / DATENSPEICHER / REGISTRES-MEMOIRE (INV List)		LABELS (Op 08) / LABELS (Op 08) / LABELS (Op 08)
A	f_p - input	0_0 indirect address	1_0 R_{11}	INV Inx CE CLR x:t x² √
B	q_p - input	0_1 q_p	2_1 $K_{max}-K$	√ 1/x STO RCL SUM y^x
C	C_2 - input	0_2 f_p	2_2 K_{max}	EE ( ) ÷ GTO X
D	C_3 - input	0_3 K	2_3 $1+\dfrac{R_5}{R_6}$	SBR − RST + R/S .
E	K - input	0_4 R_6	2_4 $\sqrt{C_2/(C_3 \cdot P)}$	+/− = CLR INV lnx CP
A'	TEXT	0_5 R_5	2_5 $R_1 = R_{11} /\!/ R_{12}$	Pgm P→R sin cos CMs
B'	PRINT	0_6 R_4	2_6 P	Rd |x| Eng t.x Int
C'	R_6 - input	0_7 C_3	2_7 GSP	Deg Pause x:t Nop Op Rad
D'	RUN-P	0_8 C_2	20 C_2/C_3	x⁻¹ Σ+ x̄ Grad St flg
E'	P-RUN	0_9 R_{12}	30 indirect address	π List Write D/z

FLAGS / FLAGS / DRAPEAUX | 0 | 1 | 2 | 3 | 4 | 5 | 6 | 7 | 8 | 9

Text in reg. 28, 29, 31-40, K in 19

P-N 0000 000 0309

000	76	LBL
001	17	B'
002	57	ENG
003	73	RC*
004	30	30
005	69	OP
006	04	04
007	73	RC*
008	00	00
009	69	OP
010	06	06
011	01	1
012	22	INV
013	44	SUM
014	30	30
015	97	DSZ
016	00	00
017	00	00
018	02	02
019	98	ADV
020	98	ADV
021	92	RTN
022	76	LBL
023	11	A
024	42	STO
025	02	02
026	92	RTN
027	76	LBL
028	12	B
029	42	STO
030	01	01
031	92	RTN
032	76	LBL
033	13	C
034	42	STO
035	08	08
036	92	RTN
037	76	LBL
038	14	D
039	42	STO
040	07	07
041	92	RTN
042	76	LBL
043	15	E
044	42	STO
045	19	19
046	92	RTN
047	76	LBL
048	18	C'
049	42	STO
050	04	04
051	92	RTN
052	76	LBL
053	19	D'
054	43	RCL
055	08	08
056	55	÷
057	43	RCL
058	07	07
059	95	=

060	42	STO
061	20	20
062	35	1/X
063	85	+
064	01	1
065	95	=
066	65	×
067	01	1
068	02	2
069	65	×
070	43	RCL
071	01	01
072	33	X²
073	85	+
074	01	1
075	95	=
076	34	ΓX
077	75	-
078	01	1
079	95	=
080	33	X²
081	65	×
082	43	RCL
083	20	20
084	55	÷
085	04	4
086	55	÷
087	43	RCL
088	01	01
089	33	X²
090	95	=
091	92	RTN
092	76	LBL
093	10	E'
094	42	STO
095	26	26
096	65	×
097	43	RCL
098	08	08
099	65	×
100	43	RCL
101	07	07
102	95	=
103	34	ΓX
104	65	×
105	02	2
106	65	×
107	89	π
108	65	×
109	43	RCL
110	02	02
111	95	=
112	35	1/X
113	42	STO
114	25	25
115	65	×
116	43	RCL
117	26	26
118	95	=
119	42	STO

120	06	06
121	01	1
122	00	0
123	42	STO
124	00	00
125	04	4
126	00	0
127	42	STO
128	30	30
129	43	RCL
130	04	04
131	22	INV
132	77	GE
133	35	1/X
134	67	EQ
135	35	1/X
136	65	×
137	53	(
138	53	(
139	43	RCL
140	08	08
141	55	÷
142	43	RCL
143	07	07
144	55	÷
145	42	STO
146	20	20
147	43	RCL
148	26	26
149	54	)
150	34	ΓX
151	42	STO
152	24	24
153	55	÷
154	43	RCL
155	01	01
156	94	+/-
157	85	+
158	53	(
159	01	1
160	85	+
161	43	RCL
162	20	20
163	54	)
164	55	÷
165	43	RCL
166	26	26
167	54	)
168	95	=
169	42	STO
170	05	05
171	55	÷
172	43	RCL
173	04	04
174	85	+
175	01	1
176	95	=
177	42	STO
178	23	23
179	65	×

180	43	RCL		240	65	×		300	95	=
181	01	01		241	43	RCL		301	42	STO
182	55	÷		242	03	03		302	39	39
183	43	RCL		243	55	÷		303	01	1
184	24	24		244	43	RCL		304	05	5
185	95	=		245	21	21		305	00	0
186	42	STO		246	95	=		306	03	3
187	22	22		247	42	STO		307	42	STO
188	65	×		248	09	09		308	38	38
189	43	RCL		249	87	IFF		309	85	+
190	23	23		250	00	00		310	01	1
191	95	=		251	02	02		311	95	=
192	42	STO		252	55	55		312	42	STO
193	27	27		253	71	SBR		313	37	37
194	43	RCL		254	17	B'		314	03	3
195	28	28		255	25	CLR		315	05	5
196	69	OP		256	92	RTN		316	00	0
197	04	04		257	76	LBL		317	05	5
198	43	RCL		258	35	1/X		318	42	STO
199	26	26		259	01	1		319	36	36
200	69	OP		260	52	EE		320	85	+
201	06	06		261	04	4		321	01	1
202	43	RCL		262	42	STO		322	95	=
203	29	29		263	04	04		323	42	STO
204	69	OP		264	61	GTO		324	35	35
205	04	04		265	01	01		325	85	+
206	43	RCL		266	36	36		326	01	1
207	27	27		267	92	RTN		327	95	=
208	69	OP		268	76	LBL		328	42	STO
209	06	06		269	33	X²		329	34	34
210	98	ADV		270	43	RCL		330	02	2
211	43	RCL		271	25	25		331	06	6
212	19	19		272	42	STO		332	42	STO
213	67	EQ		273	10	10		333	33	33
214	33	X²		274	01	1		334	02	2
215	94	+/-		275	52	EE		335	01	1
216	85	+		276	09	9		336	42	STO
217	43	RCL		277	00	0		337	32	32
218	22	22		278	42	STO		338	03	3
219	95	=		279	09	09		339	04	4
220	22	INV		280	43	RCL		340	42	STO
221	77	GE		281	22	22		341	31	31
222	33	X²		282	42	STO		342	03	3
223	67	EQ		283	03	03		343	03	3
224	33	X²		284	61	GTO		344	42	STO
225	42	STO		285	02	02		345	28	28
226	21	21		286	49	49		346	02	2
227	43	RCL		287	92	RTN		347	02	2
228	22	22		288	76	LBL		348	03	3
229	55	÷		289	16	A'		349	06	6
230	43	RCL		290	03	3		350	03	3
231	19	19		291	05	5		351	03	3
232	42	STO		292	00	0		352	42	STO
233	03	03		293	02	2		353	29	29
234	65	×		294	00	0		354	92	RTN
235	43	RCL		295	02	2				
236	25	25		296	42	STO				
237	95	=		297	40	40				
238	42	STO		298	85	+				
239	10	10		299	01	1				

| TITLE / TITEL / TITRE | 10. BP - MQ - C | PAGE / SEITE / PAGE | 1 OF / VON 3 |

TI PROGRAMMABLE
PROGRAM RECORD
PROGRAMM-BERICHT
FICHE PROGRAMME

TITLE / TITEL / TITRE	10. BP - MQ - C	PAGE / SEITE / PAGE	1	OF / VON	3
PROGRAMMER / PROGRAMMIERER / PROGRAMMEUR	Horn	DATE / DATUM / DATE	4.8.78		

| Partitioning (Op 17) / Speicher-Bereichsverteilung / Partition (Op 17) | 4 7 9 5 9 | Library Module / Software-Modul / Module enfichable | -- | Printer / Drucker / Imprimante | YES | Cards / Karten / Cartes | 1 |

PROGRAM DESCRIPTION ● PROGRAMM BESCHREIBUNG ● DESCRIPTION DU PROGRAMME

Calculate R_2, R_3, R_5, K.

R_6 will be set equal to $10k\Omega$ if not defined.

RUN-P calculates $P=R_3/R_2$ for minimal GSP.

Required K can be achieved by changing P,

C_{11} or C_{12}.

C_{12} can be set equal to zero (removed).

$$T(s) = -\frac{K\frac{\omega_p}{q_p}s}{s^2 + \frac{\omega_p}{q_p}s + \omega_p^2}$$

USER INSTRUCTIONS ● BENUTZER PLOI

STEP SCHRITT SEQUENCE	PROCEDURE PROZEDUR PROCEDURE	ENTER EINGABE INTRODUIRE	PRESS BEFEHL APPUYER SUR	DISPLAY ANZEIGE AFFICHAGE
1	Text preparation if printer is available		2nd A'	22 36 33.
2	Frequency [Hz]	f_p	A	f_p
3	Quality	q_p	B	q_p
4	C_{11}	C_{11}	C	C_{11}
5	C_{12}	C_{12}	D	C_{12}
6	C_4	C_4	E	C_4
7	if required R_6 [Ω]	R_6	2nd C'	R_6
8	Calculation of P for minimal GSP		2nd D'	P
9	RUN with given P	P	2nd E'	0.00
10	Repeat step 9 for new P			
	if required:			
11	delete print of C_{11}-Q		2nd St flg 0	
12	print C_{11}-Q (only once after each step 9)		2nd B'	
13	Cancel step 11		INV 2nd St flg 0	

USER DEFINED KEYS PROGRAMM-ADRESSTASTEN TOUCHES UTILISATEUR		DATA REGISTERS DATENSPEICHER (INV ▨) REGISTRES-MEMOIRE		LABELS (Op 08)
A	f_p	0₀ indirect address	1₀ C_{11}	
B	q_p	0₁ q_p	2₁ $(1+\frac{R_5}{R_6})\cdot q_p \cdot \sqrt{C_1/(PC_4)}$	
C	C_{11}	0₂ f_p	2₂ C_4/C_1	
D	C_{12}	0₃ K	2₃ $1+\frac{R_5}{R_6}$	
E	C_4	0₄ R_6	2₄ $\sqrt{PC_4/C_1}$	
A'	TEXT	0₅ R_5	2₅ $C_1=C_{11}+C_{12}$	
B'	PRINT	0₆ C_6	2₆ P	
C'	R_6	0₇ R_3	2₇ GSP	
D'	RUN-P	0₈ R_2	8	
E'	P-RUN	0₉ C_{12}	3₀ indirect address	

| FLAGS / FLAGS / DRAPEAUX | 0 | 1 | 2 | 3 | 4 | 5 | 6 | 7 | 8 | 9 |

© 1977 Texas Instruments

Text in reg. 28, 29, 31-40

P/N 0000 000 0309

000	76	LBL
001	17	B'
002	57	ENG
003	73	RC*
004	30	30
005	69	OP
006	04	04
007	73	RC*
008	00	00
009	69	OP
010	06	06
011	01	1
012	22	INV
013	44	SUM
014	30	30
015	97	DSZ
016	00	00
017	00	00
018	02	02
019	98	ADV
020	98	ADV
021	92	RTN
022	76	LBL
023	11	A
024	42	STO
025	02	02
026	92	RTN
027	76	LBL
028	12	B
029	42	STO
030	01	01
031	92	RTN
032	76	LBL
033	13	C
034	42	STO
035	10	10
036	92	RTN
037	76	LBL
038	14	D
039	42	STO
040	09	09
041	92	RTN
042	76	LBL
043	15	E
044	42	STO
045	06	06
046	92	RTN
047	76	LBL
048	18	C'
049	42	STO
050	04	04
051	92	RTN
052	76	LBL
053	16	A'
054	01	1
055	05	5
056	00	0
057	02	2
058	00	0
059	02	2
060	42	STO
061	40	40
062	85	+
063	01	1
064	95	=
065	42	STO
066	39	39
067	03	3
068	05	5
069	00	0
070	03	3
071	42	STO
072	38	38
073	03	3
074	05	5
075	00	0
076	04	4
077	42	STO
078	37	37
079	01	1
080	05	5
081	00	0
082	05	5
083	42	STO
084	36	36
085	03	3
086	05	5
087	00	0
088	06	6
089	42	STO
090	35	35
091	85	+
092	01	1
093	95	=
094	42	STO
095	34	34
096	02	2
097	06	6
098	42	STO
099	33	33
100	02	2
101	01	1
102	42	STO
103	32	32
104	03	3
105	04	4
106	42	STO
107	31	31
108	03	3
109	03	3
110	42	STO
111	28	28
112	02	2
113	02	2
114	03	3
115	06	6
116	03	3
117	03	3
118	42	STO
119	29	29
120	92	RTN
121	76	LBL
122	19	D'
123	43	RCL
124	06	06
125	55	÷
126	53	(
127	43	RCL
128	10	10
129	85	+
130	43	RCL
131	09	09
132	54	)
133	95	=
134	42	STO
135	22	22
136	85	+
137	01	1
138	95	=
139	65	×
140	01	1
141	02	2
142	65	×
143	43	RCL
144	01	01
145	33	X²
146	95	=
147	85	+
148	01	1
149	95	=
150	34	√X
151	85	+
152	01	1
153	95	=
154	33	X²
155	55	÷
156	03	3
157	06	6
158	55	÷
159	43	RCL
160	22	22
161	55	÷
162	43	RCL
163	01	01
164	33	X²
165	95	=
166	92	RTN
167	76	LBL
168	10	E'
169	42	STO
170	26	26
171	65	×
172	53	(
173	43	RCL
174	10	10
175	85	+
176	43	RCL
177	09	09
178	54	)
179	42	STO

180	25	25		240	22	22		300	04	4
181	65	×		241	54	)		301	00	0
182	43	RCL		242	95	=		302	42	STO
183	06	06		243	42	STO		303	30	30
184	95	=		244	05	05		304	87	IFF
185	34	√X		245	55	÷		305	00	00
186	65	×		246	43	RCL		306	03	03
187	02	2		247	04	04		307	10	10
188	65	×		248	85	+		308	71	SBR
189	89	π		249	01	1		309	17	B'
190	65	×		250	95	=		310	25	CLR
191	43	RCL		251	42	STO		311	92	RTN
192	02	02		252	23	23		312	76	LBL
193	95	=		253	65	×		313	35	1/X
194	35	1/X		254	43	RCL		314	01	1
195	42	STO		255	01	01		315	52	EE
196	08	08		256	55	÷		316	04	4
197	65	×		257	43	RCL		317	42	STO
198	43	RCL		258	24	24		318	04	04
199	26	26		259	95	=		319	61	GTO
200	95	=		260	42	STO		320	02	02
201	42	STO		261	21	21		321	10	10
202	07	07		262	65	×		322	92	RTN
203	43	RCL		263	43	RCL				
204	04	04		264	10	10				
205	22	INV		265	55	÷				
206	77	GE		266	43	RCL				
207	35	1/X		267	25	25				
208	67	EQ		268	95	=				
209	35	1/X		269	42	STO				
210	65	×		270	03	03				
211	53	(		271	43	RCL				
212	53	(		272	21	21				
213	43	RCL		273	65	×				
214	06	06		274	43	RCL				
215	55	÷		275	23	23				
216	43	RCL		276	95	=				
217	25	25		277	42	STO				
218	65	×		278	27	27				
219	42	STO		279	43	RCL				
220	22	22		280	28	28				
221	43	RCL		281	69	OP				
222	26	26		282	04	04				
223	54	)		283	43	RCL				
224	34	√X		284	26	26				
225	42	STO		285	69	OP				
226	24	24		286	06	06				
227	55	÷		287	43	RCL				
228	43	RCL		288	29	29				
229	01	01		289	69	OP				
230	94	+/-		290	04	04				
231	85	+		291	43	RCL				
232	53	(		292	27	27				
233	01	1		293	69	OP				
234	85	+		294	06	06				
235	43	RCL		295	98	ADV				
236	26	26		296	01	1				
237	54	)		297	00	0				
238	65	×		298	42	STO				
239	43	RCL		299	00	00				

212

TI PROGRAMMABLE
PROGRAM RECORD
PROGRAMM-BERICHT
FICHE PROGRAMME

| TITLE / TITEL / TITRE | 11. HP - MQ | PAGE / SEITE / PAGE | 1 OF 3 / VON / DE |
| PROGRAMMER / PROGRAMMIERER / PROGRAMMEUR | Horn | DATE / DATUM / DATE | 3.8.78 |

Partitioning (Op 17) / Speicher-Bereichsverteilung / Partition (Op 17): |4,7,9,5,9| Library Module / Software-Modul / Module enfichable: --   Printer / Drucker / Imprimante: YES   Cards / Karten / Cartes: 1

PROGRAM DESCRIPTION ● PROGRAMM BESCHREIBUNG ● DESCRIPTION DU PROGRAMME

Calculate values of the resistors R_2, R_4, R_6.

R_5 will be set equal to 10kΩ if not defined.

RUN-P calculates $P = R_4/R_2$ for minimal GSP.

Required K can be achieved by changing P and C_{12} or C_{11}.

C_{12} can be set equal to zero (removed)

$$T(s) = \frac{K \cdot s^2}{s^2 + \frac{\omega_p}{q_p}s + \omega_p^2}$$

USER INSTRUCTIONS ● BENUTZER... : D'EMPLOI

STEP / SCHRITT / SEQUENCE	PROCEDURE / PROZEDUR / PROCEDURE	ENTER / EINGABE / INTRODUIRE	PRESS / BEFEHL / APPUYER SUR	DISPLAY / ANZEIGE / AFFICHAGE
1	Text preparation if printer is available		2nd A'	22 36 33.
2	Frequency [Hz]	f_p	A	f_p
3	Quality	q_p	B	q_p
4	C_{11} [F]	C_{11}	C	C_{11}
5	only if required C_{12} [F]	C_{12}	D	C_{12}
6	C_3 [F]	C_3	E	C_3
7	if required R_5 [Ω]	R_5	2nd C'	R_5
8	Calculation of P for minimal GSP		2nd D'	P
9	RUN with given P	P	2nd E'	0.00
10	Repeat step 9 for new P			
	if required:			
11	delete print of C_{11}-Q		2nd St flg 0	
12	print C_{11}-Q (only once after step 9)		2nd B'	
13	Cancel step 11		INV 2nd St flg 0	

USER DEFINED KEYS / PROGRAMM-ADRESSTASTEN / TOUCHES UTILISATEUR		DATA REGISTERS / DATENSPEICHER / REGISTRES-MEMOIRE (INV CE)			LABELS (Op 08)
A	f_p	0 0	indirect address	1 0 C_{11}	
B	q_p	0 1		1	
C	C_{11}	0 2	q_p	2 2 C_1/C_3	
D	C_{12}	0 3	f_p	2 3 $1+\frac{R_6}{R_5}$	
E	C_3	0 4	K	2 4 $\sqrt{C_1/(P C_3)}$	
A'	TEXT	0 5	R_6	2 5 $C_1 = C_{11}+C_{12}$	
B'	PRINT	0 6	R_5	2 6 P	
C'	R_5	0 7	R_4	2 7 GSP	
D'	RUN-P	0 8	C_3	8	
E'	P-RUN	0 9	R_2	30 indirect address	
			C_{12}		

FLAGS / FLAGS / DRAPEAUX: 0 1 2 3 4 5 6 7 8 9

© 1977 Texas Instruments

Text in reg. 28, 29, 31-40

P.N 0000.000.0309

000	76	LBL
001	17	B'
002	57	ENG
003	73	RC*
004	30	30
005	69	OP
006	04	04
007	73	RC*
008	00	00
009	69	OP
010	06	06
011	01	1
012	22	INV
013	44	SUM
014	30	30
015	97	DSZ
016	00	00
017	00	00
018	02	02
019	98	ADV
020	98	ADV
021	92	RTN
022	76	LBL
023	11	A
024	42	STO
025	02	02
026	92	RTN
027	76	LBL
028	12	B
029	42	STO
030	01	01
031	92	RTN
032	76	LBL
033	13	C
034	42	STO
035	10	10
036	92	RTN
037	76	LBL
038	14	D
039	42	STO
040	09	09
041	92	RTN
042	76	LBL
043	15	E
044	42	STO
045	07	07
046	92	RTN
047	76	LBL
048	18	C'
049	42	STO
050	05	05
051	92	RTN
052	76	LBL
053	16	A'
054	01	1
055	05	5
056	00	0
057	02	2
058	00	0
059	02	2
060	42	STO
061	40	40
062	85	+
063	01	1
064	95	=
065	42	STO
066	39	39
067	03	3
068	05	5
069	00	0
070	03	3
071	42	STO
072	38	38
073	01	1
074	05	5
075	00	0
076	04	4
077	42	STO
078	37	37
079	03	3
080	05	5
081	00	0
082	05	5
083	42	STO
084	36	36
085	85	+
086	01	1
087	95	=
088	42	STO
089	35	35
090	85	+
091	01	1
092	95	=
093	42	STO
094	34	34
095	02	2
096	06	6
097	42	STO
098	33	33
099	02	2
100	01	1
101	42	STO
102	32	32
103	03	3
104	04	4
105	42	STO
106	31	31
107	03	3
108	03	3
109	42	STO
110	28	28
111	02	2
112	02	2
113	03	3
114	06	6
115	03	3
116	03	3
117	42	STO
118	29	29
119	92	RTN
120	76	LBL
121	19	D'
122	43	RCL
123	10	10
124	85	+
125	43	RCL
126	09	09
127	95	=
128	55	÷
129	43	RCL
130	07	07
131	95	=
132	42	STO
133	22	22
134	35	1/X
135	85	+
136	01	1
137	95	=
138	65	×
139	01	1
140	02	2
141	65	×
142	43	RCL
143	01	01
144	33	X²
145	85	+
146	01	1
147	95	=
148	34	√X
149	75	-
150	01	1
151	95	=
152	33	X²
153	65	×
154	43	RCL
155	22	22
156	55	÷
157	04	4
158	55	÷
159	43	RCL
160	01	01
161	33	X²
162	95	=
163	92	RTN
164	76	LBL
165	10	E'
166	42	STO
167	26	26
168	65	×
169	53	(
170	43	RCL
171	10	10
172	85	+
173	43	RCL
174	09	09
175	54	)
176	42	STO
177	25	25
178	65	×
179	43	RCL

180	07	07
181	95	=
182	34	√X
183	65	×
184	02	2
185	65	×
186	89	π
187	65	×
188	43	RCL
189	02	02
190	95	=
191	35	1/X
192	42	STO
193	08	08
194	65	×
195	43	RCL
196	26	26
197	95	=
198	42	STO
199	06	06
200	43	RCL
201	05	05
202	22	INV
203	77	GE
204	35	1/X
205	67	EQ
206	35	1/X
207	65	×
208	53	(
209	53	(
210	43	RCL
211	25	25
212	55	÷
213	43	RCL
214	07	07
215	55	÷
216	42	STO
217	22	22
218	43	RCL
219	26	26
220	54	)
221	34	√X
222	42	STO
223	24	24
224	55	÷
225	43	RCL
226	01	01
227	94	+/-
228	85	+
229	53	(
230	01	1
231	85	+
232	43	RCL
233	22	22
234	54	)
235	55	÷
236	43	RCL
237	26	26
238	54	)
239	95	=

240	42	STO
241	04	04
242	55	÷
243	43	RCL
244	05	05
245	85	+
246	01	1
247	95	=
248	42	STO
249	23	23
250	65	×
251	43	RCL
252	10	10
253	55	÷
254	43	RCL
255	25	25
256	95	=
257	42	STO
258	03	03
259	43	RCL
260	23	23
261	33	X²
262	65	×
263	43	RCL
264	01	01
265	55	÷
266	43	RCL
267	24	24
268	95	=
269	42	STO
270	27	27
271	43	RCL
272	28	28
273	69	OP
274	04	04
275	43	RCL
276	26	26
277	69	OP
278	06	06
279	43	RCL
280	29	29
281	69	OP
282	04	04
283	43	RCL
284	27	27
285	69	OP
286	06	06
287	98	ADV
288	01	1
289	00	0
290	42	STO
291	00	00
292	04	4
293	00	0
294	42	STO
295	30	30
296	87	IFF
297	00	00
298	03	03
299	02	02

300	71	SBR
301	17	B'
302	25	CLR
303	92	RTN
304	76	LBL
305	35	1/X
306	01	1
307	52	EE
308	04	4
309	42	STO
310	05	05
311	61	GTO
312	02	02
313	07	07
314	92	RTN

| TITLE
TITEL
TITRE | 12. AP - MQ | | PAGE
SEITE
PAGE | 1 | OF
VON
DE | 3 | TI PROGRAMMABLE
PROGRAM RECORD
PROGRAMM-BERICHT
FICHE PROGRAMME | |

| PROGRAMMER
PROGRAMMIERER
PROGRAMMEUR | Horn | DATE
DATUM
DATE | 31.8.78 | | | |
| Partitioning (Op 17)
Speicher-Bereichsverteilung
Partition (Op 17) | ⌊4, 7, 9, 5, 9⌋ | Library Module
Software-Modul
Module enfichable | -- | Printer
Drucker
Imprimante | YES | Cards
Karten
Cartes | 1 |

PROGRAM DESCRIPTION ● PROGRAMM BESCHREIBUNG ● DESCRIPTION DU PROGRAMME

Calculate resistors R_1, R_4, R_5, R_7.
R_6 will be set equal to $10k\Omega$ if not defined.
RUN-P calculates parameter P for minimal GSP.

$$T(s) = \frac{s^2 - \frac{\omega_p}{q_p}s + \omega_p^2}{s^2 + \frac{\omega_p}{q_p}s + \omega_p^2}$$

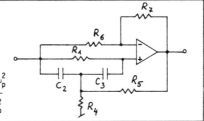

USER INSTRUCTIONS ● BENUTZER INSTRUKTIONEN ● MODE D'EMPLOI

STEP SCHRITT SEQUENCE	PROCEDURE PROZEDUR PROCEDURE	ENTER EINGABE INTRODUIRE	PRESS BEFEHL APPUYER SUR		DISPLAY ANZEIGE AFFICHAGE
1	Text preparation if printer is available		2nd	A'	22 36 33.
2	Frequency [Hz]	f_p	A		f_p
3	Quality	q_p	B		q_p
4	C_2 [F]	C_2	C		C_2
5	C_3 [F]	C_3	D		C_3
6	if other than $10k\Omega$ R_6 [Ω]	R_6	E		R_6
7	Calculation of P for minimal GSP		2nd	D'	P
8	RUN with given P	P	2nd	E'	0.00
9	Repeat step 8 for new P				
	if required				
10	delete print of R_1-Q		2nd	St flg	0
11	print R_1-Q (after step 8)		2nd	B'	
12	cancel step 10		INV	2nd St flg	0

USER DEFINED KEYS PROGRAMM-ADRESSTASTEN TOUCHES UTILISATEUR		DATA REGISTERS DATENSPEICHER REGISTRES-MEMOIRE (INV list)		LABELS (Op 08) LABELS (Op 08) LABELS (Op 08)
A	f_p	0 0 indirect address	3 0 indirect address	INV Inx CE CLR x:t x²
B	q_p	0 1 q_p	2 1 $1 + R_7/R_6$	√x̄ 1/x STO RCL SUM y*
C	C_2	0 2 f_p	2 2 $\sqrt{PC_2/C_3}$	EE ( ) ÷ GTO X
D	C_3	0 3 R_7	2 3 R_7/C_3	SBR − RST + R/S ·
E	R_6	0 4 R_6	2 4 R_p	+/− = CLR INV log CP
A'	TEXT	0 5 R_5	2 5 α	
B'	PRINT	0 6 R_4	2 6 P	
C'		0 7 C_3	2 7 GSP	
D'	RUN-P	0 8 C_2	1 8 $c^2 = C_2/C_3$	
E'	P-RUN	0 9 R_1	1 9 $6(1+c^2)^2 q_p^2/[2q_p^2(1+c^2)-c^2]$	

| FLAGS
FLAGS
DRAPEAUX | 0 | | 1 | 2 | 3 | 4 | 5 | 6 | 7 | 8 | 9 |

© 1977 Texas Instruments

Text in reg. 28,29, 31-39 ; in reg. 20: $1+c^2$

P:N 0000 000 0309

000	76	LBL	060	03	3	120	07	07
001	17	B'	061	42	STO	121	95	=
002	22	INV	062	38	38	122	34	ГX
003	57	ENG	063	85	+	123	65	X
004	73	RC*	064	01	1	124	02	2
005	30	30	065	95	=	125	65	X
006	69	OP	066	42	STO	126	89	π
007	04	04	067	37	37	127	65	X
008	57	ENG	068	03	3	128	43	RCL
009	73	RC*	069	05	5	129	02	02
010	00	00	070	00	0	130	95	=
011	69	OP	071	05	5	131	35	1/X
012	06	06	072	42	STO	132	42	STO
013	01	1	073	36	36	133	09	09
014	22	INV	074	85	+	134	65	X
015	44	SUM	075	01	1	135	43	RCL
016	30	30	076	95	=	136	26	26
017	97	DSZ	077	42	STO	137	95	=
018	00	00	078	35	35	138	42	STO
019	00	00	079	85	+	139	24	24
020	02	02	080	01	1	140	03	3
021	98	ADV	081	95	=	141	09	9
022	98	ADV	082	42	STO	142	42	STO
023	92	RTN	083	34	34	143	30	30
024	76	LBL	084	03	3	144	09	9
025	11	A	085	05	5	145	42	STO
026	42	STO	086	01	1	146	00	00
027	02	02	087	00	0	147	43	RCL
028	92	RTN	088	42	STO	148	26	26
029	76	LBL	089	33	33	149	65	X
030	12	B	090	02	2	150	43	RCL
031	42	STO	091	01	1	151	08	08
032	01	01	092	42	STO	152	55	÷
033	92	RTN	093	32	32	153	43	RCL
034	76	LBL	094	03	3	154	07	07
035	13	C	095	04	4	155	95	=
036	42	STO	096	42	STO	156	34	ГX
037	08	08	097	31	31	157	42	STO
038	92	RTN	098	03	3	158	22	22
039	76	LBL	099	03	3	159	43	RCL
040	14	D	100	42	STO	160	04	04
041	42	STO	101	28	28	161	67	EQ
042	07	07	102	02	2	162	35	1/X
043	92	RTN	103	02	2	163	65	X
044	76	LBL	104	03	3	164	53	(
045	15	E	105	06	6	165	43	RCL
046	42	STO	106	03	3	166	26	26
047	04	04	107	03	3	167	65	X
048	92	RTN	108	42	STO	168	53	(
049	76	LBL	109	29	29	169	01	1
050	16	A'	110	92	RTN	170	85	+
051	03	3	111	76	LBL	171	43	RCL
052	05	5	112	10	E'	172	08	08
053	00	0	113	42	STO	173	55	÷
054	02	2	114	26	26	174	43	RCL
055	42	STO	115	65	X	175	07	07
056	39	39	116	43	RCL	176	54	)
057	01	1	117	08	08	177	85	+
058	05	5	118	65	X	178	43	RCL
059	00	0	119	43	RCL	179	22	22

```
180   55   ÷
181   43   RCL
182   01   01
183   54   )
184   95   =
185   42   STO
186   03   03
187   55   ÷
188   43   RCL
189   04   04
190   95   =
191   42   STO
192   23   23
193   85   +
194   01   1
195   95   =
196   42   STO
197   21   21
198   35   1/X
199   65   ×
200   43   RCL
201   22   22
202   55   ÷
203   43   RCL
204   01   01
205   65   ×
206   02   2
207   95   =
208   94   +/-
209   85   +
210   01   1
211   95   =
212   42   STO
213   25   25
214   35   1/X
215   65   ×
216   43   RCL
217   24   24
218   95   =
219   42   STO
220   05   05
221   01   1
222   75   -
223   43   RCL
224   25   25
225   95   =
226   35   1/X
227   65   ×
228   43   RCL
229   24   24
230   95   =
231   42   STO
232   06   06
233   43   RCL
234   21   21
235   33   X²
236   65   ×
237   43   RCL
238   01   01
239   65   ×

240   43   RCL
241   25   25
242   55   ÷
243   43   RCL
244   22   22
245   95   =
246   42   STO
247   27   27
248   43   RCL
249   28   28
250   69   OP
251   04   04
252   43   RCL
253   26   26
254   69   OP
255   06   06
256   43   RCL
257   29   29
258   69   OP
259   04   04
260   43   RCL
261   27   27
262   69   OP
263   06   06
264   98   ADV
265   87   IFF
266   00   00
267   02   02
268   71   71
269   71   SBR
270   17   B'
271   25   CLR
272   92   RTN
273   76   LBL
274   35   1/X
275   01   1
276   52   EE
277   04   4
278   42   STO
279   04   04
280   61   GTO
281   01   01
282   63   63
283   92   RTN
284   76   LBL
285   19   D'
286   43   RCL
287   08   08
288   55   ÷
289   43   RCL
290   07   07
291   95   =
292   42   STO
293   18   18
294   85   +
295   01   1
296   95   =
297   42   STO
298   20   20
299   65   ×

300   02   2
301   65   ×
302   43   RCL
303   01   01
304   33   X²
305   75   -
306   43   RCL
307   18   18
308   95   =
309   35   1/X
310   65   ×
311   06   6
312   65   ×
313   43   RCL
314   01   01
315   33   X²
316   65   ×
317   43   RCL
318   20   20
319   33   X²
320   95   =
321   42   STO
322   19   19
323   33   X²
324   55   ÷
325   03   3
326   55   ÷
327   43   RCL
328   20   20
329   33   X²
330   85   +
331   01   1
332   95   =
333   34   ΓX
334   75   -
335   01   1
336   95   =
337   55   ÷
338   43   RCL
339   19   19
340   95   =
341   92   RTN
```

TITLE / TITEL / TITRE	13. BR - MQ	PAGE / SEITE / PAGE	1	OF / VON / DE	3	TI PROGRAMMABLE

TI PROGRAMMABLE
PROGRAM RECORD
PROGRAMM-BERICHT
FICHE PROGRAMME

PROGRAMMER / PROGRAMMIERER / PROGRAMMEUR: Horn   DATE / DATUM / DATE: 31.8.78

Partitioning (Op 17) / Speicher-Bereichsverteilung / Partition (Op 17): | 4 | 7 | 9 | 5 | 9 | Library Module / Software-Modul / Module enfichable: --   Printer / Drucker / Imprimante: YES   Cards / Karten / Cartes: 1

PROGRAM DESCRIPTION ● PROGRAMM BESCHREIBUNG ● DESCRIPTION DU PROGRAMME

Calculate resistors R_1, R_4, R_5, R_7.
R_6 will be set equal to $10k\Omega$ if not defined.
RUN-P calculates starting value of the
parameter P in the neighborhood of
the minimal GSP.

$$T(s) = \frac{s^2 + \omega_p^2}{s^2 + \frac{\omega_p}{q_p}s + \omega_p^2}$$

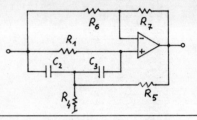

USER INSTRUCTIONS ● BENUTZER INSTRUKTIONEN ● MODE D'EMPLOI

STEP / SCHRITT / SEQUENCE	PROCEDURE / PROZEDUR / PROCEDURE	ENTER / EINGABE / INTRODUIRE	PRESS / BEFEHL / APPUYER SUR		DISPLAY / ANZEIGE / AFFICHAGE
1	Text preparation if printer is available		2nd	A'	22 36 33.
2	Frequency [Hz]	f_p	A		f_p
3	Quality	q_p	B		q_p
4	C_2 [F]	C_2	C		C_2
5	C_3 [F]	C_3	D		C_3
6	if other than $10k\Omega$: R_6 [Ω]	R_6	E		R_6
7	Calculation of starting value for P				
8	RUN with given P				
9	repeat step 8 for new P				
10	if required: delete print of R_1-Q		2nd	St flg	0
11	print R_1-Q (after step 8)		2nd	B'	
12	Cancel step 10		INV	2nd	St flg	0|

USER DEFINED KEYS / PROGRAMM-ADRESSTASTEN / TOUCHES UTILISATEUR

A	f_p
B	q_p
C	C_2
D	C_3
E	R_6
A'	TEXT
B'	PRINT
C'	
D'	RUN-P
E'	P-RUN

DATA REGISTERS / DATENSPEICHER / REGISTRES-MEMOIRE (INV ☐)

0₀	indirect address	3₀	indirect address
0₁	q_p	2₁	$1 + R_7/R_6$
0₂	f_p	2₂	$\sqrt{PC_2/C_3}$
0₃	R_7	2₃	$P(1+C_2/C_3) = \frac{R_7}{R_6}$
0₄	R_6	2₄	R_p
0₅	R_5	2₅	α
0₆	R_4	2₆	P
0₇	C_3	2₇	GSP
0₈	C_2	8	
0₉	R_1	9	

LABELS (Op 08)

INV	Inx	CE	CLR	x:t	x²
π	1/x	√	STO	RCL	SUM	y^x
EE	(	)	÷	GTO	X
SBR	-	RST	+	R/S	.
+/-	=	CLR	INV		

FLAGS / FLAGS / DRAPEAUX: | 0 | 1 | 2 | 3 | 4 | 5 | 6 | 7 | 8 | 9 |

© 1977 Texas Instruments

Text in reg. 28, 29, 31-39

P/N 0000 000 0309

000	76	LBL	060	03	3	120	01	1
001	17	B'	061	42	STO	121	95	=
002	22	INV	062	38	38	122	65	×
003	57	ENG	063	85	+	123	03	3
004	73	RC*	064	01	1	124	95	=
005	30	30	065	95	=	125	35	1/X
006	69	OP	066	42	STO	126	92	RTN
007	04	04	067	37	37	127	76	LBL
008	57	ENG	068	03	3	128	10	E'
009	73	RC*	069	05	5	129	42	STO
010	00	00	070	00	0	130	26	26
011	69	OP	071	05	5	131	65	×
012	06	06	072	42	STO	132	43	RCL
013	01	1	073	36	36	133	08	08
014	22	INV	074	85	+	134	65	×
015	44	SUM	075	01	1	135	43	RCL
016	30	30	076	95	=	136	07	07
017	97	DSZ	077	42	STO	137	95	=
018	00	00	078	35	35	138	34	ГX
019	00	00	079	85	+	139	65	×
020	02	02	080	01	1	140	02	2
021	98	ADV	081	95	=	141	65	×
022	98	ADV	082	42	STO	142	89	π
023	92	RTN	083	34	34	143	65	×
024	76	LBL	084	03	3	144	43	RCL
025	11	A	085	05	5	145	02	02
026	42	STO	086	01	1	146	95	=
027	02	02	087	00	0	147	35	1/X
028	92	RTN	088	42	STO	148	42	STO
029	76	LBL	089	33	33	149	09	09
030	12	B	090	02	2	150	65	×
031	42	STO	091	01	1	151	43	RCL
032	01	01	092	42	STO	152	26	26
033	92	RTN	093	32	32	153	95	=
034	76	LBL	094	03	3	154	42	STO
035	13	C	095	04	4	155	24	24
036	42	STO	096	42	STO	156	03	3
037	08	08	097	31	31	157	09	9
038	92	RTN	098	03	3	158	42	STO
039	76	LBL	099	03	3	159	30	30
040	14	D	100	42	STO	160	09	9
041	42	STO	101	28	28	161	42	STO
042	07	07	102	02	2	162	00	00
043	92	RTN	103	02	2	163	43	RCL
044	76	LBL	104	03	3	164	08	08
045	15	E	105	06	6	165	55	÷
046	42	STO	106	03	3	166	43	RCL
047	04	04	107	03	3	167	07	07
048	92	RTN	108	42	STO	168	85	+
049	76	LBL	109	29	29	169	01	1
050	16	A'	110	92	RTN	170	95	=
051	03	3	111	76	LBL	171	65	×
052	05	5	112	19	D'	172	43	RCL
053	00	0	113	43	RCL	173	26	26
054	02	2	114	08	08	174	95	=
055	42	STO	115	55	÷	175	42	STO
056	39	39	116	43	RCL	176	23	23
057	01	1	117	07	07	177	85	+
058	05	5	118	95	=	178	01	1
059	00	0	119	85	+	179	95	=

```
180   42  STO
181   21   21
182   43  RCL
183   26   26
184   65   ×
185   43  RCL
186   08   08
187   55   ÷
188   43  RCL
189   07   07
190   95   =
191   34  √X
192   42  STO
193   22   22
194   43  RCL
195   04   04
196   67• EQ
197   35  1/X
198   65•  ×
199   43  RCL
200   23   23
201   95   =
202   42  STO
203   03   03
204   43  RCL
205   22   22
206   55   ÷
207   43  RCL
208   21   21
209   55   ÷
210   43  RCL
211   01   01
212   95   =
213   94  +/-
214   85   +
215   01   1
216   95   =
217   42  STO
218   25   25
219   35  1/X
220   65   ×
221   43  RCL
222   24   24
223   95   =
224   42  STO
225   05   05
226   01   1
227   75   -
228   43  RCL
229   25   25
230   95   =
231   35  1/X
232   65   ×
233   43  RCL
234   24   24
235   95   =
236   42  STO
237   06   06
238   43  RCL
239   21   21
```

```
240   33  X²
241   65   ×
242   43  RCL
243   01   01
244   65   ×
245   43  RCL
246   25   25
247   55   ÷
248   43  RCL
249   22   22
250   95   =
251   42  STO
252   27   27
253   43  RCL
254   28   28
255   69  OP
256   04   04
257   43  RCL
258   26   26
259   69  OP
260   06   06
261   43  RCL
262   29   29
263   69  OP
264   04   04
265   43  RCL
266   27   27
267   69  OP
268   06   06
269   98  ADV
270   87  IFF
271   00   00
272   02   02
273   76   76
274   71  SBR
275   17  B'
276   25  CLR
277   92  RTN
278   76  LBL
279   35  1/X
280   01   1
281   52  EE
282   04   4
283   42  STO
284   04   04
285   61  GTO
286   01   01
287   98   98
288   92  RTN
```

TITLE / TITEL / TITRE	14. HPN/LPN - MQ	PAGE / SEITE / PAGE	1 OF / VON / DE 5	**TI PROGRAMMABLE**

PROGRAM RECORD
PROGRAMM-BERICHT
FICHE PROGRAMME

PROGRAMMER / PROGRAMMIERER / PROGRAMMEUR	Horn
DATE / DATUM / DATE	20.9.78
Partitioning (Op 17) / Speicher-Bereichsverteilung / Partition (Op 17)	4 7 9 5 9
Library Module / Software-Modul / Module enfichable	--
Printer / Drucker / Imprimante	YES
Cards / Karten / Cartes	1

PROGRAM DESCRIPTION ● PROGRAMM BESCHREIBUNG ● DESCRIPTION DU PROGRAMME

Calculate R_1, R_2, R_5, R_6, R_7, R_8

R_q will be set equal to $10k\Omega$ if not defined.

K will be maximum ($R_2 \to \infty$) if as 0. declared.

Otherwise $0 < K < K_{max} < 1$. With $\omega_z = \omega_p$ program

stops. Choose starting P

between 0.1-0.3.

$$T(s) = K \cdot \frac{s^2 + \omega_z^2}{s^2 + \frac{\omega_p}{q_p}s + \omega_p^2}$$

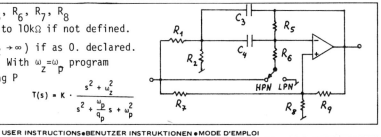

USER INSTRUCTIONS ● BENUTZER INSTRUKTIONEN ● MODE D'EMPLOI

STEP / SCHRITT / SEQUENCE	PROCEDURE / PROZEDUR / PROCEDURE	ENTER / EINGABE / INTRODUIRE	PRESS / BEFEHL / APPUYER SUR		DISPLAY / ANZEIGE / AFFICHAGE
1	Text preparation if printer is available		2nd	A'	22 36 33.
2	zero-frequency [Hz]	f_z	A		f_z
3	pole-frequency [Hz]	f_p	B		f_p
4	pole-Q	q_p	C		q_p
5	C_3 [F]	C_3	D		C_3
6	C_4 [F]	C_4	E		C_4
7	set K=0 for K_{max} or choose $0<K<K_{max}<1$	K	2nd	C'	K
8	if required R_q [kΩ]	R_q	2nd	D'	R_q
9	choose P	P	2nd	E'	0.00
	repeat step 9 in order to find an optimal solution				
10	to avoid the printing of R_1-Q		2nd	St flg 0	0.00
11	to print R_1-Q after step 9		2nd	B'	1.00
12	delete step 10		INV	2nd St flg 0	0.00

USER DEFINED KEYS / PROGRAMM-ADRESSTASTEN / TOUCHES UTILISATEUR		DATA REGISTERS / DATENSPEICHER / REGISTRES-MEMOIRE (INV Lst)		LABELS (Op 08) / LABELS (Op 08) / LABELS (Op 08)
A	f_z	0		INV __ lnx __ CE __ CLR __ x:t __ x² __ ✔
B	f_p	1		√x __ 1/x ✔ STO __ RCL __ SUM __ y^x __
C	q_p	2		EE __ (__) __ + __ GTO __ X __
D	C_3	3	see	SBR __ - __ RST __ ÷ __ R/S __ . __
E	C_4	4		+/- __ = __ CLR __ INV __ __ __
A'	TEXT	5	page 5	
B'	PRINT	6		
C'	K	7		
D'	R_q	8		
E'	P-RUN	9		

FLAGS / FLAGS / DRAPEAUX	0	1	2	3	4	5	6	7	8	9

P-N 0000.000.0309

000	76	LBL	060	03	3	120	01	1
001	17	B'	061	05	5	121	03	3
002	22	INV	062	00	0	122	03	3
003	57	ENG	063	02	2	123	42	STO
004	73	RC*	064	42	STO	124	32	32
005	30	30	065	43	43	125	03	3
006	69	OP	066	85	+	126	04	4
007	04	04	067	01	1	127	42	STO
008	57	ENG	068	95	=	128	31	31
009	73	RC*	069	42	STO	129	03	3
010	00	00	070	42	42	130	03	3
011	69	OP	071	01	1	131	42	STO
012	06	06	072	05	5	132	45	45
013	01	1	073	00	0	133	02	2
014	22	INV	074	04	4	134	02	2
015	44	SUM	075	42	STO	135	03	3
016	30	30	076	41	41	136	06	6
017	97	DSZ	077	85	+	137	03	3
018	00	00	078	01	1	138	03	3
019	00	00	079	95	=	139	42	STO
020	02	02	080	42	STO	140	44	44
021	98	ADV	081	40	40	141	92	RTN
022	92	RTN	082	03	3	142	76	LBL
023	76	LBL	083	05	5	143	10	E'
024	11	A	084	00	0	144	42	STO
025	42	STO	085	06	6	145	15	15
026	03	03	086	42	STO	146	01	1
027	92	RTN	087	39	39	147	03	3
028	76	LBL	088	85	+	148	42	STO
029	12	B	089	01	1	149	00	00
030	42	STO	090	95	=	150	04	4
031	02	02	091	42	STO	151	03	3
032	92	RTN	092	38	38	152	42	STO
033	76	LBL	093	03	3	153	30	30
034	13	C	094	05	5	154	43	RCL
035	42	STO	095	01	1	155	02	02
036	01	01	096	00	0	156	75	-
037	92	RTN	097	42	STO	157	43	RCL
038	76	LBL	098	37	37	158	03	03
039	14	D	099	85	+	159	95	=
040	42	STO	100	01	1	160	69	OP
041	11	11	101	95	=	161	10	10
042	92	RTN	102	42	STO	162	67	EQ
043	76	LBL	103	36	36	163	91	R/S
044	15	E	104	85	+	164	85	+
045	42	STO	105	01	1	165	01	1
046	10	10	106	95	=	166	95	=
047	92	RTN	107	42	STO	167	55	÷
048	76	LBL	108	35	35	168	02	2
049	18	C'	109	02	2	169	95	=
050	42	STO	110	06	6	170	42	STO
051	04	04	111	42	STO	171	22	22
052	92	RTN	112	34	34	172	43	RCL
053	76	LBL	113	02	2	173	10	10
054	19	D'	114	01	1	174	55	÷
055	42	STO	115	04	4	175	43	RCL
056	05	05	116	06	6	176	11	11
057	92	RTN	117	42	STO	177	85	+
058	76	LBL	118	33	33	178	01	1
059	16	A'	119	02	2	179	95	=

180	42	STO	240	19	19	300	23	23
181	16	16	241	65	×	301	95	=
182	65	×	242	43	RCL	302	35	1/X
183	43	RCL	243	16	16	303	65	×
184	15	15	244	85	+	304	43	RCL
185	65	×	245	01	1	305	18	18
186	04	4	246	95	=	306	65	×
187	65	×	247	35	1/X	307	43	RCL
188	43	RCL	248	65	×	308	20	20
189	01	01	249	53	(	309	65	×
190	33	X²	250	01	1	310	53	(
191	85	+	251	85	+	311	01	1
192	01	1	252	43	RCL	312	75	-
193	95	=	253	15	15	313	43	RCL
194	34	√X	254	54	)	314	22	22
195	75	-	255	42	STO	315	55	÷
196	01	1	256	20	20	316	43	RCL
197	95	=	257	55	÷	317	04	04
198	65	×	258	43	RCL	318	54	)
199	53	(	259	04	04	319	95	=
200	02	2	260	67	EQ	320	42	STO
201	65	×	261	33	X²	321	08	08
202	89	π	262	55	÷	322	35	1/X
203	65	×	263	43	RCL	323	65	×
204	43	RCL	264	18	18	324	43	RCL
205	02	02	265	95	=	325	15	15
206	55	÷	266	42	STO	326	85	+
207	43	RCL	267	13	13	327	53	(
208	01	01	268	35	1/X	328	43	RCL
209	54	)	269	94	+/-	329	23	23
210	42	STO	270	85	+	330	65	×
211	17	17	271	43	RCL	331	43	RCL
212	55	÷	272	18	18	332	21	21
213	02	2	273	95	=	333	55	÷
214	55	÷	274	35	1/X	334	43	RCL
215	43	RCL	275	42	STO	335	18	18
216	15	15	276	12	12	336	54	)
217	65	×	277	43	RCL	337	42	STO
218	43	RCL	278	01	01	338	24	24
219	11	11	279	65	×	339	95	=
220	95	=	280	43	RCL	340	35	1/X
221	42	STO	281	17	17	341	42	STO
222	18	18	282	95	=	342	09	09
223	35	1/X	283	33	X²	343	35	1/X
224	65	×	284	42	STO	344	85	+
225	43	RCL	285	21	21	345	43	RCL
226	11	11	286	94	+/-	346	08	08
227	95	=	287	85	+	347	35	1/X
228	33	X²	288	43	RCL	348	95	=
229	65	×	289	19	19	349	42	STO
230	53	(	290	95	=	350	25	25
231	02	2	291	65	×	351	65	×
232	65	×	292	53	(	352	53	(
233	89	π	293	43	RCL	353	43	RCL
234	65	×	294	11	11	354	11	11
235	43	RCL	295	65	×	355	35	1/X
236	03	03	296	43	RCL	356	85	+
237	54	)	297	10	10	357	43	RCL
238	33	X²	298	54	)	358	10	10
239	42	STO	299	42	STO	359	35	1/X

360	54	)
361	85	+
362	43	RCL
363	18	18
364	55	÷
365	43	RCL
366	11	11
367	95	=
368	55	÷
369	43	RCL
370	17	17
371	94	+/−
372	85	+
373	01	1
374	95	=
375	50	I×I
376	85	+
377	53	(
378	43	RCL
379	25	25
380	55	÷
381	43	RCL
382	24	24
383	75	−
384	01	1
385	54	)
386	50	I×I
387	65	×
388	43	RCL
389	01	01
390	95	=
391	55	÷
392	02	2
393	65	×
394	43	RCL
395	20	20
396	95	=
397	42	STO
398	14	14
399	43	RCL
400	05	05
401	67	EQ
402	35	1/X
403	65	×
404	43	RCL
405	15	15
406	55	÷
407	43	RCL
408	04	04
409	95	=
410	42	STO
411	07	07
412	55	÷
413	53	(
414	43	RCL
415	04	04
416	35	1/X
417	75	−
418	01	1
419	54	)

420	95	=
421	42	STO
422	06	06
423	43	RCL
424	45	45
425	69	OP
426	04	04
427	43	RCL
428	15	15
429	69	OP
430	06	06
431	43	RCL
432	44	44
433	69	OP
434	04	04
435	43	RCL
436	14	14
437	69	OP
438	06	06
439	98	ADV
440	87	IFF
441	00	00
442	04	04
443	46	46
444	71	SBR
445	17	B'
446	25	CLR
447	92	RTN
448	76	LBL
449	33	X²
450	01	1
451	95	=
452	42	STO
453	04	04
454	43	RCL
455	18	18
456	35	1/X
457	42	STO
458	13	13
459	01	1
460	52	EE
461	09	9
462	00	0
463	42	STO
464	12	12
465	61	GTO
466	02	02
467	77	77
468	92	RTN
469	76	LBL
470	35	1/X
471	01	1
472	52	EE
473	04	4
474	42	STO
475	05	05
476	61	GTO
477	04	04
478	03	03
479	92	RTN

DATA REGISTERS

0	indirect address (13)				
1	Qp		30	indirect address (43)	
2	Fp		31	Qp	
3	Fz		32	Fp	
4	K		33	Fz	
5	R9		34	K	
6	R8		35	R9	
7	R7		36	R8	
8	R6	values	37	R7	text
9	R5		38	R6	
10	C4		39	R5	
11	C3		40	C4	
12	R2		41	C3	
13	R1		42	R2	
14	GSP		43	R1	
15	P		44	GSP	
16	1 + C4/C3		45	P	
17	2 π Fp/Qp				
18	G				
19	(2 π Fz)↑2				
20	1+P				
21	(2 π Fp)↑2				
22	X				
23	C3C4				
24	C3C4(2 π Fp)↑2/G				
25	1/R5 + 1/R6				

226

TI PROGRAMMABLE
PROGRAM RECORD
PROGRAMM-BERICHT
FICHE PROGRAMME

PROGRAMMER / PROGRAMMIERER / PROGRAMMEUR: Horn
DATE / DATUM / DATE: 27.9.78

Partitioning (Op 17) / Speicher-Bereichsverteilung / Partition (Op 17): 4 7 9 5 9
Library Module / Software-Modul / Module enfichable: --

Printer / Drucker / Imprimante: YES
Cards / Karten / Cartes: 1

PROGRAM DESCRIPTION ● PROGRAMM BESCHREIBUNG ● DESCRIPTION DU PROGRAMME

Calculate resistors R_5, R_6, R_7, R_8, R_{10}.
R_9 will be set equal to $10k\Omega$ if not defined.
C_4 can be set to zero in case of $\omega_p > \omega_z$.
For low GSP set $C_1 = C_3 \geq C_2$.

$$T(s) = K \frac{s^2 + \omega_z^2}{s^2 + \frac{\omega_p}{q_p}s + \omega_p^2}$$

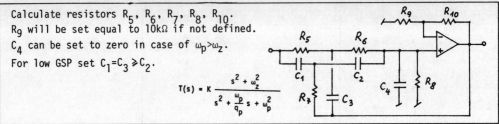

USER INSTRUCTIONS ● BENUTZER INSTRUKTIONEN ● MODE D'EMPLOI

STEP / SCHRITT / SEQUENCE	PROCEDURE / PROZEDUR / PROCEDURE	ENTER / EINGABE / INTRODUIRE	PRESS / BEFEHL / APPUYER SUR		DISPLAY / ANZEIGE / AFFICHAGE
1	Text preparation if printer is available		2nd	A'	
2	zero-frequency [Hz]	f_z	A		f_z
3	pole-frequency [Hz]	f_p	B		f_p
4	pole-quality	q_p	C		q_p
5	C_1 [F]	C_1	D		C_1
6	C_2 [F]	C_2	E		C_2
7	C_3 [F]	C_3	2nd	B'	C_3
8	C_4 [F] (for $\omega_z > \omega_p$)	C_4	2nd	C'	C_4
9	if other than $10k\Omega$ R_9 [Ω]	R_9	2nd	D'	R_9
10	RUN		2nd	E'	
	Repeat step 10 for other C_i-values				

USER DEFINED KEYS / PROGRAMM-ADRESSTASTEN / TOUCHES UTILISATEUR

A	f_z
B	f_p
C	q_p
D	C_1
E	C_2
A'	TEXT
B'	C_3
C'	C_4
D'	R_9
E'	RUN

DATA REGISTERS / DATENSPEICHER / REGISTRES-MEMOIRE (INV)

0	
1	
2	
3	
4	see
5	
6	page 5
7	
8	
9	

LABELS (Op 08)

INV   lnx   CE   CLR   x:t   x² ✓
√x̄ ✓   √x   STO ✓   RCL   SUM   yˣ
EE   (   )   ÷   GTO   X
SBR   −   RST   +   R/S   ·
+/−   =   CLR   INV

FLAGS / FLAGS / DRAPEAUX: 0 1 2 3 4 5 6 7 8 9

P/N 0000.000.0309

000	76	LBL	060	42	STO	120	03	3	
001	42	STO	061	07	07	121	95	=	
002	22	INV	062	92	RTN	122	42	STO	
003	57	ENG	063	76	LBL	123	39	39	
004	73	RC*	064	16	A'	124	85	+	
005	30	30	065	03	3	125	01	1	
006	69	OP	066	07	7	126	95	=	
007	04	04	067	03	3	127	42	STO	
008	57	ENG	068	02	2	128	38	38	
009	73	RC*	069	03	3	129	85	+	
010	00	00	070	02	2	130	01	1	
011	69	OP	071	00	0	131	95	=	
012	06	06	072	00	0	132	42	STO	
013	01	1	073	42	STO	133	37	37	
014	22	INV	074	46	46	134	03	3	
015	44	SUM	075	03	3	135	05	5	
016	30	30	076	06	6	136	00	0	
017	97	DSZ	077	03	3	137	02	2	
018	00	00	078	00	0	138	00	0	
019	00	00	079	01	1	139	01	1	
020	02	02	080	03	3	140	42	STO	
021	98	ADV	081	02	2	141	36	36	
022	92	RTN	082	07	7	142	02	2	
023	76	LBL	083	02	2	143	01	1	
024	11	A	084	07	7	144	04	4	
025	42	STO	085	42	STO	145	06	6	
026	05	05	086	47	47	146	42	STO	
027	92	RTN	087	01	1	147	35	35	
028	76	LBL	088	05	5	148	02	2	
029	12	B	089	00	0	149	01	1	
030	42	STO	090	02	2	150	03	3	
031	04	04	091	42	STO	151	03	3	
032	92	RTN	092	45	45	152	42	STO	
033	76	LBL	093	85	+	153	34	34	
034	13	C	094	01	1	154	03	3	
035	42	STO	095	95	=	155	04	4	
036	03	03	096	42	STO	156	42	STO	
037	92	RTN	097	44	44	157	33	33	
038	76	LBL	098	85	+	158	02	2	
039	14	D	099	01	1	159	06	6	
040	42	STO	100	95	=	160	42	STO	
041	15	15	101	42	STO	161	32	32	
042	92	RTN	102	43	43	162	02	2	
043	76	LBL	103	85	+	163	02	2	
044	15	E	104	01	1	164	03	3	
045	42	STO	105	95	=	165	06	6	
046	14	14	106	42	STO	166	03	3	
047	92	RTN	107	42	42	167	03	3	
048	76	LBL	108	03	3	168	42	STO	
049	17	B'	109	05	5	169	31	31	
050	42	STO	110	00	0	170	92	RTN	
051	13	13	111	06	6	171	76	LBL	
052	92	RTN	112	42	STO	172	10	E'	
053	76	LBL	113	41	41	173	43	RCL	
054	18	C'	114	85	+	174	14	14	
055	42	STO	115	01	1	175	55	÷	
056	12	12	116	95	=	176	43	RCL	
057	92	RTN	117	42	STO	177	15	15	
058	76	LBL	118	40	40	178	85	+	
059	19	D'	119	85	+	179	42	STO	

180	16	16
181	01	1
182	95	=
183	42	STO
184	17	17
185	65	×
186	53	(
187	01	1
188	85	+
189	43	RCL
190	14	14
191	55	÷
192	43	RCL
193	13	13
194	54	)
195	95	=
196	34	ΓX
197	35	1/X
198	55	÷
199	02	2
200	65	×
201	42	STO
202	26	26
203	53	(
204	02	2
205	65	×
206	89	⫪
207	65	×
208	43	RCL
209	05	05
210	54	)
211	42	STO
212	18	18
213	65	×
214	02	2
215	65	×
216	53	(
217	43	RCL
218	14	14
219	85	+
220	43	RCL
221	13	13
222	54	)
223	95	=
224	35	1/X
225	42	STO
226	11	11
227	35	1/X
228	65	×
229	53	(
230	43	RCL
231	17	17
232	55	÷
233	43	RCL
234	14	14
235	54	)
236	42	STO
237	20	20
238	55	÷
239	43	RCL

240	13	13
241	55	÷
242	43	RCL
243	18	18
244	33	X²
245	42	STO
246	19	19
247	95	=
248	42	STO
249	10	10
250	85	+
251	43	RCL
252	11	11
253	95	=
254	42	STO
255	21	21
256	35	1/X
257	55	÷
258	43	RCL
259	19	19
260	55	÷
261	43	RCL
262	15	15
263	55	÷
264	43	RCL
265	14	14
266	95	=
267	42	STO
268	09	09
269	02	2
270	65	×
271	89	⫪
272	65	×
273	43	RCL
274	04	04
275	55	÷
276	43	RCL
277	18	18
278	65	×
279	42	STO
280	22	22
281	53	(
282	43	RCL
283	22	22
284	65	×
285	53	(
286	01	1
287	85	+
288	43	RCL
289	12	12
290	65	×
291	43	RCL
292	20	20
293	54	)
294	42	STO
295	23	23
296	54	)
297	42	STO
298	24	24
299	75	-

300	01	1
301	95	=
302	22	INV
303	77	GE
304	35	1/X
305	67	EQ
306	34	ΓX
307	35	1/X
308	65	×
309	43	RCL
310	21	21
311	95	=
312	42	STO
313	08	08
314	43	RCL
315	07	07
316	67	EQ
317	33	X²
318	65	×
319	43	RCL
320	26	26
321	65	×
322	53	(
323	43	RCL
324	21	21
325	65	×
326	43	RCL
327	12	12
328	65	×
329	43	RCL
330	18	18
331	85	+
332	01	1
333	55	÷
334	43	RCL
335	08	08
336	55	÷
337	43	RCL
338	18	18
339	65	×
340	43	RCL
341	20	20
342	75	-
343	43	RCL
344	24	24
345	55	÷
346	43	RCL
347	03	03
348	54	)
349	95	=
350	42	STO
351	06	06
352	55	÷
353	43	RCL
354	07	07
355	85	+
356	01	1
357	95	=
358	42	STO
359	25	25

```
360  33  X²
361  65  ×
362  43  RCL
363  03   03
364  55  ÷
365  43  RCL
366  24   24
367  65  ×
368  53  (
369  53  (
370  43  RCL
371  11   11
372  55  ÷
373  43  RCL
374  10   10
375  65  ×
376  43  RCL
377  20   20
378  65  ×
379  43  RCL
380  13   13
381  54  )
382  34  ΓX
383  85  +
384  53  (
385  43  RCL
386  21   21
387  65  ×
388  43  RCL
389  16   16
390  55  ÷
391  43  RCL
392  09   09
393  54  )
394  34  ΓX
395  54  )
396  95  =
397  42  STO
398  01   01
399  43  RCL
400  25   25
401  55  ÷
402  43  RCL
403  23   23
404  95  =
405  42  STO
406  02   02
407  01  1
408  05  5
409  42  STO
410  00   00
411  04  4
412  05  5
413  42  STO
414  30   30
415  71  SBR
416  42  STO
417  25  CLR
418  92  RTN
419  76  LBL
```

```
420  34  ΓX
421  01  1
422  52  EE
423  09  9
424  00  0
425  42  STO
426  08   08
427  61  GTO
428  03   03
429  14   14
430  92  RTN
431  76  LBL
432  33  X²
433  01  1
434  52  EE
435  04  4
436  42  STO
437  07   07
438  61  GTO
439  03   03
440  18   18
441  92  RTN
442  76  LBL
443  35  1/X
444  22  INV
445  57  ENG
446  69  OP
447  00   00
448  43  RCL
449  42   42
450  69  OP
451  01   01
452  43  RCL
453  46   46
454  69  OP
455  02   02
456  43  RCL
457  47   47
458  69  OP
459  03   03
460  69  OP
461  05   05
462  98  ADV
463  25  CLR
464  91  R/S
465  92  RTN
```

DATA REGISTERS

0	indirect address (15)		30	indirect address (45)	
1	GSP		31	GSP	
2	K		32	K	
3	Qp		33	Qp	
4	Fp		34	Fp	
5	Fz		35	Fz	
6	R10		36	R10	
7	R9		37	R9	
8	R8	values	38	R8	text
9	R7		39	R7	
10	R6		40	R6	
11	R5		41	R5	
12	C4		42	C4	
13	C3		43	C3	
14	C2		44	C2	
15	C1		45	C1	
16	C2/C1		46	TOO	
17	1 + C2/C1		47	SMALL	
18	$2 \pi Fz$				
19	$(2 \pi Fz)^2$				
20	$(C1+C2)/C1C2 = 1/Cs$				
21	R5+R6 = Rs				
22	Fp/Fz				
23	1 + C4/Cs				
24	(1+C4/Cs)Fp/Fz				
25	1 + R10/R9				
26	$\hat{Q}$				

TITLE / TITEL / TITRE	16. HQ 5	PAGE / SEITE / PAGE	1 OF / VON / DE 5	TI PROGRAMMABLE

PROGRAM RECORD
PROGRAMM-BERICHT
FICHE PROGRAMME

PROGRAMMER / PROGRAMMIERER / PROGRAMMEUR: Horn

DATE / DATUM / DATE: 6.10.78

Partitioning (Op 17) / Speicher-Bereichsverteilung / Partition (Op 17): 4 7 9 5 9

Library Module / Software-Modul / Module enfichable: --

Printer / Drucker / Imprimante: YES

Cards / Karten / Cartes: 1

PROGRAM DESCRIPTION ● PROGRAMM BESCHREIBUNG ● DESCRIPTION DU PROGRAMME

Calculate values of resistors
for following functions:

LP = lowpass   BP = bandpass   HP = highpass

AP = allpass   BR = band rejection

$$T(s) = \frac{Y_1 Y_4 Y_5 + Y_3 Y_7 (Y_2+Y_6) - Y_3 Y_5 Y_8}{Y_1 Y_4 (Y_5+Y_6) + Y_2 Y_3 (Y_7+Y_8)}$$

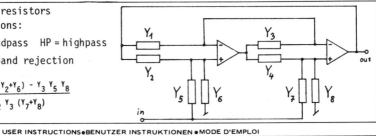

USER INSTRUCTIONS ● BENUTZER INSTRUKTIONEN ● MODE D'EMPLOI

STEP / SCHRITT / SEQUENCE	PROCEDURE / PROZEDUR / PROCEDURE	ENTER / EINGABE / INTRODUIRE	PRESS / BEFEHL / APPUYER SUR	DISPLAY / ANZEIGE / AFFICHAGE
1	enter frequency F [Hz]	F	A	F
2	enter quality Q	Q	B	Q
3	enter capacitor value C [F]	C	C	C
4	calculate optimal resistor value R_O		D	R_O
5	enter discrete resistor value R_d, which is close to R_O	R_d	E	R_d
6	run required function f' (LP→A', BP→B', HP→C', AP→D', BR→E')		2nd f'	0.00

USER DEFINED KEYS / PROGRAMM-ADRESSTASTEN / TOUCHES UTILISATEUR

A	F
B	Q
C	C
D	R_O
E	R_d
A'	LP
B'	BP
C'	HP
D'	AP
E'	BR

DATA REGISTERS / DATENSPEICHER / REGISTRES-MEMOIRE (INV)

0	
1	
2	
3	
4	see
5	
6	page 5
7	
8	
9	

LABELS (Op 08)

INV ✔ lnx __ CE ✔ CLR ✔ x:t __ x² __
√ __ 1/x ✔ STO __ RCL __ SUM __ yˣ ✔
EE ✔ (__) __ ÷ __ GTO ✔ X ✔
SBR __ − __ RST __ + __ R/S ✔ . __
+/− __ = __ CLR __ INV __

FLAGS / FLAGS / DRAPEAUX

0	1	2	3	4	5	6	7	8	9

P/N 0000 000 0309

000	76	LBL	060	95	=	120	95	=
001	42	STO	061	42	STO	121	42	STO
002	03	3	062	36	36	122	17	17
003	04	4	063	01	1	123	33	X²
004	42	STO	064	05	5	124	65	×
005	31	31	065	00	0	125	43	RCL
006	02	2	066	04	4	126	16	16
007	01	1	067	42	STO	127	95	=
008	42	STO	068	37	37	128	35	1/X
009	32	32	069	92	RTN	129	42	STO
010	92	RTN	070	76	LBL	130	18	18
011	76	LBL	071	35	1/X	131	43	RCL
012	24	CE	072	22	INV	132	01	01
013	03	3	073	57	ENG	133	55	÷
014	05	5	074	73	RC*	134	43	RCL
015	00	0	075	30	30	135	17	17
016	07	7	076	69	OP	136	95	=
017	42	STO	077	04	04	137	92	RTN
018	35	35	078	57	ENG	138	76	LBL
019	92	RTN	079	73	RC*	139	11	A
020	76	LBL	080	00	00	140	42	STO
021	61	GTO	081	69	OP	141	02	02
022	03	3	082	06	06	142	92	RTN
023	09	9	083	01	1	143	76	LBL
024	42	STO	084	22	INV	144	12	B
025	30	30	085	44	SUM	145	42	STO
026	09	9	086	30	30	146	01	01
027	42	STO	087	97	DSZ	147	92	RTN
028	00	00	088	00	00	148	76	LBL
029	92	RTN	089	00	00	149	13	C
030	76	LBL	090	72	72	150	42	STO
031	25	CLR	091	98	ADV	151	15	15
032	03	3	092	92	RTN	152	92	RTN
033	05	5	093	76	LBL	153	76	LBL
034	01	1	094	14	D	154	15	E
035	01	1	095	43	RCL	155	42	STO
036	42	STO	096	02	02	156	16	16
037	33	33	097	65	×	157	92	RTN
038	01	1	098	02	2	158	76	LBL
039	05	5	099	65	×	159	16	A'
040	01	1	100	89	π	160	02	2
041	00	0	101	65	×	161	07	7
042	42	STO	102	43	RCL	162	03	3
043	34	34	103	15	15	163	03	3
044	92	RTN	104	95	=	164	71	SBR
045	76	LBL	105	35	1/X	165	52	EE
046	22	INV	106	42	STO	166	71	SBR
047	03	3	107	16	16	167	42	STO
048	05	5	108	92	RTN	168	01	1
049	00	0	109	76	LBL	169	05	5
050	02	2	110	45	YX	170	00	0
051	42	STO	111	02	2	171	02	2
052	39	39	112	65	×	172	42	STO
053	85	+	113	89	π	173	38	38
054	01	1	114	65	×	174	85	+
055	95	=	115	43	RCL	175	03	3
056	42	STO	116	02	02	176	95	=
057	38	38	117	65	×	177	42	STO
058	85	+	118	43	RCL	178	35	35
059	02	2	119	15	15	179	03	3

233

```
180  05  5
181  00  0
182  02  2
183  42  STO
184  39  39
185  85  +
186  01  1
187  95  =
188  42  STO
189  37  37
190  85  +
191  01  1
192  95  =
193  42  STO
194  36  36
195  85  +
196  03  3
197  95  =
198  42  STO
199  34  34
200  85  +
201  03  3
202  95  =
203  42  STO
204  33  33
205  71  SBR
206  61  GTO
207  43  RCL
208  15  15
209  42  STO
210  08  08
211  42  STO
212  05  05
213  71  SBR
214  45  Y×
215  42  STO
216  09  09
217  43  RCL
218  16  16
219  42  STO
220  07  07
221  42  STO
222  06  06
223  42  STO
224  04  04
225  43  RCL
226  18  18
227  42  STO
228  03  03
229  71  SBR
230  35  1/X
231  25  CLR
232  92  RTN
233  76  LBL
234  17  B'
235  01  1
236  04  4
237  03  3
238  03  3
239  71  SBR

240  52  EE
241  71  SBR
242  42  STO
243  71  SBR
244  22  INV
245  71  SBR
246  24  CE
247  03  3
248  05  5
249  01  1
250  00  0
251  42  STO
252  34  34
253  01  1
254  05  5
255  01  1
256  01  1
257  42  STO
258  33  33
259  71  SBR
260  61  GTO
261  43  RCL
262  15  15
263  42  STO
264  07  07
265  42  STO
266  03  03
267  43  RCL
268  16  16
269  42  STO
270  09  09
271  42  STO
272  08  08
273  42  STO
274  05  05
275  71  SBR
276  45  Y×
277  42  STO
278  04  04
279  43  RCL
280  18  18
281  42  STO
282  06  06
283  71  SBR
284  35  1/X
285  25  CLR
286  92  RTN
287  76  LBL
288  18  C'
289  02  2
290  03  3
291  03  3
292  03  3
293  71  SBR
294  52  EE
295  71  SBR
296  42  STO
297  71  SBR
298  25  CLR
299  71  SBR

300  24  CE
301  71  SBR
302  22  INV
303  71  SBR
304  61  GTO
305  43  RCL
306  15  15
307  42  STO
308  07  07
309  42  STO
310  04  04
311  43  RCL
312  16  16
313  42  STO
314  09  09
315  42  STO
316  08  08
317  42  STO
318  05  05
319  71  SBR
320  45  Y×
321  42  STO
322  03  03
323  43  RCL
324  18  18
325  42  STO
326  06  06
327  71  SBR
328  35  1/X
329  25  CLR
330  92  RTN
331  76  LBL
332  19  D'
333  01  1
334  03  3
335  03  3
336  03  3
337  71  SBR
338  52  EE
339  71  SBR
340  42  STO
341  71  SBR
342  25  CLR
343  71  SBR
344  22  INV
345  03  3
346  05  5
347  00  0
348  06  6
349  42  STO
350  35  35
351  71  SBR
352  61  GTO
353  43  RCL
354  15  15
355  42  STO
356  07  07
357  42  STO
358  04  04
359  43  RCL
```

```
360   16   16
361   42   STO
362   09   09
363   42   STO
364   08   08
365   42   STO
366   05   05
367   71   SBR
368   45   YX
369   42   STO
370   03   03
371   43   RCL
372   18   18
373   42   STO
374   06   06
375   71   SBR
376   35   1/X
377   25   CLR
378   92   RTN
379   76   LBL
380   10   E'
381   01   1
382   04   4
383   03   3
384   05   5
385   71   SBR
386   52   EE
387   71   SBR
388   42   STO
389   71   SBR
390   25   CLR
391   03   3
392   05   5
393   00   0
394   02   2
395   42   STO
396   40   40
397   85   +
398   01   1
399   95   =
400   42   STO
401   39   39
402   85   +
403   02   2
404   95   =
405   42   STO
406   37   37
407   85   +
408   01   1
409   95   =
410   42   STO
411   36   36
412   85   +
413   04   4
414   95   =
415   42   STO
416   35   35
417   01   1
418   05   5
419   00   0
```

```
420   04   4
421   42   STO
422   38   38
423   04   4
424   00   0
425   42   STO
426   30   30
427   01   1
428   00   0
429   42   STO
430   00   00
431   43   RCL
432   15   15
433   42   STO
434   04   04
435   42   STO
436   08   08
437   43   RCL
438   16   16
439   42   STO
440   10   10
441   42   STO
442   09   09
443   42   STO
444   06   06
445   71   SBR
446   45   YX
447   65   ×
448   02   2
449   95   =
450   42   STO
451   03   03
452   42   STO
453   05   05
454   43   RCL
455   18   18
456   42   STO
457   07   07
458   71   SBR
459   35   1/X
460   25   CLR
461   92   RTN
462   76   LBL
463   52   EE
464   98   ADV
465   69   OP
466   00   00
467   69   OP
468   02   02
469   69   OP
470   05   05
471   98   ADV
472   92   RTN
```

DATA REGISTERS

value	text	LP	BP	HP	AP	BR
10	40	-	-	-	-	R1
09	39	R1	R1	R1	R1	R2
08	38	C1	R2	R2	R2	C3
07	37	R2	C3	C3	C3	R4
06	36	R3	R4	R4	R4	R5
05	35	C4	R6	R6	R5	R7
04	34	R6	R7	C7	C7	C7
03	33	R7	C8	R8	R8	R8

for all functions

value	exp.	text
00	ind.	
30	add.	
01	Q	31
02	F	32
15	C	
16	Rd	
17	ω_p	
18	$\dfrac{1}{Rd\, \omega_p^2 c^2}$	

TITLE TITEL TITRE	17. LPN/HPN - HQ	PAGE SEITE PAGE	1 OF VON DE 3	TI PROGRAMMABLE **PROGRAM RECORD** **PROGRAMM-BERICHT** **FICHE PROGRAMME**
PROGRAMMER PROGRAMMIERER PROGRAMMEUR	Horn	DATE DATUM DATE	6.10.78	

Partitioning (Op 17)
Speicher-Bereichsverteilung ⌊4,7,9,5,9⌋ Library Module -- Printer YES   Cards 1
Partition (Op 17)   Software-Modul   Drucker   Karten
 Module enfichable   Imprimante   Cartes

PROGRAM DESCRIPTION ● PROGRAMM BESCHREIBUNG ● DESCRIPTION DU PROGRAMME

Calculate resistor values

for LPN or HPN

Program stops if $\omega_z = \omega_p$

$$T(s) = \frac{s^2 + \omega_z^2}{s^2 + \frac{\omega_p}{q_p} s + \omega_p^2}$$

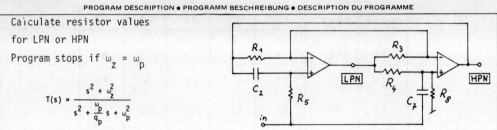

USER INSTRUCTIONS ● BENUTZER INSTRUKTIONEN ● MODE D'EMPLOI

STEP SCHRITT SEQUENCE	PROCEDURE PROZEDUR PROCEDURE	ENTER EINGABE INTRODUIRE	PRESS BEFEHL APPUYER SUR		DISPLAY ANZEIGE AFFICHAGE
1	Text preparation if printer is available		2nd	A'	34.
2	enter zero-frequency F_z [Hz]	F_z	A		F_z
3	enter pole-frequency F_p [Hz]	F_p	B		F_p
4	enter quality Q	Q	C		Q
5	enter capacitor value C [F]	C	D		C
6	calculate optimal resistor value R_O		E		R_O
7	run with discrete resistor value R_d, which is close to R_O	R_d [Ω]	2nd	E'	0.00

USER DEFINED KEYS PROGRAMM-ADRESSTASTEN TOUCHES UTILISATEUR		DATA REGISTERS DATENSPEICHER REGISTRES-MEMOIRE	([INV] [LIST])	LABELS (Op 08) LABELS (Op 08) LABELS (Op 08)
A	F_z	0 0,30 indirect addr.	1 0 R_1	
B	F_p	0 1 Q	1	
C	Q	0 2 F_p	2	
D	C	0 3 F_z	3 Text in	
E	R_O	0 4 R_8	4 reg. 31-40	
A'	TEXT	0 5 C_7	5	
B'		0 6 R_5	6	
C'		0 7 R_4	7	
D'		0 8 R_3	8	
E'	R_d-RUN	0 9 C_2	9	

FLAGS
FLAGS 0   1   2   3   4   5   6   7   8   9
DRAPEAUX

P N 0000 000 0309

000	76	LBL
001	35	1/X
002	22	INV
003	57	ENG
004	73	RC*
005	30	30
006	69	OP
007	04	04
008	57	ENG
009	73	RC*
010	00	00
011	69	OP
012	06	06
013	01	1
014	22	INV
015	44	SUM
016	30	30
017	97	DSZ
018	00	00
019	00	00
020	02	02
021	98	ADV
022	92	RTN
023	76	LBL
024	16	A'
025	03	3
026	05	5
027	00	0
028	02	2
029	42	STO
030	40	40
031	85	+
032	02	2
033	95	=
034	42	STO
035	38	38
036	85	+
037	01	1
038	95	=
039	42	STO
040	37	37
041	85	+
042	01	1
043	95	=
044	42	STO
045	36	36
046	85	+
047	05	5
048	95	=
049	42	STO
050	34	34
051	01	1
052	05	5
053	00	0
054	03	3
055	42	STO
056	39	39
057	85	+
058	07	7
059	95	=
060	42	STO
061	35	35
062	02	2
063	01	1
064	03	3
065	03	3
066	42	STO
067	32	32
068	02	2
069	01	1
070	04	4
071	06	6
072	42	STO
073	33	33
074	03	3
075	04	4
076	42	STO
077	31	31
078	92	RTN
079	76	LBL
080	91	R/S
081	91	R/S
082	92	RTN
083	76	LBL
084	11	A
085	42	STO
086	03	03
087	92	RTN
088	76	LBL
089	12	B
090	42	STO
091	02	02
092	92	RTN
093	76	LBL
094	13	C
095	42	STO
096	01	01
097	92	RTN
098	76	LBL
099	14	D
100	42	STO
101	09	09
102	42	STO
103	05	05
104	92	RTN
105	76	LBL
106	15	E
107	43	RCL
108	05	05
109	65	x
110	43	RCL
111	02	02
112	65	x
113	02	2
114	65	x
115	89	π
116	95	=
117	35	1/X
118	92	RTN
119	76	LBL

```
120  42  STO        180  15  E
121  65  ×          181  65  ×
122  43  RCL        182  43  RCL
123  04  04         183  01  01
124  95  =          184  95  =
125  42  STO        185  42  STO
126  07  07         186  04  04
127  92  RTN        187  43  RCL
128  76  LBL        188  03  03
129  85  +          189  55  ÷
130  71  SBR        190  43  RCL
131  42  STO        191  02  02
132  02  2          192  95  =
133  07  7          193  33  X²
134  03  3          194  75  -
135  03  3          195  01  1
136  03  3          196  95  =
137  01  1          197  67  EQ
138  71  SBR        198  91  R/S
139  52  EE         199  77  GE
140  91  R/S        200  85  +
141  92  RTN        201  94  +/-
142  76  LBL        202  71  SBR
143  52  EE         203  42  STO
144  98  ADV        204  02  2
145  69  OP         205  03  3
146  00  00         206  03  3
147  69  OP         207  03  3
148  02  02         208  03  3
149  69  OP         209  01  1
150  05  05         210  71  SBR
151  98  ADV        211  52  EE
152  71  SBR        212  92  RTN
153  15  E
154  33  X²
155  55  ÷
156  43  RCL
157  07  07
158  95  =
159  42  STO
160  06  06
161  01  1
162  00  0
163  42  STO
164  00  00
165  04  4
166  00  0
167  42  STO
168  30  30
169  71  SBR
170  35  1/X
171  25  CLR
172  92  RTN
173  76  LBL
174  10  E'
175  42  STO
176  10  10
177  42  STO
178  08  08
179  71  SBR
```

TITLE / TITEL / TITRE	18. GP-1	PAGE / SEITE / PAGE	1	OF / VON / DE	3	TI PROGRAMMABLE

TI PROGRAMMABLE
PROGRAM RECORD
PROGRAMM-BERICHT
FICHE PROGRAMME

PROGRAMMER / PROGRAMMIERER / PROGRAMMEUR	Horn	DATE / DATUM / DATE	9.10.78

Partitioning (Op 17) / Speicher-Bereichsverteilung / Partition (Op 17) 4 7 9 5 9
Library Module / Software-Modul / Module enfichable --
Printer / Drucker / Imprimante YES
Cards / Karten / Cartes 1

PROGRAM DESCRIPTION ● PROGRAMM BESCHREIBUNG ● DESCRIPTION DU PROGRAMME

Calculate resistor values

$$T_{HP} = K_H \frac{s^2}{s^2 + \frac{\omega_p}{q_p}s + \omega_p^2}$$

$$T_{BP} = -K_B \frac{\frac{\omega_p}{q_p}s}{s^2 + \frac{\omega_p}{q_p}s + \omega_p^2}$$

$$T_{LP} = K_L \frac{\omega_p^2}{s^2 + \frac{\omega_p}{q_p}s + \omega_p^2}$$

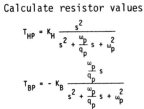
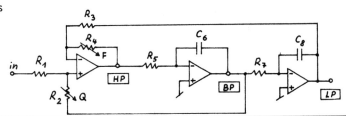

INSTRUCTIONS ● BENUTZER INSTRUKTIONEN ● MODE D'EMPLOI

STEP / SCHRITT / SEQUENCE	PROCEDURE / PROZEDUR / PROCEDURE	ENTER / EINGABE / INTRODUIRE	PRESS / BEFEHL / APPUYER SUR		DISPLAY / ANZEIGE / AFFICHAGE
1	Text preparation if printer is available		2nd	A'	34.
2	enter frequency F [Hz]	F	A		F
3	enter quality Q	Q	B		Q
4	enter capacitor value C [F]	C	C		C
5	calculate optimal resistor value R_o [Ω]		D		R_o
6	enter discrete resistor value R_d [Ω]	R_d	E		R_d
	which is close to R_o				
7	run program		2nd	E'	0.00

USER DEFINED KEYS / PROGRAMM-ADRESSTASTEN / TOUCHES UTILISATEUR		DATA REGISTERS / DATENSPEICHER / REGISTRES-MEMOIRE		(INV □)		LABELS (Op 08) / LABELS (Op 08) / LABELS (Op 08)
A	F	0₀30	indirect addr.	0	R_4	
B	Q	0₁	Q	1	R_3	
C	C	0₂	F	2	R_2	
D	R_o	0₃	KL	3	R_1	
E	R_d	0₄	KB	4	R_4/R_d	
A'	TEXT	0₅	KH	5	$1 + R_4/R_d$	
B'		0₆	C_8	6		
C'		0₇	R_7	7	Text in	
D'		0₈	C_6	8	reg. 31-43	
E'	RUN	0₉	R_5	9		

FLAGS / FLAGS / DRAPEAUX 0 1 2 3 4 5 6 7 8 9

P/N 0000 000 0309

000	76	LBL	060	42	STO	
001	34	ΓX	061	09	09	
002	22	INV	062	42	STO	
003	57	ENG	063	07	07	
004	73	RC*	064	92	RTN	
005	30	30	065	76	LBL	
006	69	OP	066	16	A'	
007	04	04	067	03	3	
008	57	ENG	068	05	5	
009	73	RC*	069	00	0	
010	00	00	070	02	2	
011	69	OP	071	42	STO	
012	06	06	072	43	43	
013	01	1	073	85	+	
014	22	INV	074	01	1	
015	44	SUM	075	95	=	
016	30	30	076	42	STO	
017	97	DSZ	077	42	42	
018	00	00	078	85	+	
019	00	00	079	01	1	
020	02	02	080	95	=	
021	98	ADV	081	42	STO	
022	92	RTN	082	41	41	
023	76	LBL	083	85	+	
024	11	A	084	01	1	
025	42	STO	085	95	=	
026	02	02	086	42	STO	
027	92	RTN	087	40	40	
028	76	LBL	088	85	+	
029	12	B	089	01	1	
030	42	STO	090	95	=	
031	01	01	091	42	STO	
032	92	RTN	092	39	39	
033	76	LBL	093	85	+	
034	13	C	094	04	4	
035	42	STO	095	95	=	
036	06	06	096	42	STO	
037	42	STO	097	37	37	
038	08	08	098	01	1	
039	92	RTN	099	05	5	
040	76	LBL	100	00	0	
041	14	D	101	07	7	
042	02	2	102	42	STO	
043	65	×	103	38	38	
044	89	∏	104	85	+	
045	65	×	105	04	4	
046	43	RCL	106	95	=	
047	02	02	107	42	STO	
048	65	×	108	36	36	
049	43	RCL	109	02	2	
050	06	06	110	06	6	
051	95	=	111	02	2	
052	35	1/X	112	03	3	
053	92	RTN	113	42	STO	
054	76	LBL	114	35	35	
055	15	E	115	02	2	
056	42	STO	116	06	6	
057	13	13	117	01	1	
058	42	STO	118	04	4	
059	11	11	119	42	STO	

120	34	34
121	02	2
122	06	6
123	02	2
124	07	7
125	42	STO
126	33	33
127	02	2
128	01	1
129	42	STO
130	32	32
131	03	3
132	04	4
133	42	STO
134	31	31
135	92	RTN
136	76	LBL
137	10	E'
138	04	4
139	03	3
140	42	STO
141	30	30
142	01	1
143	03	3
144	42	STO
145	00	00
146	71	SBR
147	14	D
148	35	1/X
149	65	×
150	43	RCL
151	07	07
152	95	=
153	33	X²
154	42	STO
155	14	14
156	65	×
157	43	RCL
158	07	07
159	95	=
160	42	STO
161	10	10
162	43	RCL
163	14	14
164	85	+
165	01	1
166	95	=
167	42	STO
168	15	15
169	55	÷
170	43	RCL
171	14	14
172	34	ГX
173	65	×
174	43	RCL
175	01	01
176	75	−
177	01	1
178	95	=
179	42	STO
180	04	04
181	65	×
182	43	RCL
183	07	07
184	95	=
185	42	STO
186	12	12
187	43	RCL
188	04	04
189	35	1/X
190	85	+
191	01	1
192	95	=
193	35	1/X
194	65	×
195	43	RCL
196	15	15
197	55	÷
198	42	STO
199	05	05
200	43	RCL
201	14	14
202	95	=
203	42	STO
204	03	03
205	71	SBR
206	34	ГX
207	25	CLR
208	92	RTN

TITLE TITEL TITRE	19. GP-2	PAGE SEITE PAGE	1 OF 3 VON DE	**TI PROGRAMMABLE**
PROGRAMMER PROGRAMMIERER PROGRAMMEUR	Horn	DATE DATUM DATE	11.10.78	**PROGRAM RECORD** **PROGRAMM-BERICHT** **FICHE PROGRAMME**
Partitioning (Op 17) Speicher-Bereichsverteilung Partition (Op 17)	4 7 9 5 9	Library Module Software-Modul Module enfichable	--	Printer YES Cards 1 Drucker Karten Imprimante Cartes

PROGRAM DESCRIPTION • PROGRAMM BESCHREIBUNG • DESCRIPTION DU PROGRAMME

Calculate resistor values

$$T_{BP} = - K_B \frac{\frac{\omega_p}{q_p} s}{s^2 + \frac{\omega_p}{q_p} s + \omega_p^2}$$

$$T_{LP} = K_L \frac{\omega_p^2}{s^2 + \frac{\omega_p}{q_p} s + \omega_p^2} ; \quad T_{-LP} = - T_{LP}$$

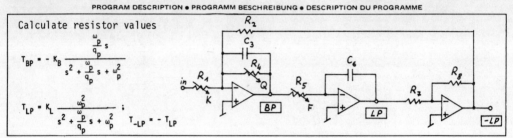

USER INSTRUCTIONS•BENUTZER INSTRUKTIONEN•MODE D'EMPLOI

STEP SCHRITT SEQUENCE	PROCEDURE PROZEDUR PROCEDURE	ENTER EINGABE INTRODUIRE	PRESS BEFEHL APPUYER SUR		DISPLAY ANZEIGE AFFICHAGE
1	Text preparation if printer is available		2nd	A'	34.
2	enter frequency F [Hz]	F	A		F
3	enter quality Q	Q	B		Q
4	enter capacitor value C [F]	C	C		C
5	calculate optimal resistor value R_o [Ω]		D		R_o
6	enter discrete resistor value R_d [Ω],	R_d	E		R_d
	which is close to R_o				
7	enter constant K	K	2nd	C'	K
8	run for bandpass		2nd	D'	0.00
9	run for lowpass		2nd	E'	0.00

USER DEFINED KEYS PROGRAMM-ADRESSTASTEN TOUCHES UTILISATEUR		DATA REGISTERS DATENSPEICHER REGISTRES-MEMOIRE (INV lst)			LABELS (Op 06) LABELS (Op 08) LABELS (Op 08)
A	F	0 0,30 indirect addr.	1 0	C_3	
B	Q	0 1 Q	1 1	R_2	
C	C	0 2 F	1 2	R_1	
D	R_o	0 3 KL	1 3	K	
E	R_d	0 4 KB	4		
A'	TEXT	0 5 R_8	5	text in	
B'		0 6 R_7	6	reg. 31-42	
C'	K	0 7 C_6	7		
D'	RUN-BP	0 8 R_5	8		
E'	RUN-LP	0 9 R_4	9		

FLAGS FLAGS DRAPEAUX	0	1	2	3	4	5	6	7	8	9

© 1977 Texas Instruments

P/N 0000 000 0309

```
000   76 LBL        060   42 STO
001   34 ΓX         061   05   05
002   22 INV        062   92 RTN
003   57 ENG        063   76 LBL
004   73 RC*        064   16 A'
005   30   30       065   03   3
006   69 OP         066   05   5
007   04   04       067   00   0
008   57 ENG        068   02   2
009   73 RC*        069   42 STO
010   00   00       070   42   42
011   69 OP         071   85   +
012   06   06       072   01   1
013   01   1        073   95   =
014   22 INV        074   42 STO
015   44 SUM        075   41   41
016   30   30       076   85   +
017   97 DSZ        077   02   2
018   00   00       078   95   =
019   00   00       079   42 STO
020   02   02       080   39   39
021   98 ADV        081   85   +
022   92 RTN        082   01   1
023   76 LBL        083   95   =
024   11   A        084   42 STO
025   42 STO        085   38   38
026   02   02       086   85   +
027   92 RTN        087   04   4
028   76 LBL        088   95   =
029   12   B        089   42 STO
030   42 STO        090   36   36
031   01   01       091   85   +
032   92 RTN        092   01   1
033   76 LBL        093   95   =
034   13   C        094   42 STO
035   42 STO        095   35   35
036   07   07       096   01   1
037   42 STO        097   05   5
038   10   10       098   00   0
039   92 RTN        099   04   4
040   76 LBL        100   42 STO
041   14   D        101   40   40
042   02   2        102   85   +
043   65   ×        103   03   3
044   89   π        104   95   =
045   65   ×        105   42 STO
046   43 RCL        106   37   37
047   02   02       107   02   2
048   65   ×        108   06   6
049   43 RCL        109   01   1
050   07   07       110   04   4
051   95   =        111   42 STO
052   35 1/X        112   34   34
053   92 RTN        113   02   2
054   76 LBL        114   06   6
055   15   E        115   02   2
056   42 STO        116   07   7
057   11   11       117   42 STO
058   42 STO        118   33   33
059   06   06       119   02   2
```

244

120	01	1
121	42	STO
122	32	32
123	03	3
124	04	4
125	42	STO
126	31	31
127	92	RTN
128	76	LBL
129	18	C'
130	42	STO
131	13	13
132	92	RTN
133	76	LBL
134	71	SBR
135	71	SBR
136	14	D
137	33	X²
138	55	÷
139	43	RCL
140	05	05
141	95	=
142	42	STO
143	08	08
144	71	SBR
145	14	D
146	65	×
147	43	RCL
148	01	01
149	95	=
150	42	STO
151	09	09
152	92	RTN
153	76	LBL
154	24	CE
155	43	RCL
156	13	13
157	67	EQ
158	32	X⫴T
159	92	RTN
160	76	LBL
161	32	X⫴T
162	01	1
163	42	STO
164	13	13
165	92	RTN
166	76	LBL
167	42	STO
168	04	4
169	02	2
170	42	STO
171	30	30
172	01	1
173	02	2
174	42	STO
175	00	00
176	92	RTN
177	76	LBL
178	19	D'
179	71	SBR

180	42	STO
181	71	SBR
182	71	SBR
183	55	÷
184	71	SBR
185	24	CE
186	42	STO
187	04	04
188	95	=
189	42	STO
190	12	12
191	35	1/X
192	65	×
193	43	RCL
194	11	11
195	95	=
196	42	STO
197	03	03
198	71	SBR
199	34	√X
200	25	CLR
201	92	RTN
202	76	LBL
203	10	E'
204	71	SBR
205	42	STO
206	71	SBR
207	71	SBR
208	43	RCL
209	11	11
210	55	÷
211	71	SBR
212	24	CE
213	42	STO
214	03	03
215	95	=
216	42	STO
217	12	12
218	35	1/X
219	65	×
220	43	RCL
221	09	09
222	95	=
223	42	STO
224	04	04
225	71	SBR
226	34	√X
227	25	CLR
228	92	RTN

FORTRAN Program Listing for a PDP-11 Computer

The main program appears on pages 246 to 248 followed by three input–output subroutines and twenty-three subroutines, one for each network. Note, however, that the circuit numbers indicated in the second format statements starting on line 0064 do *not* coincide with the circuit numbers used in Chapter 5 and in Appendices A and C. Thus, for example, the high-Q, bandpass 'type 8' circuit corresponds to circuit 17 in Chapter 5.

The input and output subroutines are written for a video display terminal. If a hard copy is required, only the output subroutine need be adapted.

All subroutines for the twenty-three networks are in accordance with the flow diagrams given in Chapter 5, except for the subroutine HLPNMQ on page 272 of the program listing. In this subroutine the starting value of the parameter P for the minimum GSP is calculated numerically, and there is no need to search for the minimum GSP by hand.

246

```
C****************************************************************C
C                                                                C
C       INSTITUTE OF TELECOMMUNICATIONS                          C
C         SWISS FEDERAL INSTITUTE OF TECHNOLOGY, ZUERICH         C
C                                                                C
C       PROGRAMER :  HANS GERBER                                 C
C                                                                C
C****************************************************************C
0001          PROGRAM BERECH
0002          COMMON/DATA1/DAT(16)
0003          COMMON /STO/STOP
0004          COMMON/FIRST/IFIRST
0005          TYPE 1
0006          ACCEPT   4,XX
0007   100    CALL CLOSE(3)
0008          TYPE 2
0009   150    ACCEPT 3,I
0010          I=I+1
0011          IF(I.LE.0.OR.I.GT.24) GOTO 150
0013          IFIRST=1
0014          GOTO (1000,502,503,504,505,506,507,508,509,510,511,512,513,514,
              1    515,516,517,518,519,520,521,522,523,524) I
0015   502    CALL LPLQ
0016          GOTO 100
0017   503    CALL LPMQ
0018          GOTO 100
0019   504    CALL LPHQ
0020          GOTO 100
0021   505    CALL BPLQR
0022          GOTO 100
0023   506    CALL BPLQC
0024          GOTO 100
0025   507    CALL BPMQR
0026          GOTO 100
```

```
0027   508   CALL BPMQC
0028         GOTO 100
0029   509   CALL BPHQ
0030         GOTO 100
0031   510   CALL HPLQ
0032         GOTO 100
0033   511   CALL HPMQ
0034         GOTO 100
0035   512   CALL HPHQ
0036         GOTO 100
0037   513   CALL APLQS
0038         GOTO 100
0039   514   I=2
0040         CALL APLQ(I)
0041         GOTO 100
0042   515   CALL APMQ
0043         GOTO 100
0044   516   CALL APHQ
0045         GOTO 100
0046   517   I=1
0047         CALL APLQ(I)
0048         GOTO 100
0049   518   CALL BRMQ
0050         GOTO 100
0051   519   CALL BRHQ
0052         GOTO 100
0053   520   CALL HLPNMQ
0054         GOTO 100
0055   521   CALL BRHLPN
0056         GOTO 100
0057   522   CALL HLPNHQ
0058         GOTO 100
0059   523   CALL GP1
0060         GOTO 100
0061   524   CALL GP2
0062         GOTO 100
```

```
0063  1     FORMAT(X,'CIRCUITS :',X,
      1            ,T20,'LOWER Q :     Q < 0.5 ',/,
      1            ,T20,'LOW   Q :     Q < 2',/,
      1            ,T20,'MEDIUM Q :  2 < Q < 20',/,
      1            ,T20,'HIGH Q  : 20 < Q')
0064  2     FORMAT(T10,'END OF COMPUTATION',T45,'(TYPE 0)',/X,
      1       ,T10,'LOW-PASS',T35,'LOW Q',T45,'(TYPE 1)',/X,
      1       ,T10,'LOW-PASS',T35,'MEDIUM Q',T45,'(TYPE 2)',/X,
      1       ,T10,'LOW-PASS',T35,'HIGH Q',T45,'(TYPE 3)',/X,
      1       ,T10,'BAND-PASS R-INPUT',T35,'LOW Q',T45,'(TYPE 4)',/X,
      1       ,T10,'BAND-PASS C-INPUT',T35,'LOW Q',T45,'(TYPE 5)',/X,
      1       ,T10,'BAND-PASS R-INPUT',T35,'MEDIUM Q',T45,'(TYPE 6)',/X,
      1       ,T10,'BAND-PASS C-INPUT',T35,'MEDIUM Q',T45,'(TYPE 7)',/X,
      1       ,T10,'BAND-PASS',T35,'HIGH Q',T45,'(TYPE 8)',/X,
      1       ,T10,'HIGH-PASS',T35,'LOW Q',T45,'(TYPE 9)',/X,
      1       ,T10,'HIGH-PASS',T35,'MEDIUM Q',T45,'(TYPE 10)',/X,
      1       ,T10,'HIGH-PASS',T35,'HIGH Q',T45,'(TYPE 11)',/X,
      1       ,T10,'ALL-PASS',T35,'LOWER Q',T45,'(TYPE 12)',/X,
      1       ,T10,'ALL-PASS',T35,'LOW Q',T45,'(TYPE 13)',/X,
      1       ,T10,'ALL-PASS',T35,'MEDIUM Q',T45,'(TYPE 14)',/X,
      1       ,T10,'ALL-PASS',T35,'HIGH Q',T45,'(TYPE 15)',/X,
      1       ,T10,'BAND-REJECTION',T35,'LOW Q',T45,'(TYPE 16)',/X,
      1       ,T10,'BAND-REJECTION',T35,'MEDIUM Q',T45,'(TYPE 17)',/X,
      1       ,T10,'BAND-REJECTION',T35,'HIGH Q',T45,'(TYPE 18)',/X,
      1       ,T10,'HIGH-/LOW-PASS-NOTCHED',T35,'MEDIUM Q',
      1       ,T45,'(TYPE 19)',/X,
      1       ,T10,'BAND REJECTION/HIGH-',/X,T10,'LOW-PASS NOTCHED',
      1       ,T35,'MEDIUM Q',T45,'(TYPE 20)',/X,
      1       ,T10,'HIGH-/LOW-PASS NOTCHED',T35,'HIGH Q',T45,'(TYPE 21)',/X,
      1       ,T10,'GENERAL PURPOSE 1',T45,'(TYPE 22)',/X,
      1       ,T10,'GENERAL PURPOSE 2',T45,'(TYPE 23)',/X)
0065  3     FORMAT(I2)
0066  4     FORMAT(A1)
0067  1000  CALL CLOSE(3)
0068        STOP
0069        END
```

```
0001          SUBROUTINE TEST(IFR,IV,IC,IR,TEX1,IN)
     C****************************************************
0002          COMMON/STO/STOP
0003          COMMON/FIRST/IFIRST
0004          DIMENSION TEX1(16),IN(9)
0005          LOGICAL*1 STOP
0006          ITOT = IFR+IV+IC+IR
0007          STOP=.FALSE.
0008          ICH=0.
0009          TYPE 10
0010          ACCEPT 20,IHI,TEST
0011          IF(IHI.EQ.0) GOTO 220
0013          DO 100 I=1,ITOT
0014          IF(TEST.NE.TEX1(IN(I))) GOTO 100
0016          ICH=IN(I)
0017          GOTO 200
0018   100    CONTINUE
0019          IF(ICH.EQ.0) GOTO 1000
0021   200    IFIRST=0
0022          CALL INPUT(IFR,IV,IC,IR,ICH,TEX1,IN)
0023          GOTO 1000
0024   220    STOP =.TRUE.
0025   1000   RETURN
0026   10     FORMAT(/X,'ELEMENT CHANGE ?',/X,' WHICH ELEMENT :',X,$)
0027   20     FORMAT(Q,A4)
0028          END
```

```
0001        SUBROUTINE INPUT(IFR,IV,IC,IR,ICH,TEX1,IN)
     C**************************************************
0002        COMMON/DATA1/DAT1(16)
0003        COMMON/FIRST/IFIRST
0004        DOUBLE PRECISION TEX(4)
0005        DIMENSION TEX1(16),IN(9)
0006        DIMENSION IH(4)
0007        DATA TEX/'(KHZ)',' ','(NF)','(KOHM)'/
0008        ITOT1=1
0009        ITOT=0
0010        IH(1)=IFR
0011        IH(2)=IV
0012        IH(3)=IC
0013        IH(4)=IR
0014        DO 200,I=1,4
0015        IF(IH(I).EQ.0) GOTO 200
0017        ITOT=ITOT+IH(I)
0018        DO 180 IJ=ITOT1,ITOT
0019        IF(IFIRST.EQ.1.AND.IJ.EQ.(IV+IFR)) GOTO 180
0021        J=IN(IJ)
0022        IF(J.NE.ICH.AND.IFIRST.EQ.0) GOTO 180
0024        J1=I
0025  115   TYPE 10,TEX1(J),TEX(J1)
0026  120   ACCEPT 20,DAT1(J)
0027        IF(DAT1(J).LT.0) GOTO 120
0029        IF(I.NE.1) GOTO 140
0031        DAT1(J)=DAT1(J)*1000
0032  140   IF(I.NE.3) GOTO 150
0034        IF(DAT1(J).EQ.0) GOTO 115
0036        DAT1(J)=DAT1(J)*1.E-9
0037  150   IF(I.NE.4) GOTO 180
0039        IF(DAT1(J).NE.0.) GOTO 160
0041        DAT1(J)=10.
0042  160   DAT1(J)=DAT1(J)*1000
0043  180   CONTINUE
0044        ITOT1=ITOT1+IH(I)
0045  200   CONTINUE
0046  10    FORMAT(X,A4,X,A8,T15,'=  ',$)
0047  20    FORMAT(F10.0)
0048        RETURN
0049        END
```

```
0001          SUBROUTINE OUTPUT(IPA,IC,IR,TEX1)
       C***********************************************
0002          COMMON /DATA1/DAT1(16)
0003          DIMENSION TEX1(16)
0004          ITOT=IPA+IC+IR
0005          DO 200,I=1,ITOT
0006          TYPE 10,TEX1(I),DAT1(I)
0007   200    CONTINUE
0008          RETURN
0009   10     FORMAT(X,A4,T15,'=',1PE10.3)
0010          END
```

```
0001          SUBROUTINE LPLQ
C****************************************************
0002          COMMON/STO/STOP
0003          COMMON/DATA1/XFR,XQP,XK,XGSP,XP,XR11,XR12,XC2,XR3,XC4
0004          DIMENSION TEX1(16),IN(6)
0005          LOGICAL*1 STOP
0006          DATA TEX1/'FREQ','QP','K','GSP','P','R11','R12','C2','R3','C4',
     1' ',' ',' ',' ',' ',' '/IN/1,2,3,0,8,10/
0007          DATA IFR,IV,IC,IRIN,IROUT,IPA,ICH/1,3,2,0,3,5,0/
0008          CALL INPUT(IFR,IV,IC,IRIN,ICH,TEX1,IN)
0009    100   XKIN=XK
0010          A = XC2/(XC4*2.*XQP*XQP)
0011          IF(A.GE.2.) GOTO 150
0013          TYPE 5
0014    5     FORMAT(/,X,'C2 >= C4*4*QP**2')
0015          CALL TEST(IFR,IV,IC,IRIN,TEX1,IN)
0016          GOTO 100
0017    150   XCHI = XC4/XC2
0018          XQHI = XQP*XQP
0019          XP = (1./(XCHI*2.*XQHI)-1.)+SQRT((1./(2*XQHI*XCHI)-1)**2-1.)
0020    160   XR1 = 1/(SQRT(XP*XC2*XC4)*(6.2831853*XFR))
0021          XR3 = XP*XR1
0022          XGSP = XQP*SQRT(1./(XCHI*XP))
0023          IF (XKIN.EQ.0) GOTO 200
0025          IF ((1-XKIN).LE.0) GOTO 200
0027          XK=XKIN
0028          XR11 = XR1/XK
0029          XR12 = XR1/(1-XK)
0030          GOTO 300
0031    200   XR11 = XR1
0032          XR12 = 1.E38
0033          XK = 1.
0034    300   CALL OUTPUT(IPA,IC,IROUT,TEX1)
0035          XK=XKIN
0036          CALL TEST(IFR,IV,IC,IRIN,TEX1,IN)
0037          IF(.NOT.STOP) GOTO 100
0039          RETURN
0040          END
```

```
0001          SUBROUTINE APLQS
     C*****************************************************
0002          COMMON/STO/STOP
0003          COMMON/DATA1/XFR,XQP,XK,XRO,XC1,XC2,XC3,XR4,XR5,XR6
0004          DIMENSION TEX1(16),IN(7)
0005          LOGICAL*1 STOP
0006          DATA TEX1/'FREQ','QP','K','RO','C1','C2','C3','R4','R5','R6',
             1' ',' ',' ',' ',' ',' '/IN/1,2,0,5,6,7,4/
0007          DATA IFR,IV,IC,IRIN,IROUT,IPA,ICH/1,2,3,1,4,3,0/
0008          TYPE 10
0009   10     FORMAT(X,'K = 1',T20,'(TYPE 1)',
             1,/,X,'K = -1',T20,'(TYPE -1)')
0010          ACCEPT 11,XK
0011   11     FORMAT(F10.0)
0012          CALL INPUT(IFR,IV,IC,IRIN,ICH,TEX1,IN)
0013  100     XH=1.-((XC1+XC2)*(XC2+XC3)*4.*XQP*XQP/(XC1*XC3))
0014          IF(XH.GE.0.) GOTO 150
0016          TYPE 5
0017   5      FORMAT(/,X,'C1 = C3 >= C2*2*QP/(1-2*QP)')
0018          CALL TEST(IFR,IV,IC,IRIN,TEX1,IN)
0019          GOTO 100
0020  150     XW=XFR*6.2831853
0021          IF(XK.EQ.1) XH1=1.+SQRT(XH)
0023          IF(XK.EQ.-1)XH1=1.-SQRT(XH)
0025          XR4=XH1/(2.*XW*XQP*(XC2+XC3))
0026          XR5=(XC1+XC2)/(XR4*XW*XW*XC1*XC2*XC3)
0027          XR6=1./(XW*XW*XC1*XC2*(XR4+XR5))
0028          CALL OUTPUT(IPA,IC,IROUT,TEX1)
0029          CALL TEST(IFR,IV,IC,IRIN,TEX1,IN)
0030          IF(.NOT.STOP) GOTO 100
0032          RETURN
0033          END
```

```
0001        SUBROUTINE BPLQR
     C****************************************************
0002        COMMON/STO/STOP
0003        COMMON/DATA1/XFR,XQP,XK,XGSP,XP,XR11,XR12,XC2,XC3,XR4
0004        DIMENSION TEX1(16),IN(6)
0005        LOGICAL*1 STOP
0006        DATA TEX1/'FREQ','QP','K','GSP','P','R11','R12','C2','C3',
          1'R4',' ',' ',' ',' ',' ',' '/IN/1,2,3,0,8,9/
0007        DATA IFR,IV,IC,IRIN,IROUT,IPA,ICH/1,3,2,0,3,5,0/
0008        CALL INPUT(IFR,IV,IC,IRIN,ICH,TEX1,IN)
0009   150  XKIN=XK
0010        XCHI = XC3/XC2
0011        XQHI = XQP*XQP
0012        XP = XQHI*(2.+XCHI+1./XCHI)
0013   160  XR1 = 1/(SQRT(XP*XC2*XC3)*(6.2831853*XFR))
0014        XR4 = XP*XR1
0015        XGSP = XQHI*(1.+XCHI)
0016        XK0 = XGSP
0017        IF (XKIN.EQ.0.OR.(XK0-XKIN).LE.0) GOTO 200
0019        XK=XKIN
0020        XR11 = XR1*XK0/XK
0021        XR12 = XK*XR11/(XK0-XK)
0022        GOTO 300
0023   200  XR11 = XR1
0024        XR12 = 1.E38
0025        XK = XK0
0026   300  CALL OUTPUT(IPA,IC,IROUT,TEX1)
0027        XK=XKIN
0028        CALL TEST(IFR,IV,IC,IRIN,TEX1,IN)
0029        IF(.NOT.STOP) GOTO 150
0031        RETURN
0032        END
```

```
0001          SUBROUTINE BPLQC
C****************************************************
0002          COMMON/STO/STOP
0003          COMMON/DATA1/XFR,XQP,XK,XGSP,XP,XC11,XC12,XR2,XR3,XC4
0004          DIMENSION TEX1(16),IN(6)
0005          LOGICAL*1 STOP
0006          DATA TEX1/'FREQ','QP','K','GSP','P','C11','C12','R2','R3',
             1'C4',' ',' ',' ',' ',' ',' '/IN/1,2,0,6,7,10/
0007          DATA IFR,IV,IC,IRIN,IROUT,IPA,ICH/1,2,3,0,2,5,0/
0008          CALL INPUT(IFR,IV,IC,IRIN,ICH,TEX1,IN)
0009    150   XC1 = XC11+XC12
0010          A = XC1/(XC4*2.*XQP*XQP)
0011          IF(A.GE.2.) GOTO 170
0013          TYPE 5
0014          CALL TEST(IFR,IV,IC,IRIN,TEX1,IN)
0015          GOTO 150
0016    170   XCHI = XC4/XC1
0017          XQHI = XQP*XQP
0018          XP = (1./(XCHI*2.*XQHI)-1.)+SQRT((1./(2*XQHI*XCHI)-1)**2-1.)
0019    160   XR2 = 1/(SQRT(XP*XC1*XC4)*(6.2831853*XFR))
0020          XR3 = XP*XR2
0021          XGSP = XQP*SQRT(1./(XCHI*XP))
0022          XK = XC11*XGSP/XC1
0023          CALL OUTPUT(IPA,IC,IROUT,TEX1)
0024          CALL TEST(IFR,IV,IC,IRIN,TEX1,IN)
0025          IF(.NOT.STOP) GOTO 150
0027    5     FORMAT(/,X,'C11 + C12 >= 4*QP**2*C4')
0028          RETURN
0029          END
```

```
0001            SUBROUTINE HPLQ
      C****************************************************
0002            COMMON/STO/STOP
0003            COMMON/DATA1/XFR,XQP,XK,XGSP,XP,XC11,XC12,XR2,XC3,XR4
0004            DIMENSION TEX1(16),IN(6)
0005            LOGICAL*1 STOP
0006            DATA TEX1/'FREQ','QP','K','GSP','P','C11','C12','R2','C3','R4',
           1' ',' ',' ',' ',' ',' ' /IN/1,2,0,6,7,9/
0007            DATA IFR,IV,IC,IRIN,IROUT,IPA,ICH/1,2,3,0,2,5,0/
0008            CALL INPUT(IFR,IV,IC,IRIN,ICH,TEX1,IN)
0009  150       XC1 = XC11+XC12
0010            XCHI = XC3/XC1
0011            XQHI = XQP*XQP
0012            XP = XQHI*(2.+XCHI+1./XCHI)
0013            XR2 = 1./(SQRT(XP*XC1*XC3)*(6.2831853*XFR))
0014            XR4 = XP*XR2
0015            XGSP = XQP*SQRT(XP*XCHI)
0016            XK = XC11/XC1
0017            CALL OUTPUT(IPA,IC,IROUT,TEX1)
0018            CALL TEST(IFR,IV,IC,IRIN,TEX1,IN)
0019            IF(.NOT.STOP) GOTO 150
0021            RETURN
0022            END
```

```
0001        SUBROUTINE APLQ(I)
C**************************************************
0002        COMMON /STO/STOP
0003        COMMON /DATA1/XFR,XQP,XK,XGSP,XP,XR1,XC2,XC3,XR4,XR5,XR6,XX1(2)
0004        DIMENSION TEX1(16),IN(6)
0005        LOGICAL*1 STOP
0006        DATA TEX1/'FREQ','QP','K','GSP','P','R1','C2','C3','R4',
           1'R5','R6',' ',' ',' ',' ',' '/IN/1,2,5,7,8,11/
0007        DATA IFR,IV,IC,IRIN,IROUT,IPA,ICH/1,2,2,1,4,5,0/
0008        GOTO (100,110) I
0009  100   TYPE 10
0010  10    FORMAT(X,'BAND-REJECTION')
0011        GOTO 120
0012  110   TYPE 11
0013  11    FORMAT(X,'ALL-PASS')
0014  120   CALL INPUT(IFR,IV,IC,IRIN,ICH,TEX1,IN)
0015  150   XCHI = XC3/XC2
0016        XQHI = XQP*XQP
0017        XP = XQHI*(2.+XCHI+1./XCHI)
0018  160   XR1 = 1/(SQRT(XP*XC2*XC3)*(6.2831853*XFR))
0019        XR4 = XP*XR1
0020        XGSP = XQP*SQRT(XP*XCHI)
0021        XR5 = I*XR6*(1.+1./XCHI)/XP
0022        XK = XR6/(XR5+XR6)
0023        GOTO (200,210) I
0024  200   TYPE 10
0025        GOTO 220
0026  210   TYPE 11
0027  220   CALL OUTPUT(IPA,IC,IROUT,TEX1)
0028        CALL TEST(IFR,IV,IC,IRIN,TEX1,IN)
0029        IF(.NOT.STOP) GOTO 150
0031        RETURN
0032        END
```

```
0001        SUBROUTINE LPMQ
      C****************************************************
0002        COMMON/STO/STOP
0003        COMMON/DATA1/XFR,XQP,XK,XGSP,XP,XPMIN,XR11,XR12,XC2,XR3,XC4,
           1XR5,XR6
0004        DIMENSION TEX1(16),IN(7)
0005        LOGICAL*1 STOP
0006        DATA TEX1/'FREQ','QP','K','GSP','P','PMIN','R11','R12','C2','R3',
           1'C4','R5','R6',' ',' ',' '/IN/1,2,3,5,9,11,12/
0007        DATA IFR,IV,IC,IRIN,IROUT,IPA,ICH/1,3,2,1,5,6,0/
0008        XP=0.
0009        CALL INPUT(IFR,IV,IC,IRIN,ICH,TEX1,IN)
0010  150   XKIN=XK
0011        XPIN=XP
0012        XCHI = XC4/XC2
0013        XQHI = XQP*XQP
0014        XPMIN = 1/(XCHI*36.*XQHI)*(SQRT(1.+12.*XQHI*(XCHI+1.))+1.)**2
0015        IF(XPIN.NE.0) GOTO 160
0017        XP=XPMIN
0018  160   XR1 = 1/(SQRT(XP*XC2*XC4)*(6.2831853*XFR))
0019        XR3 = XP*XR1
0020        XR6 = XR5*(XCHI*(1.+XP)-SQRT(XCHI*XP)/XQP)
0021        XKO = 1.+XR6/XR5
0022        XGSP = XKO**2*XQP*SQRT(1./(XCHI*XP))
0023        IF (XKIN.EQ.0.OR.(XKO-XKIN).LE.0) GOTO 200
0025        XK=XKIN
0026        XR11 = (XKO/XK)*XR1
0027        XR12 = XK*XR11/(XKO-XK)
0028        GOTO 300
0029  200   XR11 = XR1
0030        XR12 = 1.E38
0031        XK = XKO
0032  300   CALL OUTPUT(IPA,IC,IROUT,TEX1)
0033        XK=XKIN
0034        XP=XPIN
0035        CALL TEST(IFR,IV,IC,IRIN,TEX1,IN)
0036        IF(.NOT.STOP) GOTO 150
0038        RETURN
0039        END
```

```
0001          SUBROUTINE BPMQR
    C***************************************************
0002          COMMON/STO/STOP
0003          COMMON/DATA1/XFR,XQP,XK,XGSP,XP,XPMIN,XR11,XR12,XC2,XC3,XR4
              1,XR5,XR6
0004          DIMENSION TEX1(16),IN(7)
0005          LOGICAL*1 STOP
0006          DATA TEX1/'FREQ','QP','K','GSP','P','PMIN','R11','R12','C2','C3',
              1'R4','R5','R6',' ',' ',' '/IN/1,2,3,5,9,10,13/
0007          DATA IFR,IV,IC,IRIN,IROUT,IPA,ICH/1,3,2,1,5,6,0/
0008          XP=0.
0009          CALL INPUT(IFR,IV,IC,IRIN,ICH,TEX1,IN)
0010    150   XKIN=XK
0011          XPIN=XP
0012          XCHI = XC3/XC2
0013          XQHI = XQP*XQP
0014          XPMIN = 1/(XCHI*4.*XQHI)*(SQRT(1.+12.*XQHI*(XCHI+1.))-1.)**2
0015          IF(XP.NE.0) GOTO 160
0017          XP=XPMIN
0018    160   XR1 = 1/(SQRT(XP*XC2*XC3)*(6.2831853*XFR))
0019          XR4 = XP*XR1
0020          XR5 = XR6*((1.+1./XCHI)/XP-(SQRT(1./(XCHI*XP))/XQP))
0021          XK0 = XQP*(1.+XR5/XR6)*SQRT(XCHI*XP)
0022          IF(XKIN.EQ.0.OR.(XK0-XKIN).LE.0) GOTO 165
0024          XK=XKIN
0025          XR11=XK0*XR1/XK
0026          XR12=XK*XR11/(XK0-XK)
0027          GOTO 170
0028    165   XR11=XR1
0029          XR12=1.E+38
0030          XK=XK0
0031    170   XGSP = XK0*(1.+XR5/XR6)
0032          CALL OUTPUT(IPA,IC,IROUT,TEX1)
0033          XP=XPIN
0034          XK=XKIN
0035          CALL TEST(IFR,IV,IC,IRIN,TEX1,IN)
0036          IF(.NOT.STOP) GOTO 150
0038          RETURN
0039          END
```

```
0001         SUBROUTINE BPMQC
      C****************************************************
0002         COMMON/STO/STOP
0003         COMMON/DATA1/XFR,XQP,XK,XGSP,XP,XPMIN,XC11,XC12,XR2,XR3,XC4
            1,XR5,XR6
0004         DIMENSION TEX1(16),IN(7)
0005         LOGICAL*1 STOP
0006         DATA TEX1/'FREQ','QP','K','GSP','P','PMIN','C11','C12','R2','R3',
            1'C4','R5','R6',' ',' ',' '/IN/1,2,5,7,8,11,13/
0007         DATA IFR,IV,IC,IRIN,IROUT,IPA,ICH/1,2,3,1,4,6,0/
0008         XPIN=0.
0009         XP=0.
0010         CALL INPUT(IFR,IV,IC,IRIN,ICH,TEX1,IN)
0011    150  XC1 = XC11+XC12
0012         XCHI = XC4/XC1
0013         XQHI = XQP*XQP
0014         XPMIN = 1/(XCHI*36.*XQHI)*(SQRT(1.+12.*XQHI*(XCHI+1.))+1.)**2
0015         IF(XP.NE.0) GOTO 160
0017         XP=XPMIN
0018    160  XR2 = 1/(SQRT(XP*XC1*XC4)*(6.2831853*XFR))
0019         XR3 = XP*XR2
0020         XR5 = XR6*(XCHI*(1.+XP)-SQRT(XCHI*XP)/XQP)
0021         XK = XC11/XC1*(1.+XR5/XR6)*XQP*SQRT(1./(XP*XCHI))
0022         XGSP = (1.+XR5/XR6)**2*XQP*SQRT(1./(XCHI*XP))
0023         CALL OUTPUT(IPA,IC,IROUT,TEX1)
0024         XP=XPIN
0025         CALL TEST(IFR,IV,IC,IRIN,TEX1,IN)
0026         XPIN=XP
0027         IF(.NOT.STOP) GOTO 150
0029         RETURN
0030         END
```

```
0001          SUBROUTINE HPMQ
      C**************************************************
0002          COMMON/STO/STOP
0003          COMMON/DATA1/XFR,XQP,XK,XGSP,XP,XPMIN,XC11,XC12,XR2,XC3,XR4
             1,XR5,XR6
0004          DIMENSION TEX1(16),IN(7)
0005          LOGICAL*1 STOP
0006          DATA TEX1/'FREQ','QP','K','GSP','P','PMIN','C11','C12','R2','C3',
             1'R4','R5','R6',' ',' ',' '/IN/1,2,5,7,8,10,12/
0007          DATA IFR,IV,IC,IRIN,IROUT,IPA,ICH/1,2,3,1,4,6,0/
0008          XPIN=0.
0009          CALL INPUT(IFR,IV,IC,IRIN,ICH,TEX1,IN)
0010  150     XC1 = XC11+XC12
0011          XCHI = XC3/XC1
0012          XQH1 = XQP*XQP
0013          XPMIN = 1/(XCHI*4.*XQHI)*(SQRT(1.+12.*XQHI*(XCHI+1.))-1.)**2
0014          IF(XPIN.NE.0) GOTO 160
0016          XP=XPMIN
0017  160     XR2 = 1/(SQRT(XP*XC1*XC3)*(6.2831853*XFR))
0018          XR4 = XP*XR2
0019          XR6 = XR5*((1.+1./XCHI)/XP-(SQRT(1./(XCHI*XP))/XQP))
0020          XK = XC11*(1.+XR6/XR5)/XC1
0021          XGSP = XQP*(1.+XR6/XR5)**2*SQRT(XP*XCHI)
0022          CALL OUTPUT(IPA,IC,IROUT,TEX1)
0023          XP=XPIN
0024          CALL TEST(IFR,IV,IC,IRIN,TEX1,IN)
0025          XPIN=XP
0026          IF(.NOT.STOP) GOTO 150
0028          RETURN
0029          END
```

```
0001          SUBROUTINE APMQ
     C***************************************************
0002          COMMON/STO/STOP
0003          COMMON/DATA1/XFR,XQP,XK,XGSP,XP,XPMIN,XR1,XC2,XC3,XR4,XR5,XR6,XR7
0004          DIMENSION TEX1(16),IN(6)
0005          LOGICAL*1 STOP
0006          DATA TEX1/'FREQ','QP','K','GSP','P','PMIN','R1','C2','C3','R4',
             1'R5','R6','R7',' ',' ',' '/IN/1,2,5,8,9,12/
0007          DATA IFR,IV,IC,IRIN,IROUT,IPA,ICH/1,2,2,1,5,6,0/
0008          XP=0.
0009          TYPE 15
0010          CALL INPUT(IFR,IV,IC,IRIN,ICH,TEX1,IN)
0011   150    XPIN=XP
0012          XCHI = XC2/XC3
0013          XQHI=XQP*XQP
0014          XHIL=((6.*(1.+XCHI)**2*XQHI)/(2.*XQHI*(1+XCHI)-XCHI))**2
0015          XHIL=(SQRT(1.+XHIL/(3.*(1+XCHI)**2))-1.)*(2.*XQHI*(1+XCHI)-XCHI)
0016          XPMIN=XHIL/(6.*(1+XCHI)**2*XQHI)
0017          IF(XPIN.NE.0) GOTO 160
0019          XP=XPMIN
0020   160    XR1 = 1/(SQRT(XP*XC2*XC3)*(6.2831853*XFR))
0021          XRP = XP*XR1
0022          XR7=XR6*(XP*(1.+XCHI)+SQRT(XP*XCHI)/XQP)
0023          XHIL=1.-2*(SQRT(XP*XCHI))/(XQP*(1.+XR7/XR6))
0024          XR5=XRP/XHIL
0025          XR4=XRP/(1.-XHIL)
0026          XGSP=XQP*(1.+XR7/XR6)**2*XHIL*SQRT(1./(XP*XCHI))
0027          XK=1.
0028          TYPE 15
0029          CALL OUTPUT(IPA,IC,IROUT,TEX1)
0030          XP=XPIN
0031          CALL TEST(IFR,IV,IC,IRIN,TEX1,IN)
0032          IF(.NOT.STOP) GOTO 150
0034   15     FORMAT(/X,'ALL - PASS')
0035          RETURN
0036          END
```

```
0001            SUBROUTINE BRMQ
      C*********************************************
0002            COMMON/STO/STOP
0003            COMMON/DATA1/XFR,XQP,XK,XGSP,XP,XPMIN,XR1,XC2,XC3,XR4,XR5,XR6,XR7
0004            DIMENSION TEX1(16),IN(6)
0005            LOGICAL*1 STOP
0006            DATA TEX1/'FREQ','QP','K','GSP','P','PMIN','R1','C2','C3','R4',
           1'R5','R6','R7',' ',' ',' '/IN/1,2,5,8,9,12/
0007            DATA IFR,IV,IC,IRIN,IROUT,IPA,ICH/1,2,2,1,5,6,0/
0008            XP=0.
0009            TYPE 15
0010     15     FORMAT(/X,'BAND - REJECTION')
0011            CALL INPUT(IFR,IV,IC,IRIN,ICH,TEX1,IN)
0012    150     XPIN=XP
0013            XCHI = XC2/XC3
0014            XPMIN=1./(3.*(1.+XCHI))
0015            IF(XPIN.NE.0) GOTO 160
0017            XP=XPMIN
0018    160     XR1 = 1/(SQRT(XP*XC2*XC3)*(6.2831853*XFR))
0019            XRP = XP*XR1
0020            XR7=XR6*XP*(1.+XCHI)
0021            XHIL=1.-(SQRT(XP*XCHI))/(XQP*(1.+XR7/XR6))
0022            XR5=XRP/XHIL
0023            XR4=XRP/(1.-XHIL)
0024            XGSP=XQP*(1.+XR7/XR6)**2*XHIL*SQRT(1./(XP*XCHI))
0025            XK=1.
0026            TYPE 15
0027            CALL OUTPUT(IPA,IC,IROUT,TEX1)
0028            XP=XPIN
0029            CALL TEST(IFR,IV,IC,IRIN,TEX1,IN)
0030            IF(.NOT.STOP) GOTO 150
0032            RETURN
0033            END
```

```
0001          SUBROUTINE LPHQ
C*****************************************************
0002          COMMON /STO/STOP
0003          COMMON/FIRST/IFIRST
0004          COMMON/DATA1/XFR,XQP,XK,XROPT,XR1,XC1,XR2,XR3,XC4,XR6,XR7,XC,XR
0005          DIMENSION TEX1(16),IN(5)
0006          LOGICAL*1 STOP
0007          DATA TEX1/'FREQ','QP','K','ROPT','R1','C1','R2','R3','C4','R6',
     1'R7','C','R',' ',' ',' '/IN/1,2,0,12,13/
0008          DATA IFR,IV,ICIN,ICOUT,IRIN,IROUT,IPA/1,2,1,2,0,6,3/
0009          DATA ICH,IRIN1/0,1/
0010          CALL INPUT(IFR,IV,ICIN,IRIN,ICH,TEX1,IN)
0011   150    ICH=13
0012          IFIRST=0
0013          XROPT=1./(6.2831853*XFR*XC)
0014          TYPE 10,XROPT
0015   10     FORMAT(X,'ROPT',T15,'=',1PE10.3)
0016          CALL INPUT(IFR,IV,ICIN,IRIN1,ICH,TEX1,IN)
0017          XK=2.
0018          XR2=XR
0019          XR3=XR
0020          XR6=XR
0021          XC1=XC
0022          XC4=XC
0023          XR1=XQP*XROPT
0024          XR7=XROPT**2/XR
0025          CALL OUTPUT(IPA,ICOUT,IROUT,TEX1)
0026          CALL TEST(IFR,IV,ICIN,IRIN,TEX1,IN)
0027          IF(.NOT.STOP) GOTO 150
0029          RETURN
0030          END
```

```
0001        SUBROUTINE BPHQ
C****************************************************
0002        COMMON /STO/STOP
0003        COMMON/FIRST/IFIRST
0004        COMMON/DATA1/XFR,XQP,XK,XROPT,XR1,XR2,XC3,XR4,XR6,XR7,XC8,XC,XR
0005        DIMENSION TEX1(16),IN(5)
0006        LOGICAL*1 STOP
0007        DATA TEX1/'FREQ','QP','K','ROPT','R1','R2','C3','R4','R6','R7',
           1'C8','C','R',' ',' ',' '/IN/1,2,0,12,13/
0008        DATA IFR,IV,ICIN,ICOUT,IRIN,IROUT,IPA/1,2,1,2,0,6,3/
0009        DATA ICH,IRIN1/0,1/
0010        CALL INPUT(IFR,IV,ICIN,IRIN,ICH,TEX1,IN)
0011   150  ICH=13
0012        IFIRST=0
0013        XROPT=1./(6.2831853*XFR*XC)
0014        TYPE 10,XROPT
0015   10   FORMAT(X,'ROPT',T15,'=',1PE10.3)
0016        CALL INPUT(IFR,IV,ICIN,IRIN1,ICH,TEX1,IN)
0017        XK=2.
0018        XR1=XR
0019        XR2=XR
0020        XR6=XR
0021        XC3=XC
0022        XC8=XC
0023        XR7=XQP*XROPT
0024        XR4=XROPT**2/XR
0025        CALL OUTPUT(IPA,ICOUT,IROUT,TEX1)
0026        CALL TEST(IFR,IV,ICIN,IRIN,TEX1,IN)
0027        IF(.NOT.STOP) GOTO 150
0029        RETURN
0030        END
```

```
0001          SUBROUTINE HPHQ
      C**************************************************
0002          COMMON /STO/STOP
0003          COMMON/FIRST/IFIRST
0004          COMMON/DATA1/XFR,XQP,XK,XROPT,XR1,XR2,XC3,XR4,XR6,XC7,XR8,XC,XR
0005          DIMENSION TEX1(16),IN(5)
0006          LOGICAL*1 STOP
0007          DATA TEX1/'FREQ','QP','K','ROPT','R1','R2','C3','R4','R6','C7',
          1'R8','C','R',' ',' ',' '/IN/1,2,0,12,13/
0008          DATA IFR,IV,ICIN,ICOUT,IRIN,IROUT,IPA/1,2,1,2,0,6,3/
0009          DATA ICH,IRIN1/0,1/
0010          CALL INPUT(IFR,IV,ICIN,IRIN,ICH,TEX1,IN)
0011    150   ICH=13
0012          IFIRST=0
0013          XROPT=1./(6.2831853*XFR*XC)
0014          TYPE 10,XROPT
0015    10    FORMAT(X,'ROPT',T15,'=',1PE10.3)
0016          CALL INPUT(IFR,IV,ICIN,IRIN1,ICH,TEX1,IN)
0017          XK=2.
0018          XR1=XR
0019          XR2=XR
0020          XR6=XR
0021          XC3=XC
0022          XC7=XC
0023          XR8=XQP*XROPT
0024          XR4=XROPT**2/XR
0025          CALL OUTPUT(IPA,ICOUT,IROUT,TEX1)
0026          CALL TEST(IFR,IV,ICIN,IRIN,TEX1,IN)
0027          IF(.NOT.STOP) GOTO 150
0029          RETURN
0030          END
```

```
0001          SUBROUTINE APHQ
     C***************************************************
0002          COMMON /STO/STOP
0003          COMMON/FIRST/IFIRST
0004          COMMON/DATA1/XFR,XQP,XK,XROPT,XR1,XR2,XC3,XR4,XR5,XC7,XR8,XC,XR
0005          DIMENSION TEX1(16),IN(5)
0006          LOGICAL*1 STOP
0007          DATA TEX1/'FREQ','QP','K','ROPT','R1','R2','C3','R4','R5','C7',
              1'R8','C','R',' ',' ',' '/IN/1,2,0,12,13/
0008          DATA IFR,IV,ICIN,ICOUT,IRIN,IROUT,IPA/1,2,1,2,0,6,3/
0009          DATA ICH,IRIN1/0,1/
0010          CALL INPUT(IFR,IV,ICIN,IRIN,ICH,TEX1,IN)
0011   150    ICH=13
0012          IFIRST=0
0013          XROPT=1./(6.2831853*XFR*XC)
0014          TYPE 10,XROPT
0015   10     FORMAT(X,'ROPT',T15,'=',1PE10.3)
0016          CALL INPUT(IFR,IV,ICIN,IRIN1,ICH,TEX1,IN)
0017          XK=2.
0018          XR1=XR
0019          XR2=XR
0020          XR5=XR
0021          XC3=XC
0022          XC7=XC
0023          XR8=XQP*XROPT
0024          XR4=XROPT**2/XR
0025          CALL OUTPUT(IPA,ICOUT,IROUT,TEX1)
0026          CALL TEST(IFR,IV,ICIN,IRIN,TEX1,IN)
0027          IF(.NOT.STOP) GOTO 150
0029          RETURN
0030          END
```

```
0001        SUBROUTINE BRHQ
C*****************************************************
0002        COMMON /STO/STOP
0003        COMMON/FIRST/IFIRST
0004        COMMON/DATA1/XFR,XQP,XK,XROPT,XR1,XR2,XC3,XR4,XR5,XC7,XR7,XR8,
           1XC,XR
0005        DIMENSION TEX1(16),IN(5)
0006        LOGICAL*1 STOP
0007        DATA TEX1/'FREQ','QP','K','ROPT','R1','R2','C3','R4','R5','C7',
           1'R7','R8','C','R',' ',' '/IN/1,2,0,13,14/
0008        DATA IFR,IV,ICIN,ICOUT,IRIN,IROUT,IPA/1,2,1,2,0,7,3/
0009        DATA ICH,IRIN1/0,1/
0010        CALL INPUT(IFR,IV,ICIN,IRIN,ICH,TEX1,IN)
0011  150   ICH=14
0012        IFIRST=0
0013        XROPT=1./(6.2831853*XFR*XC)
0014        TYPE 10,XROPT
0015  10    FORMAT(X,'ROPT',T15,'=',1PE10.3)
0016        CALL INPUT(IFR,IV,ICIN,IRIN1,ICH,TEX1,IN)
0017        XK=2.
0018        XR1=XR
0019        XR2=XR
0020        XR5=XR
0021        XC3=XC
0022        XC7=XC
0023        XR8=XQP*XROPT*2
0024        XR4=XROPT**2/XR
0025        XR7=XR8
0026        CALL OUTPUT(IPA,ICOUT,IROUT,TEX1)
0027        CALL TEST(IFR,IV,ICIN,IRIN,TEX1,IN)
0028        IF(.NOT.STOP) GOTO 150
0030        RETURN
0031        END
```

```
0001        SUBROUTINE HLPNHQ
      C*****************************************************
0002        COMMON /STO/STOP
0003        COMMON/FIRST/IFIRST
0004        COMMON/DATA1/XFRP,XFRZ,XQP,XKHP,XKLP,XROPT,XR1,XC2,XR3,XR4,XR5
           1,XC7,XR8,XC,XR
0005        DIMENSION TEX1(16),IN(6)
0006        LOGICAL*1 STOP
0007        DATA TEX1/'FRP','FRZ','QP','KHP','KLP','ROPT','R1','C2','R3',
           1'R4','R5','C7','R8','C','R',' '/IN/1,2,3,0,14,15/
0008        DATA IFR,IV,ICIN,ICOUT,IRIN,IROUT,IPA/2,2,1,2,0,6,5/
0009        DATA ICH,IRIN1/0,1/
0010        CALL INPUT(IFR,IV,ICIN,IRIN,ICH,TEX1,IN)
0011  150   IF(XFRP.NE.XFRZ) GOTO 160
0013        TYPE 20
0014  20    FORMAT(/X,'FRP IS EQUAL FRZ !')
0015        CALL TEST(IFR,IV,ICIN,IRIN,TEX1,IN)
0016        GOTO 150
0017  160   ICH=15
0018        IFIRST=0
0019        XHI=6.2831835*XFRP*XC
0020        XROPT=1./XHI
0021        TYPE 10,XROPT
0022  10    FORMAT(X,'ROPT',T15,'=',1PE10.3)
0023        CALL INPUT(IFR,IV,ICIN,IRIN1,ICH,TEX1,IN)
0024        XR1=XR
0025        XR3=XR
0026        XC2=XC
0027        XC7=XC
0028        XR8=XQP/XHI
0029        XHI1=(XFRZ/XFRP)**2-1
0030        IF(XHI1.GT.0) GOTO 200
0032        XR4=-XR8*XHI1
0033        TYPE 31
0034  31    FORMAT(/X,'HIGH-PASS NOTCHED')
0035        GOTO 220
0036  200   XR4=XR8*XHI1
0037        TYPE 30
0038  30    FORMAT(/X,'LOW-PASS NOTCHED')
0039  220   XR5=XROPT**2/XR4
0040        XKLP=1.
0041        XKHP=1.
0042        CALL OUTPUT(IPA,ICOUT,IROUT,TEX1)
0043        CALL TEST(IFR,IV,ICIN,IRIN,TEX1,IN)
0044        IF(.NOT.STOP) GOTO 150
0046        RETURN
0047        END
```

```
0001         SUBROUTINE GP1
      C************************************************
0002         COMMON /STO/STOP
0003         COMMON/FIRST/IFIRST
0004         COMMON/DATA1/XFR,XQP,XKHP,XKBP,XKLP,XROPT,XR1,XR2,XR3,XR4,XR5,XC6
            1,XR7,XC8,XC,XR
0005         DIMENSION TEX1(16),IN(5)
0006         LOGICAL*1 STOP
0007         DATA TEX1/'FREQ','QP','KHP','KBP','KLP','ROPT','R1','R2','R3',
            1'R4','R5','C6','R7','C8','C','R'/IN/1,2,0,15,16/
0008         DATA IFR,IV,ICIN,ICOUT,IRIN,IROUT,IPA/1,2,1,2,0,7,5/
0009         DATA ICH,IRIN1/0,1/
0010         CALL INPUT(IFR,IV,ICIN,IRIN,ICH,TEX1,IN)
0011   150   ICH=16
0012         IFIRST=0
0013         XHI=6.2831835*XFR*XC
0014         XROPT=1./XHI
0015         TYPE 10,XROPT
0016    10   FORMAT(X,'ROPT',T15,'=',1PE10.3)
0017         CALL INPUT(IFR,IV,ICIN,IRIN1,ICH,TEX1,IN)
0018         XR1=XR
0019         XR3=XR
0020         XR5=XR
0021         XR7=XR
0022         XC6=XC
0023         XC8=XC
0024         XR4=XR*(XHI*XR)**2
0025         XR2=XR*(XQP*(1.+XR4/XR)/SQRT(XR4/XR)-1.)
0026         XKHP=(1.+XR4/XR)/(XR/XR2+1.)
0027         XKBP=XR2/XR
0028         XKLP=XKHP*XR/XR4
0029         CALL OUTPUT(IPA,ICOUT,IROUT,TEX1)
0030         CALL TEST(IFR,IV,ICIN,IRIN,TEX1,IN)
0031         IF(.NOT.STOP) GOTO 150
0033         RETURN
0034         END
```

```
0001        SUBROUTINE GP2
C***************************************************
0002        COMMON /STO/STOP
0003        COMMON/FIRST/IFIRST
0004        COMMON/DATA1/XFR,XQP,XKBP,XKLP,XROPT,XR1,XR2,XC3,XR4,XR5,XC6
           1,XR7,XR8,XC,XR
0005        DIMENSION TEX1(16),IN(7)
0006        LOGICAL*1 STOP
0007        DATA TEX1/'FREQ','QP','KBP','KLP','ROPT','R1','R2','C3',
           1'R4','R5','C6','R7','R8','C','R',' '/IN/1,2,3,4,0,14,15/
0008        DATA IFR,IV,ICIN,ICOUT,IRIN,IROUT,IPA/1,4,1,2,0,7,4/
0009        DATA ICH,IRIN1/0,1/
0010        CALL INPUT(IFR,IV,ICIN,IRIN,ICH,TEX1,IN)
0011  150   XKLPIN=XKLP
0012        ICH=15
0013        IFIRST=0
0014        XROPT=1./(6.2831853*XFR*XC)
0015        TYPE 10,XROPT
0016  10    FORMAT(X,'ROPT',T15,'=',1PE10.3)
0017        CALL INPUT(IFR,IV,ICIN,IRIN1,ICH,TEX1,IN)
0018        XR2=XR
0019        XR7=XR
0020        XR8=XR
0021        XC3=XC
0022        XC6=XC
0023        XR4=XQP*XROPT
0024        XR5=XROPT**2/XR
0025        IF(XKLPIN.EQ.0) GOTO 200
0027        XR1=XR2/XKLP
0028        XKBP=XR4/XR1
0029        GOTO 220
0030  200   XR1=XR4/XKBP
0031        XKLP=XR2/XR1
0032  220   CALL OUTPUT(IPA,ICOUT,IROUT,TEX1)
0033        XKLP=XKLPIN
0034        CALL TEST(IFR,IV,ICIN,IRIN,TEX1,IN)
0035        IF(.NOT.STOP) GOTO 150
0037        RETURN
0038        END
```

```
0001        SUBROUTINE HLPNMQ
C***************************************************
0002        COMMON /STO/STOP
0003        COMMON/FIRST/IFIRST
0004        COMMON /DATA1/XFRP,XFRZ,XQP,XK,XGSP,XP,XPMIN,XR1,XR2,XC3,XC4,
           1XR5,XR6,XR7,XR8,XR9
0005        DIMENSION TEX1(16),IN(9),XX(3)
0006        LOGICAL*1 STOP,OPT,RICH
0007        DATA TEX1/'FRP','FRZ','QP','K','GSP','P','PMIN','R1','R2','C3',
           1'C4','R5','R6','R7','R8','R9'/IN/1,2,3,4,6,10,11,16,0/
0008        DATA IFR,IV,IC,IRIN,IROUT,IPA,ICH/2,3,2,1,7,7,0/
0009        XP=0.
0010        CALL INPUT(IFR,IV,IC,IRIN,ICH,TEX1,IN)
0011   80   XKIN=XK
0012        XPIN=XP
0013        IF((XFRP-XFRZ).NE.0.) GOTO 88
0015        TYPE 5*
0016   5    FORMAT(/X,'NO BANDREJECT')
0017        XP=XPIN
0018        CALL TEST(IFR,IV,IC,IRIN,TEX1,IN)
0019        GOTO 80
0020   88   XP=0.5
0021        XX(2)=0.
0022        ILAUF=0
0023        OPT=.FALSE.
0024        RICH=.FALSE.
0025   89   ILAUF=ILAUF+1
0026   90   IF(.NOT.OPT) GOTO 95
0028        XP=XPMIN
0029        IF(XPIN.EQ.0) GOTO 100
0031        XP=XPIN
0032        GOTO 100
0033   95   XPMIN=XP
0034        IF(RICH) XP=XP+0.01
0036        IF(.NOT.RICH) XP=XP-0.01
0038   100  XWP=XFRP*6.2831853
0039        XWZ=XFRZ*6.2831853
0040        X=0.
0041        IF((XFRP-XFRZ).GT.0.) X=1
0043        XH1=1.+4.*XQP*XQP*XP*(1.+XC4/XC3)
0044        XH2=XC3*XWP*(SQRT(XH1)-1.)/(2.*XP*XQP)
0045        XK0=(1.+XP)/(1.+(1.+XC4/XC3)*XWZ*XWZ*(XC3/XH2)**2)
```

```
0046          IF(XKIN.NE.O.) GOTO 150
0048          IF((1-XKIN/XKO).GE.0) GOTO 150
0050          XK=XKO
0051          XR1=1./XH2
0052          XR2=1.E38
0053          GOTO 160
0054     150  XK=XKIN
0055          XR1=XKO/(XH2*XK)
0056          XR2=1./(XH2*(1.-XKIN/XKO))
0057     160  XR6=XH2*(1.+XP)*(1.-(X/XK))/(XC3*XC4*(XWZ**2-XWP**2))
0058          XR5=1./(XC3*XC4*XWP**2/XH2+XP/XR6)
0059          XH4=ABS(1.-XH2/(XWP**2*XC3*XC4)*(1./XR5+1./XR6))
0060          XH5=ABS(1.-XQP/XWP*(XH2/XC3+(1./XC3+1./XC4)*(1./XR5+1./XR6)))
0061          XGSP=(1.+XP)/2.*(XH5+XQP*XH4)
0062          XR7=XP*XR9/XK
0063          XR8=XP*XR9/(1.-XK)
0064          XX(ILAUF)=XGSP
0065          IF(XX(1).LT.XX(2)) RICH=.TRUE.
0067          IF(ILAUF.LE.2) GOTO 89
0069          IF(OPT) GOTO 600
0071          IF(XPMIN.LE.0.02) OPT=.TRUE.
0073          IF(RICH) GOTO 550
0075          IF(XX(2).LT.XX(3)) OPT=.TRUE.
0077          GOTO 560
0078     550  IF(XX(2).LT.XX(3)) OPT=.TRUE.
0080     560  XX(2)=XX(3)
0081          GOTO 90
0082     600  IF(XFRP-XFRZ) 620,80,610
0083     610  TYPE 10
0084     10   FORMAT(X,'HIGH-PASS')
0085          GOTO 630
0086     620  TYPE 11
0087     11   FORMAT(X,'LOW-PASS')
0088     630  CALL OUTPUT(IPA,IC,IROUT,TEX1)
0089          XP=XPIN
0090          CALL TEST(IFR,IV,IC,IRIN,TEX1,IN)
0091          IF(.NOT.STOP) GOTO 80
0093     1000 RETURN
0094          END
```

```
0001        SUBROUTINE BRHLPN
      C***************************************************
0002        COMMON /STO/STOP
0003        COMMON/FIRST/IFIRST
0004        COMMON /DATA1/XFRP,XFRZ,XQP,XK,XGSP,XC1,XC2,XC3,XC4,XR5,XR6,XR7
           1,XR8,XR9,XR10
0005        DIMENSION TEX1(16),IN(9)
0006        LOGICAL*1 STOP
0007        DATA TEX1/'FRP','FRZ','QP','K','GSP','C1','C2','C3','C4','R5',
           1'R6','R7','R8','R9','R10',' '/IN/1,2,3,0,6,7,8,9,14/
0008        DATA IFR,IV,IC,IRIN,IROUT,IPA,ICH/2,2,4,1,6,5,0/
0009        CALL INPUT(IFR,IV,IC,IRIN,ICH,TEX1,IN)
0010   150  XWP=XFRP*6.2831853
0011        XWZ=XFRZ*6.2831853
0012        XH=(1.+XC4*(XC1+XC2)/(XC1*XC2))*XWP**2/XWZ**2-1.
0013        XQ=1./(2*SQRT((1.+XC2/XC1)*(1.+XC2/XC3)))
0014        XR5=1./(2*XWZ*XQ*(XC2+XC3))
0015        XR6=(1.+XC2/XC1)/(XR5*XC2*XC3*XWZ**2)
0016        XR7=1./(XC1*XC2*(XR5+XR6)*XWZ**2)
0017        IF(XH) 200,220,240
0018   200  TYPE 20
0019   20   FORMAT(/X,'C4>=((FRZ/FRP)**2-1)*(C1*C2/(C1+C2))')
0020        CALL TEST(IFR,IV,IC,IRIN,TEX1,IN)
0021        GOTO 150
0022   220  XR8=1.E38
0023        GOTO 260
0024   240  XR8=(XR5+XR6)/XH
0025   260  XCS=XC1*XC2/(XC1+XC2)
0026        XRS=XR5+XR6
0027        XRH=(1./(XR8*XCS*XWZ)+XRS*XC4*XWZ-(1.+XC4/XCS)*XWP/(XQP*XWZ))
0028        XR10=XRH*XR9*XQ
0029        XGSPH=SQRT(XR5*XC3/(XR6*XCS))+SQRT(XRS*XC2/(XR7*XC1))
0030        XGSP=XGSPH*(1.+XR10/XR9)**2*XQP/((1.+XC4/XCS)*XWP/XWZ)
0031        XK=(1.+XR10/XR9)/(1.+XC4/XCS)
0032        IF(XFRP-XFRZ) 300,310,320
0033   300  TYPE 10
0034        GOTO 330
0035   10   FORMAT(X,'LOW-PASS')
0036   310  TYPE 11
0037        GOTO 330
0038   11   FORMAT(X,'BAND-REJECTION')
0039   320  TYPE 12
0040   12   FORMAT(X,'HIGH-PASS')
0041   330  CALL OUTPUT(IPA,IC,IROUT,TEX1)
0042        CALL TEST(IFR,IV,IC,IRIN,TEX1,IN)
0043        IF(.NOT.STOP) GOTO 150
0045        RETURN
0046        END
```

BASIC Program Listing for the TRS-80 Minicomputer

The program listing on the first page of this Appendix comprises the following:

Lines 30–110:   information with regard to available filter functions and corresponding circuit numbers.

Lines 120–180:   request for input of circuit number, as well as frequency and Q value.

Line 190:   branching point to the twenty-three circuit subprograms followed by two subroutines (lines 200 and 260) which are required later in the circuit subprograms.

On each of the subsequent twenty-three pages, the design subprogram for one of the twenty-three circuits given in Chapter 5 is listed.

An advantage of the TRS-80 system is that a circuit subprogram can be re-run while changing only some, but not all, of the input parameters. Thus, when depressing the ENTER key without giving a new value for the parameter in question, the old value remains unchanged in memory. On the other hand, when going to a new circuit subprogram, all variables must be set equal to zero (line 10). Since the program runs automatically, further comments should not be necessary.

The entire program is available for a nominal handling charge on tape or diskette.

```
10 CLS:CLEAR
20 PRINTCHR$(23)
30 PRINT"LOW-Q      MEDIUM-Q    HIGH-Q":PRINT
40 PRINT"1.LP-LQ    8.LP-MQ     16.LP-HQ"
50 PRINT"2.BP-LQ-R 9.BP-MQ-R   17.BP-HQ"
60 PRINT"3.BP-LQ-C 10.BP-MQ-C 18.HP-HQ"
70 PRINT"4.HP-LQ    11.HP-MQ    19.AP-HQ"
80 PRINT"5.AP-Q.5  12.AP-MQ    20.BR-HQ"
90 PRINT"6.AP-LQ    13.BR-MQ    21.L/HPN-HQ"
100 PRINT@576,"7.BR-LQ    14.L/HPN-MQ      22.GP1"
110 PRINT@640,"          15.BR-L/HPN-MQ  23.GP2"
120 PRINT:PRINT"NUMBER OF DESIRED CIRCUIT ";
130 INPUT M
140 IF M<1 THEN 10 ELSE IF M>23 THEN 10
150 CLS
160 PRINTCHR$(23):PI#=3.1415926535897932:PI=PI#
170 PRINT"FREQUENCY(HZ) =";:INPUT F:FO=2*F*PI#
180 PRINT"Q =";:INPUT Q
190 ON M GOSUB 310,590,860,1130,1370,1600,1840,2080,2360,2650,
    2900,3150,3400,3630,4010,4310,4480,4650,4820,4990,5160,
    5420,5640
200 PRINT"TYPE 1 FOR NEW RUN";:INPUT T
210 IF T<>1 THEN 10
220 CLS:PRINTCHR$(23)
230 PRINT"FREQUENCY(HZ)=";F
240 PRINT"Q=";Q
250 RETURN
260 PRINT"OPTIMAL RO(KOHM)=";RO/1E3
270 PRINT"INPUT DISCRETE VALUE NEAR RO"
280 PRINT"RD(KOHM)=";:INPUT ZZ:RD=ZZ*1E3
290 IF RD=0 THEN RD=RO
300 RETURN
```

```
310 REM <1.LP-LQ>
320 PRINT@192,"C2(NF)=";:INPUT C0:C2=C0*1E-9
330 PRINT"C4(NF)=";:INPUT C3:C4=C3*1E-9
340 H1=C2/C4/2/Q/Q
350 IF H1>=2 THEN 370
360 PRINT"C2 >= 4Q↑2*C4 !":PRINT@128,"":PRINT:GOTO 320
370 P=H1-1+SQR(H1*(H1-2))
380 R1=1/F0/SQR(P*C2*C4)
390 R3=P*R1:GSP=Q*SQR(C2/C4/P)
400 PRINT"K (OPTIONAL) =";:INPUT K1
410 IF K1=0 THEN 440
420 IF 1-K1<=0 THEN 440
430 K=K1:S1=R1/K:S2=R1/(1-K):GOTO 450
440 S1=R1:S2=1E30:K=1
450 CLS:PRINTCHR$(23)
460 PRINT"1.LP-LQ":PRINT
470 PRINT"R11=";S1
480 IF S2=1E30 THEN 500
490 PRINT"R12=";S2
500 PRINT"C2 =";C2
510 PRINT"R3 =";R3
520 PRINT"C4 =";C4:PRINT
530 PRINT"K  =";K
540 PRINT"F  =";F
550 PRINT"Q  =";Q
560 PRINT"GSP=";GSP:PRINT
570 GOSUB 200
580 GOTO 320
```

```
590 REM <2.BP-LQ-R>
600 PRINT@192,"C2(NF)=";:INPUT C0:C2=C0*1E-9
610 PRINT"C3(NF)=";:INPUT C1:C3=C1*1E-9
620 P=Q*Q*(2+C2/C3+C3/C2)
630 R1=1/F0/SQR(P*C2*C3)
640 R4=P*R1
650 GSP=Q*Q*(1+C3/C2)
660 K0=GSP
670 PRINT"K (OPTIONAL) =";:INPUT K1
680 IF K1=0 THEN 710
690 IF K0-K1<=0 THEN 710
700 K=K1:S1=K0*R1/K:S2=K0*R1/(K0-K):GOTO 720
710 K=K0:S1=R1:S2=1E30
720 CLS:PRINTCHR$(23)
730 PRINT"2.BP-LQ-R":PRINT
740 PRINT"R11=";S1
750 IF S2=1E30 THEN 770
760 PRINT"R12=";S2
770 PRINT"C2 =";C2
780 PRINT"C3 =";C3
790 PRINT"R4 =";R4:PRINT
800 PRINT"K  =";K
810 PRINT"F  =";F
820 PRINT"Q  =";Q
830 PRINT"GSP=";GS:PRINT
840 GOSUB 200
850 GOTO 600
```

```
860  REM <3.BP-LQ-C>
870  PRINT@192,"C11(NF)=";:INPUT C0:S1=C0*1E-9
880  PRINT"C12(NF,OPTIONAL)=";:INPUT C3:S2=C3*1E-9
890  PRINT"C4(NF)=";:INPUT C2:C4=C2*1E-9
900  H1=(S1+S2)/C4/2/Q/Q
910  IF H1>=2 THEN 930
920  PRINT"C11+C12 >= 4Q↑2*C4 !":PRINT@128,"":PRINT:PRINT:GOTO 870
930  C1=S1+S2
940  P=H1-1+SQR(H1*(H1-2))
950  R2=1/F0/SQR(P*C1*C4)
960  R3=P*R2
970  GSP=Q*SQR(C1/P/C4)
980  K=S1*GS/C1
990  CLS:PRINTCHR$(23)
1000 PRINT"3.BP-LQ-C":PRINT
1010 PRINT"C11=";S1
1020 IF S2=0 THEN 1040
1030 PRINT"C12=";S2
1040 PRINT"R2 =";R2
1050 PRINT"R3 =";R3
1060 PRINT"C4 =";C4:PRINT
1070 PRINT"K  =";K
1080 PRINT"F  =";F
1090 PRINT"Q  =";Q
1100 PRINT"GSP=";GS:PRINT
1110 GOSUB 200
1120 GOTO 870
```

```
1130 REM <4.HP-LQ>
1140 PRINT@192,"C11(NF)=";:INPUT C0:S1=C0*1E-9
1150 PRINT"C12(NF,OPTIONAL)=";:INPUT C2:S2=C2*1E-9
1160 PRINT"C3(NF)=";:INPUT C4:C3=C4*1E-9
1170 C1=S1+S2
1180 P=Q*Q*(2+C1/C3+C3/C1)
1190 R2=1/F0/SQR(P*C1*C3)
1200 R4=P*R2
1210 GSP=Q*SQR(P*C3/C1)
1220 K=S1/C1
1230 CLS:PRINTCHR$(23)
1240 PRINT"4.HP-LQ":PRINT
1250 PRINT"C11=";S1
1260 IF S2=0 THEN 1280
1270 PRINT"C12=";S2
1280 PRINT"R2 =";R2
1290 PRINT"C3 =";C3
1300 PRINT"R4 =";R4:PRINT
1310 PRINT"K  =";K
1320 PRINT"F  =";F
1330 PRINT"Q  =";Q
1340 PRINT"GSP=";GS
1350 GOSUB 200
1360 GOTO 1140
```

```
1370 REM <5.AP-Q.5>
1380 PRINT@192,"C1(NF)=";:INPUT S1:C1=S1*1E-9
1390 PRINT"C2(NF)=";:INPUT S2:C2=S2*1E-9
1400 PRINT"C3(NF)=";:INPUT S3:C3=S3*1E-9
1410 H1=C1+C2:H2=C2+C3:H3=C1*C2
1420 H=1-H1*H2*4*Q*Q/C1/C3
1430 IF H>=0 THEN 1450
1440 PRINT"C1=C3 >= C2*2Q/(1-2Q) !":PRINT@128,"":PRINT:PRINT:GOTO 1380
1450 H4=2*F0*Q*H2:H6=F0*F0*H3:H5=H1/H6/C3
1460 A4=(1+SQR(H))/H4:A5=H5/A4:A6=1/H6/(A4+A5)
1470 B4=(1-SQR(H))/H4:B5=H5/B4:B6=1/H6/(B4+B5)
1480 CLS:PRINTCHR$(23)
1490 PRINT"5.AP-Q.5":PRINT
1500 PRINT"C1 =";C1
1510 PRINT"C2 =";C2
1520 PRINT"C3 =";C3:PRINT
1530 PRINT"R4A=";A4,"R4B=";B4
1540 PRINT"R5A=";A5,"R5B=";B5
1550 PRINT"R6A=";A6,"R6B=";B6:PRINT
1560 PRINT"F  =";F
1570 PRINT"Q  =";Q:PRINT
1580 GOSUB 200
1590 GOTO 1380
```

```
1600 REM <6.AP-LQ>
1610 PRINT@192,"C2(NF)=";:INPUT C0:C2=C0*1E-9
1620 PRINT"C3(NF)=";:INPUT C1:C3=C1*1E-9
1630 PRINT"R6(KOHM,OPTIONAL)=";:INPUT R0:R6=R0*1E3
1640 P=Q*Q*(2+C2/C3+C3/C2)
1650 R1=1/F0/SQR(P*C2*C3)
1660 R4=P*R1:GSP=Q*SQR(P*C3/C2)
1670 IF R6=0 THEN R6=1E4
1680 R5=R6*2*(1+C2/C3)/P
1690 K=R6/(R5+R6)
1700 CLS:PRINTCHR$(23)
1710 PRINT"6.AP-LQ":PRINT
1720 PRINT"R1 =";R1
1730 PRINT"C2 =";C2
1740 PRINT"C3 =";C3
1750 PRINT"R4 =";R4
1760 PRINT"R5 =";R5
1770 PRINT"R6 =";R6:PRINT
1780 PRINT"K  =";K
1790 PRINT"F  =";F
1800 PRINT"Q  =";Q
1810 PRINT"GSP=";GS:PRINT
1820 GOSUB 200
1830 GOTO 1610
```

```
1840 REM <7.BR-LQ>
1850 PRINT@192,"C2(NF)=";:INPUT CO:C2=CO*1E-9
1860 PRINT"C3(NF)=";:INPUT C1:C3=C1*1E-9
1870 PRINT"R6(KOHM,OPTIONAL)=";:INPUT RO:R6=RO*1E3
1880 P=Q*Q*(2+C2/C3+C3/C2)
1890 R1=1/FO/SQR(P*C2*C3)
1900 R4=P*R1:GSP=Q*SQR(P*C3/C2)
1910 IF R6=0 THEN R6=1E4
1920 R5=R6*(1+C2/C3)/P
1930 K=R6/(R5+R6)
1940 CLS:PRINTCHR$(23)
1950 PRINT"7.BR-LQ":PRINT
1960 PRINT"R1 =";R1
1970 PRINT"C2 =";C2
1980 PRINT"C3 =";C3
1990 PRINT"R4 =";R4
2000 PRINT"R5 =";R5
2010 PRINT"R6 =";R6:PRINT
2020 PRINT"K  =";K
2030 PRINT"F  =";F
2040 PRINT"Q  =";Q
2050 PRINT"GSP=";GS:PRINT
2060 GOSUB 200
2070 GOTO 1850
```

```
2080 REM <8.LP-MQ>
2090 PRINT"C2(NF)=";:INPUT C0:C2=C0*1E-9
2100 PRINT"C4(NF)=";:INPUT C3:C4=C3*1E-9
2110 PRINT"K(OPTIONAL)=";:INPUT KI
2120 PRINT"R5(KOHM,OPTIONAL)=";:INPUT R0:R5=R0*1E3
2130 H1=C4/C2:H2=12*Q*Q:H3=H1*H2*3
2140 P=(SQR(1+H2*(1+H1))+1)↑2/H3
2150 R1=1/F0/SQR(P*C2*C4):R3=P*R1
2160 IF R5=0 THEN R5=1E4
2170 R6=R5*(H1*(1+P)-SQR(P*H1)/Q)
2180 K0=1+R6/R5:GSP=Q*K0*K0/SQR(P*H1)
2190 IF KI=0 THEN 2210
2200 IF K0-KI>0 THEN 2220
2210 K=K0:S1=R1:S2=1E30:GOTO 2230
2220 K=KI:S1=K0*R1/K:S2=K0*R1/(K0-K)
2230 CLS:PRINTCHR$(23)
2240 PRINT"8.LP-MQ":PRINT
2250 PRINT"R11=";S1,:IF S2<>1E30 THEN PRINT"R12=";S2
2260 PRINT"C2 =";C2,"R3 =";R3
2270 PRINT"C4 =";C4
2280 PRINT"R5 =";R5,"R6 =";R6:PRINT
2290 PRINT"K  =";K
2300 PRINT"F  =";F,"Q  =";Q:PRINT
2310 PRINT"P  =";P,"GSP=";GS:PRINT
2320 PRINT"TYPE 1 IF NEW P :";:INPUT P0
2330 IF P0=1 THEN PRINT"P=";:INPUT P:GOTO 2150
2340 GOSUB 200
2350 GOTO 2090
```

```
2360 REM <9.BP-MQ-R>
2370 PRINT"C2(NF)=";:INPUT CO:C2=CO*1E-9
2380 PRINT"C3(NF)=";:INPUT C1:C3=C1*1E-9
2390 PRINT"K(OPTIONAL)=";:INPUT KI
2400 PRINT"R6(KOHM,OPTIONAL)=";:INPUT RO:R6=RO*1E3
2410 H1=C2/C3:H2=4*Q*Q:H3=3*H2*(1+C3/C2)
2420 P=H1/H2*(SQR(1+H3)-1)↑2
2430 R1=1/FO/SQR(P*C2*C3):R4=P*R1
2440 IF R6=0 THEN R6=1E4
2450 R5=R6*((1+H1)/P-SQR(H1/P)/Q)
2460 KO=Q*(1+R5/R6)*SQR(P/H1)
2470 GSP=(1+R5/R6)*KO
2480 IF KI=0 THEN 2500
2490 IF KO-KI>0 THEN 2510
2500 K=KO:S1=R1:S2=1E30:GOTO 2520
2510 K=KI:S1=KO*R1/K:S2=KO*R1/(KO-K)
2520 CLS:PRINTCHR$(23)
2530 PRINT"9.BP-MQ-R":PRINT
2540 PRINT"R11=";S1,:IF S2<>1E30 THEN PRINT"R12=";S2
2550 PRINT"C2 =";C2,"C3 =";C3
2560 PRINT"R4 =";R4
2570 PRINT"R5 =";R5,"R6 =";R6:PRINT
2580 PRINT"K  =";K
2590 PRINT"F  =";F,"Q  =";Q:PRINT
2600 PRINT"P  =";P,"GSP=";GS:PRINT
2610 PRINT"TYPE 1 IF NEW P";:INPUT PO
2620 IF PO=1 THEN PRINT"P=";:INPUT P:GOTO 2430
2630 GOSUB 200
2640 GOTO 2370
```

```
2650 REM <10.BP-MQ-C>
2660 PRINT"C11(NF)=";:INPUT C3:S1=C3*1E-9
2670 PRINT"C12(NF,OPTIONAL)=";:INPUT C2:S2=C2*1E-9
2680 PRINT"C4(NF)=";:INPUT C0:C4=C0*1E-9
2690 PRINT"R6(KOHM,OPTIONAL)=";:INPUT R0:R6=R0*1E3
2700 C1=S1+S2:H1=C4/C1:H2=12*Q*Q
2710 P=(SQR(1+H2*(1+H1))+1)↑2/3/H1/H2
2720 R2=1/F0/SQR(P*C1*C4):R3=P*R2
2730 IF R6=0 THEN R6=1E4
2740 R5=R6*(H1*(1+P)-SQR(P*H1)/Q)
2750 K=S1/C1*(1+R5/R6)*Q/SQR(P*H1)
2760 GSP=K/S1*C1*(1+R5/R6)
2770 CLS:PRINTCHR$(23)
2780 PRINT"10.BP-MQ-C":PRINT
2790 PRINT"C11=";S1,:IF S2<>0 THEN PRINT"C12=";S2
2800 PRINT"R2 =";R2,"R3 =";R3
2810 PRINT"C4 =";C4
2820 PRINT"R5 =";R5,"R6 =";R6:PRINT
2830 PRINT"K  =";K
2840 PRINT"F  =";F,"Q  =";Q:PRINT
2850 PRINT"P  =";P,"GSP=";GS:PRINT
2860 PRINT"TYPE 1 IF NEW P";:INPUT P0
2870 IF P0=1 THEN PRINT"P=";:INPUT P:GOTO 2720
2880 GOSUB 200
2890 GOTO 2660
```

```
2900 REM <11.HP-MQ>
2910 PRINT"C11(NF)=";:INPUT C0:S1=C0*1E-9
2920 PRINT"C12(NF,OPTIONAL)=";:INPUT C2:S2=C2*1E-9
2930 PRINT"C3(NF)=";:INPUT C4:C3=C4*1E-9
2940 PRINT"R5(KOHM,OPTIONAL)=";:INPUT R0:R5=R0*1E3
2950 C1=S1+S2:H1=C1/C3:H2=12*Q*Q*(1+1/H1)
2960 P=H1/4/Q/Q*(SQR(1+H2)-1)↑2
2970 R2=1/F0/SQR(P*C1*C3):R4=P*R2
2980 IF R5=0 THEN R5=1E4
2990 R6=R5*((1+H1)/P-SQR(H1/P)/Q)
3000 K=S1*(1+R6/R5)/C1
3010 GS=Q*SQR(P/H1)*(1+R6/R5)↑2
3020 CLS:PRINTCHR$(23)
3030 PRINT"11.HP-MQ":PRINT
3040 PRINT"C11=";S1,:IF  S2<>0 THEN PRINT"C12=";S2
3050 PRINT"R2=";R2,"C3=";C3
3060 PRINT"R4=";R4
3070 PRINT"R5=";R5,"R6=";R6:PRINT
3080 PRINT"K =";K
3090 PRINT"F =";F,"Q =";Q
3100 PRINT"P =";P,"GSP=";GS:PRINT
3110 PRINT"TYPE 1 IF NEW P";:INPUT P0
3120 IF P0=1 THEN PRINT"P =";:INPUT P:GOTO 2970
3130 GOSUB 200
3140 GOTO 2910
```

```
3150 REM <12.AP-MQ>
3160 PRINT"C2(NF)=";:INPUT CO:C2=C0*1E-9
3170 PRINT"C3(NF)=";:INPUT C1:C3=C1*1E-9
3180 PRINT"R6(KOHM,OPTIONAL)=";:INPUT RO:R6=R0*1E3
3190 X=C2/C3:X1=1+X:X2=X1*X1
3200 H=6*Q*Q*X2/(2*Q*Q*X1-X)
3210 P=(SQR(1+H*H/3/X2)-1)/H
3220 R1=1/F0/SQR(P*C2*C3):R=P*R1
3230 IF R6=0 THEN R6=1E4
3240 R7=R6*(P*X1+SQR(P*X)/Q)
3250 A=1-2*SQR(P*X)/Q/(1+R7/R6)
3260 R5=R/A:R4=R/(1-A)
3270 GS=A*Q/SQR(P*X)*(1+R7/R6)↑2
3280 CLS:PRINTCHR$(23)
3290 PRINT"12.AP-MQ":PRINT
3300 PRINT"R1=";R1,"C2=";C2
3310 PRINT"C3=";C3,"R4=";R4
3320 PRINT"R5=";R5
3330 PRINT"R6=";R6,"R7=";R7:PRINT
3340 PRINT"F =";F,"Q =";Q
3350 PRINT"P =";P,"GSP=";GS:PRINT
3360 PRINT"TYPE 1 IF NEW P";:INPUT PO
3370 IF PO=1 THEN PRINT"P =";:INPUT P:GOTO 3220
3380 GOSUB 200
3390 GOTO 3160
```

```
3400 REM <13.BR-MQ>
3410 PRINT"C2(NF)=";:INPUT C0:C2=C0*1E-9
3420 PRINT"C3(NF)=";:INPUT C1:C3=C1*1E-9
3430 PRINT"R6(KOHM,OPTIONAL)=";:INPUT R0:R6=R0*1E3
3440 H=C2/C3:P=1/3/(1+H)
3450 R1=1/F0/SQR(P*C2*C3):R=P*R1
3460 IF R6=0 THEN R6=1E4
3470 R7=R6*(1+H)*P
3480 A=1-SQR(P*H)/Q/(1+R7/R6)
3490 R5=R/A:R4=R/(1-A)
3500 GS=Q*A/SQR(P*H)*(1+R7/R6)↑2
3510 CLS:PRINTCHR$(23)
3520 PRINT"13.BR-MQ":PRINT
3530 PRINT"R1=";R1,"C2=";C2
3540 PRINT"C3=";C3,"R4=";R4
3550 PRINT"R5=";R5
3560 PRINT"R6=";R6,"R7=";R7:PRINT
3570 PRINT"F =";F,"Q =";Q
3580 PRINT"P?=";P,"GSP=";GS:PRINT
3590 PRINT"TYPE 1 IF NEW P";:INPUT P0
3600 IF P0=1 THEN PRINT"P =";:INPUT P:GOTO 3450
3610 GOSUB 200
3620 GOTO 3410
```

```
3630 REM <14.LPN/HPN-MQ>
3640 PRINT"ZERO FREQ.=";:INPUT FZ
3650 X0=SGN(F-FZ)
3660 IF X0=0 THEN PRINT"NO BANDREJECT!":GOTO 3640
3670 PRINT"C3(NF)=";:INPUT C0:C3=C0*1E-9
3680 PRINT"C4(NF)=";:INPUT C1:C4=C1*1E-9
3690 PRINT"K(OPTIONAL)=";:INPUT KI
3700 PRINT"R9(KOHM,OPTIONAL)=";:INPUT R0:R9=R0*1E3
3710 PRINT"P(START BETWEEN .01 TO 3.)=";:INPUT P
3720 X=(1+X0)/2:Z0=(2*PI*FZ)↑2
3730 G=C3*F0/2/P/Q*(SQR(1+4*Q*Q*P*(1+C4/C3))-1)
3740 K0=(1+P)/(1÷(1+C4/C3)*Z0*(C3/G)↑2)
3750 IF KI=0 THEN 3780
3760 H=1-KI/K0
3770 IF H>0 THEN 3790
3780 K=K0:R1=1/G:R2=1E30:GOTO 3800
3790 K=KI:R1=K0/G/KI:R2=1/G/H
3800 R6=G*(1+P)*(1-X/K)/C3/C4/(Z0-F0*F0)
3810 R5=1/(C3*C4*F0*F0/G+P/R6)
3820 H1=Q/F0*(G/C3+(C3+C4)*(R5+R6)/C3/R5/C4/R6)
3830 H2=1-G*(R5+R6)/F0/F0/C3/C4/R5/R6
3840 GS=(1+P)/2*(ABS(1-H1)+Q*ABS(H2))
3850 IF R9=0 THEN R9=1E4
3860 R7=P*R9/K:R8=P*R9/(1-K)
3870 CLS:PRINTCHR$(23)
3880 PRINT"14.LPN/HPN-MQ":PRINT
3890 PRINT"R1=";R1,"R2=";R2
3900 PRINT"C3=";C3,"C4=";C4
3910 PRINT"R5=";R5,"R6=";R6
3920 PRINT"R7=";R7,"R8=";R8
3930 PRINT"R9=";R9:PRINT
3940 PRINT"K =";K,"FZ=";FZ
3950 PRINT"FP=";F,"Q =";Q
3960 PRINT"P =";P,"GSP=";GS:PRINT
3970 PRINT"TYPE 1 IF NEW P";:INPUT P0
3980 IF P0=1 THEN PRINT"P =";:INPUT P:GOTO 3720
3990 GOSUB 200
4000 PRINT"FZ=";FZ:GOTO 3670
```

```
4010 REM <15.BR-LPN/HPN-MQ>
4020 PRINT"ZERO FREQ.=";:INPUT FZ
4030 Z0=2*PI*FZ:Z2=Z0*Z0:X=Z0/F0
4040 PRINT"C1(NF)=";:INPUT D1:C1=D1*1E-9
4050 PRINT"C2(NF)=";:INPUT D2:C2=D2*1E-9
4060 PRINT"C3(NF)=";:INPUT D3:C3=D3*1E-9
4070 PRINT"C4(NF)=";:INPUT D4:C4=D4*1E-9
4080 PRINT"R9(KOHM,OPTIONAL)=";:INPUT Y:R9=Y*1E3
4090 C=C1*C2/(C1+C2):H1=1+C4/C:H2=1+C2/C1
4100 G=1/2/SQR(H2*(1+C2/C3))
4110 R5=1/2/Z0/G/(C2+C3):R6=H2/R5/Z2/C2/C3
4120 RS=R5+R6:R7=1/Z2/C1/C2/RS:H=H1/X/X-1
4130 IF H<0 THEN PRINT"C4>=((FZ/FP)↑2-1)*C1*C2/(C1+C2)":GOTO 4070
4140 IF H=0 THEN R8=1E30 ELSE R8=RS/H
4150 IF R9=0 THEN R9=1E4
4160 R0=R9*G*(1/R8/C/Z0+RS*C4*Z0-H1/Q/X)
4170 GS=Q*X/H1*(SQR(R5*C3/R6/C)+SQR(RS*C2/R7/C1))*(1+R0/R9)↑2
4180 K=(1+R0/R9)/H1
4190 CLS:PRINTCHR$(23)
4200 PRINT"15.BR-LPN/HPN-MQ":PRINT
4210 PRINT"C1=";C1,"C2=";C2
4220 PRINT"C3=";C3,"C4=";C4
4230 PRINT"R5=";R5,"R6=";R6
4240 PRINT"R7=";R7,"R8=";R8
4250 PRINT"R9=";R9,"R10=";R0:PRINT
4260 PRINT"FZ=";FZ,"FP=";F
4270 PRINT"Q =";Q,"K =";K
4280 PRINT"GSP=";GS:PRINT
4290 GOSUB 200
4300 PRINT"FZ=";FZ:GOTO 4040
```

```
4310 REM <16.LP--HQ>
4320 PRINT"C(NF)=";:INPUT D:C=D*1E-9
4330 R0=1/F0/C
4340 GOSUB 260
4350 C1=C:C4=C
4360 R2=RD:R3=RD:R6=RD
4370 R1=Q*R0
4380 R7=R0*R0/RD
4390 CLS:PRINTCHR$(23)
4400 PRINT"16.LP-HQ":PRINT
4410 PRINT"R1=";R1,"C1=";C1
4420 PRINT"R2=";R2,"R3=";R3
4430 PRINT"C4=";C4,"R6=";R6
4440 PRINT"R7=";R7:PRINT
4450 PRINT"F =";F,"Q =";Q:PRINT
4460 GOSUB 200
4470 GOTO 4320
```

```
4480 REM <17.BP-HQ>
4490 PRINT"C(NF)=";:INPUT D:C=D*1E-9
4500 R0=1/F0/C
4510 GOSUB 260
4520 C3=C:C8=C
4530 R1=RD:R2=RD:R6=RD
4540 R7=Q*R0
4550 R4=R0*R0/RD
4560 CLS:PRINTCHR$(23)
4570 PRINT"17.BP-HQ":PRINT
4580 PRINT"R1=";R1,"R2=";R2
4590 PRINT"C3=";C3,"R4=";R4
4600 PRINT"R6=";R6,"R7=";R7
4610 PRINT"C8=";C8:PRINT
4620 PRINT"F =";F,"Q =";Q:PRINT
4630 GOSUB 200
4640 GOTO 4490
```

```
4650 REM <18.HP-HQ>
4660 PRINT"C(NF)=";:INPUT D:C=D*1E-9
4670 R0=1/F0/C
4680 GOSUB 260
4690 C3=C:C7=C
4700 R1=RD:R2=RD:R6=RD
4710 R8=Q*R0
4720 R4=R0*R0/RD
4730 CLS:PRINTCHR$(23)
4740 PRINT"18.HP-HQ":PRINT
4750 PRINT"R1=";R1,"R2=";R2
4760 PRINT"C3=";C3,"R4=";R4
4770 PRINT"R6=";R6,"C7=";C7
4780 PRINT"R8=";R8:PRINT
4790 PRINT"F =";F,"Q =";Q:PRINT
4800 GOSUB 200
4810 GOTO 4660
```

```
4820 REM <19.AP-HQ>
4830 PRINT"C(NF)=";:INPUT D:C=D*1E-9
4840 R0=1/F0/C
4850 GOSUB 260
4860 C3=C:C7=C
4870 R1=RD:R2=RD:R5=RD
4880 R8=Q*R0
4890 R4=R0*R0/RD
4900 CLS:PRINTCHR$(23)
4910 PRINT"19.AP-HQ":PRINT
4920 PRINT"R1=";R1,"R2=";R2
4930 PRINT"C3=";C3,"R4=";R4
4940 PRINT"R5=";R5,"C7=";C7
4950 PRINT"R8=";R8:PRINT
4960 PRINT"F =";F,"Q =";Q:PRINT
4970 GOSUB 200
4980 GOTO 4830
```

```
4990 REM <20.BR-HQ>
5000 PRINT"C(NF)=";:INPUT D:C=D*1E-9
5010 R0=1/F0/C
5020 GOSUB 260
5030 C3=C:C7=C
5040 R1=RD:R2=RD:R5=RD
5050 R7=2*Q*R0:R8=R7
5060 R4=R0*R0/RD
5070 CLS:PRINTCHR$(23)
5080 PRINT"20.BR-HQ":PRINT
5090 PRINT"R1=";R1,"R2=";R2
5100 PRINT"C3=";C3,"R4=";R4
5110 PRINT"R5=";R5,"R7=";R7
5120 PRINT"C7=";C7,"R8=";R8:PRINT
5130 PRINT"F =";F,"Q =";Q:PRINT
5140 GOSUB 200
5150 GOTO 5000
```

```
5160 REM <21.LPN/HPN-HQ>
5170 PRINT"ZERO FREQ.=";:INPUT FZ
5180 IF FZ=F THEN PRINT"NO BANDREJECT !":GOTO 5170
5190 PRINT"C(NF)=";:INPUT D:C=D*1E-9
5200 RO=1/FO/C
5210 GOSUB 260
5220 C2=C:C7=C
5230 R1=RD:R3=RD
5240 R8=Q*RO
5250 X=(FZ/F)↑2
5260 CLS:PRINTCHR$(23)
5270 IF X>1 THEN 5310
5280 R4=R8*(1-X)
5290 PRINT"21.HPN-HQ":PRINT
5300 GOTO 5330
5310 R4=R8*(X-1)
5320 PRINT"21.LPN-HQ":PRINT
5330 R5=RO*RO/R4
5340 PRINT"R1=";R1,"C2=";C2
5350 PRINT"R3=";R3,"R4=";R4
5360 PRINT"R5=";R5,"C7=";C7
5370 PRINT"R8=";R8:PRINT
5380 PRINT"FZ=";FZ,"FP=";F
5390 PRINT"Q =";Q:PRINT
5400 GOSUB 200
5410 PRINT"FZ=";FZ:GOTO 5190
```

```
5420 REM <22.GP1>
5430 PRINT"C(NF)=";:INPUT D:C=D*1E-9
5440 RO=1/FO/C
5450 GOSUB 260
5460 R1=RD:R3=RD:R5=RD:R7=RD
5470 C6=C:C8=C
5480 R4=RD*RD*RD/RO/RO
5490 R2=RD*(Q*(1+R4/RD)/SQR(R4/RD)-1)
5500 KH=(1+R4/RD)/(1+RD/R2)
5510 KB=R2/RD
5520 KL=KH*RD/R4
5530 CLS:PRINTCHR$(23)
5540 PRINT"21.GP1":PRINT
5550 PRINT"R1=";R1,"R2=";R2
5560 PRINT"R3=";R3,"R4=";R4
5570 PRINT"R5=";R5,"C6=";C6
5580 PRINT"R7=";R7,"C8=";C8:PRINT
5590 PRINT"KHP=";KH,"KBP=";KB
5600 PRINT"KLP=";KL
5610 PRINT"F =";F,"Q =";Q:PRINT
5620 GOSUB 2CO
5630 GOTO 5430
```

```
5640 REM <23.GP2>
5650 PRINT"C(NF)=";:INPUT D:C=D*1E-9
5660 PRINT"K= ";:INPUT K
5670 IF K=0 THEN K=1
5680 R0=1/F0/C
5690 GOSUB 260
5700 R2=RD:R7=RD:R8=RD
5710 C3=C:C6=C
5720 R5=R0*R0/RD
5730 R4=Q*R0
5740 PRINT"TYPE 1 IF 'K' IS FOR LP";:INPUT X
5750 IF X=1 THEN KL=K:R1=R2/K:KB=R4/R1:GOTO 5770
5760 KB=K:R1=R4/K:KL=R2/R1
5770 CLS:PRINTCHR$(23)
5780 PRINT"23.GP2":PRINT
5790 PRINT"R1=";R1,"R2=";R2
5800 PRINT"C3=";C3,"R4=";R4
5810 PRINT"R5=";R5,"C6=";C6
5820 PRINT"R7=";R7,"R8=";R8:PRINT
5830 PRINT"KBP=";KB
5840 PRINT"KLP1=KLP2=";KL
5850 PRINT"F =";F,"Q =";Q:PRINT
5860 GOSUB 200
5870 GOTO 5650
5880 END
```

Testing the Programs Numerically

After writing a computer program it is necessary to ensure that the program is not only without syntax errors but also that the numerical results have been correctly computed. Thus in order to debug our programs each circuit was actually built using a set of computed component values. The expected design parameters (e.g. frequency, Q factor, attenuation) were then measured and compared with the program input values.

On the following pages two groups of numerical data are given for each network.

The values of the first group correspond to the design parameters of the circuits which were actually laboratory built and tested for the purpose of debugging the programs given in this book.

The second group indicates how a change in one or more component values results in a change in the corresponding output filter parameters, including the gain-sensitivity product. Thus, the numerical material given in this section is to be used as a tool for the testing and debugging of the given computer programs.

1.LP-LQ

```
6.6393365 03    R11
9.9590048 03    R12
       27. -09   C2
13.49059 03     R3
       3.3 -09   C4
     600. -03    K
       2.3 03    F
       1.2 00    Q
1.8652139 00    GSP
```

```
3.9836019 03    R11
       1.  90   R12
      27. -09    C2
13.49059 03     R3
       3.3 -09   C4
       1.  00    K
       2.3 03    F
       1.2 00    Q
1.8652139 00    GSP
```

2.BP-LQ-R

```
949.77374 00    R11
1.5965215 03    R12
       68. -09   C2
       15. -09   C3
7.8831221 03    R4
       1.5 00    K
       2.3 03    F
       1.4 00    Q
2.3923529 00    GSP
```

```
595.50604 00    R11
       1.  90   R12
      68. -09    C2
      15. -09    C3
7.8831221 03    R4
2.3923529 00     K
       2.3 03    F
       1.4 00    Q
2.3923529 00    GSP
```

3.BP-LQ-C

```
      68. -09    C11
      15. -09    C12
1.816083 03     R2
7.4716704 03    R3
       5.1 -09   C4
2.6071364 00     K
       2.1 03    F
       1.6 00    Q
3.18224 00      GSP
```

```
      68. -09    C11
       0.  00    C12
2.4070895 03    R2
6.880664 03     R3
       5.1 -09   C4
3.4555748 00     K
       2.1 03    F
       1.6 00    Q
3.4555748 00    GSP
```

4.HP-LQ

```
     100. -09    C11
      15. -09    C12
326.47168 00    R2
      15. -09    C3
7.1965713 03    R4
869.56522 -03    K
       2.5 03    F
       1.5 00    Q
2.5434783 00    GSP
```

```
      27. -09    C11
       0.  00    C12
1.0105076 03    R2
      15. -09    C3
9.9029742 03    R4
       1.  00    K
       2.5 03    F
       1.5 00    Q
       3.5 00    GSP
```

5.AP-Q.5

```
      68. -09      C1
     6.8-09        C2
      15. -09      C3
8.0381583 03       R4A
5.4374616 03       R5A
650.41967 00       R6A
1.6960889 03       R4B
 25.76939 03       R5B
319.1209 00        R6B
      2.5 03        F
    300. -03        Q
```

```
      27. -09      C1
     6.8-09        C2
      27. -09      C3
5.2115421 03       R4A
5.3024215 03       R5A
2.0995252 03       R6A
1.0667594 03       R4B
 25.90443 03       R5B
818.44118 00       R6B
      2.5 03        F
    300. -03        Q
```

6.AP-LQ

```
2.1624313 03       R1
      10. -09      C2
      10. -09      C3
22.143296 03       R4
 2.65625 03        R5
      6.8 03        R6
719.10112-03        K
      2.3 03        F
      1.6 00        Q
     5.12 00       GSP
```

```
1.3515196 03       R1
      22. -09      C2
      10. -09      C3
16.104216 03       R4
5.3710938 03       R5
      10. 03        R6
650.57179-03        K
      2.3 03        F
      1.6 00        Q
3.7236364 00       GSP
```

7.BR-LQ

```
370.04172 00       R1
      15. -09      C2
     100. -09      C3
9.4287247 03       R4
992.92914 00       R5
      22. 03        R6
956.81589-03        K
      2.2 03        F
      1.7 00        Q
22.156667 00       GSP
```

```
1.0132095 03       R1
      27. -09      C2
      15. -09      C3
12.75383 03        R4
2.2244192 03       R5
      10. 03        R6
818.03478-03        K
      2.2 03        F
      1.7 00        Q
4.4955556 00       GSP
```

8.LP-MQ

```
2.7457067 00        P
25.470105 00       GSP
```

```
991.99029 00       R11
       1. 90       R12
     100. -09      C2
2.7237144 03       R3
      15. -09      C4
      10. 03        R5
4.7628799 03       R6
1.476288 00         K
      2.5 03        F
      7.5 00        Q
```

```
1.5333078 00        P
30.935516 00       GSP
```

```
4.7455372 03       R11
7.0119021 03       R12
      33. -09      C2
4.3394814 03       R3
      10. -09      C4
      6.8 03        R5
4.6021254 03       R6
       1. 00         K
      2.5 03        F
      7.5 00        Q
```

9.BP-MQ-R   10.BP-MQ-C

```
15.215781 00      P          6.4407124 00      P
17.804565 00     GSP          14.08843 00     GSP

1.4128396 03     R11             68. -09     C11
915.29229 00     R12             15. -09     C12
      68. -09     C2      1.4514756 03      R2
      15. -09     C3      9.3485371 03      R3
8.4516079 03      R4            5.1-09      C4
2.9995345 03      R5      4.970735 03      R5
      11. 03      R6            15. 03      R6
      5.5 00       K      8.6694315 00       K
      2.3 03       F            2.1 03       F
       6. 00       Q             5. 00       Q


13.34444 00      P          2.500919 00      P
18.130512 00     GSP      16.541822 00     GSP

2.4766475 03     R11             27. -09     C11
       1. 90     R12              0. 00     C12
      15. -09     C2      4.2542227 03      R2
      3.9-09      C3      10.639466 03      R3
33.049473 03      R4            4.7-09      C4
2.7368193 03      R5      4.7745784 03      R5
      10. 03      R6            10. 03      R6
14.234725 00       K      11.196138 00       K
      2.3 03       F            2.1 03       F
       6. 00       Q             5. 00       Q
```

11.HP-MQ

```
65.170699 00      P
19.415779 00      GSP


100. -09     C11
15. -09       C12
370.03027 00   R2
5.1 -09       C3
24.115131 03   R4
6.8 03        R5
1.8857261 03   R6
1.1107067 00   K
2.2 03        F
7. 00         Q



11.701459 00     P
22.083997 00     GSP


15. -09      C11
0. 00        C12
2.5187373 03   R2
4.7 -09       C3
29.472902 03   R4
10. 03        R5
2.9359544 03   R6
835954 00     K
2.2 03        F
7. 00         Q
```

12.AP-MQ

```
78.117733 -03     P
17.473246 00      GSP


13.06102 03    R1
33. -09       C2
10. -09       C3
7.2215149 03   R4
1.1881686 03   R5
6.8 03        R6
2.9746737 03   R7
2.4 03        F
5. 00         Q



69.566685 -03     P
17.186565 00      GSP


27.33525 03    R1
18. -09       C2
4.7 -09       C3
13.255775 03   R4
2.2201114 03   R5
10. 03        R6
4.3922515 03   R7
2.4 03        F
5. 00         Q
```

13.BR-MQ

```
60.240964 -03     P
29.283848 00      GSP


10.686131 03   R1
68. -09       C2
15. -09       C3
14.782193 03   R4
673.05331 00   R5
5.6 03        R6
1.8666667 03   R7
1.9 03        F
9. 00         Q



79.526227 -03     P
30.42576 00       GSP


35.376656 03   R1
15. -09       C2
4.7 -09       C3
67.012608 03   R4
2.936661 03    R5
10. 03        R6
3.3333333 03   R7
1.9 03        F
9. 00         Q
```

14.HPN-MQ   14.LPN-MQ


```
   300. -03    P              200. -03    P
19.991639 00   GSP         37.729721 00   GSP


 2.554421  03  R1          3.2874103 03  R1
 3.6350018 03  R2          3.7884357 03  R2
    22. -09   C3               5.1-09   C3
    6.8-09    C4              68. -09   C4
16.750422  03  R5          8.1769184 03  R5
69.373675  03  R6         35.317329  03  R6
     5.  03   R7               3.  03   R7
     7.5 03   R8               3.  03   R8
    10.  03   R9               7.5 03   R9
   600. -03   K              500. -03   K
     2.2 03   FZ               2.5 03   FZ
     2.5 03   FP               2.2 03   FP
    10.  00    Q               6.  00    Q


   250. -03    P              200. -03    P
19.680306 00   GSP         12.109246 00   GSP


 2.6521947 03  R1          2.9779819 03  R1
 2.562408  03  R2          3.8147434 03  R2
    22. -09   C3              18. -09   C3
    10. -09   C4              10. -09   C4
13.525052  03  R5         16.580147  03  R5
78.320603  03  R6         71.612124  03  R6
     5.  03   R7               4.  03   R7
     5.  03   R8               4.  03   R8
    10.  03   R9              10.  03   R9
   500. -03   K              500. -03   K
     2.2 03   FZ               2.5 03   FZ
     2.5 03   FP               2.2 03   FP
    10.  00    Q               6.  00    Q
```

15.HPN-MQ   15.LPN-MQ


```
      68. -09    C1              18. -09    C1
      15. -09    C2             4. 7-09    C2
      33. -09    C3              18. -09    C3
      5. 1-09    C4             4. 7-09    C4
2. 3252708 03    R5       3. 5367765 03    R5
7. 4408665 03    R6       17. 081878 03    R6
704. 38495 00    R7       2. 3234298 03    R7
9. 0974377 03    R8       22. 563531 03    R8
      6. 8 03    R9              10. 03    R9
2. 5549489 03    R10      8. 3494916 03    R10
      1. 9 03    FZ             2. 5 03    FZ
      2. 3 03    FP             2. 3 03    FP
      5. 00     Q              12. 00     Q
972. 24578-03    K        811. 52543-03    K
14. 722535 00    GSP      48. 989492 00    GSP


      18. -09    C1              22. -09    C1
     4. 7-09    C2             4. 7-09    C2
      18. -09    C3              22. -09    C3
      0. 00     C4             3. 3-09    C4
4. 6536533 03    R5       2. 8937262 03    R5
22. 476155 03    R6       16. 438828 03    R6
3. 0571445 03    R7       2. 0274515 03    R7
58. 296791 03    R8       34. 057721 03    R8
      39. 03    R9              10. 03    R9
2. 2179764 03    R10      5. 5321625 03    R10
      1. 9 03    FZ             2. 5 03    FZ
      2. 3 03    FP             2. 3 03    FP
      5. 00     Q              12. 00     Q
1. 0568712 00    K        838. 61187-03    K
11. 636523 00    GSP      41. 238696 00    GSP
```

15.BR-MQ

```
       22.-09     C1
      2.2-09      C2
       22.-09     C3
        1.-09     C4
3.0142982 03      R5
 33.15728 03      R6
2.5119151 03      R7
72.343156 03      R8
      6.8 03      R9
2.7162534 03      R10
      2.4 03      FZ
      2.4 03      FP
       12. 00     Q
932.96602-03      K
34.468854 00      GSP


       22.-09     C1
      4.7-09      C2
       22.-09     C3
        1.-09     C4
3.0142982 03      R5
17.123779 03      R6
2.1119287 03      R7
77.987909 03      R8
       10. 03     R9
1.7237165 03      R10
      2.4 03      FZ
      2.4 03      FP
       12. 00     Q
931.76963-03      K
31.818059 00      GSP
```

16.LP-HQ

```
        LP

28.086166 03      R1
       68.-09     C1
        1. 03     R2
        1. 03     R3
       68.-09     C4
        1. 03     R6
876.48083 00      R7
      2.5 03      F
       30. 00     Q


        LP

86.811787 03      R1
       22.-09     C1
      2.7 03      R2
      2.7 03      R3
       22.-09     C4
      2.7 03      R6
3.1013524 03      R7
      2.5 03      F
       30. 00     Q
```

17.BP-HQ

```
        BP

      3.3 03      R1
      3.3 03      R2
       22.-09     C3
3.2766918 03      R4
      3.3 03      R6
82.208132 03      R7
       22.-09     C8
      2.2 03      F
       25. 00     Q


        BP

      2.7 03      R1
      2.7 03      R2
       27.-09     C3
2.6589098 03      R4
      2.7 03      R6
160.76257 03      R7
       27.-09     C8
      2.2 03      F
       60. 00     Q
```

18.HP-HQ

HP

```
      1.5  03    R1
      1.5  03    R2
      68. -09    C3
1.0116353  03    R4
      1.5  03    R6
      68. -09    C7
24.636988  03    R8
      1.9  03    F
      20.  00    Q
```

HP

```
      2.7  03    R1
      2.7  03    R2
      33. -09    C3
  2.38639  03    R4
      2.7  03    R6
      33. -09    C7
126.91782  03    R8
      1.9  03    F
      50.  00    Q
```

19.AP-HQ

AP

```
      1.2  03    R1
      1.2  03    R2
      68. -09    C3
1.1412511  03    R4
      1.2  03    R5
      68. -09    C7
29.256423  03    R8
      2.  03     F
      25.  00    Q
```

AP

```
      4.7  03    R1
      4.7  03    R2
      18. -09    C3
4.1585067  03    R4
      4.7  03    R5
      18. -09    C7
110.52427  03    R8
      2.  03     F
      25.  00    Q
```

20.BR-HQ

BR

```
      2.2  03    R1
      2.2  03    R2
      33. -09    C3
2.1844612  03    R4
      2.2  03    R5
87.688674  03    R7
      33. -09    C7
87.688674  03    R8
      2.2  03    F
      20.  00    Q
```

BR

```
      15.  03    R1
      15.  03    R2
      4.7 -09    C3
15.794574  03    R4
      15.  03    R5
615.68643  03    R7
      4.7 -09    C7
615.68643  03    R8
      2.2  03    F
      20.  00    Q
```

21.HPN-HQ

HPN

```
        2.7 03    R1
       22.-09     C2
        2.7 03    R3
  9.7923696 03    R4
 855.12005 00     R5
       22.-09     C7
  43.405894 03    R8
        2.2 03    FZ
        2.5 03    FP
       15. 00     Q
```

HPN

```
       12. 03     R1
        4.7-09    C2
       12. 03     R3
  45.836624 03    R4
  4.0026896 03    R5
        4.7-09    C7
 203.17652 03     R8
        2.2 03    FZ
        2.5 03    FP
       15. 00     Q
```

22.GP1

```
        1.8 03    R1
  20.020658 03    R2
        1.8 03    R3
  2.3953975 03    R4
        1.8 03    R5
       68.-09     C6
        1.8 03    R7
       68.-09     C8
  2.1385109 00    KH
 11.122699 00     KB
  1.6069649 00    KL
        1.5 03    F
        6. 00     Q
```

```
        4.7 03    R1
 230.37827 03     R2
        4.7 03    R3
  4.4635581 03    R4
        4.7 03    R5
       22.-09     C6
        4.7 03    R7
       22.-09     C8
  1.9107123 00    KH
 49.016652 00     KB
  2.0119259 00    KL
        1.5 03    F
       25. 00     Q
```

21.LPN-HQ

LPN

```
        3.3 03    R1
       22.-09     C2
        3.3 03    R3
  14.369438 03    R4
 752.50564 00     R5
       22.-09     C7
  49.324879 03    R8
        2.5 03    FZ
        2.2 03    FP
       15. 00     Q
```

LPN

```
       15. 03     R1
        4.7-09    C2
       15. 03     R3
  67.261199 03    R4
  3.5223668 03    R5
        4.7-09    C7
 230.88241 03     R8
        2.5 03    FZ
        2.2 03    FP
       15. 00     Q
```

23.GP2

```
        1. 03     R1
        1.5 03    R2
       47.-09     C3
  12.190591 03    R4
  1.2231318 03    R5
       47.-09     C6
        1.5 03    R7
        1.5 03    R8
  12.190591 00    KB
        1.5 00    KL
        2.5 03    F
        9. 00     Q
```

```
  8.1270609 03    R1
        1.5 03    R2
       47.-09     C3
  12.190591 03    R4
  1.2231318 03    R5
       47.-09     C6
        1.5 03    R7
        1.5 03    R8
        1.5 00    KB
 184.56857-03     KL
        2.5 03    F
        9. 00     Q
```

Index

Note: Numbers in **bold** type indicate pages on which definitions occur.

311